Anarchist Popular Power

Praise for *Anarchist Popular Power*:

"This is an exciting book that adds to the rich history of anarchism. An English-language history of the FAU is long overdue and Troy Andreas Araiza Kokinis's work does not disappoint. Thoroughly and sensitively researched, it places the FAU in their political and cultural context, presenting us with an understanding of a complex and flexible organization that could both work with others but still maintain its own anarchist autonomy. Books like this make one realize how much there is to learn and reflect on. Essential reading." —Barry Pateman, Kate Sharpley Library

"Troy's book is an important contribution to think about the ways in which anarchism, scarcely studied in the second half of the century, was also part of the turn of the sixties' New Left in Latin America. The so-called specifism of the FAU shows how that anarchist tradition, very influential in the Uruguay of the first half of the century, managed to rethink itself and actively influence the new cycles of social and political struggles." —Aldo Marchesi, author of *Latin America's Radical Left: Rebellion and Cold War in the Global 1960s*

"When trying to understand a period as intense as the late 1960s in Uruguay, it is greatly important to illuminate the struggles waged by so-called 'minority' political organizations. Although they were never hegemonic among the organized popular sectors, studying groups like the FAU is essential for understanding what happened beyond the scale of that which was visible. They pushed for the types of collective actions that had a broad impact both in majority parties and popular sectors of the Left, as well as other groups who organized from below." —Raúl Zibechi, author of *Territories in Resistance*

"Latin American anarchism, especially that of the Río de la Plata region, has followed unique paths and assumed different configurations depending on the historical moment that its militants' hectic political lives were going through. Some of these moments and events have been more investigated than others, either because of the access to the documents or because of the prominence of the actions. In this text, much less active decades are addressed compared to the well-studied first half of the twentieth century, and the author takes on the thorny issue of armed struggle. With a gaze that goes from north to south and then back again to think about these debates, the author goes through primary source materials from the epoch and does not escape the tensions and internal conflicts of those who took on the struggle and libertarian ideal at the same time. Troy Araiza Kokinis's proposal and the discussions that his book will undoubtedly provoke are proof of the vitality of anarchism as a crucial part of thinking about local and global history." —Laura Fernández Cordero, author of *Amor y Anarquismo*

Anarchist Popular Power

Dissident Labor and Armed Struggle in Uruguay, 1956–76

Troy Andreas Araiza Kokinis

ISBN: 978-1-84935-500-1
E-ISBN: 978-1-84935-501-8
Library of Congress Control Number: 2022948748

AK Press
370 Ryan Ave. #100
Chico, CA 95973
www.akpress.org
akpress@akpress.org

AK Press
33 Tower St.
Edinburgh EH6 7BN
Scotland
www.akuk.com
akuk@akpress.org

The above addresses would be delighted to provide you with the latest
AK Press distribution catalog, which features books, pamphlets, zines,
and stylish apparel published and/or distributed by AK Press. Alter-
natively, visit our websites for the complete catalog, latest news, and
secure ordering.

Cover artwork by Troy Andreas Araiza Kokinis

Printed in the USA on acid-free paper

For Petros Emiliano Amílcar

Si molesto con mi canto
A alguno que ande por ahí
Le aseguro que es un gringo
O dueño del Uruguay

—Daniel Viglietti

Contents

Preface

El futuro es el sur. The future is the South. I used this phrase when saying goodbye to friends from Uruguay and Argentina during our communication throughout the pandemic lockdowns. I learned the phrase from Nicolás Cuello, a fellow militant-researcher and anarchist weirdo in Buenos Aires who has been encouraging me for some time now to relocate to the South. And he is right: the future is the South. Those of us in North America and Europe should be looking toward the Global South for strategical and tactical inspiration, and for overall know-how about how to confront crisis situations with dignity and resilience, beyond symbolic gestures and slogans. In the South, they fight to win! The late urbanist and historian Mike Davis made a similar proposition in his 2010 article "Who Will Build the Ark?" There, he recognizes that poor populations in the Global South—those Frantz Fanon called the "wretched" or "damned"—have been confronting political, economic, and environmental crisis for generations. Scholars Susana Draper and Verónica Gago recognize how such a phenomenon is already occurring in the struggle for abortion rights in the United States, where the *pañuelo verde*—the green scarf that has emblematized those movements in Latin America—is a common presence at protests. In this way, they recognize the uniqueness of a moment in which North American feminists are *aprendiendo desde el sur del mundo*.[1] If we in the North, especially those "damned" people internally colonized in the heart of empire, are to have any chance at coming out of the escalating crises in a stronger position than before, then we need to look toward our

compas in the South for inspiration. One way to start is by foment-
ing relationships.

My interest in platform anarchism, and more so its Latin
American *especifista* iteration, comes from such an imperative.[2]
This strand of anarchism builds theoretical cohesion around a
specifically anarchist organization whose militants participate in
social movements with the intention of making anarchist practices
hegemonic within them. In the United States especially, platform
anarchism is all but unknown. While it has gained mention and
traction in some left circles, it remains shrouded in mystery and
misunderstanding. For most socialists, whether orthodox Marxist
or social democratic, platform anarchists still represent an "infan-
tile disorder." This perspective, borrowed from Vladimir Lenin,
sees platformists as troublemakers without a plan because of their
refusal to enter the state apparatus. Moreover, purist anarchists see
platformists as a bastardization of the ideology, sometimes referring to them as anarcho-Bolsheviks. I recall once hearing the comment: "Marxist anarchists—I have no idea how that is possible!"

While such a position may seem strange to a North American,
it makes complete sense in the Latin American context, where
anarchists are still credited with having grounded the labor movement and organized left. While the same can be said about the
first North American labor unions, this history has widely been
obfuscated. In contrast, in the River Plate region, working people
seem to know and respect this history because their unions, which
are still active and intact, have taught them this. I was often struck
by my conversations with cab drivers in Buenos Aires, of which the
following is illustrative:

Driver: "What are you doing here?"
Me: "I am doing a historical investigation of the Uruguayan
Anarchist Federation. They were exiled during the Dirty War and
were targeted as part of the pilot operation of Plan Cóndor."
Driver: "Those sons of bitches! Murderers! Thanks to an anar-
chist, we offed the first police colonel of Buenos Aires. Another
son of a bitch."
Me: "Yeah, Simón Radowitzky."

Driver: "Yes! Well, this was all before Perón. Perón made the state function for the workers. And he borrowed a lot from anarchist culture too."

Throughout the River Plate region, anarchists played a key role in the development of populist political projects. In the case of the former, anarcho-syndicalist unions integrated into the government of José Batlle y Ordóñez.[3] Some militants even embraced the label "anarcho-Batllista." In Argentina, the Peronist infrastructure borrowed from the anarcho-syndicalist model and verticalized it into the state.[4] Two decades after the heyday of belle epoque anarchism, Perón's reach was so pervasive that some labor leaders decided to abandon the red and black flag for that of *justicialismo,* the Peronist party that centered the *descamisado* (shirtless) worker as a subject of rights in the Argentine state. Historically, militants made these individual and collective decisions out of a moral conviction for a better world: they did what they thought was right under conditions of poverty, hyperexploitation, and neocolonialism.

North American anarchists have not confronted such dilemmas because the left has not provided a clear threat to power in nearly a century. This enables a purist sentiment among leftists who often only discuss strategy abstractly and who are in no way situated in spaces with potential of building toward a mass politics—in the rare case that strategy is discussed at all, beyond mere lifestyle and personal politics. In contrast, the Latin American left has made, and continues to make, bids for power. This is a result of their emphasis on strategy, consensus building to identify everyday problems and their structural origins, and the development of campaigns that go beyond lobbying and voting in an effort to transform those conditions. That is not to say that the Latin American left merely ignores the state; in fact, some of the only left-identifying statist projects of the past two decades have come from the region. However, there is a broad consensus among the left of the necessity to build *mass* movements, and what is debated are strategies about how to do so. In such conditions, anarchists have made—and remade—their politics. Moreover, the institutional left has absorbed anarchist strategy, tactics, and culture.

But conditions in Latin America are not unique solely because of the left's potential to claim state power; there is also a uniqueness to everyday Latin Americans' willingness to take risks. When crises intensify, Latin Americans act. And they do so unapologetically, because their lived experience directly reflects the immiseration and precarity brought on by centuries of coloniality. Thus, everyday people are aware of the stakes of their actions, and they organically respond to their realities in ways that are only possible from generations of practice. Crisis comes in cycles. And the cycle that hit Uruguay in the late 1960s and early 1970s provided background in which the Uruguayan Anarchist Federation (FAU) developed its politics. One militant told me: "People just acted on their own. We don't even know half of what went on, because it was impossible to keep up with." There is no North American comparison to the half decade of intensified conflict in Uruguay from 1968 to 1973.

All said, this climate of conflict was also a climate of chaos. As feminist activist Lilián Celiberti shared: "It was like we lived twenty years in only two." The social upheaval admittedly lends itself to moments of chaos in the written historical narrative. Nevertheless, I consciously set out to capture details of what everyday people were doing during this time. For in this context, it is not enough to simply write, "There was a strike." After all, the details of what took place matter. We must ask: What did these strikes look like? What were people doing at the micro level? The details can exhaust; and oftentimes the narratives relayed in this book terminate anticlimactically, without winner or loser. But, according to the FAU, all these dissident activities proved vital for the accumulation of experiences toward collective subjective transformation. As the following chapters hope to show, only through building popular power is it possible to make *socialismo desde abajo*.

Acknowledgments

I am deeply grateful to AK Press for dedicating the time, energy, and resources to publish this book. For the duration of my research project, I dreamed of and envisioned releasing my work through AK. I wanted my work to circulate among anarchists and other factions of the left, and I hope that they find my work useful when thinking about strategies and tactics in their own sites of organizing. Thank you, especially, to Zach Blue and Sam Smith for accompanying me through the editing process. And to AK for inviting me to paint the cover image.

Research for this book would not have been possible without financial support from the Fulbright Commission, Tinker Foundation, and UC San Diego's Institute of Arts and Humanities, Chancellor's Research Excellence Scholarship, and Friends of the International House.

I am incredibly grateful for the institutional, grammatical, and emotional guidance of my dissertation coadvisers, Michael Monteon and Eric Van Young. I feel very fortunate that both took me on, in each case as one of the last advisees to benefit from their lifelong dedication to Latin American history. I also benefited from the direction of Carlos Waisman, Pamela Radcliff, Wendy Matsumura, Matthew Vitz, and Nancy Kwak, whose combined expertise offered a perfect balance of support for my mixed-methods approach. I cannot imagine a better fit for me than the UCSD Department of History. Also, a sincere thank you to Aldo Marchesi, who offered his friendship and guidance during my cumulative year of research in Montevideo.

This investigation was only possible with the participation of various militants of the Uruguayan Anarchist Federation (FAU), People's Victory Party (PVP), and National Liberation Movement–Tupamaros (MLN-T), who shared their time, energy, and stories. I had the privilege of living unforgettable moments with militants and their family members who inspired me to produce a manuscript at my highest potential. Not only did they offer enriching narratives, but they also helped guide my analysis. They are: Augusto "Chacho" Andrés, Edelweiss Zahn, Lilián Celiberti, Cristina Marín, Marina Mechoso, Zelmar Dutra, América Garcia, Ana Rosa Amoros, Juan Pilo, Juan Carlos Mechoso, Sarita Méndez, Raúl Olivera, and Oscar Delgado.

Throughout my six years (2012–18) moving between California and the Southern Cone, I met fellow researchers and militants whose work has inspired me greatly. While their intellectual work is provocative and stimulating, their political work is a shining example of resilience, dedication, and self-sacrifice in hopes of making a better world. Most importantly, their companionship made my partner and I feel welcome and at home. I smile when recalling the days and nights eating, chatting, sharing, strolling, and dancing with Martín, Cuello, Sebastian, Linda, Nadia, Natalia, Pierina, Ines, Diego, Nicolás, Marcelo, Rafael, Ana Laura, Vero, Luci, Vasco, Nata, Segundo, Graciela, and Andrea. I am forever grateful for Marcos and Thalita in Buenos Aires. To welcome two strangers and a dog into their home for five weeks without asking anything in return is truly a gesture of solidarity that can only come from such political convictions and commitments as their own.

The project came together as result of over a decade of relationship building and community organizing alongside friends and acquaintances in Southern California's peripheral neighborhoods. While spending time abroad, it was always difficult to translate our subaltern realities with the hegemonic imaginary of *gringolandia* that is projected abroad via mass media. I first learned of the MLN-Tupamaros and armed struggle in Uruguay from an audio clip from Costas-Gavras's film *State of Siege* (1972) that was included in a full-length record of the Riverside-based hardcore punk band Rogue State. The band's members were from Mexico, Uruguay, the Philippines, and the US. Weird, cacophonous punk bands in the early 2000s Inland Empire micro-scene account for much of my exposure to revolutionary left ideas. Much of my analysis of race, gender, and class developed organically after sharing experiences alongside my childhood friends, including Roland, Edwin, Kevan, Josh, Nino, Ramon, Cameron, Billy, John, Alexandra, Laura, Ana, Joe, Tomas, Brent, Fritz, Joana, Romeo, Huey Itztekwanotl o))), Andy, Stefany, Tim, Tomba, and LJ.

My experience at Pitzer College was formative in my intellectual trajectory, especially my interest in Latin America and anarchism. I was unaware that anarchism had a place in academia until encountering Professor Dana Ward, who served as my guide and mentor then and thereafter. Throughout this time, I was forced to reflect upon my biracial Chicano identity and situate it among a larger Third Worldism thanks to the guidance and support of Lako Tongun, José Calderón, and Jamaica Kincaid. Moreover, I expanded my musical, and thus political, horizons as a DJ at the noncommercial radio station KSPC, where I was lucky to share time with Erica, Aaron, and Junior. Finally, I was forever shaped by my first experiences consciously applying anarchist ideas in the political organization Direct Action Claremont, where I met Maya, Chris, Kendra, Amanda, Anthony, Natty, Paul, Nathan, Pilar, Daniele, Michael, Arthur, Priscilla, Lianna, Brian, Yoatl, and Claire.

My UC San Diego graduate school experience allowed me not only to venture around the continent, but also to move throughout California to organize alongside fellow graduate student workers as a bargaining team representative for the UAW 2865 union during our 2014 contract campaign. My experience participating in the Academic Workers for a Democratic Union dissident workers' caucus offered a perspective of great use in writing this book. Moreover, the experience led me to cross paths with some of the most thoughtful and dedicated organizers and people, including Daniel, Alborz, Jeanine, Yasmeen, Nisreen, Tanner, Justin, Pablo, Nick, Josh, Jason, Katie, Shannon, Cody, Amanda, Michelle, Robert, Brenda, Duane, and Beazie. I must also recognize those fellow students and workers who participated in the formation of UCSD's Lumumba Zapata Collective and who dedicated countless days to planning for the January 20, 2017, strike on the event of Donald Trump's presidential inauguration—especially Davide, Marcela, Mychal, Bernardo, Andy, Jessica B., Jessica N., Caroline, Lisa, Luke, Sam, Maria, Grant, Luca, Ezra, Aditi, Zeltzin, Ian, Seth, and Saul, among others. Our experiences together have helped guide the analysis of this book, but most of all, they helped me grow as a person. My two years as an MA student at the UCSD Latin American Studies program led me to cross paths with Teresita, Katherine, Jacqui, Esteban, and Rafael. Our bond as a cohort showed me the power of uncompromising and unconditional care, support, and friendship. To Caribbean, Ryan, Romeo, and Alex of South El Monte Arts Posse and *Tropics of Meta* popular historiography blog: thank you for always offering a platform for me to share my ideas with a broader audience. Gratitude is due to Sky and Juan for all the help line-editing drafts of articles and grant proposals, and to Jarod for his incredible attention to detail with footnote formatting.

Much love and respect to Comunidade Pereira da Silva in Rio de Janeiro for receiving Jael, Pilona, and I for nine months during the writing of the dissertation that became this book. Their resilience, creativity, and love for life has left a lasting impact on the trajectory of my career. I aspire to create and maintain relationships based on care and support beyond the logic of the market and state as they have shown me to be possible during our brief time together.

Finally, I have benefited greatly from a support community in San Diego, where I reside and work since returning from South America in 2018. I greatly miss making music with Peter, Doga, CJ, Jack, and Hilary. I have endless gratitude for the support I have received from Pati and Katherine, Chad and my coworkers at Kilowatt Brewing, Stu and Mael, Fabian and Meera, Matias, and Farah; for the UC cognitariat fighting for a life of dignity—COLA for all!—and for Petros, who teaches me to love unconditionally.

Introduction

On October 11, 2017, I received Juliana Martínez at my Montevideo home in Barrio Sur. I had visited her home five months prior to interview her alongside fellow Uruguayan Anarchist Federation (FAU) militant Zelmar Dutra. In the initial May visit, I learned a rather superficial and linear narrative of Juliana's FAU militancy in the early 1970s: when she joined, why she joined, when she fell prisoner, and so on. Following our initial chat, we developed an amicable relationship. I often visited while she organized the FAU library, and she frequently invited me to dinner at her home. On one winter Sunday, we spent the day alongside her two lifelong friends from the armed Marxist National Liberation Movement-Tupamaros (MLN-T). We attended Montevideo's Fine Arts Museum to observe the works of Julio Mancebo, a student of the famed modernist painter Joaquín Torres-García and fellow member of the FAU's armed apparatus, the Popular Revolutionary Organization–33 Orientals (OPR-33).

The October interview was much different. Sitting comfortably in my living room, Juliana communicated more about feeling than chronology. She shared details of everyday life in the OPR-33 safe house where she lived while working at an eyeglass factory—a home that served as a key site for the meetings, propaganda production, and reconnaissance. Juliana gathered information about the daily routines of Sergio Molaguero, a member of a neofascist youth organization and son of the owner of the Seral shoe factory where, on April 12, 1971, 308 workers began a campaign for union recognition after José Molaguero insisted that they appear for work on a holiday weekend. The conflict pursued for ten months, until Molaguero conceded all the workers' demands in exchange for the liberty of his kidnapped son. The event was one of many examples of popular violence in the face of a deepening economic and political crisis between 1967 and 1973.

Juliana spent eleven years and five months in prison for her role in the kidnapping. Her participation came as part of the FAU's unique strategy to merge mass action in the labor movement with armed struggle. Unlike other armed political organizations throughout Latin America and the Third World, the OPR-33 did not identity as a vanguard. Instead, they saw themselves as a "technical apparatus" that could be called upon to intervene in escalating social conflicts. Juliana, one of myriad actors amid a historic moment of popular revolt, humbly insisted that I not use her real name. She clarified that those she cares most about participated alongside her and that she need not be glorified as an individual. She did not see the point. Instead, she insisted that the real protagonists were Seral's workers, most of whom remain unknown to either one of us. Juliana, Seral's workers, and other everyday people like them who took on a role as historical protagonists proved so threatening to capital and the state that the Uruguayan military intervened in government to suppress them. This is a story about them.

During the 1970s, Latin America's Southern Cone was a laboratory for neoliberal political economic restructuring. These experimental governments made up a region-wide network of US-supported military dictatorships, eventually consolidated under Plan Cóndor. While scholars overwhelmingly represent Augusto Pinochet's Chile as the testing ground for neoliberal policy in retort to Salvador Allende's socialist government, the Uruguayan military coup, established three months prior, marked the region's first move toward neoliberal governance in response to mass worker revolt. From December 1967 to June 1973, the half decade prior to the country's devolution into civic-military dictatorship, the Uruguayan *pueblo* (everyday people) challenged an increasingly authoritarian political framework and spiraling economic crisis through acts of solidarity, sacrifice, and disobedience.

During this era—which the FAU referred to as an era of "constitutional dictatorship"—Uruguayans saw the implementation of neoliberal political economic reforms alongside an increased use of state violence, including frequent press censorship, prohibition of strikes, growth of foreign direct investment, denationalization of industry, militarization of public space, mass incarceration, and frequent use of torture. By 1973, the state's violent tendencies would coalesce into a civic-military regime.

Uruguayan left organizations provided a variety of different, often contrasting, strategies to confront the growing political economic crisis of the constitutional-dictatorship era. I focus on the FAU, Latin America's most active anarchist organization, to broaden understandings of the Cold War–era political landscape beyond the capitalism/communism and Old Left / New Left binaries that dominate the historiography of the epoch. The FAU saw everyday people as revolutionary protagonists and sought to develop a popular counter-subjectivity by accumulating experiences that directly challenged the market and the state. The organization did not see any objective revolutionary character of the working class nor of vanguard political organizations. Instead, its militants argued that everyday people transformed into revolutionary subjects through the regular practice of collective direct action in labor unions, student organizations, and neighborhood councils. In other words, the working class was not objectively revolutionary but came into being as such through an extraparliamentary strategy that incorporated the regular use of anti-legal methods. I argue that the strategies and tactics promoted by the FAU—ones in which everyday people became revolutionary protagonists—offered the largest threat to the maintenance of social order in Uruguay and thus spawned a military takeover of the state to dismantle and deflate a vibrant popular revolt.

At their founding congress in 1956, the FAU broke from regional traditions of anarcho-syndicalism to pioneer *especifismo*, a confederation of anarchist militants who participated in and built up popular labor, student, and neighborhood organizations. Advocating for direct action tactics (i.e., strikes, sabotage, property damage, public shaming, boycotts, and political violence) and mutual aid, FAU militants set out to make anarchist ideas and practices hegemonic within mass organizations, specifically labor unions. They also created a small armed apparatus to expropriate money from banks, protect workers from police and strikebreakers, and kidnap employers. For the FAU, a revolutionary project required the empowerment and participation of everyday people who would fight for a new society in their own image. Popular power laid at the foundation of any revolutionary society and, as such, had to be *created* over time, not *taken*. Hence the FAU's slogan: "Create popular power." A study of especifismo provides a new perspective on forms of resistance at the dawn of the neoliberal era. The prevailing neoliberal ideology encourages a rupture with collective identities rooted in a shared historical experience and/or common reality and has thus necessitated new organizing strategies for advancing mass political projects. If Latin America's Southern Cone was the first site of neoliberal experimentation, then especifismo may very well be considered a foreshadowing of contemporary leftist political strategies in response to neoliberalism.[1]

With roughly eighty militants, the FAU played a key role in sparking and networking popular protagonism in workplaces, neighborhoods, and school campuses. The FAU worked in coalition with the Uruguayan Communist Party (PCU), MLN-T, and other revolutionary organizations to support a unified left project while simultaneously challenging hegemonic strategies, tactics, and discourses.[2]

Unlike other anarchist groups worldwide, which took to individualism and counterculture in response to Marxism's popularity throughout the 1960s, the FAU embraced Third Worldism and a Marxian class struggle strategy that made them a relevant force among popular social movements. Throughout the constitutional-dictatorship epoch of 1967 to 1973, the FAU and its dissident labor movement allies controlled one-third of the nation's unions in some of the most lucrative industries, especially in the private sector. The coalition endorsed a set of tactics that echoed everyday people's organic response to the political and economic crisis— one that subverted political parties' calls to use legal institutional channels and one that outlasted the MLN-T's armed strategy. At the time of the June 1973 military takeover, unruly labor provided the largest threat to political stability and status quo social relations in the country. This book situates the FAU within this climate of worker revolt.

FAU's Anarchy in a Twentieth-Century Latin American Context

Argentine historian Christian Ferrer calls anarchism a *contrapeso histórico*—a historical counterweight. He declares, "For the majority of people, anarchism, as a political ideology and communitarian project, has transformed into a mystery. It is not necessarily unknown nor unknowable, but something much like a mystery. Incomprehensible. Inaudible. Unapparent." Ferrer continues, "In every city in the world, no matter how small, there is at least one person who claims to be an anarchist."[3] Historian and political scientist Benedict Anderson also recognizes that one can expect to find a small, enthusiastic group of anarchists in every urban center, while communist groups have lost relevance and popularity after the ideology's perceived failure in the post–Cold War era. He recognizes that anarchists' inability to realize their utopian vision in the twentieth century has served as both a blessing and a curse.[4] Ferrer conveys a similar sentiment through use of a metaphor:

> Communism always seemed to be a river current that roamed uncontrollably until a natural estuary: the post-historical unifying ocean of humanity. For its critics, this river was dirty, irredeemably polluted, but even for them the current was unstoppable. Nevertheless, this river dried up, as if an overpowering sun dried it up in an instant. . . . If we continue with the hydro-metaphors, anarchism does not correspond with the figure of the river, but instead with the geyser, as well as a flood, a downpour, an underground river, an inundation, a deluge, a breaking wave, the eye of a storm.[5]

Although scholars can hardly deny the relevance of anarchism in the trajectory of the left throughout the twentieth century, few

have ventured to provide thorough investigations of the movement after the Spanish Civil War era of 1936 to 1939, which is
widely considered the last hurrah for the ideology.[6] As such, scholarship on anarchism in the Cold War–era Global South is nearly
nonexistent.[7]

At the turn of the twentieth century, anarchists played a foundational role in working-class organizations and culture throughout the continent, especially in Argentina, Chile, Cuba, Brazil,
Mexico, Panama, Puerto Rico, and Uruguay. Eugenio Tandonnet,
a French utopian socialist and follower of Charles Fourier, transported anarchist thought to Uruguay's shores in 1844. There, he
linked with recently arrived Italian exiles who shared the experience of fighting alongside Giuseppe Garibaldi in their country of
origin. The widespread study of Tandonnet's exploits emblema-
tizes a broader trend in River Plate historiography of anarchism,
which similarly focuses on its European migrant origins and circulation, especially in Argentina.[8] In 1876, anarchists in Montevideo
formed the country's first labor confederation, the Uruguayan
Regional Federation of Workers (FORU). By May 1911, FORU
organized Montevideo's first general strike, spawned by disgrun-
tled streetcar workers who challenged elite notions of progress in
the city.[9] In 1911, nearly three-quarters of the country's 117,000
industrial workers belonged to the FORU.[10]

River Plate anarchists emphasized organizational decentral-
ization and direct action tactics within the labor movement.[11] This
class-based anarchism can be traced to the influence of Errico
Malatesta, who lived in Buenos Aires from 1885 to 1889. Malatesta
recognized the frequency of victorious strikes in the region, arguing that anarchists could capture that fervor and push workers
toward forming a revolutionary consciousness.[12] Turn-of-the-
century anarchists worked in coalition with rival political organizations for the sake of strengthening the combativeness of the labor
movement. According to historian Geoffroy de Laforcade, this
"ubiquitous" and "flexible" quality "was a feature of anarchist militancy seldom considered by historians who chronicle its sectarian
fortunes."[13] Anarchists' emphasis on working-class militancy has
tricked some historians who evaluate the ideology's impact based

on its weight in working-class consciousness. For example, Latin America scholar Ruth Thompson argued that economic grievances and pragmatism proved more influential among anarchist organizations than did the ideology itself.[14] But anarchists gained popularity because the ideology directly informed the strategies and tactics used to confront those working-class grievances.

Yet regional historians trace the end of anarchist influence to the populist projects of Uruguayan president José Batlle y Ordóñez and Argentinian president Juan Domingo Perón.[15] Although both countries saw an influx of Spanish anarchist exiles who migrated to urban and rural areas to escape civil war and fascism, the Peronist experience in Argentina is commonly cited as bookending the ideology's influence in the region. Indeed, many of these Spanish anarchist exiles in Uruguay became founding members of the FAU. But Argentina's experience with Perón and the strong influence of Marxism in Uruguay, whether via the Communist Party or the MLN-Tupamaros, have cast a shadow on anarchism's activity throughout the region.

Still, little is known about anarchism's role and contribution to Cold War–era mass politics. And this remains the case in spite of the fact that New Left mobilizations sparked an upsurge of scholarly interest in anarchism throughout the 1960s. In 1965, for instance, French antiauthoritarian writer Daniel Guérin proclaimed that state communism, not anarchism, was out of touch with the needs of everyday people in the modern world in his *Anarchism: From Theory to Practice*. Historian James Joll, who concluded his monograph *The Anarchists* in 1964 with an obituary to the ideology, was forced to acknowledge that anarchism lived on in the spirit of the sixties.[16] But the initial excitement around anarchism and the New Left primarily acknowledged the ideology's influence in protest and counterculture—more specifically its broader critique of the bureaucratic nature of Soviet Communism. More recent scholars such as Arif Dirlik and Andrew Cornell have dedicated themselves to showing anarchism's influence on popular revolutionary and social movements, such as the Chinese Revolution and the US civil rights movement.[17] But this type of scholarship is rare to encounter as broader historiographical trends continue to fall short of acknowledging anarchism's existence beyond the Spanish Civil War.

The FAU's Latin Americanist anarchism broke from turn-of-the-century anarchist thought and practice to remain relevant in the New Left political trends of the time. In this sense, the FAU's contributions to anarchist political thought and strategy provide another example that challenges the unidirectional relationship between the Global North and South: namely, the FAU moved forth a post-nation-state vision for a revolutionary society in an era during which decolonial and anti-imperialist struggles were saturated with calls for nationalism. While the FAU incorporated some of this Third World nationalist discourse into their own political outlook in effort to remain relevant with the times, they proposed something beyond the globally prescribed solution offered by the left of seizing state power and transforming society from above. Whereas the postcolonial turn of the 1980s supposedly broke from the tradition of Third World nationalisms, the FAU's Latin Americanist anarchism predates such efforts to look beyond the nation-state to resolve the contradictions, challenges, and limitations imposed by the postcolonial condition. Notably, the group advocated for building popular power by growing participation in workplace and spatial conflicts to manifest the relationships and experiences necessary to wage a prolonged battle for the establishment of a nonbureaucratic socialism—one that would forego the nation-state through the implementation of democratic federalism continent-wide.[18] Moreover, the organization embraced Third Worldism as opposed to rejecting it. In their strategic cultivation of this ideology, the FAU would have concurred with scholar Vijay Prashad's observation that "the Third World was not a place. It was a project."[19]

The FAU's unique brand of politics synthesized the region's class-based anarchism with Thirld Worldism. The result was an anarchist "party" that merged traditional anarchism with New Left ideas. While the FAU membership consisted of some ex-Communists who once collaborated with the group in coalitional political spaces, the primary force behind the organization's political trajectory was likely the real impact of Marxism, and especially the presence of the Soviet Union in the Third World—something that anarchists a generation prior did not have to confront. Thus, a study of the FAU also breaks from the capitalism/communism binary that dominates Cold War historiography.

The FAU and Dissident Labor in Uruguay

Uruguayan labor has been highly understudied in both English- and Spanish-language historiography, especially during the Cold War era.[20] The study at hand borrows from a New Labor History framework to focus on everyday people rather than states, institutions, and electoral parties—a lens that coincides with a New Cold War History approach decentering bipolar political power. In its place, this book focuses on a small group of nonstate actors who played a key protagonist role in escalating social conflict. Cold War historiography tends to reproduce a unidirectional relationship between the imperial rivals (United States and Soviet Union) and "victims" in the Global South. As such, global historical accounts produced by North American scholars tend to maintain a US-centric narrative while confining Global South populations as derivative or reactive—thus failing to account for Latin American left protagonists' production of an upsurge of intellectual, strategical, and tactical innovations specific to local realities situated within a continent-wide struggle.[21]

While avoiding such easy binaries, this study also aims to escape the trap of focusing strictly on the FAU. As Geoffroy de Laforcade notes regarding early twentieth century River Plate anarchism, "The cataloging of explicitly anarchist organizations and campaigns tends to limit our understanding of the ideology's range."[22] Therefore, though this book begins by showing the organization's ideological and strategical contributions within the Latin American New Left milieu, it swiftly moves away to focus on conflicts between Uruguayan workers and management, including native-born employers that arbitrated the relationship between foreign capital and labor. The conflicts also saw significant intervention from the Uruguayan state, both as mediator via the Ministry of Labor and repressor via the police and military. While the state certainly cannot be ignored, everyday people remain central to this study.

Upon the FAU's inception in 1956, the organization set out to ignite a dissident labor movement by inserting militants into existing union structures. The first successful union battle occurred while the FAU was still in formation in 1955, when workers at the FUNSA rubber factory went on a fifty-two-day strike to protest four arbitrary firings and to split with their business-friendly union. In 1958, the newly formed union occupied the plant and put it under worker control; three members of the FAU were elected to key leadership positions. The campaigns established FUNSA as a point of reference for other dissident labor currents. FUNSA workers forged relationships with fellow autonomous unions within the Intersyndical Solidarity Commission.[23] Such unions remained autonomous from the Communist-led Uruguayan Confederation of Workers (CUT) due to conflicting positions regarding the simultaneous holding of political office and union-leadership roles, and affiliation with an international labor federation. Throughout the sixties, the FAU challenged the Communist grip over the labor movement by advocating for labor autonomy and the use of direct action or anti-legal tactics, as opposed to courts and the Ministry of Labor, to resolve workplace conflicts. Recognizing labor unions as mass organizations and thus spaces to build popular power, the FAU emphasized participation in workplace struggle as key to the formation of class consciousness.

In 1964, members of the FAU spearheaded the call to form Uruguay's first nationwide labor confederation, the National Workers Convention (CNT). Within the confederation, the FAU aligned with other dissident unionists who challenged the Communists' continued emphasis on negotiation—a coalition first evidenced by a 1967 Fight Plan (Plan de Lucha) rejected by the CNT's majority-Communist leadership. This alliance built upon the relationships established in the Intersyndical Solidarity Commission and eventually grew to encapsulate one-third of the nation's labor unions in the Tendencia Combativa (Combative

Tendency), which led some of the most dramatic and combative campaigns during the half decade leading up to the 1973 dictatorship.

From July 1969 to June 1973, Tendencia-affiliated unions were responsible for 67 percent of workplace occupations, 74 percent of strikes lasting longer than three days, and 72 percent of strikes lasting longer than ten days.[24] These unions organized prolonged work actions that often rejected legal channels of mediation, a number of which drew solidarity actions from fellow unions. The Tendencia's impact on the labor movement and on greater social relations in Uruguay is undeniable. Notably, at the time of the June 27, 1973, military coup, a majority of Uruguayan industrialists recognized the CNT as the most serious threat to national security.[25] Moreover, according to communications between US ambassador to Uruguay Ernest V. Siracusa and US secretary of state Henry Kissinger, the dictatorship's primary concern was to repress a surging labor movement rather than confronting a waning guerrilla movement.[26] After the coup, Uruguayan minister of interior Walter Ravenna identified the Tendencia's influence in the CNT as warranting military intervention and labor reform.[27] Such intriguing indicators notwithstanding, previous historiography (in both English and Spanish) provides insufficient depth to understand the broader climate of labor unrest and popular revolt in the half-decade leading up the 1973 civic-military government. Therefore, the FAU is all the more valuable to the present study as both an object of analysis and a conduit to access narratives from this climate of popular social upheaval.

The FAU and Latin America's New Left

While the term "New Left" originated to describe the Global North phenomenon of a polycentric left that moved away from the Soviet Union's influence and toward analyses of gender, race, culture, and neocolonialism, historian Van Gosse explains the global reach of the New Left by defining it as a "movement of movements."[28] Yet scholars tend to agree that the New Left was spawned out of a global youth rebellion, as George Katsiafi-cas proclaims:

> From France to Tunisia and Yugoslavia to Mexico, students
> broke with traditional political parties of the Left and the
> Right and developed new forms of organization and prac-
> tice. Their unified actions and emergent aspirations were a
> product of centuries of centralization of the world economic
> system, but at the same time, they helped define new dimen-
> sions to the global culture. New values for international and
> interpersonal social relationships quickly spread as a result
> of these movements, values which went beyond what was
> previously considered possible or acceptable.[29]

The New Left is most commonly associated with leftist ethno-nationalist groups, like the Black Panthers and Young Lords, and countercultural youth movements, like the Yippies, that thrived during the late sixties and early seventies in the United States. When broadening to a global scope of the New Left, some scholars have claimed these counter currents were spawned from middle-class youths who reproduced an *en vogue*, yet vacuous "language of dissent."[30] While these definitions help us understand the New Left's eclectic makeup, they fall short of explaining the particularities of the movement in a Latin American context.

Scholars of Latin America generally struggle when applying the term to the continent. For example, Greg Grandin provides a definition of the Latin American New Left as those organiza-tions who expressed *a will to act*. After various countries' efforts at social reform were met with state terrorism, the Cuban *foco* strat-egy offered a solution to foreseeable cycles of violence, or revo-lution and counterrevolution.[31] Jonathan C. Brown, for his part, reinforces Cuba's role as exporter of revolutionary ideology and praxis throughout the continent. Brown paints its revolutionary government as the central counterweight to US hegemony in the region[32]—a dichotomy he traces back to Régis Debray's influen-tial text "Latin America: The Long March," which advocated the continent-wide use of the foco strategy to break from Communist Party vanguardism.[33]

Many have since challenged Grandin's guerrilla-centric definition of the Latin American New Left. For instance, Eric Zolov suggests that Latin American scholars consider the polycentric definition used to describe North America's New Left. He insists that Grandin's "narrow" definition of the New Left "excludes the vast sectors of largely middle-class youth that took no direct part in armed revolutionary activities, yet who were deeply impacted by the cultural and political trends of the time," and "allows no interpretative room to address the countercultural practices found on the left, practices that have been silenced by the historical process which has tended to emphasize the overriding significance of armed revolt and repression." The author further proclaims:

> Historians require a revisionist framework that encompasses the non-armed aspects of radical challenges to political and social norms—counterculture practices, new aesthetic sensibilities, trends in film, literature, theater, music, the arts, as well as the impact of Liberation Theology and links those aspects to transnational processes, without disaggregating them from the discourses and proximity of violent revolutionary movements. Rather than viewing armed struggle—the "heroic guerrilla"—as distinct from seemingly non-revolutionary, consumptive practices ... we should regard these as twin facets of diverse and intersecting movements that confronted state power, on one hand, and patriarchal norms, on the other.[34]

In contrast, John Beverley argues that Cold War–era armed groups laid the foundation for contemporary Latin American politics by making it the only region in the world where socialism is seriously on the political agenda today. This is the case even though the popular representation of armed struggle remains one of a "Romantic adolescence" prone to "excess, error, irresponsibility, and moral anarchy." He sees this present in both popular culture, such as the 2001 film *Amores Perros*, and in the recent comments by some ex-militants, such as Beatriz Sarlo, who claimed that armed strategies should be abandoned not just because they were defeated but "because they were an error."[35] Those scholars influenced by the polycentric definition of the New Left agree that the term describes a broad movement that united various social classes, political ideologies, and revolutionary strategies in an effort to move beyond orthodox analyses and definitions of the Latin American left. According to Zolov, "In Latin America during the 1960s, to be 'on the Left' meant clearly more than choosing between the competing ideological strategies of an older Communist Party beholden to the Soviet Union's (comparatively) cautious approach to revolutionary transformation, and China's (via Cuba) brasher insistence on revolutionary action."[36] This diffuse, and often tenuous, effort to confront the challenges presented by the free market and state power resulted in a resignification of left symbols, a stretched political imagination, and experimentation with new thought and praxis.

Uruguay's 1968 differed significantly from other popular mobilizations and street confrontations that surfaced globally during the same epoch. Indeed, Uruguay saw a unique convergence between Old and New Lefts. On this aspect, Uruguayan historian Vania Markarian claims, "The violent protests of 1968 were innovative, but the novelty arose largely from the relatively widespread use of strategies, slogans, and even forms of organization that were already present in various sectors of the Uruguayan Left (mostly in minor groups)."[37] The author argues that Uruguay's student movements maintained close relations with traditional left organizations, especially labor unions. Similarly, Jeffrey Gould identifies strong linkage between the student and labor movement. While Gould is accurate to identify the continued popularity of mass politics and vanguardism, even among the New Left, he is wrong to paint the PCU as supportive of more militant strategies and tactics, especially within the CNT.[38] For while Uruguayan Communists had to contend with New Left influence in the labor movement if they wished to maintain a united labor confederation, they certainly maintained an alternative vision throughout.

While the Uruguayan case certainly shows a closer entangle-ment of the Old and New Left, scholarship on the latter focuses exclusively on the MLN-Tupamaros. Many newer works also show connections between armed struggle and counterculture, but, beyond mere lip service, they omit the place of the New Left in the labor movement. In this sense, they explore armed struggle solely through groups that applied the foco model.[39] In Uruguay, the FAU and other New Left organizations critiqued foco while still embracing the need to take up arms.[40] Yet, unlike many of their Argentine counterparts, Uruguayan scholars have not fallen into the ideological trap of painting the New Left, especially armed struggle, as separate from the working class.[41] Some North American sociologists even claim that middle classes resorted to armed struggle because their growing expectations that accom-panied regional modernization could not be met by the structural limitations of a Third World reality.[42] As an example of the cross-over between the New Left and organized labor, economist Arturo C. Porzecanski's 1974 study shows that working-class participation in the MLN-Tupamaros doubled between 1969 and 1972, from 17 to 34 percent. By the time of the June 1973 military takeover, the demographic distribution consisted of 29.5 percent students, 32.4 percent professionals, 32.4 percent workers, and 5.7 percent "other."[43] Moreover, the unidimensional category of "student," frequently utilized in dominant historiography, poses issues, as Argentine writer Pablo Possi notes. Indeed, while authors often use the term as a shorthand for "middle class," many students throughout the sixties were simultaneously workers.[44] Yet, the relationship between armed struggle and working-class sectors continues to prove evasive. For instance, in Aldo Marchesi's recent work on transnational armed struggle in the Southern Cone region, the historian admits that investigation of the topic beyond the local level primarily captures the perspectives and experiences of its mobile middle-class leadership.[45]

Meanwhile, the hegemony of the New Left (foco) versus Old Left (party) debate has led scholars to give insufficient attention to the eclectic makeup of the labor movement. Beyond the case of Uruguay, scholars have almost entirely neglected to recognize the presence and influence of anarchism among the Latin American and global New Left—a tendency especially detrimental to understanding Uruguay's Cold War–era labor movement. Internal left debates certainly identify the ideology's conceptual and tactical influences throughout the epoch. For instance, in 1971, British socialist Anthony Arblaster recognized an "anarchist revival" among the international New Left due to its antiauthoritarian character.[46] Similarly, North American anarchist Paul Goodman claimed that anarchism, not communism, was the underlying political ideological current of the 1968 student protests in the United States.[47] Both writers identified a New Left tendency to synthesize Marxist and anarchist politics. Arblaster acknowledged that while anarchist organizations were few, many New Leftists first developed an affinity for the ideology and later sought to combine it with elements of Marxism and socialism. Similarly, Goodman recognized a tension in the New Left rhetoric of "participatory democracy" (i.e., anarchism) and "cadres" (i.e., Marxism). While both scholars speak to a Global North New Left, the anarchist presence in the Latin American New Left remains understudied, although some historiographical scholarship has acknowledged the anarchist origins of the Chilean Revolutionary Left Movement (MIR) and anarchist membership in the Uruguayan MLN-T.[48] This can be seen as evidence of the effectiveness of the FAU's strategy, as members' social insertion via the Tendencia was so seamless that many scholars do not even recognize the presence of anarchism at all.

Beyond the FAU's pervasive presence in the labor movement, members participated in two of Uruguay's most important spaces for the development of New Left debate and praxis, *Época* and El Coordinador. The former, a New Left journal with participation from six political organizations, offered a venue for independent left thought outside of the Communist Party organ. The journal declared support for the 1967 Latin American Solidarity Organization (OLAS) congress verdict, which advocated for armed struggle throughout the continent. Gerardo Gatti, a FAU militant and graphic artist, maintained responsibility of the organ's printshop. However, the FAU's understanding of armed struggle differed significantly from those conceptions popular through-out the rest of the Third World. In 1966, as a result of ongoing disagreements, the FAU parted ways with El Coordinador, which went on to become Uruguay's first armed revolutionary organiza-tion modeled on the Cuban *foco* approach and eventually evolved to become the National Liberation Movement-Tupamaros (MLN-T). In mid-1969, the FAU challenged the MLN-T's armed strategy by forming the Popular Revolutionary Organization-33 Orientals (OPR-33), an armed apparatus of roughly sixty militants to confront escalating state violence. More than a guerrilla unit replicating the Cuban model, the OPR-33 operated as a "techni-cal apparatus" with clear targets and goals to support workers in labor conflicts. From 1969 to 1974, the OPR-33 carried out eight kidnappings, roughly two dozen robberies, and over thirty acts of significant property damage. The organization opposed assassina-tions and never killed a political opponent.

Contrary to the claim that Latin American armed left orga-nizations consisted primarily of naive, young middle-class males waging a belligerent war against the state, the case at hand offers an opportunity to understand a critique and alternative to the foco model advanced by an organization that shared an affinity for the use of armed struggle. The FAU's strongest presence was in Montevideo's working-class neighborhoods of El Cerro and La Teja, and the FUNSA rubber factory union. The organization merged a traditional labor union strategy with New Left armed tactics yet remained strictly committed to the former due to its mass political nature.

Finally, a thorough study of the FAU offers an opportunity to better understand predominant Uruguayan left organizations, the PCU and MLN-Tupamaros. The FAU's critiques shine a refresh-ing new light on topics of armed struggle and electoral politics that move beyond those presented by the hegemonic rival orga-nizations themselves and the state, which used a wide brush to paint the entire left as criminals and terrorists. Indeed, while left projects throughout the continent have made significant reforms in the past half century, they have holistically failed to provide sustainable alternatives the market and state. Thus, it is becoming increasingly important for historians to explore critiques of the predominant left that come from within the left itself. Sectarian rivalries aside, Jeffrey Gould accurately concludes, "The New Left provoked a virulent debate. . . . For most rank-and-file militants, however, the debate was less important than the fight for immediate objectives (however radical); the 'old' and 'new' Left thus had to coexist, even if not in harmony."[49]

The FAU was certainly a New Left organization in the Latin American context. Having formed in the Cold War era with the intention of moving away from traditional anarcho-syndicalism, the FAU introduced a novel approach to anarchism that drew influence from historical and contemporaneous ideas and strategies, including Marxism, populism, and Third Worldism, with the intention of massifying *a will to act*.

Sources and Methods

This study uses a mixed-methods approach and draws from a range of different sources. Primary-source print documents include left publications, FAU internal communications, police reports, and memoirs from state and personal archives. I rely primarily on FAU publications *Época* (1962–67), *Cartas de FAU* (1968–71), and *Compañero* (1971–73) to explore questions of the group's ideology and politics. *Época* hosted foundational conversations of a New Left coalition that would eventually become the Tendencia Combativa in the labor movement. Edited by the celebrated historian and journalist Eduardo Galeano, the journal served as a platform for six revolutionary left organizations, including the FAU. After the government shuttered it in December 1967 and outlawed all six political organizations, they were forced to operate underground.

Cartas de FAU, a weekly clandestine bulletin circulated from June 1968 to March 1971, provides the best printed documentation of the organization's public rhetoric during its three years operating underground. Roughly eighteen thousand copies were produced during the first two years of publication. *Cartas*

aimed to recruit sympathizers with the FAU's position by sharing frequent critiques of and alternatives to the Communist Party
strategy. Some militants eventually abandoned other leftist organizations to join the FAU after developing a familiarity with the
anarchists' strategy and analysis via the documents. Distribution
was risky. Indeed, anyone caught with the propaganda was subject to detention and torture. Militants located in the FAU's primary organizing sites, like the FUNSA factory or Graphic Artists
Union, distributed up to five hundred *Cartas* in their workplace.
However, those not fortunate enough to come into daily contact with revolutionary left comrades would distribute as few
as three or four.[50] On December 9, 1969, members of the FAU
expropriated three mimeographs from the ORBIS enterprise in
Montevideo's Barrio Sur. As a result, publication increased to five
thousand copies per week.[51]

Compañero served as the propaganda organ for FAU's aboveground popular front organization Worker–Student Resistance
(ROE) when it was legalized in 1971. The journal picked up
where the *Cartas* left off as a public-oriented press and continued
in-depth reports of workplace conflicts waged by unions belonging to the Tendencia. Upon seizing power in June 1973, the military dictatorship finally closed the journal and imprisoned the
editorial staff.[52]

I use the *Cartas de FAU* and *Compañero* to offer detail of everyday people's participation in labor conflicts. The publications'
editors hoped to inspire existing collective organizations to take
on roles as protagonists in a struggle against capital and the state
by reporting ongoing mobilizations, thus providing a counter-
narrative that normalized struggle as part of everyday life. After
the closure of *Época*, radical left perspective was absent from mainstream press, leaving the PCU newspaper *El Popular* as the sole
consistent aboveground source for left reporting. Whether due to
self-censorship or political opposition to the mobilizations over
ideological differences, the PCU organ often omitted details of
popular militancy, leaving *Cartas* and *Compañero* as the only documentation of many of the popular mobilizations taking place
during these years.[53]

I combine FAU publications with rival Communist Party publications to reconstruct data and narratives of the labor movement. I also utilize PCU daily press organ *El Popular* (1957–73) to quantify labor conflicts between May 1968 and June 1973. While the daily suffered frequent censorship and often its editors chose to omit details of more confrontational tactics for ideological reasons, the paper dedicated at least a full page to covering labor conflicts regardless of the union's affiliation. The extensive press coverage lends an opportunity to explore both quantitative and qualitative (tactical) differences between PCU- and Tendencia-affiliated unions. Moreover, the paper also offers the opportunity to juxtapose the party's analysis and strategy with that of the FAU.

FAU internal documents—including member profiles, planning maps for armed operations, analyses of labor actions, to-do lists, letters, internal discipline records, union records, and more—play a critical role for reconstructing the FAU's inner culture. These documents were preserved in the personal archive collections of Juan Carlos Mechoso, Martín Ponce de León, Héctor Rodríguez, Ricardo Vilaró, and Hugo Cores. In the case of the former, the contents were hidden in a secret compartment behind a safe house wall for fourteen years while FAU militants were imprisoned or in exile during the military dictatorship of 1973 to 1985.

I have interviewed twenty-seven members of the FAU who have shared in-depth personal narratives to elaborate on the events covered in the documents. Due to the overrepresentation of men in the historiography of the Cold War and New Left, I intentionally sought out women participants to represent over half my sample. Interlocutors guide me to relevant primary sources and help bring meaning to documented events by offering intimate details of personal experiences. I also rely heavily on published memoirs and personal historical research by Hugo Cores, Eleutorio Fernández Huidobro, María Julia Alcoba, Jorge Chagas, Juan Carlos Mechoso, Ivonne Trías, Universindo Rodríguez, and Augusto Andrés. While the abundance of propaganda produced by the FAU allows for a unique look at the organization's broader analysis and strategy, it does not always capture the nuances of workplace conflicts, which were often sparked by communication between the organization and one or two workers located at the site of conflict.

Oral and written testimonies have proven indispensable to the work's final chapter on the FAU's experiences with transnational state terrorism. As Italian historian Alessandro Portelli proclaims,

> There are no "false" oral sources. Once we have checked their factual credibility with all the established criteria of philological criticism and factual verification which are required by all types of sources anyway, the diversity of oral history consists in the fact that "wrong" statements are still psychologically "true" and that this truth may be equally as important as factually reliable accounts.[54]

Thus, oral testimonies allow for a more nuanced and detailed understanding of events captured in police reports, news articles, and intelligence documents from the actors' subjective viewpoints. The final chapter relies primarily on declassified correspondence between the US Embassy in Uruguay and the US State Department. While the chapter departs from its predecessors by focusing on the state as core protagonist and the militants as acted upon, it shares testimonies from some of the few survivors of Automotores Orletti, a clandestine detention, torture, and disappearance center in Buenos Aires where thirty-four members of the FAU/ROE were murdered. Together, we coproduce a narrative-analysis.

Conceptual Framework

While each chapter focuses on a different element particular to the FAU, such as ideology, structure, strategy, and/or micro-level protagonism, this book pivots around the organization to gain a window into how everyday people participated in a rapidly escalating social war. To this end, the present study offers special attention to micro-narratives and micro-gestures in attempt to capture their activity within the framework of intrasyndical debates around strategy and tactics at the union-leadership level. Here, I draw upon the scholarship of Howard Kimeldorf, who argues that labor history should move between union politics and everyday people's behavior. He recognizes that labor history has been tainted by the unfair assumption of workers as either revolutionaries or reformists—a binary he traces to the positions of Vladimir Lenin, who argued that workers would follow their "proletarian instincts" if the vanguard party could at least neutralize bourgeois hegemonic thought, and economist Selig Perlman, who argued that workers were inherently conservative and would naturally reject all radical doctrine in the absence of Leninist agitators. Regarding these assumptions, Kimeldorf jokes, "Lenin's proletarians were too stupefied by bourgeois thinking to complete the journey, while Perlman's trade unionists were too pragmatic to even begin it."[55] Thus, bread-and-butter labor struggles lead to polarizing and different conclusions. For Leninists, every act of worker resistance, no matter how small, marked a challenge to the system itself; for Perlman, workplace demands represented rearguard actions aimed at protecting diminishing economic opportunities in the face of a rapidly changing free market. Faced with this dichotomy, New Labor History moves away from unions to study working-class identity and consciousness in everyday spaces, such as churches, bars, music halls, social clubs, and the home. However, Kimeldorf offers a caveat that is instructive for the chapters that follow: a New Labor History should indeed recognize working-class subjectivity beyond the union, but it must not veer too far from unions as popular expressions of working-class interests.[56] Indeed, in the case of Cold War–era Uruguay, unions remained key spaces for everyday people's protagonism.

This study is largely guided by the Italian communist Antonio Gramsci's concept of hegemony, specifically what he called the "war of position." For Gramsci, revolution in Western Europe did not only require taking state power, or what he called the "war of maneuver." Whereas the Soviet revolution succeeded merely by claiming control over the state, in Western Europe civil society upheld liberal values of the market and state even under conditions of crisis. Thus, bourgeois ideology gained legitimacy, or hegemony, and the ruling class's ideology became the social "common sense" of everyday people. For Gramsci, the question of revolution not only revolved around taking state power but massifying counterhegemonic socialist ideas. Moreover, the counterhegemonic position itself becomes a battleground for rival factions among left groups, who struggle to win working-class hearts and minds toward their respective strategies and tactics.

In pre-dictatorship Uruguay, the Communist Party maintained hegemony over the labor movement yet remained habitually threatened by everyday people's growing militancy as they disobeyed, undermined, and/or rejected PCU hegemony in at least one-third of the country's unions, where workers elected Tendencia-affiliated leadership. This threat increased in times of crisis, when the party had to take more aggressive positions and embrace more aggressive tactics to keep up with a growingly combative base. In turn, the FAU set out to foment antagonism with the state, capital, and union officials to direct workers' discontent into an organized and prolonged Fight Plan for mass social transformation of everyday life. In a recent FAU text titled "Pueblo fuerte: Poder popular desde el libertario," the organization declares:

> The old socialists talked about creating a new civilization; Che made it popular to speak about the *hombre nuevo*. Durruti said that we will bring about a new world in our hearts. These things all allude to values—of a new form of living, of new social relations. If history has taught us anything, it is that this is not produced from above, but it requires the creation of a new social subject—and the active participation of the subject itself is fundamental for their transformation. If the social subject does not come into contact with new social forms and relations, even if they are incipient, they will not have any other points of reference beyond those that they know and tend to reproduce.[57]

While the PCU gave precedent to the *war of maneuver* and prioritized an electoral strategy, the FAU emphasized the *war of position* and aimed to make anarchist strategy and tactics the primary counterhegemonic force among the poor.

Building upon Gramsci, this study also borrows heavily from the analyses moved forth by autonomist Marxist currents in 1960s and 1970s Detroit and Turin. Autonomist Marxism challenges the Marxist-Leninist idea that the working class comes to fruition via affiliation with the vanguard party. Autonomists argue for a bottom-up model of organization centered around working-class culture and working-class struggle as the driving force of history. They argue that direct action, whether in the workplace or the social sphere, brings the working class into being by realizing a collective counter-subjectivity that exists inherently due to their class position vis-à-vis capital. The argument draws from a debate in Marxist scholarship about how the theorist understood the category of working class as a class *in* itself or a class *for* itself.[58] In the words of E. P. Thompson:

> The working class did not rise like the sun at an appointed time. It was present at its own making. . . . Class happens when some men, as a result of common experiences (inherited or shared), feel and articulate the identity of their interests as between themselves, and as against other men whose interests are different from (and usually opposed to) theirs.[59]

C. L. R. James and Raya Dunayevskaya, union and community organizers who formed Detroit's Johnson-Forest Tendency, advanced an autonomous reading of Marxism to describe the high degree of self-organization and wildcat strikes among workers in the automobile industry. They challenged the notion that workers fell victim to a logic of domination and could not move beyond a cycle of spontaneous action followed by reformist negotiations— and thus that they required leadership from an intelligentsia class (i.e., the party).[60] C. L. R. James and Grace Lee Boggs's influential text *Facing Reality* embraces workers' capacity to define and wage struggles in their own interest, especially their capacity to expand the class struggle to include questions of race and gender based on their own lived experiences, rather than due to party-leadership influence.[61] In their view, this occurs regardless of a contradictory discourse and worldview that merely reproduces hegemonic power relations while clashing with workers' lived realities. Fellow Detroit-based historian Martin Glaberman captured workers' mass refusal in *Wartime Strikes: The Struggle against the No-Strike Pledge in the UAW during World War II*. There, he examines workers' behavior when faced with the political demand to sacrifice time and wages for the war effort. While these workers overwhelmingly identified as patriots and supporters of the war, this was the period in which the union carried out the highest number of wildcat strikes.[62] As such, workers acted outside of their collective organizing body and acted on their own terms to *face reality*, even if their worldview seemed contradictory.

The autonomous Marxist analysis inspired (New Left) party dissidents in the face of an increasingly technocratic and authoritarian Soviet Union that became more visible globally after the 1956 invasion of Hungary. According to C. L. R. James and Grace Lee Boggs,

> One of the greatest achievements of the Hungarian Revolution was to destroy once and for all the legend that the working class cannot act successfully except under the leadership of a political party. If a political party had existed to lead the revolution, that political party would have led the revolution to disaster, as it has led every revolution to disaster during the last thirty years.[63]

For James and Boggs, control over production means control over workers, and thus one of the modern state's key functions is to incorporate trade unions into it. While Communist-led trade unions mediated a relationship of domination between the state and labor under capitalist social relations, a transition to bureaucratic socialism thereafter results in the submission of labor to the interests of the party.

Italian autonomist Marxists labeled their current as *operaismo*, or workerism. Italy in the 1960s saw a group of academic sociologists and union organizers coalesce around the journals *Potere*

Operaio and *Lotta Continua*. In his seminal article "The Strategy of Refusal," written amid this intellectual and political ferment, theorist Mario Tronti declares:

> Exploitation is born, historically, from the necessity for capital to escape from its de facto subordination to the class of worker-producers. It is in this very specific sense that capitalist exploitation, in turn, provokes workers' insubordination. The increasing organization of exploitation, its continual reorganization at the very highest levels of industry and society are, then, again responses by capital to workers' refusal to submit to this process. It is the directly political thrust of the working class that necessitates economic development on the part of capital which, starting from the point of production, reaches out to the whole of social relations. . . .
>
> From the very beginning the proletariat is nothing more than an immediate political interest in the abolition of every aspect of the existing order. As far as its internal development is concerned, it has no need of "institutions" in order to bring to life what it is, since it is nothing other than the life-force of that immediate destruction. It doesn't need institutions, but it does need organization. Just as there can be no classes before the workers begin to exist as a class, so there can be no revolution before the destructive will that the working class bears within itself, by the very nature of its existence, takes solid form.[64]

Moreover, such an argument should not be pigeonholed as the charge of autonomist Marxists alone. Drawing on similar logic, sociologist Alain Touraine argues for an approach centered on the *study of social action*, or social movement. He declares:

> If we often feel uncomfortable with the idea of a central social movement, it is because we are still influenced by a long tradition which identifies social movements and political action, that is, organized action aiming at controlling State power. . . . The idea of social movement interprets

very powerfully the attempts of "society" to liberate itself from "power."[65]

The autonomist tradition recognizes capitalist exploitation as pervading human relations outside the factory, especially the home and urban spaces. Italian Marxists adjusted their analysis after the country experienced mass deindustrialization throughout the 1970s. The *autonomia* (or, post-workerist) movement advanced the concept of the *social factory*, which linked housework, affective labor, cognitive labor, and globalized informal labor (especially in the Global South) with capitalist production—arguments most notably articulated by Marxist feminists. In the formative 1972 text "The Power of Women and the Subversion of the Community," Mariarosa Dalla Costa and Selma James declared:

> She could refuse to produce. In this sense, she constitutes the central figure of social subversion.... The starting point is not how to do housework more efficiently, but how to find a place as protagonist in the struggle, that is, not a higher productivity of domestic labor but a higher subversiveness in the struggle.... It does not automatically follow that to be cut off from socialized production is to be cut off from socialized struggle: struggle, however, demands time away from housework, and at the same time it offers an alternative identity to the woman who before found it only at the level of the domestic ghetto. In the sociality of struggle women discover and exercise a power that effectively gives them a new identity. The new identity is and can only be a new degree of social power. The possibility of social struggle arises out of the socially productive character of women's work in the home.[66]

In other words, workers, whether in the factory or the home, form their own collective class identity and individual subjectivities through participation in social subversion. While the domestic sphere serves as *point zero* for the social reproduction of labor power (or the feminized domestic labor necessary to reproduce masculinized value-producing labor power), the domestic sphere can be a space for counter-subjectivity and social subversion by breaking the public/private divide.

Similarly, Argentine philosopher León Rozitchner inquired about rearguard production, subjectivity, and autonomy. Speaking directly to debates between the Old and New Left, he declared:

> All of society is not solely a producer of things, but a producer of people. The entire production system falls into crisis because its production of people, which entails the production of appropriate goods, methods, and relations (divided people, unsatisfied people, people without purpose), produces crisis. Productive forces and production forms are human forms. . . . Thus, we must ask: Have we, militants of the Left, developed our own productive force? Or are we located with privilege at the margin of the system of production?[67]

Rozitchner recognized that market-oriented production created not only a material world but also social subjects. In a clear critique of reformism, he went on to accuse self-identified leftists of succumbing to a hegemonic passiveness in the everyday while only engaging politically via elections and protests. He questioned the left's ability to produce and reproduce counter-subjectivities. The answer to this question lies in an analysis of the private, or the rearguard—a site the present study lends special attention.

The chapters that follow examine the intersection of mass social movements and revolutionary aspirations during a historical moment of transition from industrial to postindustrial society, or liberalism to neoliberalism, bridged by a military dictatorship that directly attacked popular organizations. For more than a half decade prior to the country's military takeover, everyday Uruguayans embraced a unique role as protagonists challenging social domination by capital and the state. While the Soviet-influenced left aimed to channel this popular protagonism into an electoral bid for control of the state, the FAU maintained an anarchist critique of state power. Instead, they sought to build *popular power* and mass subject transformation via collective gestures of solidarity and mutual aid, primarily within organized labor, oriented toward an eventual revolutionary goal. Yet, at the moment of their protagonism, not all actors were revolutionary, nor were all of them workers—and even those who were did not solely act in response to economic conditions. Who were they? What were they doing? What were their aims? And what moved them to act?

The case at hand can be seen as a predecessor to the "new social movements" that transitioned into the twenty-first century. Scholars Sandro Mezzadra and Verónica Gago argue:

> While new struggles, movements, and practices articulated an effective critique of traditional organizations (labor unions as well as political parties), they also reactivated histories and currents of radical politics that had their origin in the 1960s and 1970s, even while emphasizing apparent programmatic differences. The issue of power was not absent from the movements' practices and discourses: however, it was mainly articulated in a "critical" way, starting with radical challenges to any understanding of politics that centered the state as its privileged site.[68]

Borrowing from the autonomist understanding of history, if everyday people's protagonism played a key role in pushing capitalism toward neoliberalism and its accompanying violent reaction from numerous states (i.e., military dictatorships and their legacy), then everyday people's protagonism will also be fundamental for moving toward an alternative.

List of Abbreviated Terms

ADEOM	Montevideo Association of Municipal Staff and Workers
AEBU	Uruguayan Association of Bank Employees
CNT	National Workers Convention
COPRIN	Council on Prices, Wages, and Productivity
COT	Textile Workers Congress
CUT	Uruguayan Confederation of Workers
FA	Broad Front
FAU	Uruguayan Anarchist Federation
FER	Revolutionary Student Front
FEUU	Uruguayan University Student Federation
FIdeL	Left Liberation Front
FOEB	Federation of Beverage Workers
FORU	Uruguayan Regional Federation of Workers
FRT	Revolutionary Workers Front
FUM	Teachers Association of Uruguay
FUS	Uruguayan Health Federation
GAU	Unified Action Group
JUP	Uruguayan Youth at Attention
MAPU	Uruguayan Popular Action Movement
MIR	Revolutionary Left Movement
MLN-T	National Liberation Movement-Tupamaros
MPS	Prompt Security Measures
MRO	Eastern Revolutionary Movement

OCOA	Coordinating Organizations for Anti-Subversive Operations
OLAS	Latin American Solidarity Organization
OPR-33	Popular Revolutionary Organization–33 Orientals
PCU	Uruguayan Communist Party
PSU	Socialist Party of Uruguay
PVP	People's Victory Party
ROE	Worker–Student Resistance
SAG	Graphic Artists Union
UF	Railway Union
UJC	Communist Youth Union
UNTMRA	National Union of Metallurgical Workers
UOESF	Union of FUNSA Workers, Employees, and Supervisors
UTAA	Artigas Union of Sugarcane Workers

1

Anarchy, *Patria, o Muerte*
Organized Labor, Armed Struggle, and the Origins of the Uruguayan Anarchist Federation, 1956–67

In April 1958, the Union of FUNSA Workers and Employees initiated a strike in response to management's arbitrary release of four workers. Management retaliated by locking workers out various times throughout the next six months. The conflict escalated on October 9, 1958, when workers responded to a lockout with a shift-long factory occupation. The day prior, management had suspended a supervisor at the INCAL satellite plant, where a team of thirty assembly-line workers did not meet the daily quota. Workers responded by implementing rolling strikes, taking two-hour breaks to disrupt the flow of production. Management contested once more by suspending the supervisor for forty-eight hours and the assembly line workers for one full day. Upon returning to the plant at six o'clock the next morning, management notified workers of the supervisor's release. Impromptu negotiations between union representatives and management failed to bring resolution to the conflict, eventually leading to a planned three-hour work stoppage to begin at 9:00 a.m. When attempting to start their shift again at noon, workers were greeted by locked doors and nonoperating utilities—a lockout. They reacted by cutting the locks and breaking in to occupy the factory.

The occupation committee consisted of FAU militants León Duarte, Washington Pérez, and seven other union delegates, who met on October 12 and decided to put the factory back into operation under workers' control if the conflict was not resolved within a week. Workers were unaware that they were making history by partaking in the first experiment of expropriation and autogestion in Latin America. FAU militant and union officer Miguel Gromaz recalls, "We were looking for something that was spectacular. We told ourselves, 'A peaceful strike is a long strike,' so we looked for something that would call attention and that could catch the management off guard."[1] One worker remembers the experience similarly, declaring, "We worked with such drive and consciousness. We didn't keep track of the time that we worked; the only thing we wanted to do was produce the same quantity of batteries as if it was a normal workday."[2] Strikers occupied the factory in shifts while sustaining a protest encampment in front of the Uruguayan parliament. They marched repeatedly to the executive palace in Montevideo's center, where they carried out frequent acts of petty vandalism and property damage. On one occasion, women of the factory used iron rods to break through the windows, allowing a flood of protesters to rush in and take over the ground floor.

Workers reimagined the occupied plant as more than a site of production and opened it to student activists fighting for co-governance of the University of the Republic. Over a hundred thousand students participated in the campaign that eventually claimed victory with the 1958 Organic University Law, which established a democratic process for administrative leadership's election by students, faculty, and alumni. Amid the struggle, FUNSA workers demonstrated solidarity by providing fourteen company-owned delivery trucks as barricades in Plaza de los Treinta y Tres, where students clashed with police while occupying the university. The trucks carried banners that read, "Workers and students united and onward!"

After three days of worker self-management, the factory bosses, under pressure from investors, returned to settle the conflict. The workers gained a 33 percent daily wage increase and management reimbursed all suspended workers with back pay. The occupation fostered solidarity among supervisors and manual workers alike. Gromaz recalls:

> The vast majority of workers who participated in mobilizations demonstrated wide agreement within the attitudes

of the union. Without this, we would not have been able
to mobilize 1,300 to 1,500 people in the street. . . . What's
more, I was always taken back that regardless of the fact that
the majority of workers were either Blancos or Colorados—
conservatives or liberals—they expressed a strong loyalty
to the union, and on many occasions put their party divisions aside.[3]

Recognizing the supervisors' sentiment, Duarte reached out to
them—a liaison that eventually led to expansion of the membership base to all 2,200 plant workers, thus birthing the Union of
FUNSA Workers, Employees, and Supervisors (UOESF).

In early 1961, FUNSA owner Pedro Sáenz sold the plant to
US-based Firestone—a development that would give new meaning to the frequent workplace strife as the site became another
emblematic example of neocolonialism throughout Uruguay and
Latin America.[4] For the next fifteen years, workers consistently
elected List 1, a radical coalitional caucus with the FAU's León
Duarte as general secretary, thus placing an anarchist at the helm
of organized labor in Uruguay's largest industrial plant.[5] Upon
assuming the role, Duarte began to work full time as a union
organizer. Management refused him access to the workplace
because he was no longer on the shop floor. Duarte subsequently
developed a knack for sneaking into the bathrooms, where he
would spend all day chatting with workers.[6] The 1958 coordination between the UOESF and the Uruguayan University Student
Federation (FEUU) took on a mythical quality due to revealing the
potential for collaboration between Old Left (labor) and a growing
and enthusiastic New Left rooted in the student movement. While
this encounter proved hopeful, FEUU secretary general Alfredo
Errandonea and secretary of union relations Hugo Cores, both
FAU militants, produced a 1958 report on student–worker relations in which they argued that the FEUU remained supportive
of labor struggles from afar via public statements but fell short
of an active relationship between themselves and the community.
They suggested increased engagement with the labor movement
through student attendance at union meetings, rearguard support,

and coordinated strikes.[7] Through such encounters, the FAU aspired to grow a relationship between the Old and New Left.

What matters here is the FAU's position vis-à-vis fellow left organizations and its contributions to founding the country's two most important left spaces over the next decade: El Coordinador (predecessor of the National Liberation Movement–Tupamaros [MLN-T]) and the National Workers Convention (CNT). While the FAU eventually declined to participate in the former due to its distance from popular movements, the organization remained committed to the latter despite remaining a minority position within it.

Latin Americanist Anarchism: A Break from Tradition

The Cold War era brought economic, social, and political crisis to Uruguay. The country's ranch economy—meat, wool, and hides—came to a halt after international demand plummeted at the end of the Korean War. Rural production remained steady at 90 percent of total exports throughout the postwar epoch, yet the total proportion of primary production for export fell from 49 to 26 percent from 1941 to 1961—numbers that continued to plummet throughout the sixties. The decline in exports brought crisis to a national economy that financed its large state bureaucracy, progressive welfare system, and import-substitution industrialization on the earnings brought in from the rural sector. As foreign markets reoriented toward Australia and New Zealand, landowners refused to invest in new technologies and agricultural stock, thus further accelerating the decline.[8]

By the 1960s, over half of workers in Montevideo labored in the public sector. Uruguay's famed proto-populist president José Batlle y Ordóñez established this trend by using government employment as reward for patronage and in exchange for social peace. He nationalized electricity, implemented the eight-hour day and compulsory rest for every five days worked, opened higher education for women, and spread public schooling to rural areas. President Batlle's reforms responded to growing militancy in the labor movement. In some ways, the government's own policies contributed to labor's combativeness, such as unrestricted immigration to political radicals from Argentina and Europe and implementation of the right to strike. According to historian David Struthers, "Batlle expanded the functions of the State to a position of 'neutrality above classes' and sought to maintain an equilibrium between an antagonistic organized labor movement and the increasingly more vulnerable urban industrialists by concessions to each, while conserving and strengthening the independence of the political system through its capacity to mediate."[9] Struthers goes on to argue that Uruguay's urban immigrant working class lacked party loyalties and thus identified with anarcho-syndicalism, which forced Batlle to make concessions for the sake of integrating labor into the state infrastructure.

Between 1908 and 1911, Uruguayan labor carried out over one hundred strikes, accounting for over five hundred thousand workdays lost. While Batlle famously blessed the 1911 general strike, he was forced to develop a progressive platform for his government and his Colorado Party due to anarchists' hold over the unions and their influence over workers' refusal to vote.[10] Anarchists would eventually lose control of the labor movement due to internal splits over relationships with the Soviet Union, which resulted in the formation of another confederation, the Uruguay Syndical Union (USU), in the 1920s. The tension was eventually compounded by the 1931–38 dictatorship of President Gabriel Terra, who censored left press and deported many labor leaders.

In 1942, the Uruguayan Communist Party (PCU) spearheaded the formation of the General Union of Workers (UGT), a new labor confederation made up of its affiliated unions. In this moment, the party made use of Soviet financing and the symbolic importance of the Russian Revolution internationally to claim hegemony in the labor movement. In 1943, the UGT supported the Law of Wage Councils, which formed a body made up of two representatives from the executive branch, two representatives of commerce, and two representatives from labor to see forth the implementation and adjustment of the minimum wage. While rival USU viewed this as a defeat representing the bureaucratization of labor, the UGT declared the Law of Wage Councils as victorious due to its guarantee of labor's representation within the state.[11]

The Law of Wage Councils would come to influence the party's line regarding social transformation and the state for the next three decades. In 1955, the widely read Marxist writer Rodney Arismendi assumed the position of PCU general secretary, arguing a unique position that challenged the Soviet-backed stage theory. While the Soviets claimed that socialist revolution in the periphery first required a national bourgeois revolution before a proletariat one, Arismendi argued that both stages could be carried out together so long as the proletariat was in command via the Communist Party in political power. He argued that such transformation could be achieved within the parameters of liberal democracy. This strategy translated into a labor movement that moved away from the direct action tactics of the Uruguayan Regional Federation of Workers (FORU) and toward negotiating within institutions.[12]

By the mid-fifties, the engorged public sector paid poorly and offered many part-time or "no-show" jobs; many public employees began working two or three jobs to survive. Moreover, the bureaucratization of the urban economy drew nearly two-thirds of the population to the nation's capital, Montevideo—leaving the countryside depopulated and impoverished. From 1952 to 1967, the role of the presidency was replaced by a National Council of Government, which consisted of nine representatives from Uruguay's two dominant political parties, the National Party (or Blanco Party) and the Colorado Party.[13] The rural crisis reverberated in the industrial sector, causing capital flight due to an unpredictable economy and a shortage of money in circulation, and thus inflation rates as high as 136 percent per year. From 1956 to 1972, gross national product fell 12 percent; per capita GNP stagnated at about $US500 for this duration as well. While Uruguayans enjoyed the highest per capita income of any Latin American country in 1956, real salaries dropped nearly 24 percent over the next decade.[14] By this time, Communists controlled nearly two-thirds of the nation's unions. However, the growing state of crisis generated dramatic shifts and new possibilities for the left.

The FAU originated under these conditions. From April 14 to May 5, 1956, Uruguayan anarchists held the National Anarchist Plenary Session (PNA). The PNA responded to a call from the International Anarchist Congress held in Paris in 1949 to create worldwide anarchist organization. At the time, Uruguayan anarchists participated across a range of organizations and popular fronts, including the *gremios solidarios* (solidarity unions), Cerro–La Teja Free Athenaeum (Ateneo Libre Cerro–La Teja), Anarchist Youth (Juventud Libertaria), and the newspaper *Voluntad*. The solidarity unions formed in the early fifties with the intention of maintaining autonomy from the Communist-led UGT. Instead, they coordinated among themselves to promote the use of direct action tactics in the labor movement. While they did not openly identify as anarchist, they had strong participation from both native-born and exiled anarchists from Montevideo's working class El Cerro–La Teja neighborhoods.[15] The Cerro–La Teja Free Athenaeum formed in 1952 as result of growing militancy among unions and the need to organize a variety of them to coordinate labor actions. While the Athenaeum declared itself politically neutral, local anarchists used it to spread their ideas and tactics to residents and fellow militants. The Anarchist Youth formed in the 1940s as a student organization within the FEUU. They belonged to the *tercerismo* movement, a broad left anti-imperialist coalition that refused to align with either the US or Russia.[16] Finally, the publication *Voluntad* was established in 1938 as an alternative anarchist perspective to the FORU's anarcho-syndicalism. In 1954, the paper moved away from individualism and embraced organized anarchism when a cadre of youths from the newly formed Cerro–La Teja Libertarian Group entered its editorial board. In the mid-fifties, the paper had upward of two thousand subscribers and was sold in more than two hundred newspaper kiosks. By 1956, the militants would be located at the heart of a historic labor conflict in El Cerro's meatpacking industry, which also drew support from eight thousand industry workers who marched for over a month from Anglo refrigeration plant in the northwest city of Fray Bentos. Anarchist militants from these four spaces became the nexus of the Uruguayan Anarchist Federation.[17]

On April 14, 1957, the FAU welcomed delegates from Argentina, Brazil, Chile, and Cuba to participate in the first-ever American Anarchist Conference in Montevideo.[18] This was an effort to bring together representatives throughout the hemisphere to promote pan-Americanism in opposition to both United States and Soviet imperialisms. Attendees recognized the continent's shared language and historical experience of colonialism as unique globally and positioned the region at the vanguard of a postnational identity. They critiqued small-nation nationalism as reactionary, bellicose, and "antithetical to an international culture," arguing instead that anarchism provided the only appropriate response to Cold War imperialism. The attendees proclaimed, "As Americans, we denounce the subdivision of the pueblo in exasperated nationalisms as a key instrument for economic exploitation, political oppression, and cultural disintegration of the continent's inhabitants. As anarchists with our international character … we will fight against existing states and superstates."[19] The conclusions of the American Anarchist Conference foreshadowed a pan-American, anti-imperialist, *ni-Washington-ni-Moscu* (neither Washington nor Moscow) perspective that eventually became hegemonic among the Latin American New Left after the 1959 Cuban Revolution.[20] Moreover, before the widespread use of armed struggle throughout the continent, FAU militants Alberto Mechoso, Enrique Constela, and Pelado Larrañaga carried out the first bank robbery in Uruguay at the Banco La Caja Obrero in Paso Molino on July 4, 1958. The small sum of money they appropriated was used to finance the FAU's print organ, *Lucha Libertaria.*[21]

Yet, the 1959 Cuban Revolution would eventually impact Uruguayan anarchism in an unforeseeable way. Whereas anarchist organizations throughout the hemisphere questioned the revolution's legitimacy or treated it indifferently, the FAU declared critical support. In October 1960, the FAU issued a statement titled, "Why Do We Support and What Do We Defend about the Cuban Revolution," declaring:

> We, who remain committed to a libertarian socialist program and who know that the Cuban Revolution is not, at

least in this moment, the type of popular revolution that
we previously promoted, believe that it can constitute . . .
the opening for a Latin American way toward socialism and
freedom. . . . For what it is today, and for what it could go
on to be, we must defend the Cuban Revolution here and
throughout Latin America.[22]

While the statement recognized the important reforms advanced
by the revolutionary government, the FAU saw the true spirit
of the revolution in common people's gestures, especially their
sacrifice and support for the guerrilla movement prior to any
state-centered revolutionary project. Everyday people's gestures, including those of non-working-class sectors such as students, peasants, small shopkeepers, and vendors, proved vital to
their taking an active role in the revolutionary process. Thus, the
Cuban's *foco* model proved that a small guerrilla cell could advance
from the countryside to seize power and make revolution in the
capital. This guerrilla vanguard, rather than an urban proletariat
insurrection, would ignite revolution with support from popular
sectors. Although foco challenged the Marxist-Leninist party vanguard, it still relied on the protagonism of a small group of people to act as revolutionary leaders. And while foco decentered the
Communist Party as the harbinger of revolution, the FAU would
eventually take issue with the guerrilla vanguard as well.

Nevertheless, the FAU's view of Cuba's significance highlighted a statement brought before the United Nations in which
the authors refused to accept the false binary between East and
West, declaring "Capitalism negates man, and communism, with
its totalitarian conceptions, negates the rights of man—that is
why we are neither." The FAU recognized this "third way" as the
"vanguard" for Latin America and the world. The FAU's declaration of support went on to draw upon lessons from the 1936
Spanish Revolution, mainly the lack of solidarity among the
Latin American left beyond proclamations of sympathy. It drew
parallels between the occurrences of 1936 and 1959, such as the
role of outside intervention by capitalist and communist global
powers. Instead, the FAU declared that the only way to avoid the

liquidation of the Cuban Revolution to both Communist states
and parties was to amplify solidarity among the Latin American
nonaligned left.[23]

The FAU's position on Cuba drew inspiration from orthodox
Marxism, populism, and democratic federalism. While they recognized that the state-centric Cuban Revolution contradicted anarchist principles, they saw it as a potential stepping stone toward
stateless socialism, or what Marx referred to as communism.
Moreover, tercerismo's emphasis on nonalignment and positive
use of the term "Third Position" showed influences from regional
populism, including Peronism, which initially drew upon symbols,
discourse, and strategies of turn-of-the-century Argentine anarchism, specifically the figure of the *descamisado* (shirtless one)—a
poor, rural, racialized internal migrant who settled in the urban
outskirts of Buenos Aires, Rosario, and Córdoba to find work in a
growing domestic industrial economy. Finally, the FAU imagined
Latin America's future as a democratic confederation, liberated
and self-organized through participatory democracy rather than
a nation-state model.[24] While Cuba did not represent this vision,
the revolutionary government's emphasis on continent-wide revolution demonstrated a shared ethos that could be pushed further
toward an anarchist horizon.

The FAU's position on Cuba sparked internal division within
the organization. Historian Eduardo Rey Tristán identifies the
two competing sides of the debate as "traditionalist" versus "New
Left." Throughout 1961, militants Lucce Fabbri and José Jorge
Martínez debated the FAU's support for Cuba in the pages of
Lucha Libertaria. Fabbri, a professor in the Faculty of Humanities
(University of the Republic) and daughter of famous Italian
migrant and anarchist intellectual Luigi Fabbri, represented a
minority position that was popular among students belonging
to anarchist collectives in the School of Fine Arts, Faculty of
Medicine, Union Group, and Comunidad del Sur housing collective. She advanced a traditional anarchist perspective of the Cuban
Revolution, which remained skeptical of any project that claimed
state power. As such, the position critiqued Fidel Castro's affinity for state capitalism, growing totalitarianism, one-party rule,

and relationship with the Soviet Union. For Fabbri, anarchism was irreconcilable with what took place in Cuba. Their strategic solution looked something like dual power, in which anarchists built cooperative alternatives to the market and state. Martínez, the elected FAU secretary, represented a majority position that was popular among founding members of the FAU active in the labor movement, including the Graphic Artists Union (SAG) and UOESF. He argued a New Left, or Third Worldist, position that saw the principal contradiction as one between imperialism and liberation.[25] Influenced by dependency theory, he viewed any bid for anarchist utopia to be impossible without intervening in a global system of extraction and exploitation—one in which the global core directly benefited from the underdevelopment of the global periphery by accessing cheap resources and labor. He believed anarchists needed to update their politics to be attuned to the rising ride of Third Worldism globally. These contrasting perspectives strongly resembled cotemporaneous polemics between Old and New Left Marxist currents.[26]

The debate concluded in May 1962 with a strong reaffirmation of the FAU's majority position in an announcement in *Lucha Libertaria*. The statement referenced militants' experiences organizing in the tercerismo movement and emphasized a commitment to an anti-imperialism that rejected both US and USSR expansion into Latin America. The FAU's position nodded toward en vogue conversations in coalitional organizing spaces, especially the student movement, where supporters of tercerismo opposed the Moscow-imposed prescription for revolution via stages, especially the replacement of old (foreign) oligarchy with a new (domestic) one and Marxist-Leninism as the sole representative of socialism. Instead, the FAU emphasized the importance of building and linking a network of self-managed production and consumption cooperatives throughout the continent to build regional solidarity and transcend the market and state. Popular liberation struggles throughout the Third World were a step in this direction.[27] Most importantly, the FAU's position on the Cuban Revolution inspired a reevaluation of their domestic strategy in Uruguay, such as the defense of popular organizations as the only true revolutionary protagonists, advocacy for a united (revolutionary) left around points of unity, shared sensibility, compromise, and a search for theoretical and ideological inspiration beyond European models.[28] These interventions established a unique mass political strategy rooted in a synthesis of traditional anarchism with Third World liberation, which entailed moving beyond the concept of a universal subject and its relationship to the market and state, and toward the incorporation of a structural analysis of global politics—one in which the "wretched of the earth" (as Frantz Fanon famously called them) had unique relationships with the global world system outside of the Marxian dialectic but nonetheless served as revolutionary protagonists.

By this time, anarchist organizations throughout the continent and around the world had begun withdrawing their support for Cuba. Among the global anarchist community, initial reports of the Cuban Revolution came from Manuel Gaona Sousa, the relations secretary of the Cuban Libertarian Association who supported Castro and sought to cooperate with the new government. In a 1961 document titled "A Clarification and a Statement by the Cuban Libertarians," Gaona denied that any anarchists had been detained or persecuted during the first years of the government. However, word rapidly circulated of the purging, imprisonment, exile, and killing of many Cuban anarchists who had initially played key revolutionary roles, especially as labor leaders in Havana. The Cuban government also suppressed the anarchist press in an era when free journalism all but disappeared.[29] On the other side of the River Plate, the Argentine Libertarian Federation (FLA) published some of the first testimonies of Cuban anarchist exiles in the periodical *Reconstruir*.[30] Yet, the FAU maintained its line of critical support in publicly oriented propaganda throughout the sixties and early seventies.

By late 1962, nearly all militants affiliated with the traditionalist current left the confederation, reducing the organization to roughly four dozen people.[31] While the two differing factions had smoothly collaborated for two years after the organization's foundation, the debate surrounding Cuba eventually pushed existing tensions over the top.[32] The "New Left" current identified more strictly as workerist, or *clasista*, and focused on building strength in mass organizations, especially labor unions. They viewed organized labor as the best avenue to build popular power through the establishment of relationships with everyday people around material-based struggles. They advocated a strict internal structure, including a central organizing committee as opposed to open assembly.[33] They emphasized organization and discipline in attempt to move toward clandestine, revolutionary armed struggle. The traditionalist current, in contrast, identified more closely with a cooperativist anarchism and sought to build alternative spaces and practices. The traditionalists sought to make cultural interventions, primarily at an aesthetic and immaterial level, and spent time building relationships with common people through community-based art projects and cooperative living experiments. They had specific concerns as students that could not be addressed by the FAU's labor-based strategy. In fact, they saw the federation's development of a stricter and disciplined internal structure as an obstruction to the student movement's autonomy and critiqued the workerist members of the FAU for pushing a party line. Strongly pacifist, they commonly dismissed their ex-comrades as anarcho-Bolsheviks or Castroists.[34]

The 1962 schism enabled each faction to pave an independent path. The FAU would organize a central committee around the group's veterans: Juan Carlos Mechoso, León Duarte, Roberto Franano, and Mauricio and Gerardo Gatti. This group would set out to build an analysis and strategy toward a unified labor confederation and accompanying armed apparatus. It was a way to ground the organization in a class-based strategy that people could take or leave upon joining. The traditionalist current, meanwhile, moved on to establish a student-worker-run campus at the School of Fine Arts, which included strong participation from community members via the extension program. In 1965, students and faculty launched a community-based art project to engage with people outside of the university by painting the facades of houses in working-class neighborhoods, such as Barrio Sur. The project, titled "Visible Sensibility," emphasized the potential for liberation through self-expression and collective labor.[35] They coalesced around a network of housing collectives, called Comunidad del Sur, which eventually grew to as many as two hundred members. Both currents maintained a distant communication via a small handful of members who continued to participate in both spaces.[36]

Inspired by Cuba, the FAU's Latin Americanist anarchism marked a break from the historical European migrant torchbearers of the movement in the region. At the turn of the twentieth century, Southern and Eastern European anarchist migrants had brought with them a global perspective rooted in their travels. While they had often been forced to migrate by exile or state repression, they laid the foundation for a global anarchist movement of the time. Workers who moved across borders found themselves in similar exploitative conditions no matter the country of their workplace—but it all seemed to fit within a more liberal-universalist worldview. Midcentury working-class Uruguayans were autochthonous. Many were born in Montevideo's western neighborhoods of El Cerro–La Teja or internal migrants from racialized regions in the northwest region of the country. The "new working class" encountered a previous generation of mostly inactive anarchist militants from eastern and southern Europe. Although they borrowed from the analyses of their immigrant elders, their life experiences were situated more strictly within the realities of midcentury Latin America and Uruguay, and they knew little beyond their local realities aside from media representations, including the excitement of poor people globally for the success of the Cuban Revolution. The FAU could not ignore that reality and thus grounded its anti-imperialist position firmly in the fervor surrounding Third World liberation.

"Words Separate Us; Action Unites Us": El Coordinador and the National Labor Convention

In mid-1962, four hundred sugar cane workers marched from Bella Unión (Artigas Department) to Montevideo, traveling six hundred kilometers from the northwest corner of Uruguay. In the 1950s, sugar cane workers began organizing to challenge widespread abuse by employers under the guidance of Raúl Sendic, a young lawyer and member of the Socialist Party of Uruguay (PSU). The Artigas Union of Sugarcane Workers (UTAA) grabbed public attention when they began coordinating frequent marches to Montevideo to demand rural labor reforms, specifically an eight-hour day, minimum wage, and expropriation of 30,000 hectares left by absentee landlords. After waging a regional campaign for nearly half a decade, they marched to Montevideo to gain more visibility. These marches revealed the tension between the countryside and Uruguay's predominately urban population. Authorities detained upward of 400 people during the UTAA march of 1963.[37]

The cane workers' struggle inspired radical left organizations in Montevideo to come together in a coalition consisting of Peasant Support Movement (MAC), Eastern Revolutionary Movement (MRO), Revolutionary Left Movement (MIR), FAU, and minority factions within the Communist and Socialist Parties. Meetings consisted of left militants who would become key figures of the revolutionary left over the next fifteen years, including Raúl Sendic, Eleuterio Fernández Huidobro, Andrés Cultelli, Hébert Mejías Collazo, José Mujica, Washington Rodríguez Belletti, Eduardo Pinela, Canario Long, Jorge Torres, Gerardo Gatti, and Vivian Trías.[38] They first gathered in late 1962 after the government implemented Prompt Security Measures (MPS), which established a state of emergency and suspended constitutional rights. The measures prohibited work actions, banned the right to assembly, enforced curfews and press censorship, and enabled authorities to detain and interrogate members of labor unions and political organizations. Under these conditions, Sendic recognized the urgency of forming an armed organization for worker self-defense after repeated experiences with state and paramilitary violence during UTAA marches and rallies.

The coalition initially drew inspiration from the revolutionary struggles in Cuba, Algeria, and Vietnam. Its members also saw themselves as a frontline response to the rise of neofascist groups that had gained traction during the recent economic downturn, many of whom frequently carried out physical attacks on

members of leftist organizations, especially youths.[39] Identifying
the imminent threat of a military coup, the coalition began to
meet frequently to develop a provocative but unpopular analysis.
Huidobro recalls the militants having come to the following conclusions in those meetings: "Uruguay will have the same destiny as
the rest of Latin America. There will be hard social conflicts, hard
repressive measures, and likely coup d'etats. There is a need to
prepare for self-defense, at the very least. There is a need to adapt,
invent, and prepare; to think about new responses and new crossroads."[40] Such perspective led those in the coalition to prepare for
what was seen to be an inevitable armed conflict with the military.
Those early meetings saw the first mention of stockpiling weapons
from the local shooting range and resulted in the formation of El
Coordinador, Uruguay's first armed left organization. To ensure
all participating organizations maintained autonomy, the coalition
operated around six points of unity: (1) Each organization would
maintain independence in anything that did not come from coordination with other groups within the coalition; (2) organizations
could freely collaborate with one another outside of the coalition;
(3) participants would keep secret all information about membership and resources; (4) organizations would share any information
regarding security and intelligence within the coalition, but there
was no obligation to share anything else; (5) organizations would
maintain their own political line and their existing affiliations with
political organizations or labor unions, in which obligations to El
Coordinador were only mandatory in cases of actions and other
coordinated efforts; and (6) acceptance of new groups to the coalition would require unanimous support and would require that
such group participate in at least one military action.[41] The coalition aimed to transcend left sectarianism and united under the
phrase of cofounder Raúl Sendic, who declared, "Words separate
us. Actions unite us." One year later, Uruguay would be plagued
by rumors of military takeover while sandwiched between dictatorships in Argentina and Brazil.

On August 1, 1963, El Coordinador carried out its first expropriation of the Swiss Rifle Club in Colonia. Members ventured
170 kilometers northwest in a Volkswagen van and returned with

twenty 1934 shotguns, five 1908 shotguns, two .22 rifles, one
Martini rifle, and 3,700 bullets.[42] In Christmas season 1963, El
Coordinador organized a series of expropriations under the name
Operation Manzanares, in which members robbed a series of food
delivery trucks belonging to the grocery chain Manzanares and
distributed the food in the working-class Montevideo neighborhood of Barrio Cerrito. Between 1963 and 1966, El Coordinador
carried out a handful of similar actions, which they signed under
the name "Hunger Commandos." Such actions gave rise to the
group's reputation as "Robin Hood guerrillas."

The coalition also organized various acts of vandalism, particularly against US-owned private firms as a means of denouncing
US intervention in Uruguay. When Uruguay broke diplomatic
relations with Cuba on September 18, 1964, militants ignited
bombs at Moore-McCormick Lines, ITT, Bayer, and Coca-Cola,
leaving some of the first references to the name Tupamaros.[43] In
the first week of May 1965, in protest of the US military invasion
of the Dominican Republic, militants set off bombs at US-owned
firms PepsiCo, Coca-Cola, International Harvester Company,
General Electric, Colgate-Palmolive, All American Cable, and
Western Telegraph.[44] These actions served as practice for what
later became a more experienced and cohesive guerrilla movement.

While El Coordinador challenged Communist hegemony by
introducing a new set of tactics in dialogue with rising revolutionary left currents throughout the continent, PCU leaders held key
positions within labor unions and ran the only viable third-party
position in electoral politics. Influenced by Marx's stage theory
of history, the party promoted a reform-oriented platform that
was standard among Soviet-linked parties worldwide. After a
1955 reform congress, however, the party combined an electoral
and syndicalist strategy and installed Rodney Arismendi as the
general secretary. Although the PCU never gained more than 6
percent of votes throughout the '50s and '60s, the party gained
weight among organized labor with help from finances coming
from Moscow. Yet, the party claimed only twenty thousand members, of which roughly eight thousand were active militants. The
PCU remained committed to an electoral political strategy and

negotiation with workplace management. Its platform sought to gain an alliance with the landed national bourgeoisie to challenge dependency on First World economies, organize the largest sectors of the working class, and increase the membership of the mass political organization Left Liberation Front (FIdeL). The party was a strong opponent of both direct action and armed struggle. Similarly, in 1964, party leader and *Marcha* editor Carlos Quijano declared, "Today, here—Uruguay 1964—with a middle class, with 250,000 public officials, with 350,000 retirees, with nationalized public services, with a weak and unorganized proletariat, with a dispersed and nonexistent peasant class: force can only bring reaction. . . . Objectively, there is no revolutionary possibility."[45] Importantly, the PCU was the only Communist Party in Latin America to remain legal throughout the height of the Cold War era.[46]

But skepticism around the effectiveness of armed struggle in Uruguay was not unique to the Communists. El Coordinador's formation also challenged Cuban revolutionaries' initial assessment of a path toward revolution in the country. In August 1961, Ernesto "Che" Guevara called armed struggle "incorrect" during a speech at Montevideo's University of the Republic. Ironically, a neofascist gang fired upon him upon leaving the auditorium. Although Che escaped unscathed, Arbelio Ramírez, a history professor, lay dead on the street thereafter.[47]

However, the FAU's participation in El Coordinador proved short lived. In 1964, FAU militants carried out their last action: an expropriation of arms from the Armeria El Gaucho, one year after the coalition's formation.[48] Sectarian conflicts grew to produce an eventual separation based on strategic differences. Most members of El Coordinador did not see a role for the organization in labor union struggles beyond that of the UTAA; rather, they looked to Che and to Mao Zedong for influence and began pooling money for boots, blankets, flashlights, and maps in preparation for a future guerrilla campaign from the rural province of Artigas.[49] But the FAU's strategy of combining armed struggle and work action pushed against the Cuban-influenced rural strategy popular among the majority of the coalition's members. As a small organization, the FAU had limited resources and thus could not commit to a coalition without full confidence in the shared strategy. Those who remained part of El Coordinador went on to form the National Liberation Movement–Tupamaros (MLN-T). At the time of the split, neither the FAU nor MLN-T claimed more than fifty militants.[50] Yet, both organizations would become the primary threats to Communist hegemony over the left.

The FAU retracted from the coalition but maintained a formal structure for weekly communication with the MLN-T, MRO, and other member organizations. They shared resources, including arms and falsified documents. The groups also continued dialogue through their participation in the independent New Left journal *Época*, the country's first broad left publication independent of party affiliation and without participation from the Communist Party. Over half a dozen left organizations participated in the journal, which sold upward of four thousand copies per week. In 1962, after four years of publishing its own independent bulletin *Lucha Libertaria*, the FAU halted its publication to participate solely in *Época*. By 1966, Eduardo Galeano—who would later pen the seminal *Open Veins of Latin America*—undertook the role of chief editor and established weekly columns from each participating political organization.[51]

The CNT People's Congress

In May 1964, conversations around a labor confederation solidified amid another UTAA protest encampment in front of the Faculty of Medicine in Montevideo. The marchers received daily support from local unions, including UOESF, SAG, and various textile plants organized under the recently formed Textile Workers Congress (COT). Daily visits to the camp brought FAU militants into frequent contact with Washington Rodríguez Belletti (UTAA), a founding member of the MLN-Tupamaros, and Héctor Rodríguez (COT), a recently expelled member of the PCU. The militants had worked together while participating in El Coordinador, but growing repression of cane workers called for a new urgency. On May 14, 1964, police attacked the UTAA encampment with tear gas and rubber bullets. With rumors of a military coup spreading, unions discussed their limited options. While many suggested a twenty-four-hour general strike, León Duarte and Héctor Rodríguez advocated an indefinite general strike with workplace occupations. Moreover, they saw the need to practice coordinating strikes and occupation tactics. The networks established throughout the UTAA struggles culminated in the Plenario General de Apoyo a los Cañeros, which called its first twenty-four-hour national general strike on June 17, 1964.

While the PCU leadership was initially reluctant to sacrifice their hegemonic position among the labor movement by forming a pluralist confederation, the June 17 general strike's success animated students and workers. A week later, sixty-five unions followed the lead of UOESF, SAG, COT, and the PCU-led Workers Central of Uruguay (CTU) to convene and discuss the formation of a nationwide nonpartisan labor confederation. By September 27, 1964, the dialoging unions elected the first Representative Table of the CNT. Regarding the confederation's founding, Gerardo Gatti declared:

> The march for land; the lack of solidarity and, in some cases, clear sabotage through a recurrent use of the same methods by the [CTU]; the police repression suffered by UTAA having gained responses solely from peace activists and some supporting organizations; the debate that all this sparked; the growing threats to union and public freedoms; the worsening economic situation—these were all factors that incited discussions about the necessity of a convention.[52]

The convention would eventually agree to organize toward a general strike and national day of action for April 6, 1965.[53]

FAU militants León Duarte (UOESF), Washington Pérez (UOESF), Gerardo Gatti (SAG), and Hugo Cores (Uruguayan Association of Bank Employees, AEBU) saw the formation of a labor confederation as key to coordinate actions between labor unions. Due to the confidence Gatti and Duarte had won among

ANARCHY, *PATRIA, O MUERTE* 53

autonomous unions over the past decade, they played an especially unique role in shaping the CNT.[54] Indeed, it required quite a bit of credence and poise to build trust across political differences that had real material consequences for everyday people who bore the brunt of these decisions. For example, El Cerro residents frequently heckled PCU organizers with sheep noises as spite for the party's role in squashing the 1956 meatpackers' strikes.[55] Thus, organizing across sectarian lines required fighting against many bad historical memories. While many unions had remained autonomous as opposed to joining the PCU-led initiatives to form the UGT and CTU, the anarchists' participation in the formation of the CNT showed the potential for a more pluralist labor confederation. The UOESF earned a nationwide reputation for its campaigns alongside students throughout the fifties, and Gatti was widely known among Communists for his work as an officer in SAG, although the artists union remained a PCU stronghold. Moreover, Communists felt threatened by growing discontent among workers within the CTU and the rising trend of laborers rejecting their unions. All these factors combined to ignite the formation of Uruguay's CNT.

The CNT's genealogy could be traced to three prior attempts to build nationwide labor confederations: the Uruguayan Regional Federation of Workers (FORU, 1905), the General Union of Workers (UGT, 1942), and the Union Confederation of Uruguay (CSU, 1952).[56] For Gatti and other FAU militants, the FORU served as a shining example for how to network and coordinate different labor unions around a central body but played too much of an ideological function for anarcho-syndicalism, which could not sustain itself politically after facing strong state-led repression. Contrarily, they argued that the UGT and CSU fell short of growing worker combativeness due to their international political associations, the former was directly linked to the Soviet Union via the PCU, and the latter eventually fell into the hands of the US-based American Federation of Labor and Congress of Industrial Organizations (AFL-CIO) after various political maneuvers enacted by a small fraction of its leadership.

The CSU was an especially interesting historical case. While

primarily an initiative of the Uruguayan Socialist Party with Juan
Acuña, José D'Elía, and Jorge Pereyra at the helm, it eventually
settled into the stewardship of the International Confederation
of Free Trade Unions. The CSU served as an alternative to the
Communists' UGT and CTU. Throughout the fifties and early sixties, it was the largest labor confederation in the country. In 1953, it
doubled UGT membership with forty thousand workers. By 1962,
the CSU claimed eighty unions among its membership. In the
early sixties, the confederation began to unravel after key member
unions, such as AEBU, voted in Communist leadership. In 1961,
the American Institute for Free Labor and Development, a subsidiary project of the US Agency for International Development,
demanded a CSU-affiliated housing cooperative be turned over
to their control. Tensions mounted when General Secretary Juan
Acuña refused and numerous Communist- and PSU-led unions
began to withdraw from the federation. Heeding the CNT call
for labor unity, Acuña retired from his position in 1965. The CSU
disbanded on June 16, 1966.[57]

Having learned from the shortcomings of such sectarianism, Gerardo Gatti and other FAU militants envisioned a labor
movement more appropriate for the historical moment, in which
the national confederation was open to all political perspectives
and all workers. Such a project would also require that the labor
movement remain free from interference by national political parties, foreign governments, and religious institutions. The CNT
structure was meant to encourage rank-and-file participation and
decision making, in which active and vibrant conversations within
fields, factories, and workshops could define a political culture
and strategy specific to the realities of the working class, without
"electoral or reformist illusions."[58]

In August 1965, the CNT hosted the Congreso del Pueblo
(People's Congress), a gathering of over 1,300 delegates and 707
organizations representing almost a million people to assess the
country's socioeconomic situation and devise a program to confront it. With PCU-affiliated and autonomous unions all committed to participate, over two-thirds of Uruguayan workers
were represented in the confederation.[59] While most attendees

represented unions, other groups included university students, retirees, and production cooperatives, among others. Even as the congress showed the left's potential to organize, it became a battle-ground for competing ideologies and strategies when participants selected nine officers to serve on the National Directory. While most belonged to the PCU, Gerardo Gatti and Héctor Rodríguez (COT) represented a challenge to the PCU line in the CNT's highest body.[60] The CNT was divided into over twenty different Zonal Committees with delegates representing each worksite in each geographical area of Montevideo and the interior. For exam-ple, Zone 20 consisted of FUNSA, Ghiringhelli, Niboplast toy factory, and eight textile factories, including PHUASA, HISISA, and Sadil—some of the most combative in the industry.

Patrons agreed upon six points: agrarian reform, import-substitution industrialization, nationalization of foreign trade, nationalization of the banking system, progressive tax reform, and extension of the social welfare system. The congress also took on complex social issues such as education—especially widespread illiteracy—and transportation. Attendees divided into workshops where presenters shared research on unemployment, hunger, edu-cation levels, banking systems, and international relations. One document proclaimed, "The word 'crisis' is not just something used for propaganda—it is our daily reality."[61]

The energy surrounding the formation of the CNT rever-berated into the streets and factories. From January 1964 to March 1965, Uruguayan workers took part in 657 work actions, including stoppages, strikes, and occupations—the total number of shift labor lost due to strikes doubled to two and a half mil-lion since the mid-fifties.[62] On October 7, 1965, the government utilized MPS security protocols to flex its power and manage labor unrest while negotiating for an International Monetary Fund (IMF) loan. One week later, the CNT called its first gen-eral strike, followed by a series of mobilizations throughout the month. In early November the government lifted the MPS but attempted to instill them once more on December 9, when both *Época* and *El Popular* received censorship notices. Again, the CNT met the decree with wide-scale strikes, putting a halt to various key industries for multiple days at a time. In response to the censorship, graphic artists and journalists carried out multiple forty-eight-hour strikes. The government retreated, calling an end to MPS two weeks later.[63]

The solidification of the CNT and rising popularity of armed struggle led to intensified government repression—especially torture—with a hemispheric reach. Indeed, the United States was already running counterrevolutionary programs throughout the continent. Uruguay-based CIA agent Philip Agee recalled a December 12, 1965, encounter with a Uruguayan Armed Forces officer with whom he was sharing information. While visiting a military outpost, Agee heard screams from the other side of the wall. Agee cringed after realizing that his information gathering was likely responsible for capturing the victim. Upon noticing Agee's discomfort, the officer raised the volume of the radio to drown out the cries with the voice of play-by-play commentary of the evening's football match. Agee retired from the CIA in 1968 and eventually published *Inside the Company*, a book that details his experiences in Uruguay.[64]

A Fight Plan

At a practical level, perhaps the most interesting and resurgent question concerned the CNT Fight Plan (Plan de Lucha). In a document leading up to the 1966 National Union Assembly, the CNT Representative Table agreed on three key elements upon which to focus in order to expand CNT membership in both Montevideo and the interior: (1) finding points of unity among campaigns in both urban and rural contexts, and building solidarity around them; (2) coordinating simultaneous actions among the entirety of the CNT to confront the government, landed oligarchy, and industrial class; and (3) utilizing coordinated action via the CNT, specifically its Zonal Committees, as a base to broaden participation from other social sectors.[65] Moreover, the Table recognized the growing climate of crisis and the necessity of going beyond defensive spontaneity and toward permanent and long-term action. Recognizing the CNT's diverse political makeup, the Table proclaimed that sectarian tensions would dissipate by leaving no workplace conflict isolated—in other words, *unity in action*.[66]

The FAU saw the CNT as having the potential to galvanize every sector of popular Uruguayan society and turn them into revolutionary protagonists.[67] The CNT Fight Plan closely paralleled the FAU's own political vision of building popular power, albeit without the strong anarchist rhetoric commonly used only within the organization. Moreover, the anarchists left a strong footprint in the federation's trajectory, most notably constitutional Article 49, which prevented CNT officers from simultaneously holding government positions. Yet, the PCU remained hegemonic among organized labor and thus became synonymous with the CNT majority.

While the CNT maintained lofty standards of nonsectarian solidarity in rhetoric, this would not always play out practically. Although the Fight Plan promised not to leave any conflict isolated, leadership's energy often went into institutional efforts. Whereas FAU militants interpreted the Fight Plan as a blueprint for a strategy of tactical escalation around the use of direct action, the CNT majority consistently respected and legitimized state institutions as avenues for resolving class conflict, whether through legal codification or arbitration. Majority-aligned unions often used short-lived tactics such as two-hour work stoppages or twenty-four-hour strikes to flex their might to the government— the mobilizations terminated with a rally in front of the parliament and a return to work the next day.

Moreover, Communist leadership often stretched themselves thin and struggled to prioritize the labor movement with their political maneuvering. Indeed, it was on such grounds that the FAU and other New Left groups critiqued the Communists' "yellow reform" campaign leading up to 1966 elections. The reform, an initiative of the PCU-centered FIdeL electoral coalition and mass front, set out to establish an executive power alongside the president and, most importantly to the labor movement, to eliminate the draconian institution of MPS. Like FIdeL's presidential ticket, the bill gained support from just over 5 percent of voters.[68]

The PCU participated in advancing the reform while simultaneously involved in the formation of the CNT. In *Marcha*, Héctor
Rodríguez declared, "They have thrown out the idea to confront
reactionary reforms with popular reforms. It seems to be a way to
enter into distracting games around constitutional reformism. . . .
Reformist projects isolate, confuse, and divide."[69] Similarly, Jacinto
Ferreyra (UOESF) proclaimed, "To enter into the game of struggling over one reformist project or the other is confusing to workers—it entails entering into the politicking and obstructive game
of the bourgeoisie. We are not opposed to reforms in order to
remain apolitical but because they do not help the process of unification."[70] In other words, Communist political wranglings gave
workers the impression that leadership was operating in the institutional sphere, although many of them distrusted it to begin with.

FAU militants raised concern over what they called fetishism
of a "utopian strong parliament." They argued that the success of
labor mobilizations should not be measured by their ability to create "sensibility" in the parliament, but instead for their ability to
win demands directed toward management or the state. In this
sense, mass action played a key role in bringing workers together
around the CNT and continued as a solidifying force in the face
of multiple government attempts to make "orange" reforms. In
a speech at the FAU's tenth anniversary celebration, Gerardo
Gatti declared:

> The conditions must be created, we say. For that we must
> unite all of those who live by working beyond the banners
> of a party. The electoral bid does not create consciousness; it
> confuses. It does not promote struggle; it paralyzes it behind
> facades. It does not aim for concrete victories; it diverts
> them. In the same way that it deviates, it also paralyzes, con-
> fuses, and divides popular mobilization and substitutes it
> with a workers' program, one that plays the game of reform
> for and against the Constitution.[71]

Gatti drew from past experiences among anarchists to warn of
the dangers of orienting the labor movement toward a specific

political party or ideology. Thinking historically about the FORA and FORU, he proclaimed, "We must evade the mistake of intending to convert unions into extensions of political parties. . . . This is the same mistake that anarcho-syndicalists fell into when they took on the difficult task of founding the first 'resistance societies' in the River Plate region."[72] Here, Gatti was especially referencing the famous 1905 fifth FORA conference in which the union declared itself committed to anarchist communism, sparking the departure of socialists and reformists from union ranks. This position was eventually overturned in 1915, leading to a split in the union.[73] Thus, not only were cotemporaneous Communists guilty of sectarianism in the labor movement, but past generations of anarchists fell short too.

Conflicting visions of the CNT went as deep as questions around nomenclature. While the autonomous unions grounding the coalition had already agreed on its name—Convención Nacional de Trabajadores (National Workers Convention)—the PCU argued for the use of "Central Única de los Trabajadores Uruguayos" (Workers' United Center of Uruguay). Thus, a debate ensued over the use of the terms *convención* versus *central*. Having initially drawn inspiration for the CNT name after the Spanish anarchist Confederación Nacional del Trabajo (National Labor Confederation), Gatti firmly rejected the use of the term "central" due to its hinting at a top-down structure under Communist control. Contrarily, Wladimir Turiansky, a high-ranked PCU official, argued, "There is a statute, there is a program, there is a declaration of principles, and thus, it is a central. But we are not going to risk the thin specter of unity that we have over a name. It is a central, meanwhile we will call it a convention."[74] Agreement around even minute questions proved difficult. Disputes around the initial direction of the CNT would result in a series of street fights throughout Montevideo in its inaugural years.[75] But militants persisted.

Yet, the FAU and PCU shared the analysis that revolution was not on the horizon. In a 1967 interview, Gerardo Gatti declared, "I emphasize that whatever direction a union takes, it will finish a conflict or struggle negotiating. Except for the case in which there is a complete triumph of the working class, something that is not possible at the moment, the correct route is negotiation."[76] The overarching question was around the role of negotiation and its prioritization vis-à-vis popular direction, considering militants had limited amounts of time and resources. The FAU critiqued the PCU for having demobilized everyday people and prevented them from sharing experiences that would make them more militant. Hugo Cores declared, "Class struggle is not only the apocalypse of the union, instead it is a determinant in the process of unity and liberation of workers and the *pueblo*. It is also what unites workers with the *pueblo* in the way that they express solidarity during conflicts."[77] Such conversations around the role of campaigns for wage increases existed within FORU at the turn of the century. The FORU generally opposed wage-based struggles for reformist ends, seeking instead to organize toward one revolutionary general strike and insurrection. Yet FORU militants like Antonio Laredo argued that workplace struggles for wage increases provided the training ground for revolutionary insurrection, specifically the use of firearms and explosives.[78] The FAU would eventually take a similar line.

Tensions between the PCU majority and dissident union currents were on public display on June 3, 1967, when the UOESF submitted a second Fight Plan to the CNT Executive Board. The document criticized the CNT majority for neglecting to devise an offensive strategy in two years since the confederation's formation. Instead it proposed that the CNT reflect on and define a set of precise, tangible, and immediate common goals for the labor movement, and to develop a strategy for winning them. While the high number of work actions, including a successful (political) general strike in 1965, proved labor's capacity to act on the offensive, the CNT's lack of orientation risked relegating the movement to the defensive. It critiqued CNT leadership for establishing a close relationship with the Ministry of Labor, including monthly conversations. The authors perceived the CNT's bureaucratization, including leadership's consensual participation in government-sponsored commissions whose members were without clear objective or function. While the CNT frequently published declarations, the authors raised concern that the confederation was in danger of transforming into a mediator between labor and the state. The document went on to advocate for the right to dignified labor (including redistribution of arable land and reactivation of factories under national control); living salaries, wages, and pensions adjusted to the rapidly surging cost of living; universal access to education; price and rent controls; and the nationalization of the banking, transportation, and meat-packing industries. The authors further suggested to build base organisms, such as committees, internal commissions, and delegate councils, and to politicize union membership against the government's increasingly frequent human rights abuses. Finally, the document concluded by advocating for the use of popular direct action as a means of raising mass consciousness, declaring, "We must decide between politicking: red tape, mediation, 'dialogue,' having our CNT run by management . . . or an offensive Fight Plan that foments consciousness by way of direct action."[79] While the Second Fight Plan grew excitement among radical tendencies in the CNT, it did not win the attention of the majority leadership.

Inspite of the increasingly vocal labor militancy, President Oscar Gestido's government stepped up repressive measures in the second half of 1967, after the IMF blamed salary increases for Uruguay's 182 percent inflation rate. Moreover, the country's key industries fell into steep economic crisis after the United Kingdom banned meat imports from the region due to an outbreak of hoof and mouth disease. In August, the government prohibited the annual meeting of the Permanent Congress of Trade Union Unity of Latin America and the Caribbean from convening in Montevideo. The same month, the military responded to labor conflict by occupying Montevideo's port and postal service headquarters. On October 9, the government implemented MPS amid renewed IMF conversations and a growing labor conflict among public bank employees (AEBU). In turn, the repressive measures forced the closure of *El Popular*, *Marcha*, and *Verdad*, a weekly bulletin published by graphic artists and journalists, amid a 114-day strike during which two hundred workers lost their jobs. By the end of the month, nine AEBU leaders and four workers were imprisoned.[80] In November, four FAU militants studying to become teachers at Montevideo's Normal Education Institute would be detained and interrogated for affiliation with the MLN-T.[81]

Meanwhile, the UOESF Second Fight Plan gained little support among the CNT Executive Board. On the evening of October 9, the CNT Executive Board met to discuss suspending a CNT-wide general strike in solidarity with bank workers. After receiving news of the MPS decree, however, the Secretariat reconvened to call for a general strike on October 11. The strike enjoyed great success, with shutdowns in some of the country's most hard-to-organize industries. Two weeks later, after the CNT threatened another twenty-four-hour general strike, the government lifted MPS.

Years later, when Héctor Rodríguez reflected on the double meaning of the strike's success in the face of an indecisive CNT leadership, he expressed confusion at the Communists' hesitation to mobilize in support of AEBU, a striking union whose PCU-affiliated caucus ran the union backed by ten thousand members in recent elections. While AEBU's leadership faced an uphill battle to achieve wage increases in the public sector, Rodríguez suggested broadening the scope toward a prolonged campaign for an increase in national minimum wage instead—already outlined the UOESF Second Plan. He concluded, "This has all occurred because the CNT majority does not believe that we are in a frontal attack with reactionary forces and that there is no risk of a political crisis. . . . If we keep silent, if we don't revise and correct our approach, we can fall into defeatism and demoralization without any reason to do so."[82] A similar pattern would reoccur over the next half decade.

Cuba: An Ideological Victory and Symbol of Revolutionary Subjectivity

Beyond the domestic questions, Uruguay's left milieu would also continue to draw influence from events abroad. While the FAU rejected foco strategy and directed political militancy toward the formation of the CNT, the organization remained attuned to national and continental conversations around armed struggle and continued to support Cuba. The FAU spearheaded the Committee for Solidarity with Cuba, including hosting the coalition's first meeting in the organization's local. Drawing participation from nearly all non-PCU-affiliated left organizations, the body maintained a strong presence in neighborhoods and factories throughout Montevideo.[83]

Yet the FAU's strange bedfellow relation to Cuba was not unique, as Communists also drew influence from the island. The PCU initially greeted the Cuban Revolution warmly but remained opposed to augmenting an armed strategy in Uruguay. In 1963, PCU general secretary Rodney Arismendi declared, "We are an echo of the continental revolutionary movement, which is bursting forth, fighting against imperialism, with its eyes on the victorious struggle of the Cuban revolution. We are a single force . . . whose heart beats in the Cuba of Fidel Castro."[84] While the party maintained allegiance to Moscow and continued with an electoral strategy, it also kept in close touch with the Cuban revolutionary government. In frequent meetings between Rodney Arismendi and Fidel Castro throughout the early sixties, both leaders agreed that armed struggle was not an appropriate means for achieving revolution in Uruguay due to the country's flat geography and high urban concentration. By 1966, the PCU's position caused dissent in the party, most notably indicated by the growth of the Eastern Revolutionary Movement (MRO), a pro–armed struggle current whose membership increased ten times to over one thousand core members by the end of the year.[85] Under pressure to keep up with a growing left alternative, the PCU advocated for other forms of political violence, such as property damage. In January 1966, the Communist Youth Union (UJC) orchestrated attacks against Pan American Airways headquarters and other US-owned commercial enterprises during a visit by IMF officials. Party leadership mandated that damage be restricted to stone throwing and prohibited the use of Molotov cocktails and other incendiary devices.[86] Eventually, the party sent a group of UJC youths to Cuba for weapons training and established a sizable weapons reserve.

In August 1967, tensions around armed struggle spilled into the international arena when 160 delegates from nine countries participated in the first conference of the Latin American Solidarity Organization (OLAS) in Havana, Cuba. The conference set out to build a consensus around the use of armed struggle on the continent. After having trained upward of five thousand revolutionaries in handling arms, the OLAS conference served as a litmus test for the formalization of organizational support behind them. Most delegates belonged to revolutionary left organizations unaffiliated with their country's Communist Parties. As such, Brazilian and Argentine parties, out of strict allegiance to Russia, declined to send delegations. The Uruguayan delegation was headed by Rodney Arismendi (PCU) and Ariel Collazo (MRO), who attended alongside other representatives from FIdeL- and PSU-affiliated organizations.[87]

The FAU sought to participate in the conference and to send militants to Cuba for training, but the Cuban government rejected their offer due to their identification with anarchism. Regardless of the FAU's participation in the Committee for Solidarity, the organization's political ideology raised suspicion among Cubans. This began in October 1966, when Haydée Santamaría, the general secretary of the OLAS organizing committee, wrote to the PCU to inquire about the FAU's presence at the conference.[88] In the end, the FAU did not send a delegate to OLAS and instead entrusted *Época*-related allies with advancing a position in favor of armed struggle. Regardless of being excluded from the OLAS conference, the FAU remained supportive of the effort to convene left organizations throughout the continent around the topic of armed struggle. To celebrate the OLAS convergence and the fourteenth anniversary of the Cuban Revolution, the FAU held a speaking series in the weeks leading up to July 26, with appearances from Eduardo Galeano and Mario Benedetti, among others. Advertising the series in *Marcha*, the FAU declared:

Aside from our support and participation for the popular

mobilizations taking place on July 26, the FAU would like to contribute to the public understanding of Latin American revolutionary experiences and, especially, take from them some conclusions that can be applied here—as they are appropriate to our reality—those of a combative orientation, without hesitations, and of an offensive struggle against the oligarchy and imperialism.[89]

While the FAU clearly recognized the importance of the Cuban Revolution at a symbolic and practical level, they always made subtle references to the specificity of the Uruguayan context and insisted on studying foreign events, as much to ask questions as to look for ready-made answers.

The ten-day conference concluded with a majority vote in favor of armed struggle. Diverging on questions of country-specific conditions, the Uruguayan delegation split down the center regarding the viability of an armed strategy and provided political theater throughout the congress when Arismendi and Collazo would break out into frequent screaming matches over their differences.[90] Of the twenty-four delegations in attendance, only the PCU and Venezuelan Communist Party did not support an armed strategy. While the former split its vote, the latter outright rejected armed struggle and was banished from further participation after accusations of Moscow-inspired sabotage.[91] The twenty points published at the conference conclusion generalized the foco strategy as viable throughout the continent. One point proclaimed, "Armed struggle is the fundamental line of Latin American revolution, and all other forms of struggle should serve, and not impede, this fundamental line, which is armed struggle."[92]

While the FAU opposed vanguardism, whether rooted in guerrilla organizations or political parties, the organization welcomed the OLAS verdict as a victory against the PCU's reformism and the hegemony of Communist parties throughout the continent. Eager to spread the word of the widespread support for armed struggle, the FAU requested permission from Galeano, *Época*'s chief editor, to use the organ's press to run off over twenty thousand copies of an OLAS special edition bulletin that included the first publication of Fidel Castro's closing speech circulated in Uruguay.[93] The special edition set out to fill a void left by the lack of coverage in the PCU's paper, *El Popular*. The FAU saw the OLAS agreement as an ideological victory that established a continent-wide block in opposition to the electoral path toward revolutionary goals. Thus, Cuba served as a symbol of a Latin American path toward socialism via armed struggle.

However, the goal of a continent-wide revolution via armed strategy soon encountered doubts following the capture and execution of Che Guevara in Bolivia, exactly two months after the conclusion of OLAS. His death put a halt to the unbridled optimism brewing among the Latin American revolutionary left just a few months prior. According to historian Aldo Marchesi, Che's murder marked a shift toward new repertoires in armed struggle, more specifically toward urban guerrilla warfare, and a geographic relocation of the focal center of armed struggle from Central America and the Caribbean to the Southern Cone.[94] It also sparked an internal battle among the left around the meaning of his life and ideas. For the FAU, Che served as a moral example due to his commitment to igniting a revolutionary protagonism in common people throughout the continent.[95] Whereas the OLAS conference concluded that it was the duty and right of Latin Americans to make the revolution, Che best embodied this ethos by taking on that responsibility subjectively. Che's concept of the *hombre nuevo* (new man)—one who would embody a communitarian attitude—represented a revolutionary mass subjectivity that the FAU set out to inspire through the accumulation of experiences among the Uruguayan working class.

The 1968 FAU pamphlet series *Rojo y Negro* would eventually dedicate significant text to an anarchist perspective on Che. In an article titled "Mijail Bakunin y Ernesto Guevara: En dos épocas una misma intransigencia revolucionaria," FAU militant Gonzalo Garcia compared Communist Party responses to Che with Marxist and social democratic critiques of Bakunin during the mid-nineteenth century. Whereas Bakunin ventured throughout Europe to participate in popular struggles, including various riots and street fights with authorities, Che had led a guerrilla campaign throughout the Global South. Both embarked on a mission to spawn popular insurrection. Moreover, both saw a key role for peripheral spaces, such as Southern Europe and the Third World, and populations, such as campesinos and day laborers, in inciting revolution.[96]

The pamphlets also contained various creative writings commemorating Che, such as a poem by Idea Vilariño and song lyrics by Carlos Molina, both fellow travelers of the FAU. Vilariño's poem expressed her disbelief at Che's death and insisted that he remained alive in the political work of revolutionaries throughout the continent. The poem radiates tenderness and compassion, for which she was already known as part of Uruguay's Generation '45 literary movement alongside Mario Benedetti and Ángel Rama, among others. Molina's lyrics declared Che immortal due to the righteousness of his ideas. Upon returning to the River Plate region after a European tour, the famous anarchist *payador* was arrested in Dorrego, Argentina, at the annual Festival of Gaucho Tradition for singing a song about Che.[97]

While Communists faced backlash for dismissing armed struggle, the party claimed Che Guevara as a martyr. Their resignification of Che stirred controversy among revolutionary left organizations who labeled the party as disingenuous and deceitful. The FAU responded by republishing a reflection from Bolivian Communist Party (PCB) member Mario Monje, who accompanied Che in his guerrilla campaign in the Bolivian highlands. The text, originally published in the magazine *Punta Final* in February 1967, decried the PCB's neglect of the guerrilla campaign. The FAU addressed the incongruences in the PCU's narrative of PCB participation in Che's Bolivia campaign: while the PCU's *El Popular* claimed that the PCB's Central Committee offered direct assistance to the guerrilla offensive, Monje proclaimed to have no organizational support until a few months before Che's murder.[98] As subsequent communications would confirm, the FAU published such declarations to push the party further left rather than to merely slander.

The OLAS decision sparked a closer relationship between the Cuban revolutionary government and the pro-Cuba MRO. In October 1967, the MRO began accepting Cuban money to assist in propaganda campaigns supportive of the Cuban model. They utilized the funds to set up numerous clandestine guerrilla training programs in the interior and to rebrand *Época* as an organ for the OLAS platform. The FAU, MRO, PSU, Uruguayan Popular Action Movement (MAPU), and MIR agreed to the organ's new function in November 1967.[99] The paper also pledged support to the CNT's Fight Plan and vowed to develop a political strategy merging labor militancy with armed struggle.[100] This "two foot" strategy was eventually taken up by the FAU.

The merger occurred amid a broader transitory climate in Uruguay. President Óscar Gestido's reign—which would last a mere nine months—marked an end to the National Council of Government and a move toward a single-man presidency. Gestido struggled to resolve the country's growing economic crisis, which saw cost-of-living increases double during his presidency. Minister of Economics Amílcar Vasconcellos initially cut ties with the IMF in search of a domestic economic solution. However, labor strife continued to escalate, resulting in a complete overhaul of economic policy and implementation of MPS once more in October 1967. A week before Gestido's sudden death in office on December 6, 1967, a CIA special report commented, "President Gestido has now surrounded himself with realist economists and the government is showing a new determination to curb Communist labor agitation."[101] His cabinet overhaul would carry over when Vice President Jorge Pacheco Areco assumed the nation's helm from 1967 to 1971.

On December 12, 1967, less than one week in office, President Pacheco Areco made his first governmental decree ordering the closure of *Época* and mandating the dissolution of all six organizations participating in its production. The reason, although never explicitly stated, seemed to concern a text published by the MLN-T regarding their relationship with the police. In the "Open Letter to the Police," the MLN-T clarified a series of events that resulted in a shootout one year prior in Montevideo's El Pinar suburbs. The group assured police that they were not interested in waging war against them but instead saw them as allies in a class war against the oligarchy. The government accused the journal of breaking constitutional law by attempting to incite treason.[102]

Over the next two weeks, police forcibly closed all six organizations' locals and detained many of the groups' primary organizers. Foreseeing the possibility of a raid, Gerardo Gatti fabricated
an archive of fake FAU documents to confuse authorities about
the group's activities.[103] The FAU relocated meetings from their
local to El Tropero (The Herder), a safe house in the Parque Rodo
neighborhood of Montevideo rented out by Idea Vilariño.[104] On
December 26, the FAU clandestinely circulated a communique
announcing the detention of six members: Gerardo Gatti, Pedro
Seré, Pedro Aurrecoechea, Julio Arizaga, Armando Cuervo, and
Carlos Machado. The communique identified the government's
attack as an effort to strike a blow against those groups on the left
most dedicated to "inspire and expand participation in struggle."[105]
Having learned from historical examples of illegalization of anarchist and other radical left press, specifically those of belle epoque-
era Barcelona and Buenos Aires, the FAU prepared to operate
as an underground political organization.[106] The December 26
communique was the first of over one hundred secretly produced
editions distributed to FAU members and supporters through
an underground network that would be used over the next three
years. The communique also responded to Areco's banning of the
Época-affiliated organizations by announcing the commencement
of the "legal dictatorship" era.[107]

In the days after the *Época* ban, the PCU made a series of statements in *El Popular* decrying the government's use of censorship as
unconstitutional. According to the CIA, "The Communists protested the government's repressive action, but in lackluster tones
that barely disguised their contentment with the misfortunes of
their rivals."[108] Unaffected by the ban, the PCU became the only
legal left organization in the country.

Conclusion

Amid the eventual fervor of mid-1968, an underground FAU bulletin reminded readers: "Our country is not an exception among
a broader Latin American historical process to fight for national

liberation."[109] The FAU's support for Cuba marked a clear break from turn-of-the-century anarchist thought and toward a Latin American anarchism—one rooted in aspirations for mass subject transformation in Uruguay and Latin America. The Cuban revolutionaries served as a moral point of reference: they challenged orthodox Marxist and liberal democratic prescriptions for social change. Their ethos and praxis of direct action followed a historical precedent of everyday people's participation in fending off foreign occupation and influence on the continent, beginning with the wars of independence. While the FAU did not support the foco model, they looked toward the spirit of the Cuban revolution as inspiration for the type of mass subject transformation via direct action they sought to foment in the CNT.

The decision to support Cuba shattered relations within Uruguayan anarchist circles and moved the FAU into closer relations with the New Left organizations networked to OLAS. Thus, 1962 marked a key moment in the organization's formation. Hugo Cores declares:

> The [FAU] has to be the only anarchist movement in the world that was equally influenced by anticolonial and anticapitalist revolutions and that stood for another very important thing ... that Gerardo, Duarte, and Raúl Cariboni defended the integration of the CNT alongside Communists. You have to keep in mind that they were doing this in '63, '64, '65, and '66, when the wounds of the Spanish Civil War were still fresh.[110]

While anarchists worldwide declined to cooperate with Communist Parties due to tensions that spilled over after the Spanish debacle, the FAU's insistence on coalition building among the left laid the groundwork for their own internal shift toward a hybrid Marxist and anarchist politics. Similarly, while the PCU remained pro-Soviet and upheld "peaceful coexistence," the party also developed close links and collaborations with anarchist, Guevarist, and Maoist groups.[111] These relationships, while riddled with tension and filled with compromise, provided an infrastructure for mass unrest that would foment rebellion over the next six years in Uruguay.

2

Dark Red, Light Black
Mass Politics and Marxist–Anarchist Synthesis, 1968

Prior to 1968, Uruguay enjoyed relative social and political stability, especially in comparison to the turbulent histories of
neighboring Argentina and Brazil. But the year brought to light
a climate fraught with conflict. While Uruguay's 1968 borrowed
from growing global countercultural trends, including rock music
and sexual liberation, it also drew strong lineage to *older* left projects that remained relevant at the time. As opposed to a reactive
explosion of repressed popular grievances, Uruguay's labor movement already showed great strike capacity, and students were well
organized and always willing to engage in street confrontations
with authorities. These trends continued to intensify in the years
following. In this way, Uruguay, like the rest of the Global South,
played an avant-garde role in shaping what became the global
sixties. Indeed, they had been preparing for it for decades—or
even centuries.[1]

By early 1968, the FAU's presence was growing in both the
labor and student movements. However, the organization's illegal status required the construction of a clandestine infrastructure so that militants could remain in dialogue regarding their
activities in these movements. Veteran militants remained in
contact at El Tropero in Montevideo's Parque Rodo, but they
hoped to purchase two safe houses with organization money, to
avoid further endangering Idea Vilariño, who had taken enormous legal and financial risks to secure that hideout. In March
1968, the FAU decided to begin robbing banks. They considered
the risks significant, based on their comrade Alberto Mechoso's

lengthy sentence for participating in the 1958 robbery of the Banco La Caja Obrero, but they were also emboldened by the left's new embrace of bank robberies as well as the growth of the MLN-T.

On March 11, 1968, a cell of six FAU militants ventured to Union Bank of Uruguay in La Teja, located on the neighborhood's main boulevard, where a significant number of FAU sympathizers labored. They had already documented general patterns in the area alongside help of the bank's employees themselves. Upon arrival, a surveillance team looked out for a group of loitering teenagers that frequented the street corner. The cell planned the arrival to coincide with closing hour. Prior to the bank's closure, a worker knocked on the main entrance to notify the team it would be left open for them to enter. The bank tellers exited through the back door, leaving the security guard alone on site. Workers previously warned the militants of his hot temper: "Be careful with the feisty Gallego—he can make your life miserable."

The operation faced complications because of the militants' work schedules. The escape team, which consisted of two textile workers from La Aurora factory, were summoned to work an hour overtime. After finishing their shift, they scoped out a nearby avenue to intercept and steal a vehicle. Upon stopping the first option, the worker entered the vehicle to find it was an automatic transmission. Bewildered by the modern setup, the militants agreed to leave it and opted for another.

As the operation proceeded, two militants stealthily entered the bank armed with iron rods. Within seconds, the duo exited calmly to the escape vehicle with the bank's entire cash deposit— only to wait nervously for an hour with bags of money in hand as the militants struggled with the car's many quirks. The engine went out twice, and the brakes required a forceful jab to stop. To make matters worse, the escape occurred at rush hour and demanded frequent braking amid bustling traffic. The occupants rocked violently back and forth as FAU militant and bank worker Hugo Cores pressed and released the brake. Cores, meanwhile, was flying high after the successful expropriation from an industry to which he belonged. It was a cartoonish spectacle. At every jerky stop he bellowed, "Arriba los que luchan!" (Hooray for those who struggle). Upon opening the bags at El Tropero, the militants found that the bills were worn and damaged, and they spent the following days repairing them with cellulose tape. Cores's phrase would become the FAU's rallying cry, and it is today used by social movements throughout the continent.[2]

Over the next five years, the FAU carried out ten success-ful expropriations, including operations at six banks and four private firms.[3] While the organization remained committed to class-based strategy and continued recognizing workers to be the traditional protagonist of social transformation, as seen by the historical left, their embrace of anti-legality—specifically armed struggle—moved them to the category of a New Left organi-zation. In the case of Uruguay, the term "New Left" gains an added level of complexity when recognizing the PCU's prepa-ration for armed struggle and embrace of counterculture, the MLN-T's nationalism, or the FAU's vanguardism. Thus, the year 1968 marked a turn toward political hybridity, coalition, and synthesis in which the entirety of the Uruguayan left underwent significant transformation, thus becoming something "new." The FAU was no exception. While the FAU clearly demonstrated what historian Greg Grandin identifies as a "will to act," the orga-nization shared the New Left characteristics of coalition building and hybrid politics. They experimented with a synthesis of tra-ditional Marxist and anarchist politics. They did so not only to remain lockstep with en vogue ideas of the time, but also because a more autonomist reading of Marx fit neatly within their under-standing of the role of workers, or *the masses*, in revolutionary transformation. For the FAU, revolution could not be achieved via policies from bureaucrats, nor did it have anything to do with individual escapism by moral imperative à la counterculture. It required a role for and participation from masses of everyday people. The group shared this perspective publicly in a May 1968 pamphlet titled *Rojo y Negro (I)*. This synthesis was the basis for *especifismo*.[4]

Especifismo, 1968, and the Uruguayan New Left

> *Since Marx and Bakunin initiated their famous debate that*
> *resulted in the division of socialism in two different tendencies,*
> *many things have happened to warrant a reevaluation of the*
> *points of view from which they departed. Of course, in the past*
> *half century of history the capitalist world has greatly changed,*
> *producing a wide variety of revolutionary experiences.*
>
> —FAU, *ROJO Y NEGRO (I)*, MAY 1968

On May 1, 1968, Uruguayan students and workers marched down Montevideo's streets commemorating the murder of the Chicago martyrs. The CNT used the march to underscore impacts of inflation, which had led to price increases of 137 percent in 1967, and another 64 percent by May 1968.[5] The crisis affected students too. The FEUU condemned the government's refusal to release annual budget funds to higher institutions, and high school students protested price hikes in their government-subsidized bus fares to and from campus. The latter had recently coalesced around the Coordinating Unit of Uruguayan High School Students (CESU), a popular organization run by the UJC. The annual march shared similar characteristics with those previous May Day gatherings throughout the sixties, including sporadic rock throwing at buses, a few dozen arrests, and the presence of UTAA sugarcane workers, who joined the march after caravanning from Artigas. However, the 1968 May Day mobilizations continued for the next month, when high schoolers rejected municipal authorities' proposal to lower bus fares, demanding instead that they extend subsidized transportation to the entire population.[6] Marches and skirmishes became a daily occurrence in the nation's capital.

Amid the May fervor, the FAU released the first edition of *Rojo y Negro (I)* under Gerardo Gatti's editorial direction. The 144-page pamphlet aimed to synthesize anarchism and Marxism, and to situate the FAU among the contemporary Latin American New Left currents. The FAU recognized the working classes, specifically the labor movement organized under the CNT, as the vanguard of revolution. According to the FAU, the past decade of political struggle in Latin America proved the need for a vanguard across the continent. They drew examples from Cuba, Guatemala, Colombia, and Venezuela, where radical left organizations developed unique relationships with popular movements and steered them *toward* the embodiment of a revolutionary character. In all four cases, radical left groups also steered popular movements *away* from domestic Communist parties, whose allegiances to Moscow limited their political activity to electoral politics and reformism.[7] Whereas anarchism historically rejected the Marxist-Leninist conception of a vanguard, recent Latin American history proved its necessity. The first few pages of the pamphlet contained the following lines:

> The Latin American left has formed itself by mechanically transferring blueprints based on conceptions that developed in very different conditions and has almost always assimilated them without any serious critique, as if to recognize them as holding an infallible universal value. . . . We cannot continue to justify the survival of stale dogmas that have caused costly sectarianism and have contributed to paralyzing false propositions. . . . In the vast revolutionary processes taking place in the Third World and Cuba, one encounters some manifestation of a vanguard, which is proving capable of dissolving these negative attitudes that have accumulated a growing baggage of historical experiences that do not match up with the classic theoretical outlines.[8]

However, labor did not assume this role objectively. Rather, it *came into being* through normalizing the use of direct action tactics within the confederation. In other words, the successful unification of labor under CNT served as an important first step toward the establishment of a broad conversation, but plenty of work remained to define a common strategy and identity independent of those prescribed by the state's definition of what it meant to belong to a union. According to the FAU, "The dominant classes tremble at pressure from the labor and popular movements, not at elections. That is why they take repressive measures against them and their publications. . . . They do not target reformists whose positions uphold and conserve the current system."[9] Direct action and confrontation served as means to "accumulate experiences" necessary to form a class vanguard. Such confrontations provided key learning experiences for workers, who could only understand the logic and functioning of the class enemy by confronting it head on. Moreover, state repression would forge new solidarities among workers, who would act collectively and selflessly to sustain the fight, thus undergoing a process of transformation into a revolutionary subject. Therefore, revolution was not the product of a single moment but instead a long process of social transformation. While many left organizations—including the MLN-T and, to a lesser extent, the PCU—insisted on the near prospect of revolution, the FAU argued that working-class activity was in a stage of *resistance* in a prolonged revolutionary process, which required working-class protagonism at the vanguard and a mass infrastructure of social reproductive labor and mutual aid in the rearguard.[10] Moreover, wide-scale change could not be implemented from above without the collective transformation of everyday people. This position lies at the heart of the FAU's conception of *poder popular* (popular power): the notion that power must be *created*, not *taken*.

The pamphlet introduced the FAU's strategy of *especifismo*, a synthesis of Marxist and anarchist currents in the form of a revolutionary political organization. After analyzing the historical processes occurring throughout the continent, specifically the use of repression by counterrevolutionary forces, the FAU recognized the need for a "combative, disciplined, and functional" revolutionary political organization embedded in popular movements to "prepare the whole pueblo and its authentic vanguards to lead the transformation processes that are inevitable if the country wishes to save itself."[11] While the attempt to accommodate Marxism was novel for the era, especifismo's genealogy traced back to the origins of anarchism. For instance, this current can be identified in the writings of Russian anarchist thinker Peter Kropotkin when he declared, "[We] consider as a definitive mistake a program which demands full agreement among participants of all details of the ideal and, besides that, the organization of an extensive group of participants before proceeding to activity among the people."[12]

The first practical example of *especifista* anarchism in the River Plate was the Argentine Anarcho-Communist Federation (FACA), a group that split from the more orthodox anarcho-syndicalist Argentine Regional Federation of Workers (FORA) in 1935. They drew influence from another local anarchist thinker, Antonio Pellicer Paraire, whose 1900 article "Worker Organization" called for anarchists to remain dedicated to economic fights in the workplace while maintaining local revolutionary cells committed to larger political questions. The FACA had strong pull in the construction workers union but saw the labor movement solely as a "field of action" and sought to mobilize "all members of society" instead. The Spartacus Workers Alliance, another anarchist group that splintered from the FACA, emphasized unity of action within the labor movement and remained open to working with Marxist political parties. Like the FAU, both organizations operated clandestinely.[13]

The anarchist political organization differed from the traditional left electoral party in its rejection of parliamentarianism and legality. Moreover, the FAU sought to challenge the conservative conception of labor unions as apolitical economic organizations, proclaiming, "Union activity alone, even with the best orientation possible, is not sufficient. The existence of an organized revolutionary political movement is a decisive factor for advancing the process of struggle in this country."[14] Whereas the labor movement already operated under the hegemony of the PCU, the anarchist organization served as a counterweight to advocate for the autonomy of popular movements while ensuring they do not lose sight of a revolutionary horizon. For the FAU, unions provided the highest form of mass organization and democracy due to their legal status, open membership, participatory decision-making process, and heterogeneous ideological makeup. Because traditional parties viewed unions as arenas in which to compete for an electoral base, anarchists had to challenge them in this popular sphere to undercut their influence and promote political independence, direct action, and class consciousness. Failure to do so voluntarily surrendered the realm of mass politics to election-oriented organizations while isolating anarchists, and anarchism, as something countercultural and disconnected. This emphasis on mass action and political organization paralleled analysis and strategy of cotemporaneous Italian autonomist Marxists like Mario Tronti, who later reflected, "Workers' struggles determine the course of capitalist development; but capitalist development will use those struggles for its own ends if no organized revolutionary process opens up, capable of changing that balance of forces."[15]

The FAU recognized that anarchism had gained a poor reputation globally for having lost its class struggle origins in exchange for countercultural practices. However, rather than revise the ideology, they set out to reconceptualize it based on merging the thought and praxis of its forefathers with that of the Cuban Revolution. They saw Cuba's use of the colors red and black as a resignification of the historical anarcho-syndicalist flag:

> The old red and black flag of the anarchists. Its vital attitude. Its libertarian communism. That is its vital message. But along the way anarchism has taken up a negative meaning, one that is not valid: individualism, spontaneity, anti-organizational, community constructivism or cooperativist or syndicalist or educationalist, a sectarian ideology, an unliberating sclerosis. . . . Well, the old anarchist flag has been planted by new hands. It is the flag of the Latin American revolution—the red and black of Fidel, of Camilo (Cienfuegos), and of Che; that of July 26, of the Assault on Moncada, of the guerrilla in our continent. It is that of the old and new causes for socialism and freedom, for anti-imperialism, and for anticapitalism. That of forging a new man and a new society. . . . In this way we are setting out to be one more of the little motors behind the broader popular movement that will march toward revolution in our country.[16]

The FAU also referenced OLAS discourse to proclaim its

commitment to building left unity via collective action. They included a text from Felix de la Uz, director of the Cuban School of Revolutionary Instruction, who emphasized a "unity in action" among the Latin American left. De la Uz challenged Communist Party claims that unity was required prior to action, proclaiming instead that unity came into being via collective action. Thus, he stressed the importance of a consensus to act as opposed to bringing together broad and diverging positions, which could only lead to concession-making and moderation.[17] The Cuban critiqued the Argentine and Brazilian Communist parties for relying on broad political fronts that included representation from the national bourgeoisie. Moreover, both parties argued that the masses were unprepared to take up arms and that armed struggle would only induce a military takeover of government. Instead, they argued the party's role was to organize the masses to prevent a coup (and maintain the status quo) while striking up political allegiances with centrist parties, whose complicity would be necessary in the case of a coup.[18] For de la Uz, the party subordinated the working class to the national bourgeoisie.

In a final effort to align the FAU's vision with that of the Cuban Revolution, the back cover of the pamphlet bore the following quote from Fidel Castro:

> The world does not need
> Guiding countries,
> Nor guiding parties,
> Nor guiding men.
> The world and more than ever
> Our Latin American world
> Needs guiding ideas.

The FAU's anarchist party set out to formally fuse two ideologies considered incompatible for nearly a century. While the Global North New Left organically merged anarchist and Marxist ideas and praxis, the FAU's Latin American anarchism set out to create a formal synthesis at an organizational, rather than personal, level.

Bankers Strike and June '68 Prompt Security Measures

Social tensions heightened as students continued marching and key industries remained in conflict beyond May 1968. In June, workers at the ANCAP utility plant occupied the La Teja refinery, causing a nationwide gas shortage. The visuals of street protests and gas queues inspired the Pacheco Areco government to present the Formula Lanza, a series of wage increases meant to curb the escalating mobilizations. The PCU and other moderate currents in the labor movement embraced the formula, promoting it as a triumph for workers. However, while the formula offered some sectors substantial gains, others, particularly those that fought most fiercely, suffered harsh retaliation. Faced with a permanent lockout in response to a four-month strike, workers at General Electric conceded a significant pay loss for strike days and the firing of all union officers for the right to return to work.[19] In recognizing that concessions frequently coincided with escalated repression, many workers saw the moment as ripe for turning up the heat against the government and their employer.

The Association of Uruguayan Bank Employees (AEBU) rejected the government's gesture and remained on strike, initially as a gesture of solidarity with ANCAP refinery workers. AEBU had earned a combative reputation as early as 1962, when dissident workers pushed contract negotiations to a strike, as opposed to previous practices of quick-to-settle bargaining. The long-fought contract also saw solidarity strikes in the textile industry. By 1964, AEBU leadership moved away from its white-collar identity to situate itself more closely to the labor movement. In 1968, Banca Oficial workers voted for the FAU- and MLN-T-led Lista 1955 caucus, making Hugo Cores the president of their public sector-wide union. The 1955 caucus later won the private banking sector union elections in 1969, giving them full control over organized labor in the financial sector. The FAU viewed AEBU's recent election of Cores as proof that state repression had radicalized workers rather than disempowered them, and that further tactical efforts would build a tighter, more cohesive movement.[20]

In response to the government's Formula Lanza, AEBU's new

leadership distinguished itself from the old guard by rejecting the proposal on the grounds that it did not meet the living-wage minimum agreed upon by membership. Moreover, AEBU leadership denounced the formula on moral grounds because it offered a higher percentage increase to white-collar bank workers compared to other working-class sectors. In stride with AEBU leadership's combativeness, a June 6 general assembly elected to continue the work stoppage and coordinate efforts with a planned teachers strike in July 1968.[21] The bank workers braved intimidation from police units, who surveyed the assembly from inside and attempted to detain union officials upon approval of the strike's extension.[22] Later that same evening, President Pacheco Areco invoked Article 168 of the new constitution to implement Prompt Security Measures (MPS). Minister of Labor Manuel Flores Mora proclaimed, "I cannot be thankful enough for the kind disposition and seriousness of CNT leaders and leadership of other unions. But my good nature, and theirs too, has been taken advantage of by the attitude of minority groups whose ignorant proposals and whose solvent behavior have made this extraordinary regime necessary."[23] He went on to assure that the MPS targeted "isolated groups that make it impossible to dialogue with workers and encourage jungle law within the student movement, burning cars and whatnot."[24] He was directly referring to the FAU and other organizations in the New Left milieu. Similarly, Minister of the Interior Eduardo Jiménez de Aréchaga declared, "The measures are meant to defend public order from the climate of violence unleashed in the streets that does not represent the real interests of the working class."[25] Scholars Howard Handelman and Vania Markarian both recognize the June 1968 MPS as a direct response to bank workers' mobilization.[26] Police forces detained and interrogated various FAU militants in attempt to find AEBU leaders, who began hiding in various safe houses upon escaping detention after the assembly. Authorities laid siege to FAU strongholds, such as the School of Fine Arts and Normal Education Institution, where swarms of riot police units, along with attack dogs, surrounded students and demanded information. The mainstream paper *El Diario* echoed the government's hostility, declaring, "The government's undeniable obligation is to combat, and more than anything, prevent anarchy."[27] To further curb the escalating class conflict, Pacheco Areco introduced a bill for the creation of the Council on Prices, Wages, and Productivity (COPRIN), which froze wages, fixed prices, and allotted a state-sanctioned mediator to labor–management negotiations. Between June 1968 and November 1971, the government maintained MPS for all but three months.[28]

The repression exacerbated divisions within the left over how to respond. Hours after the government announced the MPS decree, the UOESF presented the CNT Representative Table with a proposal for a general strike on June 18 and a long-term Fight Plan. The CNT majority approved the former in hopes that the government would retreat in the face of a one-day strike, as they had done in October 1967.[29] However, the Table rejected the latter under the auspices that prolonged and aggressive labor action would inspire a military coup. They instead suggested waging a legal struggle alongside progressive members of traditional parties in the parliament. The FAU argued that Uruguay was already under *legal dictatorship* in which the government utilized legal means to intervene in, demobilize, and dismantle social organizations in the interests of the national bourgeoisie, mainstream political parties, foreign enterprises, and imperialist nations.[30] On June 21, an article in *El Día* reported on a meeting between newly appointed Minister of Labor Julio César Espinola and CNT president José D'Elía regarding potential wage increases for public sector workers.[31] The FAU viewed such negotiations as bribery, considering workers concerns had begun to far surpass mere bread-and-butter reforms.

Opposing sectors also clashed within the FEUU regarding the urgency of a prolonged strategy and use of combative tactics. Lists of radical students from the schools of architecture, medicine, humanities, engineering, natural sciences, economics, law, and chemistry coalesced around a position influenced by the FAU, MLN-T, and other New Left organizations. On the eve of the general strike, they submitted a letter to D'Elía with their manifesto attached. The statement concluded, "FEUU should return to the path of its earlier days, with the values and tactics, to confront the reactionary police and the 'legal dictatorship' that governs both us and the labor movement."[32]

The June 18 general strike offered an opportunity for more combative unions in the CNT to set a precedent. On the eve of the larger action, the UOESF initiated one-hour rotating strikes and occupied the plant. The Textile Workers Congress (COT) called upon their twelve thousand members to barricade themselves inside their workplaces as a self-defense mechanism against police, who now had the green light to arrest and/or use force against strikers under MPS law.[33] The general strike kicked off a monthlong push with daily rallies and street actions by students and workers. The fervor provided a political opportunity for factory workers (textiles, rubber, electrical services) and white-collar employees (especially teachers, civil service, and bank workers) to meet one another; in so doing, they discovered similar conditions in their seemingly disparate industries. Crowds frequently targeted transit by blocking routes and breaking windshields in opposition to the fee hike. FAU youths from the night school led a campaign to paint buses with slogans in opposition to the MPS. Regardless of authorities' insistence that the state of siege corresponded to members of fringe groups on the revolutionary left, the government violently repressed a much broader sector of the population, including rank-and-file workers. Amid the unrest, the government began drafting hundreds of public sector bank workers and civil service workers into the Armed Forces.[34] Police squadrons patrolled public banking headquarters, such as the Central Bank, Mortgage Bank, and Stock Market. On June 24, private sector bank workers held a solidarity strike to denounce state repression against those in the public sector.[35] Wives of conscripted bank workers held a sit-in and blocked traffic on Sarandí Avenue, the main artery in Montevideo's Ciudad Vieja.[36]

On July 2, the CNT carried out another general strike that shut down major national industries and essential services, including workers in the electrical grid, sanitation, gas and petroleum, and public banking sector. Dissident workers at the Batlle Thermoelectric Central (UTE) and the ANCAP refinery remained on strike for the next two days, while contingents of textile workers occupied nearly every plant in Montevideo and its periphery. On July 3, public bank workers resisted authorities entering the Central Bank in response to a work slowdown. Bank officials then closed the site for the rest of the day. Police refused to leave the building, remaining locked inside until a military squadron surrounded the building at midnight. Soldiers beat and detained workers to ensure the eviction succeeded. The following day, private sector workers again launched a half-day strike.[37]

The government gave mixed signals regarding settling the conflict. On July 6, Central Bank president Enrique Iglesias shocked the nation by announcing the possibility of mediation between bank management and the AEBU. The next day, the Office of the President released a statement declaring the government's refusal to participate in negotiations.[38] Meanwhile, over fifty bank workers from the Villa García branch remained detained for nearly a week, and military forces occupied the ANCAP oil refinery in La Teja, threatening workers with conscription should they strike.[39]

As everyday people demonstrated a heightened militancy, the FAU insisted on disseminating an anarchist perspective, regardless of the organization's banned status. On June 20, a team comprised of Raúl Cariboni, Mauricio Gatti, Gerardo Gatti, and Elena Quinteros produced the first edition of a four-page weekly propaganda organ, titled *Cartas de FAU*. The *Cartas* circulated underground to reach an audience of roughly three thousand readers. They provided macro-level analysis, but also local-level reports on popular mobilizations, workplace activities, and popular violence. True to the FAU's position in support of resistance, the weekly paid special attention to workers' illegal activities—especially germane considering that the bulletin already circulated via clandestine infrastructure. The FAU found importance in these narratives of resistance given their omission from mainstream and PCU-related press organs. Editors encouraged readers to pass their news to trustworthy peers, *haga circular* (make it go around).

On July 17, a coalition of six unions proposed a new Fight Plan to the CNT Representative Table to broaden participation in the growing conflict. The plan's authors—UOESF, Union of BAO Workers, Glass Workers Federation, Health Federation (FUS), Ghiringhelli Union, and Autonomous Union of TEM Workers (SAOT)—called for a two-day general strike accompanied by factory occupations and sabotage to be scheduled for the first two days of August. Yet the proposal found lukewarm reception, and the CNT Representative Table approved a scaled-down version: another one-day nationwide work stoppage on August 1.[40] Regardless of this attenuation, various industries launched strikes and other work actions during the last days of July to intensify the impact. Graphic artists at Garino Hermanos, Barreiro, and Impresora Uruguay occupied their plants, and police detained various SAG officers in response, including Gerardo Gatti.

In answer to the police harassment of their officers, SAG called to extend the strike to seventy-two hours, but the CNT Representative Table again rejected the proposal. Moreover, recognizing the growing climate of repression, the Table called off stoppages in key sectors. It was too late; workers' outrage had outrun the leadership. Strikers paralyzed Montevideo by shutting down railways, textile factories, banking (insurance, savings, mortgage, stock exchange, and private sector), utility services (electricity, gas), construction sites, press, transportation, health care, and more. During the demonstrations, small incendiary devices were installed at various bank locations, train stations, and government buildings. Students threw rocks at US symbols such as Pan Am Airways and the General Electric headquarters. Moreover, clashes between strikers and strikebreakers broke out in numerous interior cities. In Salto, workers from the Federation of Beverage Workers (FOEB) and SAG smashed windows of establishments that remained open, and workers in Fray Bentos spray-painted strikebreaker's homes with slogans. Graphic artists in Salto sabotaged the newspaper *El Diario* by changing its name to *Verdad Salteña* and inserted subversive messages throughout the edition.[41]

Regardless of the successful nationwide stoppage, the CNT Representative Table maintained opposition to extending the strike for another day despite pressure from UOESF and other combative unions. On August 8, the six-union coalition organized a day of action among themselves and other radical sectors of the labor movement. They released a joint communique critiquing the Representative Table for not having returned to discuss a strategy in the days prior to the general strike. It proclaimed, "We have all contributed to forming the CNT and cannot keep going with this lack of direction, especially when the working class and pueblo legitimately want so much more than simple declarations, compromised work stoppages, and public rallies that simply depend on the authorization of the government and police."[42] The coalition's day of action saw health service workers (FUS) walk out for a half-day strike, and workers at TEM, FUNSA, Ghiringhelli, and nearly every textile factory occupy their plants. It synergized around conflicts in precarious industries, where some workers had already been sustaining occupations for weeks. For example, workers at Campomar (COT) and BAO had been occupying their factories since the beginning of June and July respectively.[43] At some work sites, the mobilizations had begun achieving notable gains against the MPS. For instance, at Garino Hermanos publishing firm, graphic artists successfully pressured management into breaking the state-sanctioned wage freeze after having stopped work twenty-four times since the June 13 MPS decree.[44] These actions and the gains achieved from them offered hope at a time when more radical factions in the labor movement felt that it was not reaching its full potential.

As the unrest accelerated, the FAU and other revolutionary left organizations remained targets of state repression. On August 9, police raided the University of the Republic and Faculty of Agronomy, Architecture, Fine Arts, Economics, and Medicine in search of UTE director Ulysses Pereira Reverbel, who had been kidnapped days prior in one of the MLN-T's first high-profile actions.[45] To avoid welcoming further repression, the MLN-T released their captive within twenty-four hours, but student unrest continued against police invasions and government interference with the university system. The Ministry of the Interior also coordinated house raids of numerous FAU militants and sympathizers.[46] On August 12, police shot dead Communist Youth (UJC) militant and Faculty of Odontology student Líber Arce. High school and university students demonstrated against the killing over the next month, often throwing rocks and Molotov cocktails, building barricades, and burning cars and storefronts. They utilized the centrally located Instituto Alfredo Vázquez Acevedo, Faculties of Chemistry and Medicine, and National Trade School (UTU) as gathering points and organizing centers. The CNT called for a day of action on August 16, which consisted primarily of walkouts during the last hour of the workday. Again, workers in textiles, health services, FUNSA, and BAO occupied their factories while graphic artists at the newspaper *El Diario* went on strike for the duration of the weekend.[47] In El Cerro, refrigeration plant workers launched a monthlong occupation of Frigorifico Nacional. Local high school students successfully warded off police evictions, even though a FAU militant from the Faculty of Medicine was hospitalized with severe head injuries.[48] Some laborers clearly won the confrontation. Among them, rubber workers at the FUNSA and Ghiringhelli factories achieved a cost-of-living wage increase.[49] More broadly, the mobilizations demonstrated everyday people's capacity for a quick response to growing state repression. Although spontaneous and reactive, the FAU saw them as a litmus for the risks people were ready to start taking.

The promising demonstrations and successful wage gains inspired the COT to resubmit the July 17 Fight Plan for approval from the CNT Representative Table. The reformed proposal called for mass demonstrations and factory occupations on September 4, followed by the launch of an *indefinite* general strike the next day. COT's proposal gave new life to the July 17 Plan, which the CNT Table delayed, but never fully rejected. However, the Table, including the COT representative on it, voted unanimously in favor of a new proposal to hold rallies on September 5 instead. One Table representative proclaimed, "There are paths already being paved at the level of Congress."[50] While this news frustrated the more radical faction of the labor movement, they were far from finished with agitating for further escalation.

The September 5 day of action again sparked intense confrontations with police and spawned two clear nuclei of social unrest: the Faculty of Medicine and El Cerro. The former, home to nearly

a dozen FAU-affiliated students and staff members, served as a
gathering point for sieges on the Legislative Palace due to its prox-
imity to the structure. It also hosted a first aid room to service
students injured during battles with police. In El Cerro, a contingent of teachers, students, and workers from BAO, FUNSA,
Alpargatas, health services, and Frigorifico Nacional barricaded
the bridge connecting the neighborhood with the city center.[51]
Again, everyday people's actions in the streets proved to be a step
ahead of labor leadership. Taking notice of the trend, the FAU
labeled the Table's timidness as traitorous, declaring:

> We are not opposed to negotiations, but they must be carried
> out above principled foundations that maintain the highest
> level of mobilization and conflict possible by the working
> class because only this guarantees and preserves its protag-
> onist and vanguard role. . . . Three months have passed in
> which we have confronted an unprecedented reactionary
> offensive. In this time span we have seen many brief work
> stoppages, sometimes even for just minutes, that did not
> cause them to stop enforcing union sanctions. There have
> been isolated strikes that, without having been surrounded
> by a broader Fight Plan, continue to be difficult to under-
> stand in their context. There are sectors that proclaim tired-
> ness and bewilderment with a more complete struggle and
> whose objectives are tangled up, one way or another, with
> mediation, contact, and negotiation.[52]

Yet the CNT Executive Board offered a different analysis of the
situation. Its leadership insisted that the labor movement was
not equipped to take on the government's executive orders alone
and instead needed to continue pushing for solutions in the parliament while simultaneously building a broader coalition with
the Uruguayan Chamber of Commerce, Catholic Church, and
Masonic Lodge. The board also saw the need to find foreign support in the International Red Cross and United Nations. The
CNT announced its position publicly at a high-profile football
match between CA Cerro and FC Rampla Juniors, where they

also invited audience members to a fundraising rally the following week.[53] Many spectators responded with mocking sheep noises, which El Cerro residents commonly used to haze party members upon encountering them in the streets—a practice that had begun following the failure of Communist-led meatpackers union campaigns in the decade prior.

As the CNT retreated, state repression continued to escalate.[54] On September 20, police shot and killed Faculty of Economics student Hugo de los Santos and UTU student Susana Pintos, both UJC militants, amid a worker–student demonstration. The government took advantage of the murders to close all school campuses in Montevideo until October 15. The government also ordered the closure of the CNT and AEBU locals—and military forces surrounded both buildings to prevent them from being used as organizing spaces.[55] By the end of September, sixty-five bankers were detained and conscripted into the military. Union officers, primarily from the AEBU, testified to having experienced home raids, physical violence during interrogations, and threats to their family members.[56] Repressive tactics previously reserved for agitators were now being used on everyday people, and they were feeling the heat.

Regardless of the heightened state repression, workers continued to be both resilient and proactive. The CNT again responded to the students' murders by calling a general strike on September 24. Leading up to the strike, state Savings Bank workers climbed to the second story to drop plastic bags filled with water onto the heads of businessmen who gathered there to inaugurate a statue to national hero José Artigas. Upon the arrival of police, workers scampered off to avoid arrest. On the eve of the strike, private bank workers held a half-day work stoppage and entered the public Mortgage Bank to distribute fliers and chant slogans. Workers at Banco Italo Americano occupied their workplace and denied management access. On September 24, a FAU–MLN-T coalition calling themselves the Comandos de Autodefensa del Pueblo (People's Self-Defense Commandos) awakened three police chiefs to the sound of Molotov cocktails exploding in their front yards.[57] Workers at the Apolo paint factory in La Teja experimented with

occupying their plants for the first time after voting a reform caucus to power in their autonomous union. The occupation lasted
into mid-October, funded by numerous "tolls" they organized
to collect contributions from passing drivers.[58] The mid-1968
responses to police murders of the politicized youths would prove
to be the most explosive of the year.

By late October, student mobilizations had fizzled out.
Uruguayan historian Vania Markarian has recognized the lull as
reflecting the "cycles of protest" historically associated with the
academic year, in which tensions often peak in May—roughly a
month and a half after the school year's fall commencement—
but eventually die out by exam season in October, as students
begin preparing for final exams and transiting into summer break.
Markarian goes on to argue that both student and labor organizations transitioned toward new forms of resistance after the events
of mid-1968.[59] During the monthlong closure of school campuses,
militants continued meeting in union locals to devise new strategies and tactics amid a growing climate of state repression.

The government also took note of its own weaknesses, reme-
diating them with an increase in military and communications
equipment, often purchased from the US government. Between
May 1968 and January 1972, the government more than doubled
Montevideo police's riot control inventory to include eleven armed
vehicles, five SUVs with chicken wire protection, three water cannons, large touring buses, one cattle truck (to transport seventeen
riot control horses of the total 160 guard animals available), two
thousand helmets (including 270 with plastic face masks), 87 plastic shields, 30 riot shields, 380 gas masks, and 99 gas guns. In
Montevideo alone, upward of 3,500 riot police were available for
mobilization.[60] In the face of such preparations, militants agreed
that the current political situation warranted the use of popular violence.

While spring 1968 marked a strategic and tactical shift in the
student movement, workers continued clashing with state forces
in Montevideo's streets into early 1969. They were not affected by
the academic year cycle. Although street skirmishes were less frequent, they were often sparked by workplace-specific grievances

and came in spurts lasting three to four days. On November 12, construction workers utilized building materials to erect barricades and block traffic in front of Plazoleta El Guacho to protest the sizeable, yet inadequate, 25 percent pay raise offered by the executive branch. Two days later, health service workers (FUS) burned debris to barricade seven main intersections in the city center. Police used water cannons and tear gas to break up protesters as they threw stones and Molotov cocktails at the portal of the Ministry of Public Health. The subsecretary of public health watched on as his car went up in flames.

On November 15, students marched in opposition to government interference in university elections, leaving the windows of eighteen banks shattered.[61] Bank tellers occupied the Banco Commercial to protest the firing of three union officials. They fled the site after police evicted the occupation by spraying tear gas into the building through a broken window. Yet, upon clearing the building, they immediately initiated a two-week long strike. In the interior, packing workers at Frigorifico Tacuarembó protested a visit from President Pacheco Areco by occupying the factory and refusing him entrance. Police detained dozens, including a priest, for distributing fliers denouncing his visit.[62] However, these actions went largely unsupported, and even antagonized, by CNT leadership.

By late December, the CNT majority's strategy to court progressive elected officials to the side of labor proved a bust when the parliament permanently established COPRIN, which regulated private sector wages and prices, and ruled on the legality of strikes.[63] The body consisted of five government officials, two labor representatives, and two business representatives. While the government had already capped wage increases at 70 percent for 1968—even though the cost of living had risen more than 200 percent since 1967—COPRIN would prove even more conservative, allowing only a 16 percent wage increase in its first year of operation. Within the first six months of its implementation, the CNT Representative Table recognized, "Every resolution of the COPRIN has been a resolution against the pueblo—authorizing increases in prices and limiting increases in wages—a

clear redistribution of income in favor of the dominant classes."[64] Furthermore, in effort to drag on conflicts and usurp union
resources, management frequently missed COPRIN-arranged
meetings but suffered no consequences on behalf of the body.[65]
Yet, COPRIN's formation would reflect one of the government's
few half-hearted attempts to curb labor conflict in a manner that
included voice from its leadership.

Dissident Labor: The Tendencia Combativa

Repeated experiences with bureaucratic shortcomings spawned
a coalition of unions under the direction of the FAU, Eastern
Revolutionary Movement (MRO), Unified Action Group
(GAU), Uruguayan Union Action (ASU), 22 de Diciembre, and
Revolutionary Workers Front (FRT). While *Época's* prohibition sought to break up the growing popularity of the six revolutionary left groups, their social insertion in labor and student
movements enabled the relationships with one another to be sustained. ASU was perhaps the most interesting fit within the coalition. As the Uruguayan national branch of the Confederation of
Latin American Christian Unions (CLASC), ASU shared a strong
anti-Communist sentiment with the FAU and other New Left
organizations. In its 1952 founding congress in Santiago, Chile,
the CLASC set out to form a Christian humanist union to combat Marxist anti-humanist, and anti-Catholic, dogma. Moreover,
they shared a similar critique of Communist bureaucracy, arguing,
"Unionism is a way in which workers can take their destiny into
their own hands and transform all of society."[66] While these groups
shared a common Communist opponent, they would coalesce
more around shared strategies and tactics. They would eventually form a dissident coalitional faction within the CNT, called
the Tendencia Combativa (Combative Tendency).[67] According to
Hugo Cores, adherence to the Tendencia came together around
three points: (1) to fight bureaucratization within the CNT; (2) to
challenge manipulation by political parties; and (3) to maintain
independence at an international level.[68]

The FAU and the GAU carried most weight within the coalition. The GAU officially formed in April 1969, but existed informally after the banning of MAPU, a social Christian organization with strong influence in COT, AEBU, Association of Electrical Workers (AUTE), Teachers Association of Uruguay (FUM), and the FEUU, especially the Faculty of Engineering.[69] The FAU had a special connection to Héctor Rodríguez, GAU's most high-profile unionist and COT representative to the CNT Executive Board, via FAU militant Raúl Cariboni, his half brother. Rodríguez was expelled from the Communist Party in 1951 after accusations of "derailment" and having a "cult of personality." Upon his departure, party membership among textile workers dropped from 517 to 19.[70] The textile industry remained one of the most lucrative national industries throughout the sixties, employing upwards of twenty-five thousand workers during high season—80 percent of its workforce women. The Tendencia's commitment to apoliticism was especially attractive to female workers, who often felt turned off by the party's dogma and unidirectional communication style. María Julia Alcoba, a COT officer and SADIL factory worker, recalls her union as women's gateway into politics. While parties remained dominated by male counterparts, women in textiles, nursing, and meatpacking identified foremost with their unions before any political party, regardless of how they voted in elections.[71] It was their close-knit group of trusted companions, and that intimacy proved key for taking risks together. Like the FAU, Rodríguez and GAU continued to challenge the PCU around interpretation of the CNT Fight Plan. While GAU did not set out to spark revolution or take state power, they advocated for a plan of escalation toward an indefinite general strike for the freedom of political prisoners, nationalization of key industries, and termination of wage freezes and MPS security measures.

The coalition had a clear strategic purpose within the CNT. The majority line, represented primarily by the PCU and Christian Democratic Party with 397 delegates, sought to organize, unify, and structure the working classes and organize them behind progressive political candidates. The minority position, represented by the Tendencia Combativa with 150 delegates, sought to confront the everyday conditions of the political and economic crisis through direct action tactics, specifically by coordinating labor actions across industries. They also worked toward building strike capacity for an indefinite general strike, although the groups differed in their respective visions of revolution and the role of a strike within it.[72] Víctor Bacchetta, student movement leader and GAU militant, explains, "The Tendencia Combativa came about as a necessary agreement of common action between distinct groups within the union movement that had substantial disagreements with the majority politics of the CNT advanced by militants belonging to the Communist Party."[73]

UOESF, AEBU, SAG, COT, FOEB, Health Services Federation (FUS), BAO soap factory workers, and the UTAA were the largest unions affiliated with the Tendencia. Each claimed membership numbers in the thousands. Moreover, AEBU and COT were the first and third most represented unions on the CNT Representative Table, with 63 and 45 delegates respectively. Tendencia-affiliated caucuses also carried considerable clout, and sometimes won out, in other large industries and professions, including the medical laboratories, railway workers, and teachers' unions, among others.[74] Lists developed around only one or two militants who laid groundwork for claiming leadership positions in the locals' elections. For example, FAU militant Gustavo Inzaurralde began agitating in the student association at the Normal Institute for Teachers, a public academy made up of primarily lower-middle-class students seeking careers in public education. Many students, whose primary and secondary education took place in clergy-led Catholic schools, were attracted to the institute because it served as a pipeline to placing teachers in underserved schools. The student union was divided into two caucuses: List 5, representing the PCU, and List 3, representing a hodgepodge of oppositional currents spearheaded by students who identified with social Christianity and liberation theology. Inzaurralde moved forth the FAU's positions within List 3, but his work was guided by an anarchist analysis of his immediate circumstances. His job as a List 3 militant was to win support for List 3's politics, not to win over people to anarchism. Yet, he would develop close relationships with List 3 rank and filers and leaders who he would eventually bring into the FAU, such as Elena Quinteros, Yamandú González, Hugo Casariego, Lilián Celiberti, and Sara Méndez.[75]

Like the experience in the textile industry, some of the most important Tendencia-affiliated unions formed after splits with their PCU-majority leadership. Throughout the fifties and sixties, the Communist-led National Union of Metallurgical Workers (UNTMRA) gained a poor reputation due to its frequent disciplining and/or purging of dissident caucuses. For example, Trotskyist factions existed in UNTMRA-affiliated factories like Inlasa and Nervión until the fifties but gave up on organizing after being frequently run out of work sites and reprimanded by union leadership for distributing dissident propaganda. In June 1966, Javier Uslenghi, a Trotskyist worker from the Bridge factory, publicly denounced UNTMRA in *Época* for having demobilized workers in preference of negotiations with management.[76] Similarly, members of the social Catholic ASU spearheaded the formation of the Autonomous Union of General Electric Workers (SAOGE) in 1958. The SAOGE spent the duration of the sixties in conflict with management and repeatedly used occupation and street confrontation to ward off police and strikebreakers. In 1961, FAU publication *Lucha Libertaria* recognized SAOGE as among the nation's most militant unions.[77]

Many autonomous unions were born of schisms in reaction to PCU management of the CTU. For example, the Autonomous Union of TEM Workers (SAOT) formed in July 1963 after membership voted 245 to 61 to disaffiliate from the Communist-led UNTMRA. SAOT moved toward the radical left after losing a 1961 strike, during which workers became disenchanted with the UNTMRA after receiving little support for the work action. The ASU had a strong influence in the decision to disaffiliate. By 1964, SAOT allied with the SAOGE to form the Executive Board of Radioelectricity, which eventually welcomed participation from fellow autonomous metalworker unions at SIAM-Sarratosa, Castells-Ferrosmalt, Regusci & Voulminot, Phillips, Radesca, Galileo, Warner's Delne, APSA, and Famesa.[78]

The Tendencia gained a unique stronghold in small, newly formed union locals such as Seral, CICSSA, and Manzanares (supermarkets), Divino, Portland Cement, ATMA, and BP Color. All would wage dramatic and important conflicts between 1970 and 1973. Minority, but nonethelesss influential, cadres of Tendencia-linked militants also existed within PCU-led unions, such as leatherworkers, shipbuilders, various agricultural workers, chemical workers, UNTMRA, sweet factory workers, newspaper vendors, and utilities workers (UTE and gas).[79] Throughout the mid-sixties, PCU leadership often struggled to call an end to strikes because workers disobeyed their orders and refused to work until winning their demands. In May 1968, a CIA special report on the Uruguayan left recognized, "Workers have on occasion accused the PCU of putting the party's safety and interests over those of the unions."[80]

Although not all member groups within the Tendencia oriented themselves toward revolution, the FAU viewed the coalition as necessary to link together organizations with shared principles and tactics. Moreover, the FAU recognized the limitations of unions on account of their open membership and mass character. Indeed, such an eclectic membership base inevitably stripped unions of any outright revolutionary potential. Nevertheless, the democratic structure of unions allowed an opportunity to form caucuses around shared values and to fight to win most of the membership's support for more combative tactics. Those experiences would then radicalize workers, ideally toward a revolutionary politics. In a communique titled "Sindicato y tendencia," the FAU declared:

> The union cannot serve as a sufficient base to construct a revolutionary movement. That is why, if we are going to advance a line of combative action among the masses, aside from participating in a union, we must come together to form a tendency.... Participation in the Tendencia requires the acceptance of a set of principles that can be shared among companions who hold different ideological backgrounds, which also clearly entails certain exclusions (such

as reformists, for example) that are essential if we are going to achieve the minimum basis for operational coherence.[81]

The wide-ranging coalition of blue-collar, white-collar, and peasant workers enabled a unique and broad-reaching network that embodied an ethos of *solidarity unionism*: namely, one in which unions share resources and support one another via solidarity strike, boycott, and sabotage. The coalition's diverse and multi-sectoral makeup required creative and innovative approaches to strategy and tactics. Many described the coalition as representative of a return to "old school"-style unionism, although the nineteenth-century anarchist influence can be seen not only in the use of direct action, but also in the assembly of a multisectoral alliance.[82] Reflecting on the Tendencia, FAU militants Ivonne Trías and Universindo Rodríguez explain:

> The Tendencia was, in the first place, a movement with all of the creativity and dynamism of any other movement, and with all of its difficulties and challenges. Its methods can be characterized by a trust in street mobilizations and the pressure of "direct action" to achieve a solution for the problems of everyday people. The Tendencia's limitations and contradictions are not enough to affirm that it was a phenomenon alien nor marginal to the Uruguayan labor movement, such as an import from the outside. It instead expressed a popular reaction that encompassed labor and student unions, as well as sectors of cultural producers, characterized by rebellion against the growing authoritarianism in Uruguayan society.[83]

Perhaps the largest wedge between the Tendencia and the CNT majority manifested in the division between union leadership in the public and private sectors. The majority line overwhelmingly controlled public sector unions, such as public administrators, utilities workers, and educators. However, Tendencia discourse frequently commented on the need to coordinate struggles in the private sector (or industrial production) with mass action in the public sector (mostly white-collar administrative work). Such unity showed sporadic signs of potential, primarily due to autonomous action of militant factions in blue-collar public industries, like railway and oil refinery workers. In 1972, teachers waged a sixty-four-day strike against an education reform bill drawing solidarity from all sectors in the CNT. State workers, however, mobilized around partial strikes and rallies. Considering over half of Uruguayans labored in the public sector, its risk aversion strongly held back the labor movement from reaching full capacity.

Finally, the strong relationship between Uruguay's private sector and foreign investment placed Tendencia-affiliated unions at the forefront of resistance to imperialism. US-based capital owned eighty of the country's largest private firms, including Portland Cement, FUNSA, Coca-Cola, General Electric, CICSSA (paper mill), Bayer, Chase Manhattan, and Citibank. Other large foreign-owned firms under Tendencia control included National Beverage Factory (German), and appliance firms TEM, Phillips, and Ferrosmalt (Dutch). Moreover, foreign firms owned much of the textile and wool industry, including Hart, Sadil, and Fibratex. While these Uruguayan factories produced for export, they often replaced labels with "Made in England" or "Made in USA" for consumption in the foreign market.[84] Combined with the Tendencia's strong presence in Administration of State Railways (AFE), Regusci Voulminot, and the meatpacking industry, the coalition controlled the country's most lucrative national industries and export infrastructure.[85] Knowing this, militants recognized the real potential for economic damage in coordinating action across Tendencia-affiliated unions alone. While there remained little hope of winning over the public sector unions to the Tendencia line, this mattered little beyond the symbolic considering the relationship of existing Tendencia-affiliated unions to global and domestic capital.

Conclusion

Regardless of the CNT's rejection of the July 17 Fight Plan, many labor unions continued to utilize radical tactics, such as street confrontations and occupations, throughout 1968. During the second half of the year, lengthy factory occupations took place in at least a half dozen factories, including General Electric, Ghiringhelli, FUNSA, Frigorifico Nacional, and TEM. Textile workers at the Campomar factory in Juan Lacazé occupied their plant for over fifty days beginning in mid-June. Graphic artists, including those at mainstream press organs, maintained daily two-hour work stoppages for three months. Workers at over two dozen work sites occupied their plants multiple times, including BAO soaps, Alpargatas, National Beverages, Inca Paints, Health Services, and various textile mills. The AEBU strike ended in a stalemate and would be reignited again the following year. Although these unions differed greatly in their political orientation, their shared tactics and analysis thrust them into a dissident coalition within the CNT, the Tendencia Combativa.

The Tendencia's diverse political makeup represented a "movement of movements." While the Uruguayan New Left did not approach questions of race and gender in the same way as their Global North counterparts, the struggles of UTAA's racialized sugarcane workers and COT's overwhelmingly female base showed an embrace of minoritized categories and "peripheral" workforces. The Tendencia remained committed to building a combative union movement around workforces historically pushed to labor's margins globally and thus moved beyond the Communist strategy of focusing on labor's most advanced industrial sectors. Moreover, to build solidarity among other everyday people, Tendencia-affiliated unions emphasized flexibility in their tactics. During the 1968 AEBU strikes, for instance, certain sectors remained on post to ensure the processing of paychecks, retirement, and social security.[86]

The FAU and other Tendencia-linked groups declared the government's austerity politics as the core source of their grievances. Indeed, they recognized the state-sanctioned wage and salary freeze as a direct attack on workers' rights because it further entrenched class disparities and illegalized labor's efforts to maintain a decent standing of living as cost of living and inflation surged. In other words, it reversed the labor movement's bread-and-butter gains of the past decade and enabled an extreme transfer of wealth into the hands of the owning class.

By the time of the July 17 Fight Plan, workers had accumulated nearly three months of experience with small-scale direct action, such as partial strikes, slow-hand strikes, and protest. Some normalized sabotage and factory occupations, and many more had their first experiences confronting police. For the FAU, these experiences served as a foundation upon which to build toward more militant forms of escalation, such as an indefinite general strike. But such goals required planning and coordination to unite around a common and combative strategy against both the politics of austerity and MPS. The FAU frequently denounced the labor movement's tendency to rely on spontaneity, or reactiveness, which could only lead to the isolation of more combative unions without a clear proactive role for the rest of the labor movement. On July 29, 1968, they declared:

> It is necessary to coordinate activity from a general level and to break away from the old routines, often done without conscience, of isolationist unionism. Now, fighting alone will only bring about defeat. We are all faced with the wage freezes and politics of repression. No one can escape from either. And there are not unions that are more, or less, important than others.[87]

The rejection of the July 17 Fight Plan and subsequent failure of the bank workers' strike proved that point.

The willingness to disobey laws and break social norms of civility demonstrated a broader sentiment of empowerment and high morale. Small factions of workers had begun setting off minor explosives causing property damage at the residences of strike breakers and management.[88] Workers and students frequently utilized company and campus materials to barricade streets, block traffic, and collect tolls. The bank workers' strike, and solidarity that accompanied it, demonstrated that amid heightened levels of state repression, including military conscription and physical violence, workers maintained tenacity and morale remained high. Regardless of the FAU's attempt at synthesis, their texts make a strong distinction between the Marxist "objective conditions" and workers' subjective willingness to fight. In some cases, workers risked salary cuts, job security, physical harm, and even imprisonment. In such cases, certain struggles took on a greater meaning to both the individual actors and the social imaginary in which moving the field of play to negotiations and/or falling short of winning demands resulted in collective demoralization and disempowerment.[89]

The FAU distinguished its position from that of the government and reformist left currents in the labor movements by emphasizing its advocacy for struggle and opposition to discourse and dialogue.[90] They accused the left of relying too much on words rather than experience, declaring:

> There is too much discourse in this country and they are all relatively the same. Confronting the oligarchy and bosses and facing the closure of one's workplace that cannot (well, they say cannot) continue in operation, illustrates more than a thousand discourses about "economic crisis". . . . You think a sugarcane worker from Artigas does not understand what is a latifundio? Or that a worker at FUNSA does not know what are the "forces of order?"[91]

The FAU called bluff on the governments' intentions to overturn its austerity politics. They insisted the calls for dialogue were disingenuous and recognized their irony amid an uneven playing field. Instead, they saw the calls for dialogue as a means for the government to buy time and offer illusions of possible solutions while waiting for the mobilizations to fizzle out. Moreover, they saw direct confrontation as a means to strengthen organizations and formulate a shared working-class interest on its own terms rather than "depending on illusions created from above that appear so favorable that many would long to return to 'normalcy.'" They recognized the futility of dialogue with authorities, proclaiming:

When the possibilities of making concessions to the oligarchy have run out; when they try in whatever way possible to
uphold the privileges of large landowners and speculators
tied to imperialism, embodied by the IMF, they replace . . .
wage increases with freezes, and dialogue with repression.
This is because the actual structures have reached their critical point and their possibilities have been worn thin. They
are dead. And, therefore, now, they try to maintain the dead
body afoot, artificially, although it is being propped up
with bayonets.[92]

For the FAU, the Pacheco Areco government, PCU, and
US-funded yellow union block all emphasized the importance of
dialogue. This left the anarchists and other direct action–oriented
organizations as a punching bag for both sides of the political spec-
trum. While the CNT coalition commenced on delicate grounds,
the PCU's reaction to the mid-1968 labor unrest proved the confederation's fragility.[93] The August 5, 1968, edition of *Cartas de
FAU* provides the best summary of the organization's position,
which they maintained over the next five years. The anarchists
responded to the one-day general strike on August 1, declaring:

The legal dictatorship imposed by the oligarchy does not
target the vacuous parliament, but instead targets radical sectors, such as workers and their unions. This is true
even among workers and organizations that do not play
with words, where no one has ever proposed a "revolutionary" general strike. Yet, this [revolutionary general strike] is
indeed something discussed among those same reformists
who promote the theory of the Apocalypse, that a revolution
will follow after a military coup, in order to justify retreating
now instead of facing up to the current reality of legal dictatorship. Through such opportunism reformists can cover
up their weaknesses. But the more combative sectors of the
working class will not be fooled, they will not fall into the
trap into which many intellectual circles fall when they confuse the Uruguayan reality with some other thesis, whether

poorly or accurately applied, from Russian, Chinese, or German theorists. Such confusion has caused some to identify a union strategy based on the progressive escalation of struggle, such as drawn-out strikes, occupations, and street actions culminating in a general strike politically oriented against the MPS, carceral system, conscription of workers, freezing of wages, and regulation of labor—a union strategy of resistance—with a plan for revolution. . . . This moment requires us to articulate actions destined to spark a prolonged resistance head on. No one considers that the popular and labor actions taking place now . . . are aimed at the immediate seizing of power. A work stoppage, sit-in, or even general strike, in this moment, does not have any other "program" beyond defending the integrity of our unions, our salaries, our work, and our limited vestiges of freedoms. The conditions are indeed there for this, but only if we act in an organized and serious manner.[94]

Regardless of differences of differences concerning strategy, Uruguay's 1968 marked a five-year span during which, according to PCU general secretary Rodney Arismendi, the country had the highest relative index of strikes, general strikes, and demonstrations of anywhere in the capitalist world.[95]

3

Alejandra and the Eagle
Mass Front and Armed Struggle, 1969

In March 1969, Gerardo Gatti visited Augusto Andrés and Edelweiss Zahn in their newly settled Barrio Pocitos apartment. Andrés, a FAU veteran and staff worker at the Faculty of Medicine, was one of a dozen members preparing to launch the organization's armed wing. Gatti took great interest in chatting with Zahn, who he had only met one time before. She was relatively unknown within political circles, although some members of the FAU recognized her as the daughter of a meatpacker from El Cerro. After over an hour of conversation, Gatti proposed that the couple take in Hébert Mejías Collazo and América García, two ex-Tupamaros who recently cut ties with the organization due to political differences.[1] Mejías and García went clandestine in December 1966 after participating in a botched robbery at the FUNSA factory. The couple parted with the MLN-T due to strategical and ideological differences. Mejías, who worked professionally as a bank teller before going underground, developed close ties with the FAU by way of Hugo Cores.

By mid-1969, the FAU had solidified plans to form its own armed apparatus after over three years of internal debate. Given their thorough studies of historical and contemporary conceptions of urban guerrilla strategy and the lessons learned from the organization's four-year stint in El Coordinador, militants understood the urgency. Mejías held skills in firearms and explosives, which he learned during multiple trips to Cuba in the early sixties. He also offered expertise in counterfeiting documents, such as national identification cards, passports, checks, and even money.

Gatti saw all these skills as useful for building and maintaining an armed apparatus within the FAU, and thus courted Mejías.

On April 27, 1969, Uruguayan media outlets reported news of an accidental explosion at a Tupamaro safe house in Montevideo's Barrio Manga. The explosion left Daniel and Carlos Betancourt, aged three and five respectively, hospitalized with severe burns. The children, who belonged to Juan Carlos Mechoso and Guirnalda Betancourt, were playing nearby as Hébert Mejías and América García offered a bomb-making tutorial. Mechoso, a member of the FAU's directorate, fled from his father in-law's home to lead an underground life for the next three years while pursued by authorities. Mejías and García, already underground, drew neighbors' attention with their ruined clothes and charred flesh as they flagged a taxi on the nearby ring road. They sought medical attention from a trusted doctor in the Tupamaro network. Daniel Betancourt, who arrived home minutes after the explosion, found his daughter amid a panic attack as she huddled over her burned children. He transported his daughter and two grandchildren to Pereira Rossell Hospital before being detained by police for interrogation. Neighbors were shocked at the incident. They recalled nothing suspicious of Mechoso's transitory hours, claiming, "He came and went from work as a graphic artist at the newspaper *El Plata* like anyone else." They remembered Guirnalda as performing the role of a typical housewife: she cared for the children and frequently tended to her garden. The explosion would mark the initiation of the FAU's armed branch, the Popular Revolutionary Organization–33 Orientals (OPR-33).[2]

This chapter explores the infrastructure and pilot implementation of the FAU's "two foot" strategy, a unique approach that combined mass mobilization and armed struggle. By 1969, the FAU realized the formation of the Worker–Student Resistance (ROE), a mass front that sought to intersect and synergize labor, student, and neighborhood conflicts, and OPR-33, a small armed apparatus that funded the organization via bank robberies and extorted managers to settle labor disputes. Pacheco Areco's heavy hand provoked a nationwide radicalization of social movements, which brought to light clear divisions among the various left camps. These differences manifested not only in public debates between labor leaders, but also in the strategic and tactical approaches of the CNT majority and Tendencia Combativa. The FAU's "two foot" strategy aimed to break PCU hegemony in the labor movement while still envisioning everyday people as the core protagonists of revolution. They sought to create a new hegemony of direct action and confrontation, including the use of armed intervention, within popular organizations. As such, the organization's role was to proactively foment and stimulate class struggle by establishing concrete infrastructural, organizational, and financial mechanisms to enable workers to act. Isolation, whether within the specific organizing site or among the broader labor movement, proved the worst-possible outcome of a campaign. The FAU's highest priority was to remain relevant in the labor movement. Regardless of the rapidly growing number of everyday people who came to embrace direct action tactics, the combination of PCU majority within the CNT, COPRIN official channels to resolve labor disputes, and Frente Amplio electoral project (discussed in Chapter 4) created a nexus of varying, but interrelated, hegemonies that pushed the FAU and other dissident workers to the fringes of popular movements.

The Organization: Fomento, Alejandra, Aguilar

The FAU's party infrastructure took on a more formal shape by early 1969. A group of veterans made up the organization's Fomento, or directorate. Its role was to link up pieces of ROE and OPR-33. All aboveground FAU militants participated in ROE (codenamed in FAU internal documents as "Alejandra"), whereas only a select few militants participated, clandestinely or semi-clandestinely, in OPR-33 (codenamed in FAU internal documents as "Aguilar"). For security purposes, the anarchists paid close attention not to mix the legal and anti-legal spheres. Moreover, the compartmentalization of tasks and growing safety risks generated a need for members to abide by strict behavioral codes and logistic responsibilities.

The FAU required all employed militants to belong to a union, student group, or neighborhood organization.[3] Militants set out to identify struggles specific to these spaces and galvanize support for an organized campaign around them. Anarchists had to remain disciplined in their efforts to capture popular grievances around which to organize mass campaigns, rather than taking on more radical campaigns supported by only a small "militant minority" of workers—even where such demands may have fit better within an anarchist set of tactics and vision of the world. Yet the FAU viewed missed opportunities as presenting even more of a difficulty—the worst-possible scenario was to lose a conflict without putting up a fight. Similarly, militants also needed to develop an awareness of when to lay rest to campaigns due to low morale or lack of combativeness from their colleagues. Without such savvy, militants risked isolation and/or were faced with having to dishonestly claim victory amid failure. Militants could avoid such scenarios only through solid relationships and trustful communication with colleagues. The FAU recognized that once a combative spirit gained footing in an organizing space, "reformists" would attack it by labeling it adventurist, fringe, or collaborationist.[4] Such attacks would likely come amid prolonged campaigns that drew heavy repression from authorities; therefore, militants would face tensions not only from management and the state but also from political rivals among the left. Recognizing the isolating effects of sectarianism, militants' fundamental task was to strike a delicate balance between popular appeal within their workplaces and the broader left milieu while advancing the combative position of the organization.[5]

FAU militants also shared responsibilities researching history and theory of River Plate anarchism and Global South revolutions. The research was synthesized and shared publicly as part of the organization's alternative perspective to that of the hegemonic left. For example, *Cartas*'s editors worked in separate teams dedicated to political formation. One team, consisting of Lilián Celiberti, Luis Presno, and Raúl Cariboni, met weekly to discuss historical and theoretical texts, especially regarding the emergent debates regarding the Soviet Union (such as the 1956

Hungarian Revolution and the Sino-Soviet split) that translated to the national context by way of the differences between the Tendencia and Communist Party. Celiberti recalls continuing the conversations late into the night while walking through Montevideo's empty streets.[6] Furthermore, teams of militants carried out a wide variety of thorough investigations to further the organization's understanding of legal codes, political opponents, and demographics. All members carried "know your rights" cards, which included legal definitions of crimes and their subsequent penalties. An internal document titled "Responsibilities for Every Militant, Every Team, Every Day" spelled out the quotidian responsibilities of FAU militants to ensure security and efficiency. Militants' tasks required close attention to the everyday spaces in which they navigated, including documentation of sites of police presence, recognition of behavioral patterns of local bosses or political elite figures, and identification of suspicious vehicles.[7]

For the FAU, membership in the revolutionary organization meant to move beyond the individual and to make sacrifices for the sake of the collective. Membership in the collective, and commitment to the collective project, was a step toward revolutionary counter-subject formation. Militants were expected to behave as *pez en el agua* (fish in the water), remaining undetectable by authorities and indistinguishable from their peers while in public.[8] The organization even enforced an unofficial dress code that aimed to avoid unwarranted attention and the individual desire for superficial bids for attention: beards, long hair, and shabby clothes were highly discouraged.[9] In this way, the FAU's anarchism shared much more in common with Latin American Marxist and Third World liberation organizations than it did with anarchist tendencies in the Global North.[10]

Fomento: The Directorate

The FAU directorate consisted of veterans Gerardo Gatti, Mauricio Gatti, Juan Carlos Mechoso, Hugo Cores, Raúl Cariboni, and León Duarte. They focused primarily on building strategy, producing analysis and propaganda, mounting connections between the labor and student movements, and coordinating actions between the popular and armed fronts. The directorate differed significantly from its Trotskyist democratic centralist counterpart in that ROE and OPR-33 cells could discuss their proposals and decide among themselves whether to accept tasks. Lilián Celiberti, a Normal School student and intermediary between the directorate and both feet, recalls never having questioned the organization's structure because of its organic fluidity in decision-making processes.[11] While she came to question the male-dominated directorate after embracing feminism in the 1980s, she recalls having welcomed the veterans' role because of the knowledge and wisdom that they offered as a result of experience. While most FAU militants joined the FAU after being radicalized in the struggles of the late sixties, the directorate's veterans had been involved with the organization for more than a decade.[12]

Alejandra: Worker–Student Resistance

The FAU had been seeking to build an interlocking network of worker and student militants since the 1958 Organic University Law, which brought strong acts of solidarity between striking FUNSA workers and combative students in the FEUU.[13] But throughout the sixties, the organization directed its energy toward building up the CNT and Tendencia. By late 1968, the momentum of the student movement organically synergized with that of the labor movement, and the FAU used the intergenerational ties to form the Worker–Student Resistance (ROE). For many students, especially high schoolers, the May 1968 episodes served as their first experiences with street protests and their first confrontations with state authorities. In the University of the Republic, these newly radicalized students primarily gravitated toward the PCU's Communist Youth (UJC) wing, which served as the major left force within the FEUU.[14] University students also flocked toward the newly formed the Revolutionary Student Front (FER), a New Left student group that informally served as recruiting base for the MLN-T. However, many freshly energized high schoolers were not yet networked into an established political project. Given this potential, as well as Communist dominance in the University, the FAU therefore sought to build ROE chapters in local high schools—especially those in El Cerro, La Teja, and Colón—which would deepen the organization's influence and presence in all three peripheral working-class neighborhoods.

Soon thereafter, ROE developed a strong presence in at least sixteen different Montevideo high schools. They also built a strong university and technical school student base at the UTU's night school and the Faculties of Fine Arts, Medicine, Agronomy, Humanities, Social Sciences, Architecture, Economics, Chemistry, and Education. With less than five hundred militants, ROE would play a key role in the next half decade of the Uruguayan social conflict. According to a 1972 internal survey distributed to eighty ROE militants in the El Cerro–La Teja zone, the group was 55 percent male and 45 percent female, including eight young mothers. The average age was twenty-one years old, with more than half below twenty years old. The youngest militant was sixteen, and the oldest was thirty-five. Over 62 percent were students, and 20 percent of the students held a job as well. Occupations included factory workers, "handymen" (*changas*), hospital employees, a plumber, a shoemaker, and a handful unemployed (including one "without stable housing"). More than three-quarters reported having no prior experience in a political organization.[15]

As a "mass front" organization, ROE was open to militants of all political persuasions who shared a commitment to escalation of social conflict through coordination of struggles and the use of direct action. Although the FAU grounded ROE's infrastructure and strategic framework, the popular organization refrained from making direct references to anarchism.[16] ROE served as the primary vehicle by which the FAU agitated to make direct action and anti-legality hegemonic within the labor movement. Due to the requirement that all FAU members carry out political work at the site of their employment, all of the organization's militants participated in the ROE. As part of a broader FAU strategy to expand the Tendencia, ROE militants were tasked with identifying the most

combative circles within each union and to assist in forming them
into caucuses based on a shared set of goals and objectives specific
to their organizing site. These caucuses were then networked into
the Tendencia by means of their ROE contact, who could serve
as a liaison for coordinating direct action campaigns alongside
other workers.[17]

Students and workers planned alongside one another in the
union halls of the Bakers Union in La Teja and UOESF in the
city center. The Bakers Union had been an anarchist stronghold
since the beginning of the twentieth century, while the UOESF
local served as a headquarters for other rubber workers unions,
like Ghiringhelli and Fanaesa, as well as for many other centrally
located unions who did not have their own local, including TEM,
CICSSA, PepsiCo, FUS, Seral, and at least a dozen more. The
union halls served a variety of functions beyond a meeting space,
including concert venue, social center, and even refuge for home-
less militants without work.[18]

Tactical escalation required high levels of organization
to maximize the impact of actions and to lessen security risks.
Therefore, students and workers planned meticulously beforehand, leaving little room for spontaneity. Scouts would research a
site before a manifestation, while others would keep watch during
the gathering. All illegal actions were carried out by experienced
militants, who had physical and technical skills that enabled them
to properly execute the task and subsequently evade authorities
if necessary. The organization kept track of militants' abilities
and called upon them for tasks specific to their skill set. The
most common street actions were *relámpagos*, or lightning actions,
which the organization defined as under-five-minute actions—
such as vandalism, traffic stops, graffiti campaigns, and/or building administration takeovers—carried out by highly coordinated
"disciplined groups" amid demonstrations. The organization
expected each participant to commit to their respective roles and
see the actions through.[19]

Due to the limitations of networks insular to the union
world, the worker-student coalitional strategy proved important: maintaining the Tendencia's infrastructure required popular

participation beyond union officers and rank and file. While union officers primarily dedicated themselves to planning and bureaucratic responsibilities, rank and filers balanced between their workplace responsibilities, assembly participation, and mobilization. This often led to the neglect of research, information gathering, propaganda distribution, and more. ROE thus completed many of these quotidian tasks as a gesture of student solidarity with the labor movement. For example, in El Cerro a ROE team produced a thoroughly researched profile of the neighborhood, including the location and hours of shift changes of all factories in the area. The profile included locations and operating hours of schools, bars, and cafés. Militants referenced the neighborhood profile when outreaching to workers and members of the community. For security purposes, many internal documents were signed off as "CNT – Comisión Juvenil" and dated 1965—some were written exclusively in code.[20] This was a security protocol in preparation for the potential seizure of documents by police raid. ROE also participated in various local neighborhood organizations, such as the Support Committee for Popular Struggles in La Teja and the El Cerro Neighborhood Commission, which represented upward of forty-five thousand families. The former represented a coalition of workers, students, and shopkeepers who alerted the community of local social conflicts by painting on walls, whereas the latter served as a renters union.

The ROE encouraged a proactive role for those outside of the organized labor infrastructure, especially students, *amas de casas* (homemakers), small vendors, and the unemployed. The FAU's initial vision for the mass front came after realizing the limitations of labor unions and the necessity to build a rear guard based on mutual aid and collective social reproduction. Unions, including combative tendencies within them, fell victim to a structure that prioritized salaries and other workplace issues, and thus struggled to incorporate participants beyond their membership base. An April 1970 communique declared:

> There are many people in the neighborhoods who are not members of labor unions but who are prepared to fight,

and who have organized among themselves to do so. The Tendencia realistically cannot provide a backbone for this reality. Instead, we should develop . . . the coordination of activities among groups who share our tendencies within the same zone or neighborhood, and thus open a real possibility for all those who wish to participate in the struggle to do so whether or not they are affiliated with a union: non-unionized factory or shop workers, students, unemployed, and amas de casas should have the chance to participate in the fight.[21]

Uruguayan left organizations broadly sought to connect with students, but the FAU's call to unemployed youths and amas de casas were especially unique. Some scholars have identified the left's failure to challenge traditional gender roles as marking an epoch of "regression" during the fifties and sixties.[22] For example, the PCU's *El Popular* continued to depict women in the domestic sphere, including weekly columns dedicated to cooking recipes and beautification. While the FAU did not promote a discourse of gender liberation akin to early twentieth-century anarcha-feminism, which promoted free love and liberation from the domestic sphere, the organization saw amas de casas as protagonists in a broader class struggle and sought to find a role for them within ROE's rearguard support network.

Similarly, the ROE recognized women and shopkeepers in La Teja for offering support behind industrial conflicts, declaring, "They have given a hand to those who are fighting for the dignity of all of us. There is a role for everyone; and there is no place for any one person to come away feeling like a hero. There is no such thing as an isolated act. With every act we construct something bigger."[23] Women played an increasingly important role as part of the FAU's prisoner solidarity network, in which mothers and spouses transmitted information and transferred care packages to imprisoned loved ones as repression increased.[24] Thus, unemployed and nonwage workers, including small shopkeepers, prefigured a non-market-oriented and solidarity-based economy through their gestures of mutual aid.

The protagonists' multisectoral categories consolidated as *el pueblo* (the people). The FAU, like other contemporaneous left organizations in the River Plate region, borrowed heavily from populist discourse to redefine popular protagonism beyond the term "working class." While anarchism had a rich history of organizing popular sectors outside of the Marxist purview, such as peasants, street peddlers, and vagrants, the regional term *pueblo* also carried anti-imperialist notions. Argentine philosopher Ernesto Laclau calls the term an "empty signifier"—so much so that it could be defined and redefined to incorporate sectors ranging from peasants to middle classes in the name of a shared political objective.[25] While the FAU's use of the term recognized the importance of a broad alliance of protagonists, the organization still centered labor conflict as central to social transformation. This differed greatly from the strategy of the MLN-T. While the Tupamaros similarly recognized "all sectors of the poor" as revolutionary protagonists, they did not have a clear role for the working class prior to the organization's Marxist-Leninist reformation while exiled in Chile in 1973.[26]

Finally, the worker–student coalition sometimes created tensions between both groups. Augusto Andrés recalls students' response to the campus closures in September 1968:

> Pacheco closed the middle schools, high schools, and the UTU so the youngsters invaded the faculties. Up until then, control of the campuses was the responsibility of unionized staff workers. The FER and ROE, each on their own, expropriated two rooms where furniture and files were kept in the Faculty of Medicine—they began to use them without consulting anyone. There, they began to use paint, cardboard, and papers. They kept gasoline there too, and it got all dirty. Conflicts began to develop between them and unionized staff. In FUNSA it was something similar. The youngsters of the ROE began to operate in the main room and then occupied the secretariat that is in the entrance—they often answered the phone, and there were always a dozen militants at a time. The FUNSA workers began to retreat.

They would meet in the bar nearby, which was almost theirs anyway.[27]

Aguilar: Popular Revolutionary Organization–33 Orientals

By mid-1969, the FAU established OPR-33, a small armed apparatus that began with roughly twenty militants. Unlike ROE, all OPR-33 militants were also members of the FAU. More than a guerrilla wing, OPR-33 served as a "military-technical apparatus," with clear targets and goals within existing campaigns and social conflicts. The FAU's directorate modeled OPR-33 after the Spanish Civil War–era Iberian Anarchist Federation (FAI), a confederation of small affinity groups that carried out direct action and political work parallel to the National Confederation of Labor (CNT). While rumors throughout the 1930s ran wild of a FAI dictatorship within the CNT, militants such as Francisco Ascaso and Buenaventura Durruti, who had participated in the Nosotros affinity group, insisted on maintaining the CNT as a politically neutral body for the expression of working-class interests. In a 1933 FAI meeting, Durruti had declared:

> The F.A.I. advises the workers of the C.N.T. to be prepared for any eventuality. You control the factories and the places of work. Remain with them. Do not abandon them. Let the councils of workers and technicians start to operate the factories. They will be the basic organizations of the new social and libertarian economy. The anarchists will fulfill their duty, as always, by being the first in combat. . . . A defensive posture means the failure of every insurrection. The occupation of the factories without coordination with forces outside is doomed to failure in isolation.[28]

In this way, anarchists would provide a complementary armed function to the revolution while maintaining workers as its core protagonists. OPR-33's genealogy can be traced to turn-of-the-century debates among the transatlantic Spanish-speaking anarchist community in the River Plate.[29] OPR-33 militants worked in cells of three to six members who all performed tasks and contributed to the same specific function. For security purposes, militants did not know other members outside of their cell.[30]

The branch possessed no more than a dozen pistols and five shotguns, and most had only practiced shooting on two or three occasions. However, members were well versed in street fighting and often carried bats and pipes on them, which they sometimes used to combat scabs and members of fascist organizations in retaliation for attacks on workers, comrades, and family members. The FAU took a very strong stance against killing political opponents—an opposition not so much moral as strategic, given the tendency of the broader population to misinterpret assassinations. In other words, the social psychological impact of assassination tactics was bound to lose the support of the public, and such circumstance was never worth the risk.[31]

The FAU was very particular about OPR-33 recruitment, which kept membership low, especially in comparison to the MLN-T. One militant recalls having recognized OPR-33's unique makeup upon meeting MLN-T militants in jail: the latter consisted of a mixed-bag of socialists, communists, liberals, and Christian Democrats, many of whom were drawn to the organization out of altruistic interests.[32] Recruits for OPR-33 were invited based on their trustworthiness rather than their knowledge and comprehension of en vogue arguments around left strategy and armed struggle. The FAU intentionally recruited fellow workers who demonstrated an affinity for militant direct action into the OPR-33. As a result, many recruits came from the UOESF and SAG, where FAU presence was strong, and workers already had much experience with direct action in their own workplace. Working-class members always made up at least half the militants in the organization.[33] Such emphasis on working-class participation strongly distinguished the OPR-33 from the MLN-T, who drew their membership primarily from professional classes and students. Notably, a CIA report on the MLN-T declared:

> The leaders of the Tupamaros are mainly members of the
> intelligentsia and young professionals. The great majority of
> recruits over the years probably have come from the ranks
> of university students. . . . To some extent, it appears to be a
> case of sons and daughters rebelling against their fathers, as
> many of the terrorists come from relatively advantaged and
> at times prominent families.[34]

While the CIA's pseudo-Freudian analysis may be better read as
a projection of their own insecurities and internalized patriarchy,
they accurately recognized the well-off background of a sizable
number of MLN-T militants, who found their political feet in the
university rather than the labor movement.

OPR-33 militants were held to high standards of discipline
because the FAU acknowledged the potential for disequilibrium
within the group as result of building and maintaining armed cells.
The organization was highly cognizant of the broader New Left
tendency to fetishize armed struggle as the sole path toward transforming into a revolutionary subject, which often bred a sense of
elitism among guerrilleros.[35] Juan Carlos Mechoso recalls seeing
Tupamaros flaunting their weapons, keeping them tucked in their
pants while in public. The FAU viewed such gestures to be signs
of vanity and individualism, or reproductions of an elitist system
of values that insisted upon ascribing varying degrees of importance to different members of society.[36] Yet, the strict code of conduct developed a more reclusive and private subjectivity. Lilián
Celiberti recalls a clash between the militant profiles of those in
Alejandra, who acted as public figures via the Tendencia, compared
to Aguilar, who acted privately via OPR-33. The latter were much
more reserved. She recalls transitioning from her role as intermediary from the former to the latter as causing a sense of bewilderment,
as if they were two completely distinct political organizations.[37]

The FAU's directorate divided OPR-33 militants into three
different compartments based on their roles: Cholas, Intelligence,
and Violencia FAI. Cholas, or action groups, carried out high-risk
and tactically developed actions—primarily kidnappings and
armed expropriations. These militants were the most competent

in weapons handling. While most maintained normal lives as students or workers, some lived clandestinely due to being wanted by authorities.

Intelligence groups performed information gathering to lay the foundations for the armed actions of Cholas. Intelligence tasks often required months of astute investigation of physical spaces and people. Teams would take pictures, document schedules, locate nearby police and military outposts, identify emergency escape routes, and more. Due to the longevity of their investigative assignments, this required militants to be competent performers. Militants would spend hours loitering at park benches, factory parking lots, sidewalk corners, and storefront verandas, where they had to act the part of an ordinary citizen going through an ordinary day's routine. Much of the intelligence work never resulted in an OPR-33 intervention but remained on file for potential use in the future.

Violencia FAI (VF) performed the task of normalizing popular violence amid social conflicts. Formed within the OPR-33 two years after its foundation, the FAU's directorate saw the need to bridge the armed apparatus more directly with the mass front. Often participating in the ROE, VF militants were responsible for tactical escalation during rallies and/or strikes. They performed community self-defense, which could entail armed security for striking workers or physically confronting strikebreakers and police. As protagonists in their own workplace conflicts, they laid the foundation for future class-based violence and sought to plant the seed of a popular militia among the working classes. Last, VF militants assisted and complemented Cholas by performing reconnaissance and driving escape vehicles.[38]

Each OPR-33 cell had one *encargado* (head), who was responsible for keeping contact with the directorate by way of an intermediary and for organizing information within the group. Cells elected their encargado based on a survey process, which included questions about each militant's teamwork, discipline, capacity for self-criticism, organizational skills, demonstrations of solidarity, and punctuality.[39] Although the directorate assigned the cells with tasks based on the climate of union conflicts, militants debated their responsibilities internally before consenting to carry them out. Cells often declined tasks based on their own self-perceived limitations; in such cases, Fomento simply assigned them to other cells. The consent process differed dramatically with other armed organizations throughout the continent. For example, the MLN-T permitted cells to debate, but it prohibited militants from disobeying orders from their superiors and even punished them with sanctions for doing so.[40]

The FAU's extralegal activities required a complex infrastructure and an extended support network of sympathizers. Accordingly, the OPR-33 surveyed all its members and sympathizers to document the skills and resources they had to offer the organization. To prevent risking a leak of the participants' identities to state authorities, these profiles were hidden in a *pozo* (hidden wall compartment) at a FAU safe house on the outskirts of Montevideo.[41] For example, some of the profiles included personal details of woodworkers who had been contracted to construct secret holding rooms in safe houses for kidnappees.[42] Many sympathizers did not participate in the organization beyond offering their homes as future refuge for clandestine and/or wanted militants. In fact, to maintain a "clean house" and low profile, those offering safe houses were often asked to refrain from participating in any further militancy. Sympathizers with higher social class positions were very important because of their networks within broader communities with means. In one example, an economics professor linked the OPR-33 to a friend's private aircraft, which was used to fly escaped prisoners across the river to Argentina.[43] Sympathizers also participated in the FAU's Solidarity Commission, which kept in regular contact with imprisoned members and their families. Many of OPR-33's small-scale robberies served to raise funds for imprisoned members or to offer stipends to family members and sympathizers who were sustaining clandestine militants.[44] Imprisoned militants often communicated by means of *pastillas*, or pills. The encrypted notes were written on cigarette papers and wrapped in nylon thread, then passed by mouth to visitors.[45]

Labor Action and Armed Struggle

A report titled "Standards for Mass Level Work (1)" in the May 19, 1969, edition of *Cartas de FAU* spells out the FAU's strategy, situating it within left debates of the era. The document's argument addresses conditions specific to Uruguay, where rank-and-file union militancy and armed struggle had both obtained high levels of organization and achieved significant success. The piece directly criticizes the PCU, declaring:

> In spite of accumulated experiences and practical everyday evidence, there are still those that insist on presenting the two methods as exclusive and incompatible when really, they are just different levels of the same struggle that can, and should be, convergent and harmonious. There are those who continue to create an artificial tension between mass action and armed struggle, union mobilization, and direct action. . . . Following such a trajectory one is destined to suggest, "The conditions are not there yet—we should stick to legal propaganda, nonviolent action, and electoral fronts." In the same spirit they also argue, "First we organize the party."[46]

While legal means such as electoral politics and aboveground press had successfully won wage increases and workplace rights historically, they were not enough to break the austerity politics of the moment.[47]

Furthermore, the FAU argued that everyday people's development of political consciousness and counter-subjectivity presented itself in various stages and that a political organization's role was to escalate class conflict by empowering them to act collectively and autonomously, and to use direct action. They labeled the first stage as agitation, which included rallies, fliering campaigns, mural paintings, and protests to lay the foundation for a later confrontation. The second stage included work stoppages and strikes, which served the purpose of making workplace-specific gains. In the third stage, people participated in street actions with low levels of confrontation to move public opinion and galvanize workers, both within the acting union and more broadly, and to normalize the presence of a combative strategy. Finally, they would participate in direct action to defend workers from scabs, state authorities, and paramilitaries, radicalize workplace-specific conflicts, and otherwise damage the economic interests of the owning class.[48] Thus, ROE and OPR-33 served as militant sectors within the labor movement that could be mobilized to escalate existing conflicts to stages three and four: ROE laid the site-specific groundwork for dissident workers to coalesce around an organized union caucus and provided an infrastructure to link them with other dissident currents throughout the country; OPR-33 provided the tools and skills necessary to move beyond labor-based tactics and toward normalizing, and preparing for, confrontations characteristic of an insurrection.[49]

The FAU's "two foot" strategy was unique among contemporaneous revolutionary groups globally. Indeed, Abraham Guillén's *Strategy of the Urban Guerrilla* offers the only conception of guerrilla warfare that resembled the FAU's position.[50] Guillén, a Spanish anarchist exile living in Uruguay at the time of the book's release, was inspired by both the MLN-T and the OPR-33 although he saw the latter as more accurately fitting his theories on urban guerrilla warfare. His theory of the urban guerrilla is widely considered the first direct challenge to Che's *foco* theory. Before moving to Uruguay, Guillén had resided in Argentina, where he had written extensively on economics from an "anarcho-Marxist" perspective. The writings gained enough traction to influence major congressional votes under the first government of Juan Perón. Guillén was eventually arrested after accusations of belonging to the Uturuncos—Argentina's first guerrilla organization, formed in 1955 after Perón's overthrow.

Guillén moved to Uruguay in 1962.[51] Although Guillén resided in Montevideo, members of the FAU recall little contact between him and the organization. Throughout this investigation, interlocutors referenced only one encounter in 1966, in which Guillén spoke to a crowd of less than a dozen people at the FAU's local in El Cerro. Carlos Marighella's *Minimanual of the Urban Guerrilla* was released three years later in Brazil, but, like nearly all theories of revolutionary violence from the epoch, diverged strongly from the "two foot" strategy in its advocacy for direct confrontation with authorities.[52] Marighella's ideas were more in stride with Argentina's PRT-ERP, which combined the Leninist strategy of the vanguard Workers' Revolutionary Party (PRT) with a foco-influenced armed apparatus, the People's Revolutionary Army (ERP). The group gained ground in Córdoba between 1969 and 1975. While the ERP lent armed assistance to various labor conflicts, the apparatus also waged various spatial battles, such as sieges on military barracks and a 1975 rural guerrilla campaign in Tucumán Province. Such paramilitary-style operations veered drastically away from the FAU's conception of armed struggle.

Finally, the "two foot" strategy served as a compromise between the even further contrasting strategies of the MLN-T and PCU. The MLN-T sought to drive a wedge between the masses by forcing them to choose between joining the armed struggle or side complacently with counterrevolution. They envisioned themselves at the vanguard that was accelerating society into a new stage of armed struggle between the masses and the state—one in which previously used tactics of protest and strikes were no longer adequate tools of resistance. Unlike the FAU, the MLN-T refused to enter forums for debates among the left; instead, they claimed that they could lead by example in their practice.[53] The MLN-T, for its part, rejected the PCU's argument that foco tactics contradicted a mass strategy. In a document titled "Foco o partido—falso dilemma," they clarified their concept of armed propaganda, declaring, "The kidnapping of a hated person from the regime in power registers with the masses and transforms the life of the country more than any publication or public rally of the traditional left." They drew from examples of China, Russia, Cuba, and Algeria to shed light on historical cases in which parties organized for the creation of an armed apparatus. While the MLN-T accurately recognized a false dichotomy between mass politics and armed struggle, they fell short of offering a revolutionary strategy beyond arming the pueblo. Thus, their writings never resolve a contradiction between the vanguard role of the armed apparatus and the role of the masses.[54] The FAU viewed this strategy as a pipe dream and felt it would inevitably confine everyday people to the role of passive observers of MLN-T actions.

1969: Meat Processing Plant and Bank Workers on Strike

On April 18, 1969, Minister of Commerce and Industry Jorge Peirano Faccio terminated fourteen thousand meat processing plant workers' right to two kilos of meat, per person, at the end of each shift—a prized benefit that had been earned nationwide by striking workers in the 1940s and '50s. The decree was part of a larger plan to restructure the processing industry, including the liquidation of El Cerro's Frigorifico Nacional and its division into smaller private industries in the interior of the country, where labor was easier to control and less organized. The plan entailed targeting other unionized meat-processing plants nationwide, such as Comargen, Cruz del Sur, Sudamericano, Casablanca, and Anglo. Frigorifico Nacional workers responded with a strike and occupation under the coordination of the Autonomous Meatpackers Federation (FAC). They also set up an encampment in front of the El Cerro Refrigeration Establishments—an El Cerro-based cooperative of 1,800 workers that collaborated with the government to demonstrate worker support for the new decree. Workers from Casablanca and Anglo, located in the interior cities of Paysandú and Fray Bentos respectively, marched to Montevideo to participate in the protest camp, encountering various waves of police violence along the way.

The campsite received support from thousands of sympathizers in the El Cerro–La Teja neighborhoods. The FAU's networks in local neighborhoods and middle schools played a key role in offering solidarity to the strikers. The ROE implemented roadblocks and *peajes* (tollbooths) to collect money from passing drivers. Students carried out daily expropriations of supermarkets and food delivery trucks to gather sustenance for the encampment. One report in *Cartas* claimed, "In the aisles of Manzanares, not a single food product remained." Upward of thirty people, militants and common people alike, participated in these frequent supermarket raids.[55] The occupation tactic required workers hold out inside Frigorifico Nacional and thus led El Cerro's amas de casas to take on a unique role in the home and community. Their domestic labor assumed new meaning as the backbone of labor strife, as they frequented local fruit stand vendors to request food donations and cooked large meals in a communal pot to feed their husbands. They also did the laundry to assure their spouses had clean clothes. At night, they roamed the city posting fliers and painting walls to provide updates of developments throughout the conflict.[56] Over eleven different unions affiliated with the Tendencia Combativa set up donation boxes in their union locals. The Railway Union (UF), the site of the ROE-affiliated Worker Dignity caucus, refused to transport cattle and offered limited service throughout the interior—actions undertaken in solidarity with strikers and to pressure the state-owned railway services into paying their withheld salaries from April and May.[57] When companies turned toward trucks to transport meat instead, two were mysteriously set on fire.[58]

Not only did striking workers face off against management, but they violently confronted police and strikebreakers as well. In early May, an MLN-T and OPR-33 coalition organized alongside striking workers to establish a community self-defense network. Augusto Andrés recalls:

> There were moments that resembled an insurrection. There were enormous barricades made with cut-down trees set ablaze. Police on horseback forcing children off the street were confronted by mothers, who struck them with whatever they had in their hands. . . . At nighttime, students dressed in all black climbed the trunks of trees on Calle Grecia and launched steel pellets at police patrols with slingshots.[59]

After being evicted from their encampment in front of the Frigorifico Carrasco factory, striking workers confronted police with bats and knives. When the police unit that led the eviction took over their encampment and began using it as a base for further eviction operations, workers laid siege to the site and reclaimed it for their own use. For example, an unclaimed bomb blew up the front door of ex-police commissioner Besio Viña's home after he was rumored to be using his newly opened bar as a recruitment center for scabs.[60]

In mid-May the CNT held its First Ordinary Congress, which shed light on clear strategical differences between the CNT majority and the Tendencia. The gathering brought together 603 delegates representing seventy-one unions nationwide. The Tendencia introduced its May 1969 Fight Plan, which aimed to coalesce organic expressions of solidarity with the meat-processing-plant workers into a coordinated plan to fight the broader grievances of workers nationwide, such as the wage freeze, mass layoffs, union busting, and salary cuts. The coalition announced its opposition to the COPRIN and argued for its abolition. It also called for the nationalization of the meatpacking industry and reinstatement of workers' right to two kilos of meat.[61] Finally, the Tendencia's Plan recognized a serious disconnect between mobilization efforts of private versus public sector workers and sought solutions for addressing it.[62] AEBU issued a statement echoing the plan, declaring, "It is correct that we should not be using a general strike for the sake of it, but it remains incorrect to limit its use solely in the face of a military coup. Doing so puts workers in the defensive against a military intervention, a weapon of capitalism and imperialism."[63] The plan was voted down, 397 to 150, along caucus lines. Instead, the congress resulted in a CNT-wide strike on June 11, which left Montevideo and the interior paralyzed for one day while resulting in the arrest of upward of five thousand workers.[64]

While the Tendencia's motions did not win majority throughout the CNT, its combative spirit grew across industries where its militants maintained a stronghold. In early June, FUNSA workers participated in elections to reaffirm León Duarte and ROE's List 1 at the union's helm.[65] The PCU-aligned List 5 frequently accused union leadership of "adventurism" in an intense campaign to change power dynamics, but they fell short with only 15 percent of the total vote. After the victory, List 1 announced: "Workers should be united against management, the government, and capitalism . . . without opportunism and without demagoguery. . . . Against sectarianism and dialogue without struggle. For an offensive Fight Plan to confront capitalism and its reaction. For solidarity with all workers in conflict, with politically persecuted, and with political prisoners."[66] Aside from the nod to anticapitalism, statements such as these demonstrate FAU militants' propensity to take radical positions without going beyond workers' threshold to lose their support.

On June 16, 1969, AEBU assembled for the largest gathering of locals in the union's history. There, they agreed to begin partial rolling strikes at different bank locations to initiate a campaign for a break from International Monetary Fund influence while also supporting the striking meat-processing-plant workers. AEBU president Hugo Cores, who by now served on the FAU's directorate and as vice president of the CNT, remained committed to unifying the CNT around an escalation strategy to break the wage freeze. A day after the assembly, Pacheco Areco's government implemented MPS for the second time in less than a year, both induced by AEBU's strike call. Beyond prohibiting strikes and escalating repressive policing tactics against work actions, the measures also censored major news outlets *Acción*, *Extra*, *BP Color*, and *El Diario* for twenty-one days and closed *El Popular* for one month.[67] Anticipating the popular response, the government's press censorship sought to obfuscate the deluge of work actions that took place for two weeks after the MPS announcement.[68]

The wave of illegal work actions extended nationwide, including wildcat strikes, sabotage campaigns, vandalism, and censorship defiance. The revolt saw over five hundred detentions, including that of José D'Elía, the standing president of the CNT. Railway workers continued to refuse to transport meat, and bank workers intervened in the supply chain by refusing to process checks for the meatpacking plants. On June 26, electrical-grid workers at the state-owned UTE launched an industry-wide strike in reaction to militarization—a forced draft of striking workers in the industry. Montevideo was left without electricity for five hours when workers at the Batlle Thermoelectric Central sabotaged the grid, and rolling blackouts continued throughout the city for the next week. The El Cerro encampment continued to resemble a war zone with nightly clashes between strikers and police, often in the dark.[69] The strike drew a violent response on behalf of the state, including the opening of a new detention center at the abandoned lighthouse station on Isla de Flores, a small island thirty-four kilometers offshore from Montevideo.

Journalists and graphic artists defied their newly prescribed role as mouthpiece for the government. Rather than legitimize press censorship by continuing production of Ministry of Interior reports, they implemented an industry-wide strike of their own. Workers at *Extra* occupied the plant, using the printing machinery to barricade the doors. Police refrained from evicting them after warning that doing so could destroy the company's machinery. At *El País*, the nation's largest newspaper and government-sympathetic press outlet, a group of writers associated with the police filed reports that defied the strike. Upon encountering them in the street, ROE militants chased the writers into the bathroom at Montevideo's historic Bar Tasende, where they hid out for two hours only to be beaten physically upon leaving.[70] In one evening, two hundred journalists and graphic artists were arrested.[71]

Montevideo's chaotic environment led New York governor and Alliance for Progress representative Nelson Rockefeller to cancel a visit to Montevideo and instead take refuge in Punta del Este. The days leading up to his scheduled visit saw over twenty attacks on US-owned private firms scattered throughout Montevideo. A Tupamaro cell set fire to Uruguay's General Motors headquarters. Following Rockefeller's arrival, students and workers responded by leading a protest caravan to Punta del Este. Waving the flags of Vietnam and Cuba, demonstrators denounced Rockefeller as a symbol of US aggression and imperialism abroad. The FAU trumpeted their anti-imperialist position by using red and black balloons to raise a large banner proclaiming "Death to Empire" in Montevideo's Plaza de Libertad.[72]

On June 30, after two weeks of rolling work stoppages and solidarity strike actions, 8,500 bank employees at 105 bank locations initiated what would become a seventy-three-day strike demanding full nationalization of the banking sector and a break from IMF restructuring, a minimum wage equivalent to basic living standards, the return of fired workers, and the right to strike.[73] That day, delegates from AEBU, UOESF, FUS, COT, and FUM presented the CNT Representative Table with a proposal for a CNT-wide indefinite general strike on July 2. The Table voted against the proposal following the lead of the AUTE's chief representative, Wladimir Turiansky, who announced that the union's PCU-led leadership had called off the electrical workers' strike earlier that same morning. CNT leadership opted instead for a thirty-six-hour strike, during which partial services would be sustained for the first twenty-four hours. They defended the decision based on the logic of a "wear-down strategy."[74] Utilities workers later testified that the decision was made unilaterally and without their consultation.[75] Martín Ponce de León, a GAU militant and AUTE officer at the Batllé Thermoelectric Central, proclaimed:

> We considered it inexplicable and incredibly erroneous that the AUTE delegation in the CNT voted against a confederation-wide general strike while its own membership was on strike. That united struggle of the whole labor movement, something that AUTE leadership argued didn't exist as a justification not to go on the offensive in 1968; that united struggle that thousands of UTE workers were waiting for in the streets and the jail cells. . . . That united struggle never happened—not because there were not conditions nor reasons to do so, but because there were people who saw it as tactically inconvenient. Instead, they preferred to wage a struggle that didn't include everyone—just AUTE—so the CNT limited itself to a solidarity strike.[76]

Turiansky, a PCU militant, proclaimed that the strike had begun as a defensive mechanism against military conscription. While some sectors maintained a strike, many workers suffered detention and forced conscription after being arrested at their homes. He declared, "Knowing beforehand that this strike would be waged under completely unfavorable conditions . . . the AUTE Congress of Delegates, having reunited the evening of July 25, elected the only path: *the path of dignity.*"[77]

The July 2 general strike saw strong police repression against the nation's most combative industries. At FUNSA, striking workers were surrounded by a squadron of forty military trucks and a small tank while holding a rally outside of the factory. Soldiers fired above workers' heads to intimidate them, striking many of the valves that ran alongside the factory walls. That evening, the Metropolitan Guard detained León Duarte at his home. Workers responded the following morning by prolonging the strike and demanding Duarte's release. They initiated daily marches alongside workers from Cuopar, an adjacent textile factory under worker occupation, with whom they barricaded streets and painted delivery trucks and buses with the slogan "Freedom for Duarte—Down with the Measures!" After five days on strike, the conflict escalated into a monthlong occupation of the plant.[78] In mid-July, the UOESF submitted a letter to the CNT general secretary reaffirming the June 30 Fight Plan.[79]

On July 15, an OPR-33 cell broke into the National History Museum and expropriated the flag of independence, leaving the following communique:

> The pueblo responds by recovering the custody of the flag that once waved so gracefully. Under its motto the first independence was won: Freedom or death! Today, Uruguayans again face the despotism of the oligarchy. With the persecution of workers, with terror, by converting Isla de Flores into a jail, they try to silence our protest. Allied with the octopus of foreign interests, they take from the country and increase their fortunes. It is time for this flag to stop being used as a museum piece in the insulting possession of *vendepatrias* [sellouts].
>
> Now the flag of "the 33" will wave again above the popular struggle.[80]

The same evening, another band of OPR-33 militants broke into the Banco Commercial and poured acid on their IBM computer, causing it to short-circuit and sizzle within minutes. The group left a statement declaring solidarity with the striking bank workers and denouncing the Banco Commercial's complicit role in finance imperialism via the IMF.[81]

Two weeks later, the Armed Forces occupied all state-owned finance institutions nationwide to force them open and conscript strikers to the military.[82] Management and other bank officials maintained restricted services at some locations due to a conscription-induced personnel shortage, but many bank locations had remained closed for nearly a month. The Ministry of the Interior announced the closure of AEBU locals nationwide, along with a search warrant for union leaders, who had been directing the strike clandestinely. Workers responded by targeting management's homes with vandalism and terror. In a series of attacks, they attempted to seal their front doors shut with tar while launching Molotov cocktails through the windows. In response to the military's intimidation, roughly 330 bank tellers returned to their posts in defiance of the strike. By that afternoon, a mob of students and strikers set two cars ablaze—the first belonging to Citibank's manager, and the second to the manager of the Collection Bank.[83]

The militarization of the finance district intensified throughout the week, during which the banking industry slowly resurrected. On July 29, a caravan of military vehicles carrying detained bank tellers arrived from interior cities San Ramón and Treinte Tres. Authorities increased the number of Montevideo tellers to 427 after mandating they work in the capitol's banks or face conscription. The next day, the number of workers increased to 576. Feeling pressured, strikers and students made plans to set fire to more bank manager's homes. The unrest sparked Undersecretary of Industry Washington Cataldi to offer mediation on behalf of the state.

On July 31, AEBU and Uruguayan Bank Association representatives met and agreed upon a settlement favorable to the union. However, Cataldi dragged his feet on formally announcing the agreement in hopes that the strike would wind down without implementing a new contract. He foresaw that numbers of strikebreakers and detainees would increase into the weekend to curb the strike's momentum. However, their numbers decreased, and labor combativity continued to escalate. Indeed, strikers read into the strategy and proved unfazed. On August 1, hospital staff and textile workers held solidarity strikes. Protesters in Ciudad Vieja slashed bus tires, using the stalled vehicles as makeshift barricades to prevent transit from entering the Financial District. After the weekend passed without any legal headway, the strike continued the following Monday.[84]

In the first half of August, nearly five thousand bank workers gathered in separate meetings to discuss strategies for maintaining the strike. They reevaluated tactics for communicating with strikebreakers. While they had previously used shame and confrontation, such as public tarring and circulation of blacklists with personal information, they decided to do more outreach. This plan, called Rescue Operation, saw a strong decrease in strikebreaking at over a dozen banks, including Citi and Banco do Brasil. Workers rotated calling in sick en masse, leaving banks with only two or three employees on hand and thus forcing closures.[85] Strikers continued attacks on bank property. At the Banco Commercial, a team of workers ransacked administrative offices, dragging out furniture and filing cabinets and setting them ablaze in broad daylight. That same evening, four banks burned to the ground. Students entertained themselves by breaking bank windows and throwing Molotov cocktails between classes.[86] By early September, President Pacheco Areco called for the militarization of private banks as well.

On September 9, the MLN-T kidnapped Gaetano Pellegrini Giampietro, secretary of the Uruguayan Bank Association and head director of SEUSA, the editorial firm for both *El Diario* and *La Mañana*. Pellegrini, whose father had served as minister of labor in Italian dictator Benito Mussolini's government, acted as a spokesperson for management's hard-line stance throughout the conflict. The guerrillas demanded settlement favorable to the workers within forty-eight hours.[87] In response, Minister of Labor Jorge Sapelli shared news of secret negotiations between the government, Carlos Gómez, and CNT president José D'Elía that had commenced days prior. The announcement accompanied a call for an AEBU general assembly to discuss a potential settlement. Gómez, who represented the PCU-affiliated minority caucus within the union, argued that settlement offers were growing progressively worse since July 26. He claimed that the strike's continuation would at least preserve the union's legal status and achieve the reinstatement of all conscripted workers. AEBU leadership argued that a settlement would maintain IMF control over Uruguay's financial system while abandoning the 181 workers who lost their jobs during the conflict. Moreover, they accused D'Elía and Gómez of misrepresenting the membership base. On July 12, bank employees voted to settle and return to work the next day. For Hugo Cores and other Tendencia militants, the maneuver caused an irreparable loss of trust.[88]

Adding to the bankers' defeat, the meat-processing-plant workers' strike ended with the permanent closure of El Cerro's main source of employment, Frigorífico Nacional, and initiated an extended process of closing all other meat-processing plants in the neighborhood. Management relocated nine hundred plant workers to new firms in the interior, where they hoped to take advantage of a rural population desperate for work and lack of union presence. The plant's closure led to a six-month conflict over worker compensation and reimbursement for the factory's auctioned machinery. To ensure productivity, military personnel established a presence at packinghouses throughout the country, and freelance truck drivers began transporting butchered meat in response to rail workers' refusal to do so.

Conclusion

By the end of these conflicts, eight hundred labor organizers and 5,600 workers had been detained and/or imprisoned.[89] Workers in both unions suffered harsh blows on behalf of management and the state. Out of 8,500 total bank workers, upward of one thousand bank employees were arrested throughout the conflict. Authorities detained Hugo Cores after both major strike campaigns were in full retreat. Punishment for participation was cruel: Cores and other AEBU leaders were harshly tortured.[90] Moreover, police ordered hundreds of electrical workers to stand for eighteen hours in front of the UTE headquarters; one UTE worker died while imprisoned.[91] Two thousand bank workers were marked as deserters for evading military conscription, and 181 bank employees remained without their jobs.[92] The repression of AEBU rank and file affected the April 1970 union elections, which saw participation from nearly six thousand workers who selected the PCU-affiliated List 3 by a 154-vote margin. Election participation fell by 25 percent compared to the previous year—many of the more radical workers remained in prison, while more conservative workers turned away from union participation in general.[93] By the end of the year, dozens of union officers began living clandestinely. According to MLN-T commander and ex–bank worker Eleuterio Fernández Huidobro, "The 1969 bank strike was one of the largest and best organized in the history of the country."[94] But it still fell short.

The 1969 conflicts provide the clearest example of diverging positions within the CNT.[95] The May 15 Fight Plan best reflected that of the Tendencia, which advocated for a coordinated and prolonged strategy of escalation grounded in an ethos of solidarity unionism.[96] While the call fell upon deaf ears among the CNT's majority, they would soon find a new bedfellow. The Pacheco Areco government's poor handling of the conflicts created a political crisis within the Colorado Party: Congressmen Zelmar Michellini and Alba Roballo left the party, while General Liber Seregni retired from his position in protest.[97] All three soon after participated in the formation of a left electoral coalition alongside the PCU in 1971.

Amid the conflicts, FAU militant and UOESF secretary Washington Pérez drafted a letter to the CNT Executive Board on behalf of the union declaring that the only way to put a stop to wage freezes, state repression, massive layoffs, and increasing poverty was to coordinate a CNT-wide indefinite general strike. He recognized workers' autonomous tactical escalation among PCU-led unions, like AUTE, AFE, and postal workers, and critiqued the majority leadership for bypassing internal processes to put an end to strikes, such as in the cases of the AEBU and AUTE.[98] The Tendencia, for its part, saw these calls for deescalation as undermining the full potential of a labor federation by returning to a strategy of site-specific, isolated conflict that could at best produce spontaneous action. The PCU, in contrast, saw the 1969 strikes as drawing energy away from the effort to build an electoral project.

After the conflicts of 1969 lost steam, Héctor Rodríguez (GAU) and Mario Acosta (PCU) publicly debated the diverging positions of the Tendencia and PCU in a series of articles over the next six months. Rodríguez, who published his position in the New Left journal *Marcha*, claimed that support for the 1969 Fight Plan was a "moral imperative" and a warranted response to keep up with government repression "punch for punch." He accused Acosta and the PCU of offering mixed messages. On one hand, the party emphasized caution, claiming that an indefinite general strike call would unleash the violent full force of the state apparatus and would eventually bring on the illegalization of organized labor. But Rodríguez emphasized that this concern was unique to the PCU as the sole legal entity on the left. However, he argued, the party's rhetoric offered false myths of hope and invincibility. As evidence, he pointed to PCU declarations such as the following from an article in *El Popular*: "No force is strong enough to stop a united pueblo—neither MPS, nor strong governments, nor military takeovers, nor dictatorships."[99] For Rodríguez, such mixed messages were of great concern.

Acosta, who published a series of rebuttals in *El Popular*, proclaimed that the entire year of labor activity could not be reduced to the twenty days of mobilization in late June. He recognized that the government had implemented MPS for a combined nine months out of the year, which created a quotidian feeling of shock among workers, leaving them unable to sustain the level of resistance seen midyear. Moreover, Acosta emphasized that the working class had not yet reached a position to take institutional political power and thus implement the necessary structural reforms to ensure successful transformation.[100]

For those in the Tendencia, these preoccupations proved insufficient. GAU organ *Lucha Popular* further blamed the CNT majority for the year's shortcomings, declaring:

> The losses suffered by some important sectors of the labor
> movement have been consequences of the perilous battles
> and the erroneous orientation of the majority leadership of
> the CNT. The advances that they have produced in the con-
> struction of the Tendencia have the capacity to transform
> into a real direction, with a plan to wage an offensive battle,
> in the CNT program.[101]

However, the article also hinted at the organization's own move
toward an electoral strategy. The 1969 conflicts led GAU to realize that most workers followed the PCU's electoral strategy and
thus to reform their own positions. The public debate between
Héctor Rodríguez and various representatives of the Communist
Party—including Mario Acosta, César Reyes Daglio (SAG), and
Wladimir Turiansky (AUTE)—continued into February 1973.[102]

These diverging strategical visions would play out repeatedly over the next four years. The core tension revolved around
the question of legality. Whereas the PCU aimed to maintain its
legal status, Tendencia-aligned organizations had already illegalized and thus did not respect legal rulings or state institutions.
Moreover, the MLN-T and OPR-33 interventions in the conflicts
showed the possibility of coordinating labor conflict and armed
struggle. Hugo Cores recalls:

> What set [the FAU] apart from the PCU in the everyday life
> of unions had to do with our conception that gave credence
> to workers' capacity for rebellion and theirs which saw polit-
> ical action as channeling support for elections. . . . For us,
> if the legitimacy of the capitalist state relied on violence—
> which, beginning in 1968, we are talking about a constitu-
> tional dictatorship—our practices should not express any
> fetishization of legality. It was the state that violated the
> law. . . . The struggle, as we saw it, was to remain firm against
> an ongoing persuasion and coercion—the violent deception
> that upholds domination.[103]

4

¿Tiempo de Lucha? ¿Tiempo de Elecciones?
Peripheral Conflicts and Election, 1970–71

In the latter half of 1970, the OPR-33 embarked on a series of expropriations to raise funds for self-sustenance. By this time, roughly a dozen militants had already begun living clandestinely. Of the five operations, only one terminated successfully. In December 1970, OPR-33 coordinated three simultaneous actions under the name Operation Apretesis. Militants entered the homes or offices of three national elites and forced them to fill out checks. Two of the actions failed—one in numerous arrests, the other in a shootout. The successful action was carried out against Cándido Eizmendi, who signed a check for $14 million (approximately $56,000 USD in 1970) that was immediately cashed.[1]

One of the failed operations sought to gather a signature from Pedro R. Core, a right-wing banker rumored to sit below a portrait of Spanish dictator Francisco Franco in his office. With falsified identification cards in pocket, militants entered the Uruguay Chamber of Commerce and visited Core's office on the sixth floor. To ease their entry, the militants conjured a story in which Washington Pérez, an ignorant yet bossy latifundista from the interior, had arrived in Montevideo eager to purchase urban real estate. Pérez was accompanied by Selva Artigas, who played his sister, and Augusto Andrés, who played his financial adviser. Ivonne Trías kept lookout on the street while the other three ventured inside.

Upon exiting the elevator, the militants were greeted by two janitors who had not been present at that hour during reconnaissance visits. They stared firmly as the group moved down the hall.

Clearly, they were aware of something. After picking up on the janitors' strange vibes, Pérez suggested aborting the operation and returning to the elevator. Andrés pressed the button to go down, but it was blocked. Police arrived at the scene and arrested all three militants, who were charged soon after with possession of falsified documents.[2] They were lucky to have been caught before carrying out the action itself.

On January 6, 1971, Augusto Andrés arrived at Punta Carretas prison, where he was greeted by a dozen fellow imprisoned FAU militants. His comrades hurried to update him of their recent political falling-out with the MLN-T. His heart was heavy upon hearing the news. While passing time on the patio the next day, Andrés encountered Eleuterio "El Ñato" Fernández Huidobro, an old friend and member of the MLN-T. The two had developed an amicable friendship beginning in 1969, when both organizations had initiated weekly coordinating meetings in a Barrio Buceo safe house. They would rideshare and often arrived early to the meeting house. Passing the time, they shared maté and chatted about topics beyond the purview of political strategy, like recent bar fights and who played the best *tambora* among their Afro-Uruguayan neighbors. In prison, militants from both organizations resentfully observed their conversation: subordinate members of the MLN-T were surprised to watch one of their leaders break character to interact with a member of a rival group. After the chat, Andrés declared his intention to break the silence between both two groups, but comrades warned him of the dangers of getting too close and leaking too much information. Two weeks prior, imprisoned MLN-T leadership affirmed the group's adhesion to the Broad Front (FA), a left electoral coalition centered around the PCU and Christian Democratic Party. While the FAU remained loyal to an anti-legal strategy, the Tupamaros were moving toward a ceasefire and participation in aboveground politics. Andrés recalls his comrades' advice to terminate communication across organizations, saying, "They were right—I returned to our anarchist circle."[3] With both groups pursuing divergent strategies, information leaks had become too risky.

Throughout 1970 and 1971, small and newly formed unions

waged a series of fights that were synergized and triangulated via ROE. These burgeoning unions were key as roughly 90 percent of Uruguay's factories and workshops employed less than twenty workers.[4] By midyear, overall cost of living had increased 105 percent. Meanwhile, COPRIN authorized private sector salary increases by only 50 percent;[5] workers in some industries saw upward of 31 percent reductions in real wages.[6] Others feared unemployment as they witnessed management gradually reduce personnel until eventually closing down factories.[7] In El Cerro, unemployment reached 25 percent in 1971.[8] While owners of small and medium-sized factories scrambled to maintain profit margins, workers challenged massive layoffs, backpay, wage cuts, and union busting. The 1972 "year of fury" brought the highest number of labor actions in the country's history. Meanwhile, the years 1970 and 1971 are remembered for the successful formation of the Broad Front electoral coalition that laid claim to being the formal (and legal) representative of workers' interests. While the CNT majority directed efforts toward this end goal, they further neglected to develop an offensive Fight Plan. Moreover, as a result of their inability to split energies between the electoral and syndical fronts, they left an opening for the FAU and other Tendencia-affiliated lists to gain strength within the labor movement, especially among small, newly formed unions waging battles with management for recognition. While the period saw three general strikes, it did not see any CNT-wide coordination in the nation's largest industries like in 1968 and 1969. However, the period proved key for grounding solidarities and developing shared praxis among workers from smaller firms. Moreover, the gap between the public and private sector's combativeness grew even larger after a June 25, 1970, law recognized all public workers to be providers of "essential services" and prohibited them from striking.[9]

From 1970 to 1971, Uruguayan workers carried out at least 120 work actions. The two-year period saw at least fifty-three occupations, of which forty-two were carried out by Tendencia-affiliated unions. The period also saw at least fifty-six strikes lasting more than three days and thirty-six strikes lasting more than ten days. Tendencia-affiliated unions carried out forty-five of the former and twenty-seven of the latter. Workers at Decovid and Hermanos Carino printing press struck for over seven months, including a plant occupation at the former. Workers at six foreign-owned medical laboratories occupied their plants for over eighty days. COT called industry-wide occupations and two weeks of rolling strikes. Workers on *Zurzul*, a cargo ship, forced the vessel to dock four days in Montevideo after workers occupied it and demanded nearly two years of back pay. Despite their alignment with the CNT majority, workers at five different metallurgy plants occupied them for over twenty days. After management closed the Erosa metallurgy factory due to the accumulation of U$110 million in debt, workers occupied it for ten months. They eventually experimented with self-management for twenty-five days and demanded the plant's nationalization. The period saw four other experiments with autogestion, including multiple days of free train transport and health services. After management fired a union delegate of the Lanasur textile factory (COT), workers defied a lockout, placing the plant under worker control. After management at Bio, Gramon, Atenas, and Bayer failed to comply with a COPRIN ruling in favor of wage increases, medical laboratory workers (SIMA) at all four sites implemented autogestion. Meanwhile, graphic artists at the Catholic news organ BP Color (SAG) printed various editions under worker control amid a three-week dispute, during which they utilized the daily editions as a mouthpiece for their perspective on the conflict. Through diverse means, workers were aggressively taking control of their situation.

In a March 1971 internal document, the FAU affirmed the rising trend of direct action as reflective of workers' growing distrust of political institutions and political parties' capacity to resolve their increasingly harsh economic and social problems. The document proclaimed:

> At the level of mass action, the rising conflicts are confirming the validity of popular direct action as an effective response to the situation that everyday people find themselves in at the current historical conjuncture. . . . Neither political repression nor reform efforts have proven capable

of restraining mass action and pacifying it in turn for an "electoral exit," a proposal offered from above which claims to offer "solutions" for everyday problems. The gradual radicalization of the class struggle exceeds those previously seen . . . and they impede the construction of the "electoral peace" that reformists want to offer while at the meantime they continue to use repressive measures.[10]

The growing number of workplace conflicts drew interunion solidarity. Workers found refuge in the UOESF local, where Tendencia-affiliated locals met to organize over two dozen conflicts. In March 1970, over three hundred workers at the Ghiringhelli plant concluded a two-month conflict with rolling strikes and occupations. The conflict saw a two-week occupation after management announced the layoff of over half the workforce. Although the plant's workers recently voted to replace the long-standing Tendencia-aligned leadership with a CNT majority list, they looked toward their old guard for orientation in the face of management's offensive.[11] FUNSA and BAO workers occupied their respective plants in solidarity, while ROE militants gathered students and community members from La Teja, El Cerro, and Colón to set up toll booths in front of the plant in support. In mid-1970, workers at Decovid used the UOESF local to lay the infrastructure for a six-month factory occupation. Workers frequently demonstrated gestures of solidarity that transgressed left divisions. For example, BAO workers donated U$300,000 to 150 striking workers at the occupied Erosa metallurgy factory, although it was run by a majority-affiliated list. Local merchants and neighbors also helped sustain the occupation by donating food and household goods.[12]

This coordination proved most fruitful for organizing boycotts. During a three-month conflict at ATMA plastic factory, a dozen unions gathered to declare a boycott of the company's products at their workplaces; FUNSA workers further crippled production by refusing to deliver essential rubber products to the plant.[13] In August 1970, ROE militants organized a boycott of Pepsi products to support 450 workers carrying out two months of rolling strikes and plant occupations in opposition to layoffs.[14] Due to the firm's reliance on national infrastructure to transport their products, the ROE's strength in the railway union proved especially impactful. In October 1971, ROE militants set fire to the Divino mattress storefront in Barrio Sur. After management suspended twenty-three workers for refusing to comply with a bimonthly payment plan, plant workers remained on strike for eight months. Again, railway workers lent their support by boycotting shipment of Divino mattresses throughout the country. The conflict terminated in favor of the workers, who gained management's recognition of the union, full staff rehiring, and back pay.[15]

At Portland, a mill owned by US-based Lone Star Cement Corporation, workers occupied and held management hostage for one week in the plant's office. In 1968, workers had formed a splinter union after discovering a bribing network linking union leadership and management. In October 1971, workers discovered the presence of four infiltrators from the US-backed Uruguayan Institute for Syndical Education and responded by purging them from the union. In pursuit of their demand for health care and updated machinery at the aging plant, workers first initiated a slow-hand strike, cutting production to 10 percent; three days later they occupied the plant using a gasoline tank truck as a barricade. Over the next four days, AFE conductors slowed trains when passing the occupied plant and allowed workers onboard to circulate fliers and a donation box. The weeklong conflict terminated in a settlement favorable to workers' demands, including an extensive workplace health inspection, wage increase, holiday bonus, and retirement severance after twenty-five years.[16]

The frequent and sustained conflicts, interunion solidarity, autonomous labor action, and community solidarity demonstrated the labor movement's swift recovery from the past two years' defeats. Unraveling some of these threads, this chapter explores a handful of labor conflicts that took place at smaller work sites during this period. Whereas Uruguay's left largely shifted focus toward an electoral strategy in preparation for the November 1971 elections, the FAU continued to emphasize everyday people's protagonism as the sole means of creating power. While the CNT majority viewed labor action, especially in smaller industries, as peripheral to a campaign strategy, the increasing number of labor conflicts and growing labor militancy proved that workers would not be pacified by the prospect of an electoral win. Moreover, the COPRIN's ambivalent role in the face of management's growing antagonism showed the state's limited capacity to resolve a growing hostility induced by economic crisis. Instead, workers confronted their realities by utilizing a variety of direct action tactics coordinated alongside other unions.

"In Support of TEM: Direct Action at Every Level"

In mid-1970, a medium-sized factory of metalworkers organized a combative campaign that drew participation from various Tendencia-affiliated unions while getting little attention from PCU labor officers. On April 16, Minister of Industry Dr. Julio Sanguinetti visited the Canadian- and US-owned TEM kitchen appliance factory in Montevideo's Barrio Maroñas.[17] Sanguinetti arrived with a team of photographers, who sought to capture images of the plant's workers greeting him with warmth while steadily at work. TEM management mandated workers to clean the floors and machines in preparation for the spectacle. Upon the minister's arrival, a voice shouted, "Hora!," to announce a work stoppage. All five hundred plant workers responded by leaving the factory and refusing to pose for photographs. One worker described the factory floor as having taken on a "deathly silence," in which the minister and his crew anxiously navigated the space searching for an appropriate site to capture a photograph. TEM management responded by suspending all five hundred workers for six days without pay. When workers returned to the plant, their employers presented them with a prewritten letter of apology and required each worker to sign it before starting the shift, but most of the workers refused. Management retaliated with massive layoffs.[18]

In attempt to divide the workforce and curb unrest, TEM subsequently accepted all but thirty-nine of the fired workers back to the plant; all those left jobless belonged to the Tendencia-led SAOT. In answer, the SAOT launched a 112-day strike under the call "All, or no one!" ROE supported the effort by organizing a boycott of TEM products and raised money for striking workers and their families by setting up tollbooths in front of the University of the Republic. Other Tendencia-affiliated unions demonstrated solidarity through workplace sabotage. Various radio station broadcasters contacted the strikers to notify them that they would no longer offer TEM advertising space on their shows. Workers at Acodike, a gas company, blocked the shipment of three thousand propane tanks to the TEM factory. Bank tellers initiated a slowdown strike on all TEM-related transactions, refusing to process them for weeks at a time and thus delaying profit revenues.[19] Bus drivers responsible for the route leading to the TEM factory redirected their journeys to avoid stopping there.[20] In all of these ways, the strike offered prime evidence of the potential of solidarity unionism.

After one hundred days of striking, the conflict saw a wave of tactical escalation. On July 17, ROE militants launched a sabotage campaign against kitchen vendors who dismissed the boycott. In a coordinated effort, roughly four dozen pairs of ROE militants entered stores on Avenida 8 de Octubre, emulating newly wed couples. While one member distracted the retail workers by expressing interest in certain stovetops and ovens, the other snuck away to pour acid into TEM appliances or paint them with the words, "Fabricated by novice strikebreakers." The vandalism was accompanied by a public propaganda campaign that painted "Do not buy TEM products—they might burst" on walls throughout Montevideo, hinting at the potential for malfunction due to the damage induced by the acid. By the afternoon, some kitchen setups began smoking. Two days later, police responded to the vandalism by arresting over a dozen of the most active SAOT workers in a wave of home raids. Consequently, the ROE activated its prison solidarity commission in collaboration with families of the detained. Students then embarked on a public shaming campaign by covering Avenida 18 de Julio with union propaganda, leading to various detentions for breach of the peace.

On the morning of July 21, workers at nearby factories initiated a work stoppage and convened at the intersection of 8 de Octubre and Corrales, where they met up for a rally alongside workers from FUNSA and COT. After a series of speeches, the mob marched down the avenue toward the city center. However, after proceeding only a few blocks, they met a police barricade. Confined to the street where the conflict initiated, distraught students and workers attacked various vendors who continued to sell TEM products, including Bazar Lamar, where marchers dragged stove sets into the street to use as a barricade and set them on fire. Others tossed Molotov cocktails into the store, igniting a fire that required two fire crews to extinguish. Solidarity marches took place in various ROE strongholds, including Zona Norte, Sayago, Carrasco, Colón, and Peñarol. Upward of three dozen retail workers at various appliance stores began a solidarity strike. In one march, an OPR-33 militant experimented with a newly encountered Molotov cocktail recipe, which he used to set ablaze a plant manager's car that was parked in front of the TEM administrative offices.[21] As street violence escalated, a dozen TEM workers took refuge in the United Methodist Church and initiated a hunger strike. A banner that hung at the doors of the church read, "Then they spat in his face, they punched him, and others slapped him (Matthew 26:67)."[22] ROE saw the importance of maintaining a delicate balance between fighting management and winning public opinion. In this case, workers used nonviolent protests tactics and spirituality to appeal to public morality.

On July 24, students at the Instituto Alfred Vásquez Acevedo, Montevideo's largest high school, set up barricades on Avenida 18 de Julio denouncing a recent audit of the public school system. They also declared solidarity with TEM strikers. Upon drawing attention from police, the high school students took refuge in the University of the Republic, where they linked with more strike sympathizers. The skirmishes continued throughout the morning, resulting in more vandalism of TEM products. The march culminated in a rally inside the Methodist church, where speeches were read by the head priest, hunger strikers, a student, and one worker from FUNSA who declared:

> And there are no conditions? And there are no conditions
> for fighting? ... Working every day in the unions, organiz-
> ing the resistance, acting with and among the people ... and
> acting out of practical solidarity in model struggles like that
> being waged by the workers of TEM, we are starting to pave
> a new path. With their lives, their struggle, and their sacri-
> fice for the cause of the people, Che Guevara and Camilo
> Torres show us the path, that with the everyday militancy
> we are going to follow. And like this, fighting, as said by
> Buenaventura Durruti, labor militant from Spain, "We will
> make a new world because we carry it in our hearts."[23]

The speech directly challenged the PCU's reformism, in which
party leaders often labeled direct action tactics as "adventurist"
and "misguided." Moreover, the speech highlights the FAU's
syncretism of left political symbols and figures, referencing two
recently martyred Latin American revolutionary figures for the
sake of maintaining popular relevance while situating their ethos
and spirit alongside that of a more obscure anarchist historical
figure, Durruti.

On July 26, the Senate intervened and pushed for mediation
between the union and management. Five days later, management
rehired all five hundred workers at the plant and agreed to a 4
percent "productivity" wage increase.[24] Reflecting on the triumph,
striking workers recognized the essential role of those outside the
factory. Their victorious communique proclaimed:

> *Compañeros*, you are a pillar in the victory that the pueblo will
> pull off against the millionaire gringo management of TEM.
> This victory is not only by the TEM workers, but instead by
> all the workers, and from a will to fight—one that is rooted
> in a combative unity of the pueblo, and one that can defeat
> the bully management.[25]

Similarly, one SAOT leader declared, "Given the selflessness and
sacrifice of the striking workers, the strike became a central concern and welcomed solidarity from broad sectors of the pueblo."[26]

Notwithstanding the popular support, the conflict failed to draw the attention of the PCU-run UNTMRA or the CNT majority. The officer quoted above went on to lament the lack of interest from the CNT Strike Commission, which did not inquire with union leadership about the nature of the conflict until the seventieth day of the strike. The officer recognized the conflict as a clear example of the disconnect between the CNT's strategy and the reality of everyday people's strong combativeness. He went on to praise the support from ROE and Tendencia-affiliated unions— especially UOESF and AEBU—declaring:

> We believe that the CNT statute and program are good things. The CNT draws membership from the great majority of the Uruguayan working class. However, we find issue with its current direction, whose tactics are not sufficient for confronting the current dictatorship. Regardless, we believe that our union should affiliate with this organism. Other unions find themselves in a similar situation—taking issue with the current direction—but they, bank workers, FUNSA, teachers, and textiles, participate in it anyway.[27]

Similarly, another SAOT officer proclaimed, "We believe that the CNT does not utilize the full potential of the labor movement."[28]

Yet, the PCU's dissatisfaction with SAOT's tactics remained clear. While the party organ, *El Popular*, covered the conflict in the first two months of negotiations within COPRIN, it offered no reporting on any of the illegal actions that repeatedly took place in the final weeks. In all fairness, the organ was censored for eleven days beginning on July 24. Netertheless, when coverage resumed, it omitted details of the SAOT's more combative tactics even if it spoke fondly of the hunger strike. To save face, *El Popular* published an article titled "From the Beginning We Extended Solidarity to the Workers at TEM," including testimony from workers at Galmisa metalworks, who convinced their management to boycott sales of galvanized plates to TEM and collected donations to support workers.[29] However, the gesture was interpreted as a desperate attempt to remain relevant and instrumentalize the SAOT struggle. After the long campaign, SAOT expanded to include all wage-earning workers at the plant and thus changed its name to Union of TEM Workers and Employees, modeling the move after UOESF.[30]

To Unite Fighting, to Divide Voting:
The FAU and the Broad Front, 1971

For nearly two years prior to the November 1971 elections, left organizations channeled political energy into building and campaigning for the Broad Front coalition. PCU general secretary Rodney Arismendi, MLN-T leader Mauricio Rosencof, and Christian Democratic Party politician Juan Pablo Terra helped marshal the coalition, recruiting ex-Colorado Party member General Líber Seregni to run as the FA presidential candidate. The PCU identified their strategy as "the least painful road to socialism," by which the party rejected armed struggle while emphasizing the importance of courting the military. According to Arismendi, the state remained susceptible to outside influence in certain areas, such as public administration and education, but maintained a bourgeois monopoly on violence via the military, which had never seen the influence of popular sectors in its directorate. However, the growing reform faction among the military leadership provided a possible opening should a left government gain access to the state. Arismendi saw critiques of elections, parliamentarianism, and broad coalition building as historically revisionist for assuming such strategy could only lead to a synthesis of capitalism and socialism (i.e., social democracy) and not to the "destruction of the bureaucratic-military machine of the bourgeois state."[31] For PCU leaders, elections offered a unique opportunity, considering their rare status as one of the only Communist parties in Latin America not yet banned. In a July 6, 1971, speech to members of FIdeL, Arismendi proclaimed:

> Revolution is the product of a united people, the product of
> a united working class, of the working masses, of the most

advanced sectors and the anti-imperialists. There is no other war toward the liberation of the people on earth. . . . Dear friends: to speak of electoralism as creating a clash between the campaign work and revolutionary work is old news and was resolved forever by Marx, by Engels, by Lenin, by Fidel Castro, by our beloved and dear *compañero* Guevara in his old polemics against the anarchists and other *infantalistas* of the left.[32]

The PCU looked toward the Soviet revolution as an example of a unified pueblo that included peasants, workers, and soldiers. Its leadership argued that in Uruguay, the FA coalition offered an opportunity to coalesce these sectors around a political project, seeing this as a prerequisite for any revolutionary endeavor.

The FA hoped to achieve three main objectives: agrarian reform, nationalization of banking, and nationalization of foreign commerce. The objectives overlapped to form a broad economic program. Agrarian reform aimed to resolve the massive rural exodus by shifting production into the hands of small producers. While less than one-third of the national population worked the land, the decline of rural industries endangered some of Uruguay's most important urban industrial sectors, such as textiles, wool, and leather goods. There just wasn't enough raw product to draw from domestically. Through nationalization of foreign commerce, the FA sought to use the state to ensure that foreign enterprises purchase raw resources at market value rather than buying them low and selling the finished product high for Uruguayan consumption. The FA also claimed that such interventions reflected a Uruguay-specific revolutionary program, declaring, "Revolution is the only thing that cannot be imported nor exported. . . . No one is going to invent the Uruguayan path except for us Uruguayans, and it is based on our way of seeing our own reality."[33] The FA set out to develop a program that permitted "an organic national link" and brought together "cadres from hundreds of movements . . . and that created thousands of forms of struggle, whose originality and contributions we should validate and respect."[34]

In December 1970, the MLN-T expressed frustration with the electoral coalition but nonetheless saw potential in the mobilizations leading up to and after the vote. In one communique, the MLN-T declared, "In our support of the Broad Front, we understand that its principal task is to mobilize the working-class masses and assure that this labor does not start and end with the elections."[35] The MLN-T acknowledged a "false dilemma" between *foco* strategy and party politics. They saw themselves as providing "armed propaganda" for constructing a political party. In other words, for the MLN-T, the armed apparatus served to raise revolutionary consciousness and to express the urgency and viability of a revolutionary moment.[36] Eventually, in October 1971, they agreed to a ceasefire out of respect for the electoral process.

The FA held its first public rally on March 26, 1971, commencing the year's campaign around the call "el pueblo unido" (the people united). Over two hundred thousand braved autumn rain to participate in what *El Popular* declared as the largest political rally in Uruguay's history.[37] The months leading up to the official announcement saw a hopeful narrative among the left, including a Gallup poll that reported 35 percent support for the FA among Uruguayans.[38] Although the FAU officially declined to endorse and attend the founding rally as a political organization, a handful of members arrived to scope out the atmosphere. Some felt isolated and envious while viewing the excitement and fervor of such a large gathering of fellow workers, neighbors, and radicals.[39]

The FAU, for its part, saw the FA's use of the CNT infrastructure as traitorous to the initial mission of the labor confederation, which aimed to maintain the autonomy of the labor movement by means of apoliticism, or nonaffiliation with a political party. Moreover, rather than maintain the autonomy of existing social movements, the FAU saw the FA's electoral strategy as co-opting them into a liberal democratic framework and thus legitimizing its hegemony for making politics. In the 1971 CNT Congress, the Executive Board amended Article 49 to allow for CNT officers to hold government positions yet kept the clause preventing references to the CNT in campaign rhetoric.[40] The FA's formation also brought about a split within the Tendencia. Adding to the complication, the GAU and MRO decided to join the electoral coalition as a gesture of left unity. Along with more radical members of the PSU, they formed the Corriente, playing the role of militant minority within the FA. The FAU and Revolutionary Communist Party (Maoist) were the only left organizations to decline participation in the coalition.[41] FAU militants Hugo Cores, Gerardo Gatti, and Mauricio Gatti spent the majority of 1970 in prison and thus were absent from the conversations about where to direct the energy and momentum of the CNT.[42] Cores was again arrested in April 1971. He remained in prison for the duration of the year, eventually reuniting with sixteen other FAU militants behind bars. Between their absence and party members' focus on the campaign, the confederation would prove uncoordinated.

"Voting Does Not Solve the Problem of Power"

Guided by an anarchist perspective, the FAU recognized the limitations of the electoral strategy from its inception because the left was not in position to take power. Instead, electoral participation served the role of building consensus around political pluralism in a liberal democratic framework while halting the left's charge to build popular power. As a June 1969 communique notes:

> The electoral campaign is the means by which the oligarchy seeks to reestablish dialog with the working class and recuperate their influence among them disguised as their representatives. The unpopularity and lack of prestige of politicians and politicians in general is evident. . . . They aim to "reactivate the political life" destined to reinstate the mainstream political parties to their importance and gravitational function in the national politic. This would be achieved as the result of an election campaign that generates expectations, hopes of renewal, and after a massive propaganda campaign that mobilizes old sentimental values that remain effective in many sectors. In the end this will only open the door for reactionary interests. . . . To divide the

pueblo around empty slogans and banners, in an electoral
bout practically inconclusive, avoiding that in the struggle
for revindication and real solutions to the grave problems
that affect them. Through action, everyday people come
together around concrete motives. In elections, everyday
people divide among themselves over abstract pretexts and
utopic illusions. . . . Those who never really divide themselves
between banners and parties remain united in defense of their
positions vis-à-vis the pueblo, are the privileged members
of the dominant classes. Their circumstantial disagreements
and conflicts never make them lose sight of their common
interests as a class. They never cheat respect and thus . . . they
continue promoting that the elections are the only "correct"
form for the pueblo to express its opinions. . . . Thus, faced
with the intentionally confusing maneuvers of reaction, and
faced with the attempts to derail the pueblo toward the electoral route, there is only one response: escalate and broaden
the struggle. We must unite to break the austerity politics of
wage freezes. We must spread solidarity to unions involved in
conflicts. We must drive forward with all our energy a popular organization. . . . We must combat every tendency to subordinate the activity of popular movements to the interests
and perspectives of electoral candidates.[43]

Referencing the shortcomings of the 1969 conflicts due to lack
of long-term and sustainable escalation strategy, the FAU argued
that the left remained in a phase of *resistance*, in which militants
were still laying the foundation for a prolonged struggle with
capital and the state.[44] In other words, everyday people required
more experiences as protagonists *via* direct action and mutual
aid to advance further toward the formation of revolutionary
counter-subjectivities that could take an active role in the implementation of a new mode of political economy beyond the market
and the state. Instead, the electoral route, like foco, relegated the
population to the passive and disempowered role of spectators.

The Broad Front eventually finished third, with 19.6 percent
of the vote.[45] They foresaw an inevitable loss in the elections,

regardless of rumors of 30 to 40 percent support based on Gallup poll surveys. They also envisioned such a loss as having devastating consequences on working class morale.[46]

The FAU's pamphlet *¿Tiempo de lucha? ¿Tiempo de elección?* directly countered Communist arguments regarding the state. The FAU recognized that the state has two functions: to provide services and maintain order. Yet, they claimed that the state's primary commitment was to the latter. Most importantly, they argued that the state was not neutral and could not be utilized as an instrument to challenge the interests of the oligarchy and bourgeoisie. Moreover, they looked toward history to claim that any government's attempt to significantly challenge ruling-class power would inevitably result in a military takeover.[47] The FAU viewed the recent struggles at small and medium-sized firms as proof of labor's unity in the face of worsening economic realities. Whereas workers could potentially think, feel, and vote against their own interests, their shared economic condition moved them into the role of protagonist in their neighborhoods and workspaces. They simply needed more experience to ensure a subjective transition. A November 1970 article in *Cartas* proclaimed:

> The reformist leaders cling more and more to their policy of confronting the struggle at the mass level to avoid tensions and channeling the generalized malaise of the people toward the electoral opening, where it will materialize, without risks, for the system in obtaining some legislative seats. However, under the pressure of increasingly difficult living conditions, people naturally tend to adopt attitudes and combative positions as soon as they are lowered from the unalterable and rarefied climate of union "summits" to the reality of concrete action between the people . . . workers who, at the time of voting, have opted for the most diverse hairs, which had the most diverse beliefs or opinions (white or red, believers or atheists) at the time of facing the prepotencies or the revived ones of the above, they unite closely, in the hard fight and without returns, in that eternal war, between the exploited ones and the exploiters.[48]

But not all was lost in the climate leading to the election. Throughout 1971, ROE grew not only among combative sectors of the labor force but also among students. In April 1971, the ROE took advantage of a government lift on press censorship and began releasing *Compañero*, a biweekly newsletter under the editorial direction of León Duarte. The paper's content paid special attention to the labor conflicts by Tendencia-affiliated unions. By this time, the FAU infrastructure had grown to be upward of two hundred active militants who advanced and reproduced the organization at various levels of participation. The growth was primarily due to ROE's popularity among workers and students, which had gained a reputation for winning dramatic labor conflicts in coordinated efforts with the storied UOESF. Many of the newer members were high schoolers from El Cerro–La Teja. For example, Juan Pilo joined the ROE at age thirteen and began distributing copies of *Compañero* to nearly a hundred subscribers throughout La Teja; most were purchased by members of the Bakers Union. One afternoon, while Juan was waiting outside a union hall with papers in hand, an unknown man approached him and asked for a copy. Juan responded with the paper's cost; and the man responded, "I am Duarte, you know?"[49] The anecdote demonstrates the ROE's large growth and local emphasis: new members could not identify core militants due to the organization's widespread reach and emphasis on maintaining a low profile.

Regardless of the organization's legal status, participation in the ROE and other left youth organizations became increasingly risky throughout the election year. In May, the government mandated that all households register their family members at local police stations; in effort to prevent political meetings, police subsequently monitored houses for gatherings larger than the registered number. The program's architects, who drew inspiration from Nazi anti-espionage, hoped that its implementation would inspire a social fear of gathering in private spaces.[50] The increasing criminalization of popular political activity left youths vulnerable to attacks by fascist groups and the police, who sometimes acted jointly. On May 31, 1971, a group of students affiliated with the far-right Uruguayan Youth at Attention (JUP) collaborated with plain-clothes police to violently attack high school students in Colón, a ROE and UJC stronghold. The JUP identified as anti-communist, with the primary goal of maintaining the "law and order" status quo of Blanco and Colorado political hegemony. The group also accommodated a radical wing oriented toward street violence modeled after Spain's falangist "blue shirts." The JUPistas identified their dissident peers to the group of middle-aged men, who mounted an attack on the playground that left forty injured, including one in critical condition.[51] In October 1971, a middle school student in Bauza threatened a teacher with a revolver after faculty members broke up a JUP rally on campus.[52]

The focus on national elections also opened opportunities for ROE-linked caucuses to win union elections, as the PCU and PSU remained preoccupied. One of ROE's biggest wins came in the UF, a twelve-thousand-strong union that stretched out across Uruguay's nationalized railway system, the Administration of State Railways (AFE). Upon nationalization of the railways in 1952, the UF developed close ties with mainstream political parties dating back to the Battlista populist project, thus gaining AFE workers a reputation as some of the most conservative in the country. AFE workers watched the street conflicts of the late sixties from a distance and condemned more militant actions, such as tollbooths and property damage. But they faced a tactical and moral crossroads beginning in 1969, when the government began radically slashing funding to the industry, giving preference to the construction of a private bus infrastructure instead. The rail industry was already highly neglected: workers frequently loaded railcars built in 1872. Nearly half of the country's locomotives remained out of operation, and workers received "monthly" paychecks every forty-five days.

With a small nucleus of under two dozen militants, the ROE-affiliated Worker Dignity caucus won the UF elections in 1971. Their victory reflected more of a change in workplace culture than an outright ideological shift among the railway's employees. Raúl Olivera, a FAU militant and UF officer, remembers workers welcoming more radical tactics after recognizing there was no other alternative. They found themselves replicating tactics used by the student movement, such as blanketing the street with spike strips to prevent police vehicles from approaching train stations during strikes. Amid one conflict, workers expropriated operating machinery from the Peñarol neighborhood station, holding it hostage until management agreed to demands.

While workers previously refused to align with students for questions of disparate class interests, they maintained a firm link with the ROE contingent from the UTU. By 1971, this relationship proved vital as students played an important role distributing propaganda via fliers and murals to grow zonal solidarity around the worker's conflict in the face of the industry's liquidation. Workers returned support for students by implementing political strikes in opposition to police violence against the student movement, including six students assassinated by Armed Forces between 1971 and '72. The ROE caucus not only embraced combative tactics but also introduced the first female UF representative. These events and conflicts led to the formation of new solidarities among AFE workers, who could no longer rely on institutionalized channels of representation. On March 24, 1972, workers placed the railways under worker control for two days and offered passengers free rides from rural areas to Montevideo. They also refused to transport military supplies. Olivera recalls the union circulating the following phrase: "Fight against the bosses and for public opinion."[53] However, this change of guard did not expand to the rest of the labor movement.

On June 23, 1971, the CNT held its Second Ordinary Congress in Montevideo. In a statement addressing congress attendees, PCU prime secretary Rodney Arismendi hinted at the CNT's role in the Broad Front project, declaring, "Today an unforeseen trajectory has opened to the pueblo—that of taking over the government. While recognizing the importance of not derailing the specific function of our unions . . . the unifying function of the CNT has contributed to this new situation."[54] Delegates from the Tendencia denounced the PCU's manipulation of process and use of the platform for election campaigning. For example, the Federation of Maldonado Industrial and Commercial Employees, a Tendencia-linked union representing over one thousand workers in the interior, was prohibited from participating in the congress for failing to pay dues.[55] A UF delegate asserted:

> There has not yet been any real joint effort to confront the oligarchy. . . . Those unions who have come out to fight did so alone in most cases. They received no mass support from the CNT, which merely released some declarations of support. . . . As the result of the lack of a Fight Plan, today there are very important unions that remain semi-paralyzed after having exerted themselves alone and without the support of the rest of the workers.[56]

Beyond participation in workplace conflicts, the FAU sought to maintain connections to popular neighborhoods by redistributing resources in Montevideo's periphery. Such actions took new meaning during the 1971 election season, as many among the left saw the electoral coalition as a real possibility to take power. On August 6, 1971, the Dia del Niño (Children's Day), an OPR-33 cell broke into the Plastlit toy factory and began filling large sacks with toys. The expropriation went smoothly and without interruptions, but upon arriving to the distribution point in Barrio Cerrito the operation went poorly: children began fighting over the toys, and teenagers harassed younger children to take their toys. After a few hours, the FAU militants ended the action with a poor taste in their mouths. Some militants returned a few days later to sign off on the action by leaving a photocopied image of the independence flag. A group of mothers came outside to take the fliers and burned them; others called the police, who sent search teams throughout the city to find "Los 33." The militants realized that they had lost popularity in the neighborhood after consistent visits from Colorado Party affiliates who came to distribute spaghetti and blankets in the months prior as part of the electoral campaign. The action would be one of the FAU's last neighborhood redistribution efforts, as militants redirected energy and resources into labor conflicts and political prisoner support. As such, the left's overall ability to connect with peripheralized populations appeared to be losing ground. While the FA relied strongly on the CNT infrastructure to collect votes, the community's reaction proved that the labor-based strategy had not gained equal footing among the unemployed and *amas de casas*.

"All or Nothing": The Three Fs and CICSSA

Yet all was not lost in the labor movement. UOESF would continue to prove itself as an example for smaller unions to replicate. Moreover, they began to work alongside radical union allies more formally, specifically beverage plant workers and health service workers. The coalition would come to identify as *los tres F* (the three *F*s): FUNSA, FOEB, and FUS. They would forge a front at a moment in which each local was experiencing its own heightened conflicts. On April 20, 1971, an OPR-33 cell broke into the FUNSA rubber factory to expropriate a collection of arms from management's office. The operation was one of four raids to steal arms from known collections of business firms and individuals.[57] A week later, the UOESF published the following statement regarding the local's role in the growing climate of unrest among small and medium-sized workforces:

> We have nothing to hide regarding the use of our union hall—it is regulated and public, and we are notorious for what we do here. . . . If a union hall should function as a social club, then it should be a bastion of student militancy and for the people. . . . It should serve as a bastion, like a binding center, for all the FUNSA union to come together with other unions, and with students that invigorate the space with their enthusiasm, with the youth of the pueblo that struggle against its oligarchy. In our local, our beloved local, they have planned, programmed, and pushed forward some of the hardest-fought battles and conflicts against the dictatorship. . . . It was the center of restlessness and hopes, of happiness and deception. . . . This is the use of our local and we are proud and honored that we can serve the student and worker pueblo, as they have served us too.[58]

The UOESF local hosted Sunday afternoon meals commonly attended by community members and guests from ally unions. The support network often extended into León Duarte's home, where fellow organizers gathered frequently to seek consultation.[59] The UOESF maintained its commitment to solidarity unionism primarily by offering support for smaller union struggles largely ignored by the CNT majority. Indeed, the union's unique role as referent proved key to moving the labor movement further toward the strategies and tactics encouraged by the FAU and the Tendencia.

While UOESF remained outspoken in its support for direct action, the union rarely entered conflict with management beyond verbal negotiations. FUNSA's workers largely entrusted and respected Duarte's negotiation skills and remained prepared to act should bargaining efforts fall short. Moreover, most of the union's radical activity concerned moral and political questions rather than bread-and-butter issues. But that changed as stratification intensified. In late August 1971, the UOESF called for a boycott of FUNSA's products in demand of a cost-of-living wage increase. Regardless of the union's militancy and notable gains over the past decade, management enjoyed an annual profit margin five hundred times greater than employees' yearly salaries. Upon receiving the demand, management insisted the issue be presented before the COPRIN, but the latter responded by asserting that the claim be handled at management's discretion. In a maneuver that further surpassed the COPRIN's function, management announced they would accompany a wage gain with augmented prices and increased productivity.[60]

Leading up to the UOESF's boycott call, an OPR-33 cell kidnapped Luis Fernández Lladó, a member of FUNSA's shareholder board of directors. His father, Saturnino Fernández, served as the board president. The kidnapping was meant to intervene in a labor conflict at Frigorífico Modelo in Tacuarembó, where workers labored in twelve-hour shifts and where Lladó served as vice president. The armed cell held Lladó for fifty-one days after kidnapping him while en route to his local butcher shop. On October 9, Lladó's father delivered US$200,000 in ransom and brokered a settlement of the FUNSA conflict in exchange for his son's release.[61]

A similar climate of conflict existed in factories organized by the FOEB. On August 12, 1970, over four hundred workers at PepsiCo commenced a two-month strike in response to management's firing of Douglas Lacuesta, a union steward who recently requested management provide workers with boots and gloves. Lacuesta also served as the Pepsi plant–based locals' representative to FOEB, which represented seven thousand workers throughout the industry. The union petitioned COPRIN's intervention to remove chief director Ignacio Aguerre from decision making over labor. Aguerre was a frequent collaborator with the Uruguayan Institute for Sindical Education—he sent six supervisors to the school in hopes of breaking the plant's union—and served as the chief director for TEM. The union accused him of creating the workplace conflict to pressure COPRIN into approving the company's outstanding request for price increases. In November 1969, the company's four largest beverage producers petitioned COPRIN, with Pepsi uniquely threatening a lockout to leverage the request.[62] The union's request drew mediation from the Ministry of Labor on September 3; however, Aguerre left the meeting in outrage before his turn for getting questioned.[63] Instead, company lawyer Daniel Jiménez de Aréchaga proposed a plan titled "Internal Labor Regulation," which banned the distribution of union propaganda within the plant, prohibited workers from leaving their section, mandated workers clock out when going to the bathroom, granted management authority to search the locker room, and forbid the use of the telephone. The plan consisted of ninety-three new rules in total.[64] On September 22, the union rejected COPRIN's mediated solution for leaving Aguerre in place and neglecting to rehire Lacuesta.[65] Two days later, plant foreman Heber Chechile fired a shot from his car window as he drove past a group of strikers in Montevideo's center, leaving one assembly line worker with a bullet in the knee.[66]

The conflict drew widespread support, including from the CNT, which called for a boycott of Pepsi products and collected over U$40,000 in donations from supporters.[67] On September 15, the CNT North Zone held a two-hour work stoppage, halting production in surrounding textile, metallurgy, and chemical factories; students and teachers also walked out to join the rally in front of the plant.[68] A day later, Tendencia-affiliated unions held a two-hour work stoppage to gather at the UOESF local for another solidarity rally.[69] The plant's eighty-strong fleet of delivery drivers expressed solidarity with the striking assembly line workers. Elcio Mancini, president of the Cargo and Transportation Workers Union (SUTCRA), proclaimed:

> We express full support to the PepsiCo workers and our comrade delivery drivers whose labor remains halted at the fault of plant manager Ignacio Aguerre. We denounce management's bad attitude that has deliberately provoked this conflict in attempt to break the PepsiCo workers union. SUTCRA remains committed to our classist line and will always be side by side with the workers in conflict. Our union demands an immediate resolution to this situation.[70]

On October 16, 1970, Pepsi plant workers negotiated an agreement to all four strike demands, including a joint labor–management committee to negotiate workplace conflicts, a loan reimbursement for lost time, Aguerre's removal from his acting position, Chechile's forced resignation, and Lacuesta's rehiring without penalty.[71]

A year later, on October 22, 1971, the Uruguayan Health Federation, an MLN-T stronghold, occupied *mutualista* (private, dues-based) clinics throughout Montevideo and offered free medical services for two weeks. These "Popular Hospitals," a tactic utilized on four different occasions, responded to the yearlong conflict between workers and management at Montevideo's ten largest private hospitals that, combined, serviced over eight hundred thousand patients annually.[72] While each hospital local negotiated separately with private management, the federation enabled all workers to coordinate both demands and labor actions to make a stronger impact on industry.

The conflict was a culmination of organizing that had begun one year prior. In July 1970, an assembly of three hundred FUS delegates representing over thirteen thousand health service workers voted to initiate a campaign for nationwide free health service with worker participation in its directive. The campaign began with two separate forty-eight-hour and seventy-two-hour strikes within the same month. In October, various acts of police repression, including a bloody bludgeoning of three workers at Hospital Británico's entrance, swiftly radicalized the conflict. On October 27, workers responded by implementing the first Popular Hospital and issued free services for two days; workers at IMPASA and the Italian Hospital followed their lead.[73] Meanwhile, students and staff at the Faculty of Medicine camped in front of the recently closed residency clinic, which shut its doors due to loss of funding. The clinic lacked medicine and hygiene products, leaving staff so dramatically under-resourced they could not adequately change patients' bedsheets. The government's U$2.3 billion debt to the university forced the closure of various campus resources, including labs and cafeterias, and left students with scholarships without stipends. One student declared, "We conceived of the encampment as a propaganda method to reach the everyday worker, the housewife, the man in the street. The encampments are everyday evidence of the 1,800 scholarship students who cannot continue studying, who must return to the interior with their careers on hold."[74] The encampment at the Faculty of Medicine drew support from health service workers in the public sector organized under a separate union. Although they could not legally strike, they presented the COPRIN with a parallel list of demands and utilized the encampment to draw public sympathy.[75] In late 1970, FUS retreated from further labor actions and announced they would integrate the free health service and wage increase demands into the CNT program.[76]

By October 1971, the entire health industry spiraled into labor conflict. Health service workers protested management's failure to comply with a September ruling by the COPRIN, which approved an immediate 27.2 percent wage increase, the six-hour day, and a salary bonus for night shifts and skilled labor. On October 26, FUS initiated a campaign for a 50 percent salary increase as living costs continued to rise. They began by implementing Popular Hospitals that drew participation from unionized doctors who offered free service to roughly three hundred people each day. Many doctors were recent graduates of the Faculty of Medicine, a longtime feeder of militants to both the FAU and MLN-T—the Uruguayan Medical Union (SMU) was an especially important MLN-T stronghold.[77] Doctors maintained their own set of demands, including pay bonuses for performing surgeries and paid transportation costs to and from work. The conflict also intersected with workplace occupations at Omega and Warner Lambert, two pharmaceutical laboratories. Both laboratories belonged to Union of Drug and Allied Industries (SIMA), a federation of lab workers that coordinated occupations across five different labs during a three-month conflict over pay increases one year prior.[78] Moreover, the November 1970 conflict had ignited a union drive at the US-owned Warner Lambert laboratory. By mid-October 1971, Warner Lambert's two hundred workers had maintained a two-month occupation in protest of management's firing of a union militant for insubordination. The campaign drew solidarity from FUS; Faculty of Medicine Administrative Employees (FUFEMM), who refused to distribute the company's products; and SAG, who refused to print the company's labels.[79]

By November 1971, various hospitals agreed to settle the conflict, agreeing to a month paid vacation and time and a half for nightshifts.[80] The conflicts in the health service industry calmed down until March 1972, when FUS and SMU launched another bid for universal healthcare accompanied by demands for wage increases, pension reform, and freedom for political prisoners. Beginning in October 1972, FUS embarked on a fifty-two-day strike demanding universal healthcare and back pay from as far back as 1967. Regarding the 1972 campaign, one FUS steward proclaimed, "The current government, while installing fascism through concentration camps, state of siege, violent attacks, torture, and assassinations . . . on the other hand proposes for the 'humanization' of medicine. The people know that a humanization of medicine is only viable if it is framed in the total change of the structures of the country."[81] The campaign for universal free health service would eventually come to fruition under the Broad Front government in 2005.

During this two-year time span, the three Fs established themselves as bastions for a combative unionism. As hotbeds for the FAU and the MLN-T, these unions had an ideological clarity guiding their actions from the start. But other unions organically developed their combativeness when confronting their immediate situation, and through that process often turned to support from militants like Duarte, Gatti, and Pérez. The close relationships forged at the UOESF local built trust and opened possibilities for OPR-33 interventions in workplaces with little to no FAU presence.

In mid-1971, CICSSA's 250 pulp and paper mill workers waged a three-month campaign for union recognition. The plant's North American owner, known throughout Uruguay as "Gringo Brown," openly boasted that he had saved up thirty million dollars to bust any unionization efforts. Workers had organized an unsuccessful campaign for union recognition three years prior, during which a strikebreaker assassinated CICSSA employee Urián Correa amid a confrontation at the picket. When management obligated workers to sign off on a contract amendment that would forfeit their benefits, workers responded with another union drive campaign. Brown pushed back by firing the entire workforce.[82]

On June 23, 1971, the OPR-33 hatched a plot to kidnap Dr. Alfredo Cambón, a lawyer and legal adviser to both CICSSA and FUNSA management. Cambón was also founder of the Neighborhood Collaboration Commission, a neighborhood watch organization that collaborated with police units to enforce the recently implemented neighbor registry.[83] Upon taking a trip to Germany, Brown entrusted Cambón with control of CICSSA. FAU seized the opportunity to confront Cambón, having already gathered information on him due to his affiliation with FUNSA. Disguised as a moving crew, the armed cell approached the lawyer's home and greeted him bedside with a 9mm pistol. Upon transferring him to a "people's cell," they demanded he contact his family to request they deliver groceries and supplies to the workers' encampment at the gates of the plant; his son soon delivered the goods personally. After two days of interrogation, during which Cambón promised to resolve the conflict by the end of August, the OPR-33 released him.[84] To keep up the pressure, two weeks later a mob of students and workers set fire to Brown's car while it was parked in front of the Legislative Palace, where he was visiting the minister of labor.[85] Throughout the campaign, police shot and wounded five strikers, leaving one in critical condition. On July 24, 1971, the campaign also saw the death of Héber Nieto, a ROE militant and construction school student, who was shot with a sniper rifle at a tollbooth organized to support the workers.[86] Historian Clara Aldrighi later discovered that the assassin's .225 Winchester was one of four donated by CIA agent Dan Mitrione to the Uruguayan secret police in 1969.[87] Two days after Nieto's assassination, sixteen unions called for an indefinite general strike against state repression.[88]

In early August, CICSSA workers won union recognition. Brown initially attempted to rehire only a portion of the workforce, but this did not fly with the union. Management eventually agreed to rehire the entire staff and pay forty days back pay with help from a loan by the national social security fund. Regarding the experience, one worker declared:

> In the conflict we established a unity among our coworkers, which was something that we did have prior. We got to know one another by sharing *mate* and meals, and during the sleepovers. This was the most important result of the occupation. There were eighty of us who cohabitated and did things together that we had never done throughout the ten or twelve years that we had worked together. Now, it is like we are all brothers. . . . We also discovered the support of groups from the outside, like students. We did not understand the logic behind what students were doing previously, such as socking someone in the face or burning a car. Now, after having gone through this with our own bodies, we understand it all. . . . We recognize that what the students do is very fruitful. They come out to work (tollbooths, signs, mobilizations) and to defend us.[89]

Elections: Fervor, Fear, and Failure

However impressive, many of the struggles listed above were lost in the election fervor leading up to November 1971. Aware of the volatile situation in labor relations, the Pacheco Areco government broadened repressive measures beyond that sphere by maintaining strong influence over media and militarizing public space in the months prior to the election. On September 10, the government censored four FA-affiliated press organs, including one for six months.[90] On October 30, a group of FA supporters were detained on Montevideo's Playa Ramirez after setting up a day camp on the beach with umbrellas featuring the coalition's logo.[91] Meanwhile, the government made use of media coverage around recently completed infrastructural projects, such as National Highway Routes 5 and 26, to simultaneously campaign for the Colorado Party. The repression extended beyond the state apparatus, including numerous JUP attacks on FA locals.[92]

Amid the fervor, sixteen FAU militants remained indefinitely detained in the Punta de Rieles "special holding centers." All those detainees were ROE militants, including Gerardo Gatti, Washington Pérez, and Hugo Cores, who had contracted hepatitis during his more than six months of detention.[93] Other prisoners included Darío Espiga, an active militant in the TEM and CICSSA struggles; Eduardo Dean, a shoemaker and student; Lilián Celiberti, a middle school teacher; José Caraballa, a student at the technical university; and Ruben Prieto, a student in the Faculty of Education and union delegate, among others. Various FAU militants moved in and out of prison during the months leading up to the election: if authorities considered militants useful sources of information, they could be detained repeatedly, even after serving jail terms.[94] Although Pacheco Areco denied their imprisonment to the press, word of the militants' detention spread widely in left political circles, inducing sympathy from the FA.[95] Although the two organizations took different positions on the elections after working closely together for nearly a decade, the GAU remained in solidarity with the FAU. On November 22, all sixteen political prisoners launched a hunger strike to bring light to their torture and to decry the undemocratic conditions under which elections were being held. Family members moved between the First Military Division, General Command, and Ministry of the Interior searching for answers, but no one accepted responsibility or revealed the location of the prisoners. On election day, *Ahora*, the Broad Front newspaper, published an article titled "Hunger Strike in the Prisons: Those Kidnapped by the Government Cannot Vote Today," which questioned Pacheco Areco's claims of free elections due to significant numbers of the population being held in prison. The article also contained a powerful statement by the medical doctors union, which recognized the illegality of the prisoners' detention and identified prisoners' devolving health as due to poor conditions and torture.[96]

On November 29, Uruguayans voted in favor of the Colorado Party candidate Juan Bordaberry, who won the presidency by less than a 1 percent margin with 40.6 percent of the votes. The Blanco Party took second, and the FA placed third with only 18.3 percent of the vote total.[97] The following day, an OPR-33 cell kidnapped Michèle Ray, a foreign journalist and the wife of famous French–Greek film director Costa-Gavras. Ray, a sympathizer with armed struggle who had been kidnapped by the Viet Cong while reporting on the Vietnam War in 1967, is rumored to have collaborated with the FAU to manufacture a sensationalist event that would communicate OPR-33's commitment to armed struggle and anti-legality vis-à-vis the FA's shortcomings.[98] Ray was staying in the home of María Esther Gilio, a Uruguayan journalist with close ties to the MLN-T. The two women developed a friendship while Gavras and Ray visited Uruguay to investigate for the 1972 film *State of Siege*. Upon releasing Ray a few days later, OPR-33 shared a communique reinforcing the limitations of the elections. Ray aided by distributing the content to foreign media sources.

On January 4, 1972, the ROE held its first postelection rally, where Gerardo Gatti, Hugo Cores, and León Duarte, all recently released from detention, delivered speeches. Appearing gaunt and malnourished from the torture and hunger strike, Gatti reminded attendees of the importance of maintaining an independent labor movement, free of state direction and intervention.

He proclaimed:

> This is why we give importance to union action as one of
> the key areas of direct action at a mass scale. Why should
> we give it such recognition in this country and why is this
> not the case in other countries of the continent? Here, we
> have a syndicalist movement, complete with its limitations
> and defects, with its diversity of conceptions for its direction,
> with "unevenness" in its tradition and organization, and with
> all of this, it is not a vertical syndicalism, it is not a yellow
> syndicalism. Even in the worst historical times of weakness
> and division, it has not welcomed state regulation.[99]

Conclusion

Between 1969 and 1971, labor won a 16 percent wage increase.[100]
However, the cost of living continued to rise, with 35.8 percent
increase in housing costs and 50.3 percent increase in food costs.[101]
While workers at FUNSA enjoyed the fruits of a successful campaign to increase wages, management petitioned COPRIN to
double the market price of the firm's products. Throughout 1971,
over one hundred firms requested permission for price increases
from COPRIN.[102] In the wool industry, firms responded to the
upsurge of labor conflicts by firing over 75 percent of the industry's workforce; to compensate, wool and textile investors instead
imported as much as forty million pounds of contraband wool
from abroad.[103] The years saw an upsurge in workplace conflicts,
but, according to the FAU, there was still no clear role for the CNT
among them. Moreover, the government-sanctioned COPRIN
was proving increasingly incapable of resolving tensions between
labor and management, and when intervening, it did so in favor
of the latter.

The struggles of 1970 and 1971 would foment new solidarities
independent of the CNT. Workers established regional solidarities across different industries, such as in Carrasco, where workers
at CICSSA, Seral, and Portland linked and coordinated actions.

The period also laid the foundation for what would become the most visible representation of the Tendencia coalition, the three *F*s. Finally, the period saw greater unity between the labor and student movements. Whereas some unions doubted the utility of working alongside the student movement, the bond strengthened throughout the era as both movements coordinated actions while maintaining boundaries and autonomy.

The Broad Front's failed electoral bid closed the door on a legal route to political and economic change in the near future. Yet, everyday people's living conditions showed no signs of recovering to their precrisis levels, and the government remained steadfast in upholding the MPS. The hegemonic left could no longer rely on rallying people around the hope of change from above and thus had to look within for answers to growing unrest among popular classes. Left leadership, specifically those among the PCU who occupied visible platforms in the parliament and the CNT leadership, needed a strategy that matched the urgency of its rhetoric. Increasing working-class militancy, especially in the nation's majority small industrial firms, required a new and thoughtful response from movement leaders better attuned to the base.

5

To Know Half a Person
Social Subversion, Internal War, and
Military Takeover, 1972–73

At a Montevideo bar, Juliana's lover returned to the table after using the pay phone. "It happened," he said. She smiled back, and the two continued their evening out. In an effort to avoid drawing unwarranted attention, they fought their instinct to celebrate. On May 11, 1972, an OPR-33 cell kidnapped Sergio Molaguero, a member of the JUP and son of the Seral shoe factory owner. Juliana Martínez, a sunglass factory worker and recent dropout of the School of Fine Arts, and Ana Rosa Amorós, a bank worker at the state-owned Social Security Institute, had carried out two months of reconnaissance to lay the groundwork for the operation. The women lived semi-clandestine lives while maintaining Casa Emma, a FAU/OPR-33 safe house named after the anarcha-feminist Emma Goldman.

This chapter explores the period between January 1972 and June 1973, when the Broad Front's defeat forced the left to shift focus toward extra-parliamentary strategies, especially within the labor movement. The period saw dramatic changes in the left milieu, such as increased labor militancy among PCU-affiliated unions and a new void created by the Tupamaros's military defeat in April 1972. While the FAU remained committed to its "two foot" strategy, half of its core leadership and the entirety of its armed apparatus was in exile in Buenos Aires by end of 1973. Yet, the brief period of heightened labor unrest reflected the potential of the CNT and the possibility for armed direct action to complement it. This relationship is further explored in the case of the 1972 kidnapping of Sergio Molaguero.

In 1972 alone, public sector workers participated in 134 strikes, 351 work stoppages, and seven occupations; private sector workers participated in 130 strikes, ninety-five work stoppages, and eighty occupations; students participated in fifty-six strikes and forty occupations.[1] The period saw a boom in work actions because industries began coordinating days of action, including across sectarian lines. On July 5, COT and UNTMRA coordinated to occupy over one hundred factories for two days. The CNT made three calls for general strikes *with* workplace occupations as part of a campaign for a 40 percent wage increase. Although the campaign sparked widespread work actions across most of the country's main industries, COPRIN offered a 20 percent raise while simultaneously authorizing price increases for consumer goods in September. Factory occupations remained common in the textile industry, which saw upward of 2,500 layoffs by mid-1973. But PCU stronghold sectors such as metallurgy, yarn, and tannery also began to use the tactic. In one case, metalworkers at Etchepare Gil occupied their factory for one hundred days after seventeen union delegates fell to detention. Interior cities experimented with municipal-wide strikes. In Juan Lacazé, all factories stopped production for three hours to demand union recognition for workers at Indelaco (FOEB). In Maldonado, workers frequently walked out to join the Montevideo Association of Municipal Staff and Workers (ADEOM) on indefinite strike after not receiving their salaries for five months. Railway and health service workers placed their industries under worker control on numerous occasions throughout the year. Finally, teachers nationwide launched a sixty-four-day strike against an education reform bill drawing solidarity from all sectors in the CNT. The "year of fury" marked a shift in CNT majority strategy to begin utilizing more combative tactics, including in the public sector. However, while organized labor was growing its capacity, it was still having only marginal effects on COPRIN rulings.

By this time, union membership had increased 13 percent nationwide, primarily due to the successful union drive campaigns waged by workers at small plants—most of which had had to overcome strong resistance from employers. In May 1972, the

CNT National Gathering of Shop Committees received 1,800 delegates from six hundred locals. In an opening statement, the Representative Table warned of a possible coup d'état on the horizon and reaffirmed the CNT's commitment to "achieve structural transformations that will create the conditions so that exploitation of man by man will disappear."[2] The Gathering concluded with a reaffirmation of the CNT Program, including escalation of the campaigns against wage freezes and state of internal war, but rejected a Tendencia-backed proposal to withdraw the CNT delegate from the COPRIN.[3] For the FAU and the Tendencia, the only solution was to increase labor antagonism to capital and the state.

State of Internal War

While labor militancy escalated, so did state repression against the entirety of the left in response to the Tupamaros's growing capacity for armed direct action. In the first quarter of 1972, the MLN-T successfully carried out over seventy armed actions.[4] On April 15, 1972, the Coordinating Organizations for Anti-Subversive Operations (OCOA), or Joint Forces, declared a "state of internal war."[5] One day prior, the MLN-T had assassinated four Joint Force members to avenge their participation in paramilitary groups and torture centers. The April 15 counterinsurgency operation resulted in eight Tupamaro deaths and the arrest of numerous high-ranking officers, including Eleuterio Fernández Huidobro and David Cámpora. That same evening, a Joint Forces team raided the PCU central headquarters. On April 17, a Joint Forces operation resulted in the deaths of eight party leaders at the PCU local in Paso Molino. The military attack at Paso Molino sought to invalidate the Communist Party by provoking it to move toward an armed strategy à la *foco* and thus distract from its mass activity in organized labor.[6] By September 1972, authorities captured MLN-T leaders José Mujica, Mauricio Rosencoff, and Raúl Sendic in a sweeping operation. Upward of five thousand people were prosecuted by military courts on charges of sedition, including a handful of FAU militants.[7] The MLN-T responded to the repressive climate by carrying out upward of thirty assassinations in the first nine months of 1972, but this would prove insufficient.[8] The massive offensive eradicated the MLN-T infrastructure from the officer to rank-and-file level.[9] The Tupamaros would never recover.

By mid-1972, the FAU produced an internal document that assessed the circumstance of the revolutionary left, specifically the shortcomings and subsequent defeat of the MLN-T. The anarchists allotted the MLN-T's failure to their use of the foco strategy, one that put their armed organization at risk by acting as a disparate paramilitary force as opposed to serving as a tool for escalating mass social conflict.[10] According to the FAU, the MLN-T did not lack connections to popular movements out of neglect, but they had failed to strike a balance between armed struggle and mass action due to their prioritization of the former.

While the FAU expressed disagreement with the MLN-T's foco strategy, which had caused a political antagonism between the two groups throughout the 1960s, the organization expressed a heartfelt solidarity with fallen members of the MLN-T and a sincere sadness regarding the loss of an accomplice. One communique proclaimed:

> Until today, armed activity was predominately oriented around the foco conception. We disagreed with this conception from the very beginning—we saw and highlighted its weaknesses ... and we oriented our practice along an alternative line. Against all else, above our own shortcomings, our own mistakes, time and actions have given us reason. We do not rejoice in seeing so many of our comrades from the MLN-T murdered, tortured, and imprisoned after all that marvelous effort they have made to build up a revolutionary movement in the recent years. We cannot be satisfied with the fact that what we predicted years ago is now coming true. Those dead are our dead. Those tortured are our tortured. They are just as much comrades as those comrades of our own organization, who today are now enduring savage

torture themselves, and are putting their lives out there to
defend the principles, life, and line of our organization.[11]

The FAU viewed the MLN-T as one of the few Latin American
revolutionary organizations to move beyond the foco strategy,
specifically through their use of an urban guerrilla strategy. Yet
although the MLN-T's tactics represented an attempt to depart
from foco orthodoxy, they were still informed by and unable to
fundamentally break from the strategy throughout their ten years
of activity.[12]

The FAU offered four main critiques of foco strategy. First,
they critiqued the sense of urgency to initiate armed struggle
due to *objective* conditions, such as the technological underdevelopment of Latin American states (particularly militaries), the
economic impoverishment of most Latin American populations,
and the popularity of revolution in the collective imaginary. This
urgent posturing caused expectations of immediate results, which
did not manifest aside from various reform-minded concessions
in the political arena.[13]

Second, the FAU critiqued foco's assumption that armed
struggle would radicalize people ideologically or that worsening
subjective conditions would have them join the revolutionary
movement—despite guerrilla military victories. Thus, military
victories did not provide the means for ideological development
among the masses. Instead, the strategy converted the idea of
insurrection into a grand myth—something achievable upon the
advancement of the guerrilla vanguard and thus detached from
everyday life. It traced this myth to the earth-shattering events of
the Paris Commune of 1871, the Russian Revolution in 1917, and
the Spanish Revolution of 1936, which saw the masses running to
the streets to construct barricades and defend a set of ideals rooted
in a certain revolutionary praxis. In the case of Spain, decades of
anarchist organizing in opposition to oppressive factory exploitation, rural servitude, and the capitalist city spawned the formation
of schools, unions, social centers, and defense committees that
fomented working-class solidarity and identity. But the insurrec-
tionary *moment* continued to play a role in the left's imagination

and to offer a prescription for achieving a revolutionary situation. Whereas collective direct action provided a clear, proactive role for everyday people, foco strategy constrained everyday people to the role of witness to a military theater.[14] The FAU was not alone in this analysis. Abraham Guillén, the MLN-T's guiding strategical influence, argued that the organization's strategy was limited to encounters between the guerrillas versus the army and/or police, which ended up with "the people [being] caught in the middle."[15]

Third, the FAU viewed foco as unique to rural areas, where guerrillas could "strike and disappear" and always stay in movement. While they recognized the MLN-T's innovative contribution to the expansion of foco to the urban sphere, this did not mean they agreed with it. Instead, urban guerrillas served to complement their rural counterparts by laying the foundation for their eventual arrival to the metropole and thus the final victory against capital and the state. Instead, the FAU looked toward historical examples of urban armed struggle in the anarchist tradition, specifically those of Spain's CNT-FAI, who built a revolutionary movement strong and broad enough to defend working-class interests.

Finally, the FAU challenged the action/repression dialectic, or the assumption that generalized state violence would motivate everyday people to action. Instead, they argued that as repression increased, the armed apparatus would assume a more privileged, or vanguard, role. Such polarization would create an opportunity for the state to mobilize behind the "old ideological myths of bourgeois liberalism," such as elections and legality, which were more likely to win the support of everyday people due to the state's hegemonic position. The state could therefore isolate the guerrilla. In their view, while foco strategy often gained ground toward national liberation, such as sparking foreign capital flight due to fear of political instability, it only strengthened the relationship between the domestic military and national bourgeoisie, thus doing nothing to challenge the fundamental social relationship under capitalism—the subjugation of labor to capital.[16]

The FAU's internal document assured that the MLN-T's failure was due to their replication of the foco model, not the result of their use of an armed strategy. In fact, the FAU offered a reassurance of their commitment to armed struggle, declaring: "The process of deterioration is clearer than ever. Nothing indicates, therefore, that we must change our own strategy. . . . [T]he armed struggle takes on a fundamental role."[17] The document concluded: "Are the comrades who have participated in foco strategy revolutionaries? Yes. Is foco an efficient revolutionary strategy? No. Instead, foco is an erroneous strategy that is negative and dangerous for making the revolution."[18]

Seral, Sergio Molaguero, and the Women of Casa Emma

Gender roles in '60s and '70s Uruguay did not undergo the transformative explosion that occurred in places like the United States, UK, and France. Indeed, relative to the "swingin' sixties," changes in Uruguayan society were quite moderate. Various interviewees referenced miniskirts and hot pants as an indicator of publicly visible changes of the time, but traditional gender expression and relationships remained much intact. Because it remained common to live at home until marriage, youths broadly struggled to find space for sexual expression.

Membership to a left organization often required even further compromise beyond the expectations of the home. As noted by Uruguayan historian Vania Markarian, left militants' private lives were "subordinate to the demands of their political activities."[19] Militants faced a dilemma in which the utopian horizon conflicted with the crushing reality of a heavily regulated clandestine life, imprisonment, and torture. Women militants recall feeling liberated by their participation in a political project with different goals beyond that of the prescribed role of women in the heteronormative nuclear family, but much of their activity remained in the domestic sphere. This contrasted strongly with myths around highly sensual and sexually liberated guerrilla women; in reality, their political obligations simply did not allow for such a thing. Moreover, the Uruguayan left's classist emphasis led it to straggle behind many of the progressive ideas around gender of the time. Even among the left, childrearing remained expected of the mother rather than shared; and homosexuality was often seen as "fragile" and "weak." Yet, women militants broadly express having felt emancipated through their participation in OPR-33 and other armed left organizations of the time.

FAU's coordination between armed cell and mass front is best represented in the May 1972 kidnapping of Sergio Molaguero. Armed operations not only required a complex network for dialogue between those underground and above, but also among intelligence gatherers and supporters who laid the groundwork behind armed interventions. Indeed, such invisibilized and under-documented labor served as a lynchpin for armed organizations throughout the continent. Women protagonists predominately participated in revolutionary organizations in this way.[20] Like their MLN-T rivals, the FAU did not advance a clear gender analysis, nor did they incorporate demands for gender equity into a revolutionary vision. Whereas the MLN-T saw gendered domestic labor as oppressive and sought to liberate women from this sphere, the FAU recognized domestic workers as potential protagonists acting from within the space of the domestic sphere.[21] Women commonly served as *encargadas* (heads) of mixed-gender surveillance cells, which entailed taking on more organizational and cognitive labor, such as filing documents, identifying and solving problems, synthesizing information, and remembering deadlines.[22] While responsibilities followed the normative gendered expectations at the time, female militants recall feeling equal to their male counterparts within the organization due to a general understanding of the importance of all political work, no matter what form, in sustaining and advancing the revolutionary cause. As OPR-33 militant Edelweiss Zahn recalls, "Intelligence was no small task."[23]

Women militants embraced a counter-subjectivity that required sacrifice and compromise in their everyday lives to fit the mandates of a political strategy amid conditions of social war. Ernesto "Che" Guevara famously labeled this transformation as the *hombre nuevo* (new man), a clearly gendered descriptor that omits the ways in which women militants throughout the continent took on revolutionary subjectivities. Women militants resignified their everyday labor in the rear guard and thus provided an integral, yet invisibilized, role in maintaining a revolutionary infrastructure. Whereas the traditional role of household labor had served to reproduce "value-producing" (male) labor power, the women of Casa Emma contributed to socialized struggle by redirecting home labor to a political organization antagonistic to both the market and the state. Rather than produce and reproduce value, OPR-33 expropriated and redistributed value from the possession of banks and business owners as part of an anticapitalist and anti-statist project. As such, their decision to compromise and sacrifice in the name of a revolutionary project challenged liberal feminist understandings of autonomy as rooted in personal choice and option, or "living a life of one's own choosing."[24] On the contrary, upon choosing to join the organization, militants' capacity to make life choices thereafter was extremely compromised.

For OPR-33 militants, disciplined commitment to a greater struggle proved fundamental to their personal liberation. In the case of Casa Emma, militants' everyday life subverted hegemonic gender roles and thus took on a unique counter-subjectivity. Rather than exacerbate a tension between public and private, or *calle* (street) and *casa* (house), women militants labored primarily from the home—albeit with the intention of having a social impact far beyond the domestic sphere. They acted as much more than supporters: their labor was primary and fundamental.[25] Moreover, Uruguayan women's participation in the burgeoning global sexual revolution was a class marker—most FAU militants came from working-class backgrounds, and sexual expression was of less concern, at least. Ana Laura Di Giorgi, a historian of Uruguayan feminism, declares:

> Participation in activities that defined a particular youth culture, including the possibilities to enjoy sexual liberation . . . depended much more on one's class position than the traditions of their family. It required material, cultural, and symbolic resources—to purchase modern clothing, to dance to rock n' roll in the clubs, to sing in English, to disavow one's father with a miniskirt, to go to the pharmacy and purchase

a pill, and to be capable of not coming home to sleep in one's
family home.[26]

While some FAU militants participated in youth countercultural
spaces, particularly among artist and rock-music circuits, this
was not an overall site of struggle for the group. Women militants recall lukewarm feelings toward sexual liberation and free
love. Although some were interpolated by its message and even
embodied it in practice, they did not find interest in advancing it
as a cause, whether at the mass scale or as integral to the FAU's
internal politics

It is important to situate women's reproductive labor in the
narrative the OPR-33's kidnapping of Sergio Molaguero in 1972.
While narratives of armed intervention in the Southern Cone
remain well documented in police files and media outlets, little is
known about the everyday lives of militants nor the broad organizational infrastructure within which these actions occurred—especially the key contributions of women. Media representations and
scholarly analysis commonly reinforce a gendered hierarchy of
labor by rendering it invisible or secondary due to its location in
the rear guard. Yet, a study of this labor with attention to autonomy and compromise offers a unique insight into revolutionary
left counter-subjectivity at this historical conjuncture of ampli-
fied social war.

Ana Rosa Amorós and Juliana Martínez, the Women of Casa Emma

Ana Rosa, Juliana, and two male militants made up Torres
(Tower), an OPR-33 intelligence cell that operated out of Casa
Emma, where both women resided.[27] Ana Rosa, a bank teller at
the state-owned Social Security Bank (BPS), began participating
in the FAU as a collaborator in 1969. Throughout high school, she
belonged to the Catholic Association of Students and teachers,
a Montevideo-based liberation theology project lead by Father
Jorge Techera. The bank teller's union, the AEBU, remained
a FAU stronghold beginning in 1968 under the helm of Hugo

Cores. A fellow bank worker recruited her after a brief conversation about her prior political militancy. She began participating by distributing *Cartas de FAU*, the organization's illegal underground newsletter. Ana Rosa also collaborated by storing the *Cartas* and other FAU-related materials, such as auto parts and hardware, in her family home. Her father, who served as deputy representative of Rivera Department, held parliamentary immunity due to his role in national politics. As such, her class position deviated significantly from that of other FAU militants. In mid-1971, Ana Rosa joined OPR-33 and accepted the responsibility for operating the safe house.[28]

Juliana joined the cell after one year participating in ROE. In 1970, she moved to Montevideo from the northeast border town Chuy and began her trajectory as a student at the School of Fine Arts. While Juliana had not been politically active prior to arriving, she was moved to participate in an anarchist political project after her cousin gifted her Daniel Guérin's *Anarchism: From Theory to Practice*.[29] However, she remembers struggling to comprehend the complex debates surrounding the ideology during student union meetings, where the FAU's brand of Latin Americanist anarchism often clashed with a more traditionalist vision popular among Fine Arts students and Comunidad del Sur.[30] She eventually joined ROE and participated in various solidarity campaigns with striking factory workers. An intermediary later approached her about taking on intelligence-gathering responsibilities in OPR-33. She recalls joining without second thought, even after being warned that participation would likely result in imprisonment, exile, or execution. Juliana moved into Casa Emma in late 1971, soon after dropping out of school to begin working full time in an eyeglass factory.[31]

The quaint house was in Montevideo's Brazo Oriental neighborhood. The women, both in their early twenties, claimed to be students—a narrative that helped explain the frequent visits from youth members of the organization. While they received a small stipend from the organization, the women worked in the formal sector to pay for rent and living costs. They kept up the home's maintenance, received a daily newspaper, and hired a gardener to visit once a week. "We were two people living a normal life. . . . We had a life that resembled everyday life in the rest of the country," Ana Rosa recalls.[32]

Yet, the domestic sphere doubled as the site of their political militancy. They hosted weekly meetings where participants sought to develop a shared analysis of national politics. The FAU published content from these conversations in *Cartas*, drawing upon it to develop appropriate strategies and tactics for its mass front. The women studied daily newspapers to compile scrapbooks of politicians, factory owners, and members of neofascist organizations in effort to preempt intelligence gathering for potential interventions. They filed the albums in secret compartments (*pozos*) fabricated behind dressers and vanities within the house. Finally, the women participated in physical training exercises, including weightlifting, aerobics, and self-defense. Ana Rosa recalls frequently practicing lifting one another up off the ground in a drill to simulate assisting a fallen team member while running from authorities. Such drills and training were part of daily life.

The home served as a space of refuge but also required attention to detail to avoid unwarranted attention from neighbors. The women had to pay close attention to symbols and references to politics within the home. Prior to one meeting, when a visiting militant noticed they had decorated a vanity dresser with a red and black ribbon, he demanded they remove it for security purposes should the house be visited by police.[33] Juliana spent hours in front of the house with yarn and a crochet hook imitating hand motions, although she did not know how to knit. She recalls feeling anxiety about household malfunctions that necessitated a repairman or plumber to enter the home. They both developed basic handyman skills in order to keep the house "clean," or free of outside presence that might reveal its political function. To this end, the organization also relied on its own network of trusted repairmen who shared common skills and were available on call.[34]

Due to security precautions, relationships within the armed cell remained limited. The women knew one another, their neighbors, and fellow members of OPR-33 by way of an alias. But safeguarding personal information was very important for the resident militants and visitors alike because revelations could compromise a fellow militant should another member be caught and interrogated. These security measures became even more important when hosting clandestine members, who sometimes passed time at the house before leaving the country to evade warrants. They interacted with a strict focus on political labor, taking caution not to stray into any personal information about their interests, backgrounds, or identities. (In one noteworthy gesture of trust, however, a visiting militant shared her real name with Ana Rosa.) None of the four Torres militants had any contact with the FAU nor OPR-33 outside of their intermediary and those who passed through the house.[35]

The women's political labor required them to compromise their social lives outside of the organization. While they participated in social activities popular among Uruguayan youths, such as moviegoing and nightlife, they could not share information regarding their activity with anyone, even their closest friends. Within left circles, youths knew that their friends could potentially be participants in clandestine armed organizations. This mandated a social code in which such inquiries and topics of conversation remained taboo. They distanced themselves from friends and family members to maintain boundaries. Juliana recalls feeling anxious when converting previously substantive relationships into superficial encounters. She had to close doors and establish boundaries with people that must have seemed arbitrary to her interlocutors. While, to avoid raising suspicions, she remained in touch with people from her past life, she struggled to balance between maintaining the facade of her previous self and her militant counter-subjectivity.

Romantic life was even more compromised. The militants' universe of potential love interests was limited to those they met within the armed wing of the organization. They could not date outside of this circle, because sharing information regarding their activities, even within the confines of a romantic relation, could compromise both people's security.[36] This became even more complicated if one member of the couple was fully clandestine. Juliana recalls balancing her relationship with security needs after authorities issued a warrant for her arrest in July 1972. Henceforth, she maintained relationships with her fully legal partner and friends but feared for their safety should authorities come looking for her while they were together. She remembers feeling like she was putting the people closest to her at risk. "Sometimes the flow of life brought you into situations in which you would be together with people. The idea was to do so as little as possible, but sometimes it just happened," she shared.[37]

Militants sometimes struggled to strike a balance between their desires and needs as individuals, and their responsibilities to the organization. They often felt guilty for not attending worker solidarity actions, such as picket lines and rallies, even when the timing clashed with other responsibilities in the rear guard.[38] Juliana remembers having little time for leisure, and social life could never come before organizational obligations. For instance, she attended one of Montevideo's many beaches only once while living in the safe house—an experience she shared with fellow members of Torres. The day trip brought her a feeling of joy and freedom not replicable elsewhere in the city.[39] But the feeling was fleeting.

Seral: A Fight for Dignity

On April 12, 1971, over three hundred workers at the Seral shoe factory began a campaign for union recognition after plant owner José Molaguero insisted they appear for work on a holiday weekend.[40] A group of eighteen workers from the vulcanization section refused to comply due to having planned a fishing trip together. After Molaguero fired the entire section, the plant's workers responded with a strike. They lamented management's frequent firings, refusal to pay maternity leave and overtime, child labor practices, and denial of break time. Molaguero had gained notoriety for personally entering the women's restroom to mandate workers return to their posts if they took longer than two minutes.[41] The sole competitor to FUNSA's national monopoly over athletic shoe production, Seral had developed a reputation for using a strong hand.

On April 22, Seral management resolved the strike by recognizing the collective bargaining unit and reinstating all fired workers.[42] Julio Ojeda, the union's elected general secretary, was a ROE militant. He and five coworkers served as liaisons between the Seral union and the FAU.[43] Seral workers looked to the UOESF as a point of reference because of their hard-fought campaign against anti-union employer Pedro Saen, on which account leadership selected León Duarte as an outside consultant. They gathered frequently in the UOESF local to meet with members of the ROE, including students from local high schools and fellow independent unions, such as Portland Cement and the CICSSA paper mill.

Although the union had earned recognition, Molaguero continued with draconian measures on the shop floor. Foremen painted the factory walls with tar to prevent workers from leaning on them for rest. They prohibited conversation and penalized workers with two hours lost pay if they were caught laughing. On May 14, 1971, management fired thirty-two underage workers after a law was passed to limit child labor to six-hour workdays. After over a month of failed negotiations, Seral's workers again went on strike and won their rehiring after twenty-four hours.[44] This conflict reignited the membership base to begin pursuing outstanding demands of the company.

On August 26, 1971, management closed the plant after four months of stalemate negotiations regarding salary increases, workload, maternity leave, and child labor practices. Molaguero, the sole proprietor of the enterprise, enjoyed earnings one thousand times higher than the average worker's annual salary. Rather than capitulate to a Ministry of Labor ruling in favor of the Seral union, Molaguero had opted to simply shut down the factory, firing all 308 employees.[45] Workers had frequently utilized partial and slowdown strikes throughout the negotiations, and they met the lockout with an occupation. After only three days, however, police raided the plant takeover and forced workers out at gunpoint.[46] With support from ROE, Seral workers then launched a boycott campaign against Seral brand shoes.[47]

Molaguero responded by activating his son's networks within the neofascist Uruguayan Youth at Attention (JUP) to recruit strikebreakers.[48] Intimidation became commonplace. Nelson Hardoy, a shift manager and JUP member, provided the names of union agitators to local police, who frequently raided their homes amid the standoff. Demonstrations outside the factory often drew violence from strikebreakers. In one case, a JUP member struck a child in the face while he was distributing fliers in front of the plant. Police frequently arrested workers and their family members during public gatherings. Three workers and two minors were detained for distributing fliers, another five workers spent three days in prison for painting a wall with propaganda, and a hired driver of a *perifoneo* (mobile loudspeaker) was detained for twenty-four hours. Family members commonly faced harassment from police officers upon visiting detainees. Montevideo's subcommissioner of police once insulted a group of workers' wives, insisting, "Go wash yourselves, filthy women!"[49]

On December 8, 1971, some forty workers set out on a forty-two-kilometer caravan march from the Seral plant in Santa Lucía, Canelones. Setting out with no destination, the "March for Dignity" sought to galvanize support throughout the Montevideo metropolitan area. It made stops at various factories in the country's interior, where workers camped and fraternized before arriving to Montevideo. Upon weaving through the city, eleven workers were detained before the march finally settled in Cerro Norte. Within a week the encampment grew to nearly a thousand. Police eventually raided the camp, forcing the marchers to relocate to San Rafael Church in El Cerro, where a dozen workers then initiated a hunger strike for over one week. On Christmas Eve, a group of fifteen Seral workers and ROE militants escalated the conflict by vandalizing storefronts of vendors who did not respect the boycott, including the pro shop at the Punta Carretas Golf Club. The group also used Molotov cocktails to set fire to Casa Sanz, Montevideo's oldest sporting goods store, causing upward of U$10 million of damage.[50]

The conflict continued into the new year. Authorities repeatedly evicted various protest encampments as workers settled and resettled throughout the city. In April 1972, León Duarte began closely conversing with Seral's ROE caucus to consider the possibility of an armed intervention on behalf of OPR-33. Duarte's internal reportback to the FAU acknowledged: "It seems to be that Molaguero, the son of the owner and active shareholder in the company, has been insulting workers, groping female staff members, and encouraging a crackdown on the factory's workforce. He seems due for a kidnapping. It's clearly time to look beyond union action for a resolution of the dispute."[51] Upon receiving confirmation from Seral's ROE caucus, a FAU intermediary relayed the task to Torres.

Members of Torres unanimously accepted the task of surveilling Molaguero.[52] Juliana recalls, "There was no discussion. It was clear because our job was simply to support the labor movement. There was no doubt among any comrade. And we knew that this kidnapping target had a girlfriend in Canelones."[53] Seral's workers shared plentiful tips regarding Sergio Molaguero's 1955 Ford Thunderbird and his weekly pattern of visiting the nearby town. The team selected Juliana and Ramon to frequently visit the house and confirm the information. Twice a week, they traveled sixty kilometers each way to pass three hours together on a park bench, where they simulated flirting while surveilling the area. They held hands, cuddled, giggled, and played with each other's hair.[54] These gestures reflected a simulacrum of love and intimacy—both of which were limited due to their involvement in clandestine political labor. OPR-33 information teams often feigned romance while scouting targets because public displays of heteronormative romantic love proved least likely to raise suspicion. The frequency of such interactions sometimes resulted in both militants falling in love with one another.

After two weeks scouting, Juliana's reconnaissance schedule had become aligned with the schedules of Molaguero and that of the owner of the Divino mattress factory, another potential kidnapping target, where workers maintained a campaign for union recognition for over a year. She could not balance all three responsibilities, so she quit the factory job, thus beginning to rely on the organization for day-to-day living expenses. She dedicated herself fully to rearguard political labor. The decision represents a compromise that made her economically dependent on the organization yet independent of market social relations. In other words, she gained autonomy by disavowing her role as a wage laborer while embracing a singular role as protagonist in social subversion.

After five weeks of surveillance, the team compiled a detailed report identifying Molaguero's commuting patterns and the girl-friend's home, along with important geographical markers in the surrounding area, such as bridges and pastures for hiding. They passed their typed report to an intermediary who they met on a Montevideo side street.[55] Waiting patiently for further direction, Juliana continued scouting at Divino.

On May 11, a cell of four OPR-33 militants disguised them-selves as military servicemen and set up a checkpoint along National Route 11. They had failed in four previous attempts, including one in which a risky error led to stopping a local pol-itician.[56] This time, however, the disguised militants successfully detained Molaguero, transporting him to a "people's jail" in El Cerro—the very jail cell that had held French journalist Michèle Ray a year prior. Neighbors would later testify to having heard construction noises from the home nearly a year earlier, but they had given it little thought considering the frequent informal build-ing in the poor neighborhood.[57]

The FAU subsequently presented Molaguero's father with a list of demands, including back pay for striking workers; school supplies for local students; one hundred pairs of jeans, jackets, and shoes for children in a local slum; and publication of the agreed-upon terms in all five mainstream press newspapers.[58] Amid negotiations between the organization and Molaguero's law-yer, Joint Forces detained León Duarte and three other FUNSA workers, accusing them of participation in the kidnapping. There, workers responded by occupying the factory for the duration of their two-week detention.[59] On July 19, José Molaguero met all demands, and his son was released. Media outlets reported that he was malnourished and had lost twenty-five pounds due to receiving a daily meal of rice, cheese, and an apple. He decried the persistent playing of "protest music," such as Carlos Molina and Daniel Viglietti.[60]

A day after his release, Joint Forces raided Casa Emma, capturing Ana Rosa Amorós and Enylda Silveira Griot inside. The latter, also a FAU militant, had arrived the week prior after a warrant was issued for her arrest due to her role as one of Molaguero's captors. Enylda's presence would change the patterns of the home.

The weekend before the raid, Enylda had occupied the home alone while Juliana and Ana Rosa ventured to the interior to visit family, as they did every Sunday. While there, she turned on the stove to get some extra warmth. Soon it began emitting smoke, so she moved it outside. A worried neighbor visited the home, but, to avoid raising suspicion, Enylda did not answer the door. The neighbor, who sent her granddaughter to the home each week for tutoring, became concerned and notified police. In the meantime, Ana Rosa and Juliana returned from their getaway. A Joint Forces team arrived hours later and immediately identified Enylda from wanted photos. Ana Rosa denied any involvement in OPR-33 and insisted that Enylda was staying at the house after separating from her husband. She failed to convince the authorities but managed to remove a deodorant bottle from the bathroom window facing the street—an agreed-upon alarm signal—thus warning Juliana upon her return.[61] Before settling back into the home, Juliana ventured to her lover's house to wind down the weekend. Upon returning to the home later that evening, a nearby shopkeeper intercepted her. The shopkeeper, a member of the Communist Party, dashed toward her to give her a wine bottle upon seeing her walk down the street. While simulating a chummy encounter, he warned her that the house was occupied by Joint Forces who awaited her return. She kissed his cheek and continued walking. She escaped into hiding with a warrant out for her arrest after police found documents revealing her identity inside the home. The Casa Emma raid commenced a series of operations that would break the FAU/OPR-33's social and material infrastructure over the next few days. Thus, rather than utilize the established network of clandestine safe houses, Juliana would have to rely on family and friends. She soon left for Buenos Aires with a fake passport but felt estranged and feared being captured in a foreign country. Returning to Uruguay one month later, she managed to evade capture for a time but was eventually arrested in March 1973.[62]

Juliana spent eleven years and five months in prison following her conviction by a military court for subversion (membership in a revolutionary organization), accomplice to kidnapping, and possession of fake documents. Ana Rosa served two years in prison for subversion. Authorities frequently raped and tortured both women while imprisoned. The torture tactics often relied on appeals to affect. For example, interrogators frequently threatened to show Ana Rosa the fetus of her stillborn child, who she had birthed shortly after arriving to prison. She recalls the difficulty of remaining noncompliant, declaring:

> There were things that we knew, like half the person. But we were accustomed to the role of using an alias, one could not give [the authorities] more information than what one knew. Sharing too much information was dangerous. It had nothing to do with the other person being bad or anything—me, I think that all of us in some way took in the enemy. In my case, I never thought that the torture I would receive was going to be so gutting. And that the rape would be so widespread. . . You think that you are brave, but then there are so many ways that they could break you down and manipulate you. Really, you feel like you are in the hands of monsters. You try to defend yourself, but there were so many things that kept happening. Then, after nine months my entire team ended up falling.[63]

Ana Rosa suffered extreme back problems that left her immobile for the duration of her sentence. Guards began treating her for tuberculosis. Upon learning of her condition, her father, who was exiled to the French Basque Country after the coup, petitioned for her release for medical reasons, with support from the International Red Cross. The appeal was successful and she left to Australia where, soon after, she learned she was misdiagnosed: doctors and prison guards commonly colluded to issue experimental medical treatment to prisoners for false medical diagnoses. She remembers feeling like a "lab rat" after learning she was negative.

On the same day as the Casa Emma raid, León Duarte (UOESF), Washington Pérez (UOESF), Gerardo de Avila, (UOESF), Julio and Hilda Ojeda (Seral), and four other Seral workers were detained for connection to the kidnapping and alleged membership in OPR-33. The raids also saw the arrests of Alberto Mechoso, Augusto Andrés, Ivonne Trías, and "La Malet," some of whom served prior sentences but received warning that they could be detained thereafter for more interrogation. In a show of defiance, FUNSA workers occupied the plant, publishing a communique recognizing the suspicious timing of Duarte's detention: he was scheduled to mediate negotiations between Seral workers and management, who were finally at the table after ten months of conflict.[64]

The detainees arrived at the Fifth Artillery Regiment, where Joint Forces authorities used a variety of torture tactics in hope of extracting information. To avoid revealing their activity to the guards, detainees feigned ignorance, while seeking to obscure their connections. For instance, Washington Pérez lunged toward Andrés and attempted to punch him upon his arrival— an act meant to indicate they had not been in collaboration. He then yelled profanities and accused Andrés of serving as an agent provocateur who collaborated with the FUNSA management. Days later, Generals Manuel Cordero and Washington Varela introduced Andrés and Trías to see if they knew one another. Both refrained from acknowledging one another and sharing politically sensitive information, even under pressure from waterboarding. Meanwhile, imprisoned MLN-T leadership and Uruguayan Joint Forces continued to negotiate a permanent ceasefire—conversations that arguably led to more frequent and brutal torture tactics against imprisoned members of the FAU as authorities hoped they could pressure the organization into following in the footsteps of their rivals. Andrés remembers Alberto Mechoso and Ivonne Trías receiving the harshest treatments, the latter of whom once attempted suicide by slitting her own wrists after undergoing extreme torture.[65] Duarte's high-profile status led the Uruguayan parliament to formally acknowledge his torture and demand his release.[66]

The mid-1972 defeat of the MLN-T created further division between the FAU and PCU. In the absence of the MLN-T, the FAU represented the largest threat to PCU hegemony over the left. Indeed, the growing militancy of everyday workers proved the possibility for a new alternative, one rooted in mass protagonism rather than the activity of a small guerrilla vanguard. Tensions climaxed when the PCU mobilized its majority within the CNT to release a statement publicly denouncing the ROE. The statement, which came after skirmishes between the rival factions during a march, labeled the ROE as "having nothing to do with the labor movement" and claimed that the gesture represented a "divisive and adventurist line." In a subsequent communique, the PCU accused ROE of serving as a front for the CIA—a label the party had previously reserved to describe the armed activity of the MLN-T but now redirected toward the worker–student organization.[67] For the FAU, the PCU's "sectarian" rhetoric served to distract from the CNT leadership's recent decision to cancel a general strike call.[68]

On August 23, the ROE held a rally of support for León Duarte and Washington Pérez at the Artigas Theater. Upward of five thousand attended the event, which was disguised as an homage to the Italian American anarchists Nicola Sacco and Bartolomeo Vanzetti, political prisoners the United States murdered by electric chair in 1927. The rally hosted speeches by Hugo Cores, Gerardo Gatti, Héctor Rodríguez, Enrique Erro (Popular Union–National Party), Armando Rodríguez (March 26 Movement–MLN-T), Zelmar Michelini (*Agrupación Avance*–Broad Front), and a delegate from the Argentine CGT (CGT-A).[69] Aside from the FAU, all Uruguayan organizations in attendance belonged to the Corriente (Current), a radical faction within the Broad Front now searching for alternatives to an electoral strategy. Mario Benedetti, a famous writer and member of the Corriente, exclaimed, "Perhaps the grand defeat was necessary to remove an electoral strategy from its near-sacred position. . . . This kind of lesson can only be learned with experience."[70] Speakers frequently

reiterated the importance of unity in action, while none emphasized political parties or elections. On the contrary, many bluntly
denounced sectarianism. While speakers notably differed in the
intensity of their rhetoric, they shared common ground in their
tactful critique of the Communist Party. Zelmar Michelini's declaration is illustrative:

> There has been so much time lost trying to figure out where
> one does political work, the group to which he belongs, or
> the label upon his forehead. This fight must be understood
> and must be felt inside, and it is not the moment for trea-
> tises or useless thoughts, nor to uphold artificial precon-
> ceptions. . . . Those who enter into this struggle to establish
> divisions beyond the question of tactics establish barriers
> that sharply separate those who are in the fight, and that is
> deeply wrong. These people do not understand the meaning
> of history. I repeat that they are longing for the feelings of
> solidarity that we here have. It is very easy to be alongside
> someone with whom you always agree; it is very easy to fight
> side by side with someone who shares all the same ideas. The
> depth of life is beyond discrepancies, it is understanding the
> meaning of struggle.[71]

Similarly, Gerardo Gatti decried:

> We need unity among the working class. We need unity
> to fight. But this fight of the working class should not be
> reduced solely to them. We think that this class is funda-
> mental, that it is the primary force, but we should be able
> to, all of us, without sectarianism, with flexibility, to unite
> the working class with all of the population who works and
> suffers and wants to change their conditions.[72]

Finally, Hugo Cores proclaimed, "The problem is not one of discussion and dividing ourselves, but instead to go out into the street
and fight, to occupy factories, to organize ourselves and fight . . .
because we are living in a difficult moment in which we cannot

show any weakness. One in which we cannot give any sign of division." He drew from examples of military boycotts in FUNSA and
Alpargatas, where workers refused to produce military supplies.
On the day of the rally, railway workers announced they would
permanently stop transporting military personnel.[73] In contrast,
the PCU declined to echo the call to free political prisoners out of
fear of reprisals from the Armed Forces. Instead, the party insisted
that the CNT remain committed to labor-specific issues rather
than take up political positions.[74]

Buenos Aires (Re)querido

After the rally, Joint Forces issued arrest warrants for FAU-ROE
militants Hugo Cores, Gerardo Gatti, Elvira Suárez, Kimal Amir,
Sara Lerena de Goessens, María Selva Echagüe, Darío Espiga,
Carlos Goessens, Rubén Rodríguez Coronel, Silvia Valerón, and
Gonzalo Vigil. Forced into hiding, some militants began swiftly
exiling to Buenos Aires. The FUNSA plant remained occupied
for over one hundred days until León Duarte, Washington Pérez,
Julio Ojeda, and Gerardo de Ávila were eventually released in
mid-November 1972. Workers received the prisoners with a rally
at the UOESF hall. De Ávila had endured such brutal torture that
he could not address the crowd by voice, so he instead waved and
blew kisses from the stage.[75]

While militants celebrated their comrades' arrival, Alberto
Mechoso and Ivonne Triás remained in detention, where they
continued to undergo torture for their refusal to share information about OPR-33. Authorities claimed they were responsible
for Molaguero's kidnapping. Meanwhile, however, they plotted
a prison break among themselves. As the planned date of escape
approached, guards coincidentally mandated Trías to solitary con-
finement and assigned a single soldier to watch over her, nullifying
the militants' initial plan to escape together. On November 21,
1972, Alberto Mechoso broke from his cell, jumped the prison wall,
and ran toward the North Cemetery. After crossing the Arroyo
Miguelete, he flagged down a *juntapapeles* (scrap collector) on a

horse and buggy. The two men exchanged clothes before the informal worker offered his humble getaway vehicle. Mechoso maneuvered the horse and buggy through a police-ridden Barrio Cerrito until reaching the home of a friend and ex-colleague from his days working in the Swift refrigeration plant. Gatti and Duarte arrived at the refuge the next morning to transport him to a FAU safe house in Ciudad Vieja, where a medic treated him for fractured ribs and amputated numerous fingers. After two weeks of recovery, Gerardo Gatti invited longtime friend Eduardo Galeano—who had published his seminal *Open Veins of Latin America* the year prior—to meet and conduct an interview with Mechoso.[76] For his own security purposes, Galeano used an alias and fabricated the interview's suburban Madrid location to give the impression that Mechoso had already fled the country. The interview provided detailed descriptions of the Joint Force's various torture methods, including sessions of electrocution and waterboarding that lasted up to three hours. He also testified as to having witnessed rape and genital electrocution as common practice against female prisoners. Mechoso concluded the interview by proclaiming:

> If there is anything that feels good when inside the prison underworld of my country, in the middle of electrocutions and waterboarding, it is knowing that one always must be in the trenches. I am going to return to the trenches once more with the people of my class. Fighting. There, I am going to reunite with my family and my brother, who is also currently suffering persecution as well.[77]

Recognizing the difficulty of maintaining Mechoso's safety within Uruguay, the FAU utilized networks from its sympathizers list to arrange for Mechoso's escape to Argentina via private airplane. After one month in hiding, Mechoso departed from Uruguay's Melilla Airport to Buenos Aires under the alias Alfredo Leizagoyen Cantonet. One week later, his wife traveled via commercial airliner under the alias Delia Toribia Rodríguez.[78] Mechoso and other FAU exiles spent the next six months laying an infrastructure for others to join them in exile across the River Plate.

In the Face of a Coup, General Strike

The first half of 1973 saw at least ninety-five labor actions nationwide, including thirty-three strikes lasting three or more days, twenty-four of which included occupations. Nearly half the conflicts were waged by Tendencia-affiliated unions. Of the twenty-four occupations, seven were carried out by textile unions, including La Industrial (fifty-one days), Montegal (twenty-seven days), and Industria Este (twenty days). CICSSA, another Tendencia-affiliated union, carried out a thirty-six-day occupation. Metalworkers (UNTMRA) showed a growing radicalism regardless of the PCU-aligned leadership, occupying at four different work sites. Finally, this era also saw two CNT-wide general strikes, including one with over half a million participants on June 21, the eve of the coup d'état.

The question around the military had haunted conversations on the left for years leading up to the coup. The cleavage between revolutionaries and the PCU deepened after the Uruguayan military began openly intervening in politics in February 1973, when the Armed Forces released the cryptic "Communiques 4 and 7," which some on the left interpreted as nods to an ally force within the ranks. One part read:

> The Armed Forces neither adhere nor adjust their mental outlooks to any specific politically partisan philosophy but seek to adjust their beliefs and orient their actions according to the native and original concept of an ideal Uruguay . . . which will offer the greatest well-being and happiness to all its sons. This concept will be achieved with the creation and consolidation in all Uruguayans of the mystique of Uruguayanness, which consists in recovering the great moral values of those who forged our nationality and whose basic facets are patriotism, austerity, disinterest, generosity, honesty, self-denial, and firmness of character.[79]

PCU leaders, who maintained frequent conversations with factions in the military for nearly a decade, saw the announcements as reflecting a potential turn toward a progressive military takeover, like the military-led and Marxist-oriented Peruvian Revolution of 1968. The PCU strategy remained in line with Lenin's prescription to inspire a mutiny within the armed forces and court them to the side of revolutionaries. In the week following the communiques, CNT majority leadership and the PCU Central Committee secretly met multiple times with high-level officers to discuss a tactical agreement between the military, CNT, and PCU. Publicly, CNT leadership reiterated its call for a general strike in the face of a coup d'état with numerous public statements.[80] But Communist organs repeated, "There is no conflict between civil power and military power, instead it is between oligarchy and pueblo."[81] Party leadership proposed converting May Day 1973 into a festival to celebrate the new favorable political circumstance. On May 23, Secretary General Rodney Arismendi declared, "No one doubts that there are now circumstances for more unity among the pueblo. . . . Now it is time that a worker, a student, a professor, a peasant, and a soldier join in the street and act together."[82]

While the hope offered by the communiques eventually proved false, they succeeded in creating a crisis of legitimacy for the Uruguayan government. Rather than implement structural reforms to combat the mounting economic and political crisis—which included a 94 percent rise in cost of living since 1972—President Bordaberry made space for the Armed Forces as the new "locus of power."[83] In early April, the government announced the formation of the National Security Council (COSENA), a vehicle for involving the military in political decision making. The body coalesced representatives from all three branches of the Armed Forces and key government cabinet members.[84] While the February communiques opened frequent dialogue between CNT leadership and Coronel Ramón Trabal, a rank officer with populist sympathies, the government's announcement solidified the prevailing line of conservative General Gregorio Álvarez within the military. On April 9, COSENA blamed the CNT for creating an economic crisis and announced its intentions to modify labor laws, specifically the right to strike.[85] Advocates argued that labor had become too politicized. Thereafter, the military declared their plan for national development to be "irreconcilable" with the interests of the CNT.[86] In one dramatic move, military officials took over the direction of train services. The UF, which had operated services under worker control numerous times throughout 1972, frequently disobeyed strike prohibitions for public sector workers. While the new military directorate announced their intentions to salvage a failing public transport industry, they also used the industry as a laboratory for the Armed Forces' further participation in politics.[87]

In a scathing critique of the Communist Party's position, the FAU highlighted what seemed to be increasingly absurd justifications for a strategy involving the Armed Forces. Some CNT leaders claimed that military repression had toned down dramatically since September 1972[88]—perspectives perhaps influenced by deferential treatment from the state. In early May, the Bordaberry government prohibited a ROE rally in Montevideo. A week later, the Joint Forces detained Tendencia-affiliated militants throughout the country, including Sergio Benavidez (president of the Fruit and Vegetable Union–Salto) and his wife, Arturo Echinique (delegate of the Mercedes Roundtable), and Julio Arizaga (delegate of the UTU Staff Union).[89] Feeling the heat, the FAU insisted upon moving beyond Marxist-Leninist dogma, which fetishized a key role for the military. Instead, the anarchists argued that the threat of military involvement in politics was now serving as a chip to coerce consent around labor reform. On May 31, the UOESF rejected COSENA's offer to release union delegate Celso Fernandes in exchange for a public statement in support of anti-labor legislation. The union made the following declaration:

> At this moment, with as much clarity as possible, we convey our position of open and absolute rejection of any law or decree that implies restricting, preventing, or limiting union activity. . . . These are unrestricted and unalienable rights that the working class has conquered in this country in hundreds of tough struggles for union freedoms during almost a century of trade unionism.[90]

Moreover, the CNT responded to the labor reform bill with a variety of planned mobilizations over the next three weeks. They included a two-hour work stoppage in the private sector on June 7; manifestations across the banking and meatpacking sectors between June 11 and 15; a two-hour work stoppage by public administration workers on June 14; private sector worker manifestations in front of COPRIN between June 18 and 22; a gathering of food service, health service, and bank workers on June 22; and a series of rallies in support of teachers between June 25 and 29. The FAU called the response "absolutely insufficient given the gravity of the situation." Not only did the itinerary fail to intersect conflicts by allotting industries specific days, but it also failed to synergize energy around existing conflicts in TEM, CICSSA, ATMA, family services, Cativelli, HISISA (COT), and the Central Bank (AEBU). All were actively engaged in strikes and occupations.[91]

On June 27, 1973, a guard transmitted a government communique throughout the hallways of Punta de Rieles women's prison: in order to "revitalize the nation," President Bordaberry, Ministry of Interior Colonel Nestor Bolentini, and Minister of Defense Walter Ravenna had signed a decree to dissolve the parliament. After hearing the news, Juliana and a half dozen cellmates, all Tupamaras, crammed together and gazed out a small window overlooking a workshop across the street. They eagerly awaited any indication of a strike in response to the military takeover. Beginning a decade prior, founding members of the CNT moved urgently to form the confederation to confront a foreseeable future dictatorship with what they saw as the working class's most effective weapon: a general strike.

True to its word, the CNT responded by launching a fifteen-day general strike. In La Teja, the ANCAP chimney was no longer emitting smoke. Essential services, such as electricity, water, telecommunications, and health care, operated under workers' control. FUNSA workers occupied the plant and hung a banner from the entrance declaring "Down with the fascist dictatorship!"[92] Soon, Joint Forces surrounded the eighteen square blocks of the FUNSA plant, where they remained throughout. Recognizing the symbolic importance of FUNSA within the labor movement, they directed significant resources into repressing the occupation. Faced with a potentially violent confrontation, workers inside kept the lights and machinery running to give the impression of an operating assembly line. They hoped that authorities would refrain from entering if they knew they would be faced with shutting down the complex and expensive machines themselves.

In an effort to curb the unrest, the government prohibited public and private assemblies "with political ends." Three days later the government banned the CNT, forced its offices to close, and ordered the arrest and trial of all officers for the crime of "delinquency."[93] By the first days of July, the Armed Forces began clearing out factories and taking them over to prevent workers from returning to occupy the sites. However, workers entered and refused to leave anyways. The FAU and GAU utilized a clandestine communication network to update workers about activity going on within their own plants or those within their vicinity.[94] Organizers convened in the home of ROE militant Jorge Zaffaroni to produce propaganda, which they later printed at the UOESF local and distributed factory by factory.[95] Héctor Rodríguez recalls:

> Construction sites resembled piles of iron and concrete. You could only see frozen machinery, immobile. Inside the occupied factories, workers not only recognized the importance of achieving a minimum level of self-organization to maintain the occupation, but very important tasks were performed in the neighborhoods throughout the strike, such as distributing bulletins and information on small pieces of paper to the entire population.[96]

After one week, CNT leadership began to question whether to maintain the strike. The PCU identified the strike as a "small gesture" and saw severe tactical limitations due to lack of support from the Blanco and Colorado parties. While neither traditional party took a position on the military coup, the CNT and their student movement allies were isolated as the only clear protagonists with little capacity to gain support beyond those already aligned with the left. Contrarily, the Tendencia set out to "win" the strike at "whatever price necessary." Delegates Héctor Rodríguez and León Duarte identified severe risks in losing: sliding into a Brazil-style military dictatorship potentially meant the end of organized labor.[97] The stakes were high. But it was becoming clear that the situation was not sustainable.

On July 4, the key industries of collective transportation, railways, and municipal workers began returning to work. That same day, the government announced arrest warrants for fifty-two CNT delegates. Recognizing the CNT's incapacity to maintain the strike, UOESF officers, including Duarte, began to advo-cate for negotiating with the military to avoid harsh retaliation on behalf of the state. Occupation Committee delegates Alberto Márquez and Luis Romero reached out to Colonel Barrios, an Armed Forces contact with whom the UOESF previously estab-lished contact during negotiations to free Duarte and Pérez from detention. In exchange for ending the occupation, UOESF lead-ers demanded that no workers be arrested for their participation. Duarte and others recognized that labor was no longer on the offensive but instead fighting to return to pre-civic-military status quo. As such, they saw the best potential outcome to be the legal-ization of the CNT and release of all political prisoners. FUNSA workers exited the plant on July 6 and returned the following day to work. Angry with the decision to end the occupation, workers called for an emergency assembly and unanimously decided to reoccupy the workplace. Joint Forces responded by breaking in to remove the workers—remaining inside as a symbolic gesture. Recognizing they had no way out, Duarte reached out to fellow Tendencia delegates from Portland, COT, and UNTMRA to request further negotiations with the military and plea for the best possible outcome amid a devolving situation. As the Tendencia sought an exit strategy at FUNSA, ANCAP management replaced striking oil refinery workers with busloads of scabs from Southern Brazil. Joint Forces broke into the homes of bus drivers and forced them to work at gunpoint; some accompanied workers along their transit routes to curb any attempts of subversion.[98] By the strike's second week, labor militancy had transcended even the most radical of its leadership, who turned to negotiation in the face of an increasingly violent situation. Rather than experiencing an explosive moment of autonomy and self-management, such as the experience in Barcelona in July 1936, Uruguayan workers were isolated and lacking a mass consensus around the meaning of the strike and how to sustain it.

On July 11 the CNT Representative Table called the strike's end. Subsequently, the saga at FUNSA would play a key role in forcing other Tendencia-affiliated unions into submission. As the symbol of the labor movement's most radical potential, the UOESF's defeat marked a turning point in working-class morale nationwide. The general strike sparked the civic-military government to use a variety of repressive measures to break the CNT's infrastructure. In response to the official end of the strike, the UOESF published a statement with ally unions FOEB and FUS proclaiming, "The level of escalation brought on by the occupied factories eloquently signaled the strength and vanguard role of the working class in the struggle for liberation."[99] The document emphasized the existing high levels of working-class consciousness and the need to continue to channel such energy into a coordinated Fight Plan via base-level organizing. "The three Fs"—FUNSA, FOEB, and FUS—concluded by taking a slight jab at the PCU majority for lifting the strike, declaring, "No union was defeated. What was defeated was a style, a method, and an approach to union labor."[100] In other words, their own participation in calling an end to the strike was not a mere product of the moment, but instead a consequence of lacking in preparation due to a failed approach to organized labor in the years leading up to the coup. While CNT leadership decided not to take advantage of other moments of labor unrest to implement a general strike from the offensive, it was forced into calling one by mandate as a safeguard. This was not an empowering position to be in.

The government's punishment for strike participation proved harsh. The PCU's *El Popular* was closed for ten editions beginning June 30; *Marcha* and *Compañero* were closed for two editions on July 10.[101] On July 4, the government passed a decree permitting employers to fire workers suspected of union organizing, leading to nearly two thousand layoffs. Unions with a strong connection to the Tendencia suffered disproportionate firing. For example, of the 225 metalworkers laid off, ninety-six belonged to TEM and ATMA; the former suffered more firings (sixty-seven) than any metallurgy plant in the country.[102] The textile industry was hit especially hard. Combined with the past two years of personnel downsizing, over twenty-five hundred textile workers were out of work by September 1973. At the National Beverage Factory, one hundred transport workers were laid off and twenty-seven workers were arrested, including the general secretary and secretary of FOEB.

While FUNSA workers did not suffer any layoffs, León Duarte was again detained alongside two other UOESF officers. The plant's workers were especially concerned about devolving situations in neighboring plants and responded by sending 0.5 percent of their weekly salaries to support fired and/or imprisoned workers from Textíl Ferres, *La Mañana*, *El Diario*, Textíl Campomar (de Juan Lacazé), Lanasur, AFE, Optilon, Ardea, Sapelli, Amdet, TEM, CICSSA, and Dique Nacional, among others.[103] The UOESF also raised funds by hosting a benefit concert at the local. ROE organized a campaign to collect food donations of one kilo of meat every Friday.[104] In the two months after the coup, *Compañero* published dozens of interviews with workers who maintained strikes and occupations, and others who had recently lost their jobs. FAU-ROE used their press organ as a platform to maintain communication and dialogue, but repression was too great, and they could not realize their goals. Hugo Cores recalls, "There were many people among the ROE who I never saw again."[105]

On July 31, 1973, police detained six members of AFE's Worker Dignity caucus after entering the union local during a meeting. Raúl Olivera, Luis Raimundo, Óscar Rodríguez, Luis Peña, and Naydú Sosa remained in prison for the duration of the dictatorship. On August 24, the government prohibited all forms of "interunion organizing by way of the CNT."[106] Police occupied various union locals, including UNTMRA and SUNCA; the CNT local was converted into a detention and torture center.[107] On December 14, FAU militant and UF officer Gilberto Coghlan died after being taken from his cell to the middle of a soccer field, where drunken officers waterboarded him to the point of cardiac arrest.[108]

Labor militants continued meeting secretly with help from students, who maintained at least thirty meeting spots on various campuses throughout Montevideo. In late October, GAU militants accidently set off a bomb in the Faculty of Engineering, resulting in the death of a professor who also belonged to the group. The military responded by occupying the University of the Republic and closing it down for the remainder of 1973. The offensive saw the arrest of dozens of GAU militants, demobilizing one of the FAU's closest allies. Moreover, the military occupation forced the closure of all thirty organizing spaces.[109] As the Tendencia's infrastructure deteriorated, León Duarte, Washington Pérez, and Miguel Gromaz went into hiding, releasing the final edition of *Compañero* on November 6, 1973. Three weeks later, the government passed a new decree to dissolve and declare "illicit" all Uruguayan left political organizations, including the FAU-ROE, PCU, PSU, GAU, and nine others. All political activity involving a banned political organization now constituted a crime of "subversive association" or "assistance to a subversive association." Alongside the prohibition of left organizing, the government also mandated the closure of *Compañero*, *El Popular*, *Marcha*, *Crónica*, *Ahora*, *Vea*, *El Oriental*, and *Última Hora*, thus eliminating all left perspective from public circulation. León Duarte was detained one week later. Within the next three years, twenty-six national newspapers and five local newspapers, including various church-related publications, would receive cease-and-desist orders from the state.[110]

Duarte remained in detention for the first months of 1974. Authorities assured UOESF leadership that his capture would be brief. Meanwhile, General Hugo Chiappe Posse, who led the interrogations, sought to build a "non-red" labor union confederation outside of the CNT structure. His "nationalist central" followed Benito Mussolini's corporatist model and would be channeled vertically into the military government. Moreover, the new central would break the CNT's class-struggle foundation, replacing it with one of labor harmony, with the state as mediator. He hoped to take advantage of tensions between the PCU major-ity and Tendencia Combativa, and recognized Duarte's key lead-ership role among the latter faction when offering him a position in the Ministry of Labor. Duarte declined, proclaiming, "There is only one central: the CNT. I am a delegate of the CNT. My responsibility is to the CNT. . . . I recognize that those of you who speak to me are on one side and the working class is on the other."[111] In May 1975, León Duarte and Washington Pérez crossed the Río de la Plata to join fellow members of the FAU-ROE in exile.

Conclusion

Between November 1971 and June 1973, Uruguayan workers car-ried out upward of nine hundred work actions, including at least two hundred occupations. The CNT coordinated over a dozen days of action across industries, including four general strikes. Of the total work actions, 22 percent included occupations. In a dra-matic change compared to previous years, CNT-majority-affiliated unions accounted for 41 percent of occupations, 37 percent of strikes lasting longer than three days, and 34 percent of strikes last-ing longer than ten days.[112] While the FA's electoral defeat forced majority-affiliated union leadership to discover new approaches outside of the electoral strategy, the rank and file demonstrated an impressive propensity to act by foregoing legal processes and embracing direct action tactics instead.

One of the longest and most dramatic strikes took place at the Seral factory, where workers waged a ten-month campaign that concluded victoriously after intervention from the OPR-33. The balance between mass protagonism (ROE) and armed action (OPR-33) provides the best example of the FAU's "two foot" strat-egy. Moreover, a narrative analysis of the event centering wom-en's reconnaissance labor offers a unique opportunity to demystify the multiple forms of political labor behind the growing popular unrest. While everyday people certainly embraced a role as pro-tagonists, the tactical forms utilized throughout the epoch were made possible by a complex, overlapping social infrastructure maintained by political organizations. Within that infrastructure, women's reproductive labor played a primary role.

August 1972 marked a unique moment in which the FAU-ROE stood as the sole challenger to the PCU's hegemony over the left. The MLN-T ceasefire shifted emphasis toward building popular power, coinciding with rising militancy within the labor movement. Moreover, state repression against high-profile union organizers León Duarte and Washington Pérez inspired solidarity across factions of the left, which drew local comparisons to world-wide experiences during the Sacco and Vanzetti affair. Finally, the PCU's stigmatization of the FAU-ROE—something addressed by numerous speakers during the rally in support of Duarte and Pérez—revealed a prevailing tension within the left. While the Uruguayan Communist Party certainly showed an exceptionalism by remaining open to contemporary influences, especially cultural ones, they maintained a rigidity, orthodoxy, and dogmatism that upheld the old-versus-new divide, specifically the "revolutionary parliamentarian" strategy and privileged role of the vanguard party. These strategical and tactical differences, and the shifting coalition formations around them, presented clear tensions that proved irresolvable even in the face of rising state repression. Moreover, the historic moment showed potential for a vibrant new coalition outside of the electoral framework—one rooted in mass action rather than voting. The shifting political field clearly surfaced after the PCU announced its position on "Communiques 4 and 7" in February 1973 and continued into the June 1973 general strike.

Strategic differences between the Tendencia and CNT majority carried over into the 1973 general strike. While Tendencia-affiliated unions demonstrated intentions to force the civic-military government into submission by withholding their labor, the majority-aligned unions representing essential services proved ill prepared to continue beyond the first week. Arguably, the workers' inexperience with sustaining large-scale work actions left them without the necessary infrastructure to hold out. As such, their return to work left more militant sectors isolated and forced an end to the strike. Thus, while workers showed an increasing combativeness throughout 1972, the PCU's impact remained strong.

Regardless, President Bordaberry justified the Armed Forces' role in government by pointing toward its victory against the MLN-T in April 1972. He insisted that the military's participation in politics represented a compromise between "chronic anarchy" and a "true military takeover."[113] The civic-military government prioritized labor reform upon taking power. Minister of Defense Walter Ravenna, for his part, declared commitment to "uprooting the Marxist infiltration of Uruguayan society." He recognized the influence of organizations "further to the left than Communists" and insisted that "there was no turning back possible; there would be no mediation or negotiation."[114] The government enjoyed strong support from Uruguayan industrialists who shared the opinion that the CNT, not the MLN-T, was the largest threat to national security in the country. Over half proclaimed "control of labor unrest" as the government's largest accomplishment; of those who mentioned the MLN-T, nearly half saw the guerrilla movement and labor unrest as part of a coordinated left conspiracy[115]—a phenomenon scholar José Nun has called the "middle-class military coup."[116] Over the next twelve years, the US-based AFL-CIO contributed upward of US$160,000 annually to form the General Confederation of Uruguayan Workers (CGTU), a new trade union central in opposition to the CNT. According to a clandestine periodical titled *Carta*, the US embassy acted in collaboration with Uruguayan ex-delegate "J. Betancourt" to bring instructors from Central America to the Uruguayan Institute of Union Education, a local branch of the American Institute for Free Labor Development.[117] As the most important organizations on the Uruguayan left lay in shambles, the outlook for workers proved disastrous: real salaries nationwide would decrease by 50 percent in the first five years of the new government.[118]

6

The Garage Was Not a Garden
Exile Strategy, USAID, and the Argentine Clandestine Detention, Torture, and Extermination Center "Automotores Orletti," 1973–76

The jungle is very big,
There is plenty of room for all the animals,
And no one would lack a thing,
If everyone were able to work.

The animals love the jungle very much,
The rivers and the trees,
Its land and its fruits . . .

The animals that work
Have realized that
In the jungle there are many things to fix.
They gather around a little fire
And they start talking.

If someone comes to bother
the owl upon the branches
Is the one responsible for calling out.

One day without being seen, a hunter arrives in the jungle
Of the jungle, he does not understand a thing.
He does not care if the animals live better.

—MAURICIO GATTI, 1972

In 1974, Uruguay's famed cartoonist Walter Tournier released his first animated short film based on a prison letter from FAU militant Mauricio Gatti to his daughter, Paula.[1] The letter and film, both titled *En la selva hay mucho por hacer* (In the jungle there is much to do), depict Uruguay as a free territory inhabited by wild animals who cooperate and live in harmony until being disrupted by the arrival of a hunter, who begins capturing them to send to the zoo. Some of the animals identify the hunter and set up an alert network, but they are captured first. They eventually escape the zoo by boat and then return to the jungle, where the rest of the animals have warded off the encroaching zookeepers. At the time of its writing, the narrative translated for Paula the FAU's exile strategy: one in which everyday people would overthrow the dictatorship and pave the path for the exiles' return. However, this proved to be a fantasy.

Alberto Mechoso's jailbreak and subsequent exile led the way for what would become a FAU mass exodus to Buenos Aires. Beginning in late 1972, many FAU militants were forced underground, while the already-clandestine OPR-33 militants began the journey toward Buenos Aires.[2] Most exiles belonged to the armed faction, which found itself isolated as the only armed group in Uruguay after the MLN-T agreed to a ceasefire and subsequently suffered mass arrests in April 1972.[3] The FAU's strong presence in the graphic artists and bankers unions allowed the organization to counterfeit passports, national identification cards, and even money.[4] Recognizing the importance of working in coalition, the FAU made an easy decision to divide forces on both sides of the River Plate; after all, staying in Uruguay meant being forced to operate as a small, isolated organization of a few hundred anarchists. Instead, they followed exiled left groups from throughout the continent to Argentina—the only Southern Cone country that had not fallen to military rule as of late 1973.

While exiled in Buenos Aires, the FAU remained independent of formal left coalitions but continued collaborating with other New Left organizations to fortify a cross-border resistance network between both countries. They funded these efforts with ransom money acquired by kidnapping Dutch businessman Federico

Hart and extorting him for US$10 million. Lured by the prospect of recovering the massive sum, the Uruguayan Armed Forces and Argentine Secretariat of Intelligence collaborated to permanently disappear thirty-five FAU militants at the Buenos Aires-based clandestine detention, torture, and extermination center, Automotores Orletti. In all likelihood, the operation was the first of Plan Cóndor, a transborder policing and surveillance infrastructure that would plague the Southern Cone and Central America for the next decade. Yet, as word of the Uruguayan government's over seven thousand political prisoners and frequent use of torture gained wider circulation abroad, the dictatorship found itself the target of an international human rights campaign lead by Amnesty International and the Bertrand Russell (International War Crimes) Tribunal.

This chapter sets out to achieve three main goals. First, I identify the FAU as a relevant political organization among the Latin American left milieu exiled in Argentina between 1973 and 1976. In doing so, I show the benefits of moving away from the "heavyweight" left organizations in the region, specifically Argentina's Guevarist People's Revolutionary Army (ERP) and Peronist Montoneros, and Uruguay's PCU and MLN-T. The FAU advanced its own political vision and strategy as an independent organization, while still working in coalition with other groups in the New Left milieu. They not only played a protagonist role in the decade leading up to the 1973 Uruguayan civic-military coup but continued influencing strategies and tactics for resistance to dictatorship from abroad. As such, the organization acted as one of many lynchpins in the region's transnational left. They represent one of the many exiled Latin American left organizations that crossed paths in Argentina before the country became the last Southern Cone government to fall under military dictatorship on March 24, 1976.[5]

While much has been written about the region's transnational state terror networks, little has been written on the transnationality of the region's left.[6] Among the few scholarly studies on the subject is Aldo Marchesi's recent historiographical contribution, which shows that Southern Cone national liberation movements operated regionally and thus cannot be explained by what the author calls a "national-foreigner dichotomy."[7] Moreover, Vania Markarian shows how exiled Uruguayan congress members effectively launched a campaign to politically isolate the Uruguayan military dictatorship from abroad by mobilizing a human rights discourse.[8] Like other exiled organizations at the time, the FAU sought to maintain a balance between the changing internal dynamics induced by exile and a firm political position rooted in a local Uruguayan reality in which most of the organization's militants were no longer present.

Next, I follow FAU militants to their incarceration at Automotores Orletti in mid-1976, which served as the Argentine headquarters for Plan Cóndor. Of the 172 Uruguayans disappeared throughout the Dirty War era, 119 were disappeared in Argentina—thirty-four of them members of the FAU.[9] John Dinges, a *Time* and *Washington Post* journalist who extensively covered Plan Cóndor, has recognized that the operations against Uruguayans in Argentina resulted in the largest group of Plan Cóndor disappearances.[10] More broadly, the Orletti case demonstrates how transnational state terror came as a response to the deterritorialization of the left post-1973. Although a small and under-resourced organization, the FAU's continued commitment to political coalition building abroad made them an important target of both Uruguayan and Argentine governments. Recognizing the FAU's low-profile membership, international obscurity, and strength in the domestic labor movement, the multinational military offensive against them served as a pilot run for Cóndor. As a result, the FAU suffered more deaths than any other Uruguayan organization abroad. Moreover, by the end of 1976, the only surviving members still located in Uruguay were in prison—the rest were killed or exiled.[11] Thus, the FAU's exile experience, especially their confrontation with regional security, serves as a key case study for understanding both Plan Cóndor state offensives and the popular human rights campaigns that followed.

Finally, both Argentine and Uruguayan governments kidnapped, detained, and tortured FAU militants and other Uruguayan political exiles while simultaneously communicating with US State Department and embassy officials regarding activities in the region. The case shows a clear tension between the State Department and CIA's explicit and implicit support for the formation and implementation of a transnational state terror network on one hand, and the US Congress's effort to defund the Uruguayan civic-military government due to extreme human rights violations, on the other. Scholar Katheryn Sikkink emphasizes that although human rights became central to US foreign policy toward Latin America, they led to a practice of "mixed signals" due to differing internal visions regarding Cold War strategy.[12] Incongruence within the US government eventually led Uruguay's Joint Forces to develop an assassination plot against US House representative Edward Koch and fabricate a raid on a fictitious FAU safe house under the codename "Chalet Suzy." While the rumored operation against Koch aimed to intimidate US politicians who voiced concerns about human rights in the Southern Cone, the Chalet Suzy spectacle sought to court sympathy and justify continued access to funding from the US Agency for International Development (USAID). Both indicate the civic-military government's deception in the face of despair. Coinciding with the Argentine government's escalating belligerence, Chalet Suzy marked a turning point in US *discursive* support for Plan Cóndor. The case offers insight into how US congressional politics clearly affect the decisions of foreign governments. While regional governments doubtless enjoyed US assistance and support, they did not serve solely as puppets. In fact, much of their autonomous activity induced tension in their relationships with the US government. Regardless of growing debate around lexicon, the US government maintained significant financial support for both governments throughout their tenure.

To Endure Doing: Exile as Political Strategy

In the months following the civic-military takeover, roughly sixty FAU militants fled to Buenos Aires, where they intended to continue advancing an anarchist political project and lay the groundwork for a coalition of left resistance alongside other exiles. Buenos Aires served as more than just a refuge for wanted militants. Alberto Mechoso and three others spent the year prior laying an infrastructure for OPR-33 to take advantage of Argentina's democratic political climate to raise money and resources via expropriations. The decision to relocate the OPR-33 to Buenos Aires caused a small schism in the organization. One small team of four militants insisted on remaining in Uruguay to wage direct war against the Armed Forces rather than fight from the rear guard. This group, called El Libertario, argued that the move toward military rule required a reconsideration and reframing of the armed strategy, moving away from the "two foot" model and more toward *foquismo* (foco theory). In April 1974, police raided a bar in Barrio Maroñas that produced a shootout with three members of the splinter organization. The exchange saw the deaths of FAU militant Julio Larrañaga and officer Nelson Vique; while militants Idilio De León Bermúdez and José María Seque successfully escaped.

The FAU's directorate split the organization across the River Plate. Hugo Cores, León Duarte, Carlos Coitiño, Raúl Olivera, Mariela Salaberry, and Jorge Zaffaroni Pérez represented the directorate in Uruguay, which consisted mostly of ROE militants who continued organizing at the mass level. Those in Montevideo maintained a small printing press for producing pamphlets and fake national documents, and a small laboratory for making explosives.[13] The FAU recognized that the dictatorship would maintain power for at least a decade and thus committed itself to a strategy they referred to as *durar hacienda* (to endure doing).

Borrowing from the Cuban Revolution, militants still understood their role as that of a "little motor" behind popular mobilization. Conceptually, they thus viewed their role abroad as one of "helping to elevate working-class moral, combating calls for demobilization and surrender, reporting on and making sense of acts of resistance, and maintaining networks of solidarity with political prisoners."[14] They traced the lineage of their political activity to a long history of anarchists waging struggles in places outside of their countries of origin.[15] Practically, the FAU prioritized four main endeavors that aligned with an overall strategic vision for building resistance: (1) to produce and disseminate propaganda on both sides of the River Plate; (2) to amplify and proliferate an international smear campaign against the dictatorship by drawing attention to human rights; (3) to maintain the use of direct action, specifically property damage against elite holdings, in an effort to demonstrate the dictatorship's permeability; and (4) to establish a communication network for strategic planning around points of unity between exiles and militants back home. In these ways, the organization situated itself as both part of a national and regional struggle to "liberate the River Plate." Moreover, they continued to see themselves as part of the broader continent-wide struggle of the epoch and continued using the Cuban revolutionary call, *Hasta la victoria siempre* (Onward to the final victory).[16]

Regardless of the FAU's intentions to realize a coalition of resistance from abroad, including the participation of progressive politicians, they continued to see everyday people as the main protagonists of resistance. In a communique directed toward fellow Uruguayans in exile, the FAU proclaimed:

> The resistance struggle is possible, and in our country, there is a resistance. There are frequent examples of this. They do not consist of spectacular acts that result in immediate triumphs or generate feelings of success. They are instead constant everyday acts in which the pueblo is principal actor. . . . For this reason, Uruguay is set up for a long and tolling struggle for socialism and the forging of popular power."[17]

While challenging the dictatorship would not grant immediate results, the effort was not seen to be in vain. Although many on the left insisted on waiting out the regime, the FAU viewed dissident acts as seeds for building class power and forging new subjectivities in a prolonged process of social transformation.

While the anarchists envisioned a prolonged struggle against the dictatorship, they remained skeptical of reaching solutions via institutional politics. They pushed back against the PCU's continued faith in a progressive mutiny from within the military, insisting, "The pueblo should not subordinate itself to the spirit of February by waiting, still, for the fulfillment of Communiques 4 and 7."[18] For nearly a year and a half after the military coup, the still-legal PCU continued aspiring to collaborate with a progressive sect within the military. Perhaps the best example of this intention can be found in the publication of an aboveground military bulletin titled *9 de Febrero*, which received backdoor funding and influence from the party.[19] While the military demonstrated clear signs of internal incoherence, it had without doubt demonstrated a commitment to dismantling organized labor and the left prior to and after the coup.[20] In contrast, the FAU espoused a view that reflected an influence from both orthodox Marxist and New Left ideals, one that saw politics and government as "superstructure" to working-class struggle and the forging of the "hombre neuvo." The search for political solutions only disempowered everyday people who had already demonstrated, by instinct, their willingness and knowledge of how to subvert to regime. Thus, the pueblo's organic response to the dictatorship offered an opportunity to accumulate experiences necessary for a transformation of collective subjectivity.

With their militants' relocation to Buenos Aires, the FAU shared a position similar to that of other exiled left organizations from Uruguay, Bolivia, and Chile who had also moved there as conditions in their home countries proved too hostile. While the Tupamaros stumbled through exile for three years before reorganizing around a Marxist-Leninist position and eventual membership in the Revolutionary Coordinating Junta (JCR), the FAU did not face the same serious challenges of reevaluating strategy, ideology, and internal organization.[21] The JCR was an international coalition of the Marxist guerrilla organizations including Argentina's ERP, Chile's Revolutionary Left Movement (MIR), Bolivia's National Liberation Army (ELN), and the MLN-T. In 1974, the four groups coalesced around a joint paramilitary strategy in Argentina, the last country in the Southern Cone to avoid falling to dictatorship. The JCR saw Argentina as host to the decisive battle in the region's prolonged war between guerrillas and the state.

Notably, the FAU did not join the JCR, due to its contin-
ued emphasis on *foco* strategy.[22] In the second half of 1973, the
FAU instead initiated a dialogue among the entirety of the
Uruguayan left, including progressive factions within the Blanco
and Colorado parties, in hopes of forming a National Resistance
Front (Frente Nacional de Resistencia). The conversations marked
a noteworthy shift in the Uruguayan left. In November 1973, the
Revolutionary Workers Front (FRT) and Revolutionary Student
Front (FER), two Marxist organizations previously associated with
the MLN-T, merged into the ROE.[23] By October 1974, National
Resistance Front conversations eventually solidified into a coalition spearheaded by Enrique Erro and Zelmar Michelini in
collaboration with the GAU, PCR, and MLN-T ("New Times"
faction). The coalition, named the Artiguist Liberation Union
(Unión Artiguista de Liberación), intentionally excluded the PCU,
marking a rejection of the Broad Front and an end to Communist
hegemony within coalitional left spaces.[24] The Broad Front, for
its part, critiqued the party for having placed too much hope in
organizing a progressive military sector. Erro especially accused
the PCU of tanking the preparation of the 1973 general strike in
hopes of reaching a negotiation with military leaders.

Again, the FAU did not formally join the coalition, but the
anarchists continued working alongside various individuals and
political factions within it.[25] For instance, FAU exiles linked up
with members of the anarchist organization La Protesta and the
left-wing Peronist Armed Forces (FAP).[26] The anarchists' emphasis
on Third World liberation and mass politics posed a challenge for
relating with Argentine anarchist groups. Instead, the FAU sought
political alliances elsewhere. Reflecting on the parallels between
the FAU and Peronists, Hugo Cores declared:

> It had nothing to do with the Peronist doctrine, with the
> figure of Perón and his unions. We didn't like any of these. . . .
> You're Uruguayan with a fresh defeat on your back . . . and
> suddenly in a country where a popular movement is going
> to win after eighteen years. . . . Their emotional drive was
> appealing to us. They were very different from the arrogant

and well-dressed Argentines we had met. These Peronists
were like brothers to us. They dressed badly, talked badly,
and were very friendly."[27]

Local contacts aided the new arrivals by producing and circulating a document of fifty words forbidden to use in Buenos Aires.
After all, any subtle marker of difference could flag the exiles as
suspicious, including use of a Uruguayan Spanish lexicon rather
than *porteño* (Buenos Aires vernacular).[28] The most common way
to distinguish Uruguayan migrants was through their use of "ta"
as a substitute for "está bien." Sara Méndez recalls her first taxi
ride upon arriving to Buenos Aires, in which she commented,
"ta, ta, ta" to indicate arrival to her destination. Instantly drawing a mental link to the Tupamaros, the cab driver turned around
and glared, inquiring, "Tupa?!"[29] He assumed she was a member
of the MLN-T.

Many militants felt insecure and overwhelmed by the new
political landscape in Buenos Aires. Local armed groups such as
the ERP and Montoneros demonstrated a level of military sophis-
tication that far surpassed that of the FAU. Both organizations
also dwarfed the anarchists in numbers: ERP had roughly two
thousand members, while the Montoneros had upward of five
thousand.[30] Subscribing to a paramilitary model influenced by
Maoism and foco strategy, they saw themselves as a revolutionary
vanguard whose role was to confront the military directly. Due to
mandatory military service in Argentina, Montonero and ERP militants were much more advanced in weapons handling. Whereas
the FAU operated with a couple of shotguns and a handful of pistols, their Argentine counterparts stockpiled hundreds of assault
rifles and submachine guns. Moreover, both groups operated an
underground factory to produce over five hundred JCR-I submachine guns.[31] By 1975, the groups had assassinated over one hundred military and police servicemen and wounded roughly three
thousand more combined.[32]

While the FAU remained opposed to the foco strategy, its
directorate still emphasized the role of kidnapping, extortion, and
robbery to accumulate resources for resisting the dictatorship. To

raise money for the militants' relocation and housing costs, as well as resistance efforts back home in Uruguay, OPR-33 began meeting in the home of anarchist sympathizer and budding Argentine film maker Aída Bortnik to plan future activities.[33] In late July 1973, OPR-33 carried out their first kidnapping operation abroad, targeting the manager of the Argentine PepsiCo corporation, Nelson Laurino Penna. While the OPR-33 cell captured Laurino Penna successfully, nearly two months of negotiations between the FAU and representatives from Pepsi's international headquarters failed to bring about resolution. Pressured by the arrest of two militants, and the uncertainty of operating on a new terrain, the anarchists released the captive without collecting ransom.[34]

Federico Hart and Funding a Transnational Infrastructure

On March 16, 1974, OPR-33 targeted the Dutch Argentine wool exporter Federico Hart, a known white-collar crook who had been convicted of contraband in 1957 by a Uruguayan court. The FAU selected Hart knowing that public opinion was already strongly against him. After roughly two months of scouting the residence, a team made up of Alberto Mechoso, Iván Morales, and Adalberto Soba kidnapped Hart from his suburban Buenos Aires home. Gerardo Gatti handled negotiations over the next five months while Hart remained captive in a basement room. Throughout his time in holding, Hart denied his identity, instead presenting himself as Lebanese-Palestinian and speaking only in French. Upon negotiating with Hart's family, Gatti demanded US$2 million for his release, but a flawed communication led the familiar contact to seek *diez* (ten) rather than *dos* (two) million dollars in ransom. The Harts paid the sum in hundred-dollar bills for a total that weighed over one hundred pounds—money used by the organization to purchase safe houses throughout the city.[35]

Days after Hart's kidnapping, the FAU and GAU collaborated to hold a public rally at the Buenos Aires Boxing Federation. Now that the ROE had absorbed FER-FRT members previously affiliated with the MLN-T, the event brought together upward of five thousand attendees, including Zelmar Michelini, Enrique Erro, and Enrique Rodríguez (PCU). Event organizers also invited representatives from some of Argentina's largest political organizations, including the Radical Civic Union and Peronist Youth. Although the event had no scheduled speakers, both Erro and Rodríguez asked to speak over the megaphone. After a brief argument around who would speak first, Erro took the mic and publicly denounced "those who supported Communiques 4 and 7" without naming the PCU nor its individual delegates. He called them traitors to the working class and condemned their decisions for continuing to induce state violence against the left. He concluded by acknowledging that the government's main targets remained those militants most active in the street while the Broad Front maintained a passive approach that continued to seek a solution within the Armed Forces.[36] The crowd's majority MLN-T, Montoneros, and PRT-ERP broke into a chant, "Tupas! Tupas! Tupas!" Rodríguez then took over the megaphone, to the sound of boos and hisses. After numerous attempts to initiate his speech, he forfeited his speaking role to an eruption of applause and chants.[37]

On June 2, 1974, ROE hosted another rally on a street corner in Barrio Almagro to celebrate the anniversary of the largest CNT general strike. Under the title Operation Gris, the Argentine Federal Police arrested over a hundred Uruguayan exiles, including nearly three dozen OPR-33 militants, and charged them with unlawful assembly.[38] While detainees were released only days later, the list of names and addresses served as the basis for future operations against FAU-ROE and other exiled Uruguayans in the country.[39] The maneuver came two months after a meeting between security officials from Argentina, Brazil, Bolivia, Chile, Paraguay, and Uruguay in Buenos Aires to discuss "coordinated actions against subversive targets." By this time, the region's police forces welcomed a 600 percent increase in US funding for anti-narcotics efforts, which doubled as financing for anti-subversion. Historian J. Patrice McSherry argues that the February 1974 meeting and subsequent operation, such as Gris, represent a prototype of what would eventually consolidate as Plan Cóndor in November 1975.[40]

Over the next two years, the FAU utilized US$500,000 of the Hart ransom money to fund a transnational infrastructure that included houses, vehicles, propaganda material, and public transportation costs.[41] While the ransom money enabled most militants to keep their personal homes "clean" of political activities, a handful lived on site and served as caretakers of FAU meeting spaces and warehouses in the Buenos Aires periphery. Caretakers received monthly stipends to ensure their presence at the space.[42] In one case, three mothers disguised a FAU local as a daycare. Convening at the site in the morning, the women later received their own children, who their partners dropped off en route to work. Other militants arrived early to construct a soundproof basement located ten feet below the building, which would serve as the future home of a newly purchased industrial printing press— the FAU's first upgrade from the mimeograph. However, due to the difficulty of transporting such a large machine without raising suspicions, the printing press was never delivered to the local. Instead, it remained unused in Alberto Mechoso's home, while the FAU printed propaganda on borrowed machinery from PRT-ERP and Montoneros.

By this time, FAU-ROE propaganda had become much more centralized due to the difficulty of maintaining more diffuse methods of print production and distribution under the dictatorship. Recognizing the inevitable prohibition of aboveground press, the FAU initiated a new clandestine media titled the *Boletín de la Resistencia*, which was first circulated in July 1973. It reported on national politics, labor actions, solidarity campaigns from abroad, and state repression, in the process connecting the diaspora with those who remained in Uruguay. The bulletin sought to inspire political activity among the half a million exiles living abroad and insisted that they maintain a community together, thus creating a new battle front from which to strike the dictatorship. Unlike many historical political organizations who used exile as means to move further underground, the ROE called for high visibility from abroad as a tactic to challenge the new meanings prescribed to national symbols and national identity on behalf of the dictatorship. The *Boletín* contained images of ROE solidarity in exile, such as banner drops at soccer stadiums in Argentina, murals on the streets of Paris, and denunciation of torture in the Swedish press. Images of international solidarity were meant to lift everyday people's morale and demonstrate exiles' refusal to abandon the struggle against dictatorship back home, regardless of the new spatial reality.

Members of the ROE distributed the bulletin anonymously in workplaces and on campuses, leaving them in public spaces. Like the previous FAU literature, the *Boletín* included a section calling on workers to submit workplace grievances for publication in future editions. Militants identified fellow workers and students who expressed interest in the material through casual conversations without releasing their identities as distributors. If a colleague happened to express serious interest, militants might slip a copy of the bulletin in a frequently transited space accompanied by a note with information about the time and place for future bulk distribution. Members of the ROE would punctually leave boxes of content in the arranged site, often a centrally located plaza, then leave the premises without encountering any of the volunteer distributors.[43]

On account of new legal codes that prohibited political propaganda within Uruguay, militants innovated new methods for distributing propaganda. One device, called a "flier thrower," could be made of a shoebox or food can with a small firework attached. Militants adjusted the wick to allow for over a minute before detonating to prevent being caught near the explosion. Upon placing multiple devices in a public space, hundreds of quarter-sheet *mariposas* ("butterflies," or fliers) would trickle down after the initial shock of a small bang. François Graña recalls:

> The flier thrower had a real propagandistic affect, but it also had an extra charm: it was a prank to throw in the faces of the repressors. It would be enough to have only been recognized by the onlooking pedestrian accomplices, even those who would not dare to pick up a flier, for it to have been a successful action. The tin can was a more efficient vessel because it did not take up that much space and could fit in

a purse, small bag, or backpack. It was very easy to leave it wherever, and the explosion, strengthened by the tin itself, made a lot of noise.[44]

Militants also devised new methods for communicating on both sides of the river. The FAU, for instance, devised a special tactic to use international mail services to send propaganda from Argentina to Uruguay. They sent up to a dozen packages at a time without return addresses to a mix of random addresses, military officers, and one FAU militant located in Uruguay—often Elena Quinteros, who managed the organization's Montevideo local. Each box consisted of propaganda material and a cover letter, declaring, "This material is for dispersal. Do not feel obliged to read it or distribute it. Feel free to discard it." The tactic was intended to confuse authorities about who was an actual member of the organization should they interrupt mail correspondence. The tactic became even more useful after the government implemented Decree 450/975 of June 5, 1975, which directed postal authorities to confiscate all "Marxist and antidemocratic" correspondence in the mail.[45]

Print propaganda was accompanied by a sustained wall-painting campaign that utilized a slogan, "Resistencia vencera" (Resistance will overcome), that was widely circulated among Tendencia-affiliated unions during the 1973 general strike. The organization initially drew inspiration for the slogan from another phrase being circulated around Argentina, "Perón volvera" (Perón will return). They adopted a similarly styled logo, an *R* above a *V* to remain discreet while appealing visually to a regional population already familiar with the famous Peronist "victory" symbol. Propaganda also made frequent use of images of the national independence flag to draw on the commonsense knowledge of its capture by OPR-33 in 1969. Like the FAU's use of the ROE as a popular space for anarchist practice without the necessity of anarchist ideological affinity among members, "Resistencia" served as a new signifier for a mass front behind which were militants of the FAU. Everyday people knew this as result of the frequent use of the "Libertad o muerte" (Liberty or death) flag in print propaganda.[46]

ViloX, a New Brand of Politics

In June 1975, nearly fifty FAU-ROE militants met in Buenos Aires for ten days to complete the final deliberation of an organization-wide congress that had begun eight months prior. This transnational forum had drawn participation of 90 percent of the FAU's membership, totaling upward of three hundred militants, who met clandestinely in four-day increments in the months prior to the final deliberation, which saw an affirmative vote to change the FAU's name to the People's Victory Party (PVP).[47] The PVP maintained the same "two foot" strategy, but Gerardo Gatti, Maricio Gatti, León Duarte, and Alberto Mechoso took over the Fomento's regional duties while Hugo Cores and Luis Presno laid groundwork for new branches among exiles in Europe. They shrunk the armed apparatus to include only eleven militants divided into three different teams, but they grew the size and resource allocation for internal propaganda to better fit the mandates of transporting information between both countries. The military apparatus carried out only one operation, which took place on January 11, 1976. A team lead by Mechoso placed small bombs at various sites in the upper-class city of Punta del Este, including the iconic Hotel San Rafael, two country clubs, a marina, and numerous yachts. While the operation failed to inflict considerable damage upon the target sites, it nevertheless demonstrated the vulnerability of the dictatorship.[48] Moreover, the action demonstrated a reconceptualization of the armed apparatus as a means of spreading propaganda rather than solely as a tool for escalating workplace conflict. In some ways, the operation showed the influence of FER-FRT militants who came from the Tupamaro tradition of "armed propaganda."

In a creative attempt to break the civic-military government's censorship efforts, the PVP launched a publicity campaign disguised as an advertisement for a fictitious Belgian cosmetics line called ViloX. The organization published advertisements that blanketed full pages with the company logo in mainstream press outlets, such as *El País*. The logo coincided with PVP propaganda clandestinely circulating within factories. In one bold effort,

ViloX sponsored the Uruguayan wing of the fifth annual Rutas de América bicycle tour. The sponsorship included various banners located along the competition route, a frequently aired television commercial, and brand placement on three different competitors' jerseys.[49] Similar to the Punta del Este bombing operation, the ViloX campaign set out to disrupt the dictatorship's narrative that dissident political movements had been eradicated. Moreover, the joking nature of the campaign, including various witty product slogans, attempted to shine a humorous light upon a gloomy climate in effort to raise popular morale.

Regardless of the prospects for a continued militancy from abroad, the FAU-PVP was a weakened and compromised organization after suffering nearly a decade of repression. Augusto Andrés reflects on the time in exile:

> In Argentina I was not doing well. It was very difficult to adapt. It felt like I needed to be in our own country, and things just took much longer to do. Because overall I was just not doing well. In Argentina, no one was doing well. . . . Everyone who went there did so feeling pressured because you feel like you are abandoning everything. We were under a moral pressure. It was like schizophrenia because at the same time I realized that I had to leave, I also realized that I had nothing to do there. We got together to see who we had lost and who was going to be next. What was this for? To do politics? No. We were just subsisting. We stretched out our lives a bit, but it was nothing else. It's true there was always a good atmosphere between us, something that did not exist in other organizations and parties that I knew, but that is not sufficient.[50]

Plan Cóndor's Pilot Plot

> *They say that Uruguay has set up a base in the Argentine*
> *territory but it would be completely unheard of that the Argentine*
> *government would permit that, within its own territory, armed*

forces from a foreign country to install an operation base, venture
around the city armed, carry out operations, detain persons, etc.
(. . .) Such fictitious histories could only be made in the mind of a
novelist.

—MAJOR JOSÉ NINO GAVAZZO, 1976

On April 14, 1975, Argentine police detained Hugo Cores in his La Plata home. Internal police memos claimed to have discovered a plot to transport "extremists" and arms between Argentina and Uruguay through use of a small boat stolen from a private dock in the Tigre suburb.[51] Cores was detained in a larger sweep that included members of the MLN-T, including Andrés Cultelli, who was accused of traveling with false documents.[52] During the first week of Cores's detention, Uruguayan police tortured him in an effort to obtain information about the location of the Hart ransom and the Uruguayan independence flag. They also questioned him extensively about the whereabouts of Gerardo Gatti and León Duarte. Cores's detention drew international attention, including a letter published in the Buenos Aires newspaper *Última Hora* signed by organizations and individuals, including the Italian Confederation of Workers Unions (CSIL), the French General Confederation of Labor (CGT), and public intellectuals including Roland Barthes, Alain Touraine, and Gabriel García Márquez.[53] Upon his release in December 1975, Cores moved to Paris where he linked up with other Uruguayan exiles to found a European faction of the ROE within the Committee for Uruguayan Political Prisoners' Defense. PVP militants who remained in Uruguay suffered torture during this same period. In May 1975, Carlos Coitiño, an AEBU steward, was detained and held at an artillery facility, where he suffered daily torture sessions that ultimately left him in critical condition, including electrocution to sensitive areas of the body, waterboarding, and being forced to stand on two feet for multiple days without food or water.[54] The militants' experiences with torture foreshadowed what others would come to experience some months later.

With news of torture rapidly surfacing out of the Southern Cone region, the US State Department remained committed to downplaying human rights violations and even painting the Uruguayan government as victim. In a May 1975 conversation between Secretary of State Henry Kissinger and Uruguayan foreign minister Juan Carlos Blanco, both agreed that the rise in human rights discourse was a result of left intellectuals' influence in global media outlets. Kissinger ventured to play the victim card for the US government regarding global opinions on the Vietnam invasion and domestic poverty rates, declaring:

> We should discuss some time how the left-wing and the intellectuals are demoralizing public opinion on every issue. In Europe, 90 per cent of television is controlled by extreme leftists and intellectuals and they are preventing the public from receiving a fair perception of events and of reality. I saw a survey of television programming in the Netherlands, Britain, Germany, and one other country, and it indicated that nothing favorable about the United States is being shown. The Viet Cong are depicted as heroes, the United States as an ogre, and U.S. farmers as being poor and oppressed. I don't know where you'd find such farmers in the United States. Only eight per cent of our population are farmers, and they are not noticeably poor. Perhaps the Mexicans are. But the left-wing extremists are demoralizing public conceptions.[55]

In this same conversation, both parties identify the need for inter-American cooperation to combat armed groups. Blanco contended:

> We need completely new reforms. We are trying to develop our own solutions to the political crisis facing Western civilization. The second most important thing is that we must solve the problem of subversion and terrorism. Many may have thought when this first started that this only happened in countries with military governments, or as the result of

tyranny, or because of social injustices. But now we have it
in Argentina, Chile, Paraguay, Bolivia, Venezuela, Colombia,
Central America, Mexico, and even Western Europe. . . . In
Western Europe, it can be stopped without altering the life
of the country. But in our own country, it destroyed our
small defenses, and we have had to fight for our life. We do
not ask others to do it for us; we will do it ourselves, and we
will continue to do it. But these subversive movements are
all inter-connected. We can fight them in our country, but it
is difficult when they get assistance from abroad.[56]

While Southern Cone governments broadened their scope
to embark on a regional offensive against subversion, the US
embassy emphasized Uruguay's internal improvements on human
rights. The embassy's narrative suggested committing to isolate
the Uruguayan government's actions to within its own borders,
rejecting US presence in security efforts, and minimizing the
role of imprisonment and torture.[57] US embassy official Russell
E. Olson downplayed reports of torture to "rumors" and insisted
that political arrests had dropped significantly. He acknowledged
the continued use of "some torture" of prisoners, but he insisted
that the July 31st death of a political prisoner—news of which had
been recently released—remained an isolated incident that was
"absolutely contrary to policy and intent."[58] Meanwhile, whether
Olson knew it or not, the reality was far more chilling: more than
twenty political prisoners had been tortured to death since the
military coup, including FAU-ROE militant Gilberto Coghlan.[59]

The potential for international collaboration became even
more realistic when officers from fifteen Latin American countries
met in Montevideo at the Eleventh Conference of Latin American Militaries. With the meeting's October 1975 commencement,
Uruguay's Joint Forces launched "Operation Morgan" against
the PCU. The offensive resulted in the detention of roughly five
hundred party members and dealt a decisive blow, ultimately
leading to twenty-three disappearances, sixteen deaths by torture, and forced exile of all party leadership over the span of the
next decade.[60] The PVP responded by calling for isolated PCU

militants to find refuge by linking up with the Resistencia, whether in Uruguay or in exile abroad. A document released shortly after the offensive summarized the contentious history of the FAU and PCU by specifically highlighting PCU leadership's repeated efforts to isolate and disassociate from radical elements of the left amid moments of state repression. When the 1972 counterinsurgency offensive broke the party, various PCU leaders appeared on television and radio stations to express repentance for their affiliation with it. Yet the PVP made a clear expression of solidarity with those victims of state repression, declaring:

> There continue to be great differences between our orientation, conceptions, and political practice and that of the Communist Party. Like always, we argue strongly and openly against dialogue as a substitute for struggle, and against the positions that intend to place popular movements as a caboose for the political and owning classes. . . . And like before, we continue to distinguish the distinct methods that should be utilized to resolve the contradictions at the core of the pueblo with those that we have reserved for the real class enemy. When forces on our side are struck, the entire popular movement is struck, and there is no room for sectarianism. . . . For that reason, to the militants of the Communist Party that have resisted torture, to those who have distributed propaganda clandestinely, to those who have lost contact and look to rearm their political cadres, to those who know that the task at hand is difficult but do the impossible to complete it, to those we say: *compañeros* of the Communist Party, *arriba los que luchan!* [Hurray for those who struggle][61]

PVP emphasized the shared conditions, experiences, and class positions among militants to push for a unified left, and the statement's distinction between the official PCU line and the moral and practical actions of individual militants demonstrated a commitment to practical collaboration beyond ideological and theoretical differences.

Operation Morgan drew the attention of Amnesty International and the Bertrand Russell Tribunal. The human rights organizations were nearing completion of their reports on both Uruguay and Argentina with the assistance of Zelmar Michelini, Wilson Ferreira Aldunate, Héctor Gutiérrez Ruiz, and Hugo Cores, who spoke at a Russell Tribunal press conference in Rome in December 1975. Denouncing Operation Morgan, Cores shed light on the five thousand political prisoners in Uruguay. He acknowledged the nearly two dozen militants recently killed during torture sessions and warned of the potential for more murders of political prisoners after the Morgan offensive. Graciela Tabey, a PVP militant who testified alongside Cores, also recalled her experiences being tortured while detained in Buenos Aires.[62] Following the Uruguayan government's October 1973 prohibition of domestic press from wiring stories concerning "the political, economic, or social situation in Uruguay" to foreign media outlets, the February 1976 Bertrand Russell Tribunal and various Amnesty International reports throughout the same year played key roles in transmitting what was taking place within Uruguay to government officials and the general public abroad.[63] The reports accompanied Ferreira's growing condemnation of the US embassy, US government, and global financial institutions for serving as accomplices to the Uruguayan government. Ferreira, who maintained a distance from revolutionary left groups and considered himself a "defender of Western Civilization," recognized that the United States had armed the Bordaberry regime with more financial assistance than any previous Uruguayan government.[64]

US officials remained in denial. Anticipating the Amnesty International and Bertrand Russell reports, US ambassador to Uruguay Ernest Siracusa called a meeting with Uruguayan foreign minister Juan Carlos Blanco to insist both countries maintain a friendly relationship and expressed concern over growing criticisms. Although Siracusa recognized some validity in both reports, he insisted they were "propagandistic distortions" based on incomplete information.[65] A *Washington Post* article quoted US ambassador Siracusa declaring that the Amnesty International report was greatly exaggerated.[66] The silence and cover-up opened the door for Uruguayan security forces to participate in forms of state terrorism at a regional scale.

On March 24, 1976, the Argentine Armed Forces overthrew President Isabela Perón, leaving the entire Southern Cone region under military dictatorship. From March 1976 to December 1983, the Argentine military embarked on the Process of National Reorganization, during which they systematically targeted members of leftist political organizations, trade unionists, clergy, peasants, and intellectuals while simultaneously liberalizing the national economy. While US secretary of state Henry Kissinger was warned of the "potential for a good deal of blood" following the military's takeover, he insisted, "I do want to encourage them. I don't want to give the sense that they're harassed by the United States."[67] The new military government plugged into a regional network of shared intelligence services initiated by the Chilean National Intelligence Directorate (DINA) at a late November 1975 meeting in Santiago. The network, called Plan Cóndor, linked military intelligence services of Argentina, Bolivia, Brazil, Chile, Paraguay, and Uruguay to combat subversion in a so-called "psycho-political war."[68] Participating governments looked toward the International Criminal Police Organization (INTERPOL) as an example, but they sought to build a more specific computerized database, called Contel, which documented organizations and individuals "connected directly or indirectly with subversion." The project's visionaries designed modern communication systems to collectively compile individual profiles, document counterinsurgency operations, and track suspects' movement across borders.[69] Perhaps the most useful communications tool proved to be a telex electronic messaging system located at US military facilities in the Panama Canal Zone.[70]

While unaware of the newly established regional intelligence structure, US House representative Edward Koch felt a heightened sense of urgency to pursue sanctions against Uruguay after the military coup in Argentina. On May 7, the US House Foreign Operations Subcommittee approved an amendment to prohibit transfer of US$3 million in USAID money allotted to Uruguay for fiscal year 1977. The amendment swiftly passed and moved to vote as a congressional resolution in the Senate.[71]

Upon news of the amendment's approval, US ambassador Siracusa telegrammed the State Department to reinforce the embassy's opposition and to emphasize that the measure, passed in vain, would only jeopardize US regional interests while failing to enact the changes it set out to accomplish. He hinted that Koch and others were delusional, claiming that the amendment had passed because of their "perception of the human rights situation in Uruguay."[72] Both the US State Department and US Embassy in Uruguay continued to downplay, or outright deny, the ongoing human rights offenses in the region in hopes of deterring congressional action. According to Uruguayan historian Vania Markarian, US officials, specifically those in the State Department, were concerned that Uruguay's damaged reputation would jeopardize its ability to play a "moderating and constructive role in the Organization of American States." They feared that strong policies in opposition to human rights violations would weaken their ability to exert influence over the growing wave of bureaucratic authoritarian regimes in the Southern Cone region. As result of an absence of US influence in the region, the authoritarian governments would become isolated from the United States's "cognitive universe" and respond by launching even bloodier counterterrorism campaigns in the future.[73] However, such offenses had already begun.

On May 20, 1976, a Uruguayan Joint Forces unit operating in Buenos Aires assassinated exiled politicians Zelmar Michelini and Héctor Gutiérrez Ruiz—paramilitaries abducted both men from their homes on May 18, 1976. Their tortured bodies were found stuffed into a car with two dead Tupamaros three days later. While the Uruguayan government denied responsibility for both murders, officials accused the men of membership in the JCR. The assassinations represent two high-profile cases during an increasingly chilling climate. Beginning late April, ten unidentifiable cadavers washed up along Uruguay's shores in the eastern department of Rocha. A peasant made the initial discovery of a "white lump" that was eventually found to be a "semi-decomposed young man, hogtied and blindfolded." Within the next week, a series of bodies washed up on the shore nearby.[74] News of the dead bodies sparked fear within the PVP because militants Ricardo Gil, Elida Alvarez, Eduardo Ferreira, Ary Cabrera, Telba Juárez, and Eduardo Chisella had disappeared from their Buenos Aires homes during the first days of April.[75] Moreover, OPR-33 militants Juan Carlos Mechoso, Alfredo Pareja, Raúl Cariboni, and Héctor Romero had also mysteriously vanished from their cells in Montevideo's cruelly named Libertad Prison in late April.[76] Hugo Cores's contact with European press outlets launched a wave of commentaries from foreign newspapers, including *Le Monde* and *Le Quotidian de Paris*. As result of word spreading throughout the European press, Amnesty International London telegrammed President Bordaberry and Foreign Minister Blanco to express concern and demand the bodies be identified.[77] While the Uruguayan government maintained the narrative that the bodies belonged to Asian fishermen, a competing INTERPOL report demonstrated that the bodies had been previously mutilated—some even shot numerous times.[78] On May 22, the Uruguayan government held a press conference presenting the four prisoners in uniforms and shackles. The men appeared alive after enduring one month of interrogation and torture during which authorities hoped to extract information about the location of the national independence flag. While the press event offered proof of life of the four prisoners, word had yet to surface regarding the whereabouts of the other six missing militants.[79]

A month after the internationally organized political assassinations and cadaver scandals, US secretary of state Kissinger met with Argentine foreign minister Admiral César Augusto Guzzetti in Santiago, Chile. The June 6, 1976, meeting took place on the eve of a wave of state-sanctioned violence in Argentina, including the kidnapping and detention of numerous PVP militants. The conversation focused primarily on the supposed relocation of a half million leftist exiles from Uruguay, Chile, Paraguay, and Bolivia to Argentina. Upon learning of the large exile community in Argentina, Kissinger responded, "You could always send them back." In a rare show of empathy, Guzzetti acknowledged the moral questions around sending exiles back to their home countries, considering the known human rights violations in Chile and Uruguay. Kissinger cynically responded, "Have you tried the PLO

[Palestine Liberation Organization]? They need more terrorists."
As the conversation deepened, Guzzetti made the first known
references to Plan Cóndor, to which Kissinger reacted with tacit
approval. Guzzetti declared, "The terrorist problem is general to
the entire Southern Cone. To combat it, we are encouraging joint
efforts to integrate with our neighbors." Kissinger responded by
making clear that he saw regional economic uplift and integration as key to defeating "internal subversion," further declaring, "If
there are things that have to be done, you should do them quickly."
Kissinger went on to warn Guzzetti of the growing domestic
pressures to intervene in human rights but assured the admiral,
"We want you to succeed. We do not want to harass you. I will do
what I can."[80]

Regardless of the meeting, internal communications between
the US Embassy in Uruguay, US National Security Council, and
US State Department show a shared commitment to spreading misinformation, specifically the denial of the international
cooperation of Cóndor-affiliated governments. Regarding the
murders of Michelini and Gutiérrez Ruiz, the National Security
Council insisted, "There is no evidence to support a contention
that Southern Cone governments are cooperating in some sort of
international 'Murder Inc.' aimed at Leftist political exiles residing
in one of their countries."[81] Similarly, the US Embassy in Uruguay
telegrammed the US State Department to comment on the recent
murders in Argentina, in which Ambassador Siracusa proclaimed:
"We know of no evidence to indicate that the recent deaths of
Michelini, Gutierrez, and Mr. and Mrs. Whitelaw, have been the
result of any GOU [government of Uruguay] action, or desire, or
by 'arrangement'. . . . We have no evidence to support allegations
of international arrangements to carry our such assassinations or
executions." He continued by acknowledging that the embassy
was indeed aware of Uruguayan officials traveling to Argentina
and Chile for the purpose of interrogating Uruguayan prisoners
but emphasized that officials preferred to keep detainees alive for
the purpose of extracting information.[82] He never recognized the
relationship between interrogation and torture.

El Jardín: Automotores Orletti

Taking Kissinger's suggestion seriously, the Argentine Armed Forces moved quickly to disappear foreign and domestic leftists within their borders. On June 9, a squadron of men dressed in civilian clothing kidnapped PVP militant Gerardo Gatti from his Buenos Aires home. The kidnappers knew that Gatti belonged to an organization in possession of a large sum of money. During the kidnapping, they took the equivalent of US$100,000 that they found hidden in a box at Gatti's home. They first brought Gatti to a Federal Police outpost and then transferred him to a clandestine holding center four days later, where he underwent frequent interrogations under the command of Aníbal Gordon, a civilian employee of the Argentine Secreteriat of Intelligence (SIDE) and leader of the neofascist organization Argentine Anticommunist Alliance (AAA, or Triple A). Gordon notified Gatti of his intention to recover $10 million of the ransom money in exchange of for his release and the release of ten other detained Uruguayans. On the day of Gatti's arrival to the clandestine site, a group of Triple A members broke into the home of Washington Pérez and transported him to a holding center blindfolded, alongside his son. Pérez, who had arrived broke to Buenos Aires, no longer participated in the organization, and worked selling newspapers at a small stand in front of Café Monterrey.[83] Nevertheless, Gordon hoped to use Pérez as an intermediary between Gatti and the rest of the PVP. Over the next three days, Pérez was transferred to and from the holding center five times to communicate between Gatti and the rest of the organization.[84] The visits were brief and monitored by guards. Pérez felt overwhelmed and could not help but focus his energy on the growing infection on Gatti's left wrist as result of torture.[85] After the first four attempts to communicate between parties by use of word of mouth, PVP sent Pérez to deliver an envelope containing a written proposal of their demands, including proof that Gatti was alive. Gordon responded to the request with a counterproposal accompanied by a photo of Gatti and Pérez together holding a copy of the day's newspaper. The photo would become the last image captured of Gatti, who by that time had communicated to Pérez that he had experienced various torture sessions during which he was hung by his arms from the ceiling. He warned, "Be careful, these are the same people that killed Michelini and Gutiérrez Ruiz."[86]

On June 23, Pérez returned to the detention center to present a counterproposal on PVP's behalf. Augusto Andrés recalls a collective feeling of confidence among members of the group, saying, "When Gatti fell, we gathered and unanimously said to ourselves: we'll wait. We had full confidence in Gerardo."[87] By now, the organization had accumulated plenty of experience negotiating freedom for political prisoners in both Uruguay and Argentina. Yet, this time proved different. Pérez recalls being met with the response that "these people are fucking around too much. We are going to have to clean out about twenty or thirty. We'll have to kill them . . . so that they shape up."[88] Over the next month, twenty-six PVP militants and five members of their families—including two spouses, two toddler-aged children, and one militant's father—were kidnapped from their Buenos Aires homes and detained in the back room of a vacant Barrio Floresta mechanic shop, known as Automotores Orletti. Prior to the sweep, the Uruguayan Army Intelligence Department had submitted a list of sixty-four PVP militants to the Contel shared intelligence database.[89] The Uruguayan government also initiated a domestic offensive, including the kidnapping and permanent disappearance of Elena Quinteros, who sought refuge in the Venezuelan embassy but eventually fell captive to the Joint Forces in a raid on June 26. Augusto Andrés recalls the kidnapping of his wife and fellow PVP militant Edelweiss Zahn in Buenos Aires:

> Early morning of July 14, 1976, Edelweiss and I arrived at the house of Margarita Michelini to drop off our children. She was not there. We waited ten, fifteen minutes, and then left with great anxiety because Marga was always on time.
>
> We took the train to Rivadavia station, only thirty meters from our old house on Dehesa Street, which we had moved out of a few days prior. What were we coming back to? To get two bags filled with clothes and food that we had

left near the front door. Were they essential? No. But we felt committed to gathering our belongings that were purchased with the collective's money.

"Stay with the kiddos. I will be back in five minutes," said Edel. "*Dale* [Go on]," I answered. Feeling uncertain and unconvinced, I stayed behind with our children, Julia (5) and Diego (3). I waited five minutes, ten minutes, and it kept getting later. So, I left the children sitting alone at the station while I walked slowly to get some cigarettes at a kiosk located across the street from our house. My mouth is dry, and my legs are heavy. I try to smile. The man, usually talkative, recognized me and turned pale. He makes gestures with his mouth while his eyes dance wildly. I returned to pick up the kiddos at the station, and we took the train to go meet up with another comrade, Ana Quadros, as planned. Ana organized contacts with Leon "Loco" Duarte, who was key to many things in the organization. I left the children sitting at the door of a corner store and walked down the opposite side of the sidewalk, half a block from the appointment. It is a busy avenue. I took another turn down a parallel street looking, realizing something strange. I am distressed and arrived at the appointment at the exact time. No one. I waited a little longer than five minutes and then walked away slowly. I sit on a bench, and I try to think. I feel total anguish because Ana is very responsible. I do not know what to do. Suddenly I am moved—forty-five minutes ago I left my children at the door of a cafe! I feel like a Nazi criminal.

I go back to find them there, accompanied by Daniel Bentancur, an old El Cerro comrade and member of the organization. Daniel and Dorita, another comrade, came walking down the street and saw a couple of scared-faced children at the entrance to the café, and Dorita said: "I think they are the children of the *pelado*." It was a miracle inside the Cóndor. They take me to Sandra's house, today a psychologist, who takes me to the attic. Today Sandra still remembers and tells me: "You were shocked, and it was hard

for you to talk, just like your children, who looked at you
without speaking."

That's how things ended on July 14, 1976, and there was
nothing to celebrate. . . .

Then there were people in a hurry to leave for Europe,
including someone from the emergency lists. And other
cases like mine, of suicidal behavior. For months I continued with my children in that infernal Buenos Aires, the scar-
iest things had already happened, and I rejected going to
the United States as a refugee. Carter had accepted me and
our two children. Then, I passed on Sweden and Switzerland
despite the desperation of Guy Prim, a Frenchman and head
of the UNHCR in Argentina. I took the last plane out, on
December 14, bound for Paris, alongside Senator Enrique
Erro and Ignacio Errandonea, brother of our missing comrade Pablo, and some other survivors. I wanted to pay for the
sin of being alive, the sin of not having shared the fate of all
the others, of Edel and Gerardo in the first place.[90]

Automotores Orletti operated from May to November 1976,
during the immediate months after Argentina fell under military
dictatorship. The space, which housed the telex communication
machine linked to other countries in the region, operated as the
primary site for implementing Plan Cóndor in Argentina. Roughly
three hundred detainees, most of whom were political exiles from
other countries in Latin America, entered the site, of whom only a
few dozen would ever leave.

Aníbal Gordon managed Orletti's primary operators, including the Argentine SIDE, the Uruguayan Defense Intelligence
Services (SID), and the Triple A.[91] SID deputy directory and colonel José Fons linked the Uruguayan Armed Forces to Plan Cóndor
after serving as the country's representative for the operation's late
1975 founding meeting in Santiago. SIDE officer Rolando Oscar
Nerone headed a special task force within the Triple A to pursue
and kidnap leftist exiles in Buenos Aires. The task force included
Juan Gattei, a recipient of a USAID scholarship in 1962 and
employee of the Department of Foreign Affairs within the Federal

Police—a branch overseen by CIA station chief M. Gardener Hathaway.[92] Inside Orletti, Uruguayan colonel José Nino Gavazzo led torture and interrogation practices against Uruguayan detainees alongside fellow Uruguayan officers who belonged to the sixty-person strong División 300, including Colonel Manuel Cordero. At this time, Gavazzo was also employed as plant manager at Frigorífico Comargen in Las Piedras, Uruguay.[93] Orletti also welcomed authorities from Bolivia, Chile, Paraguay, and the United States, who sent CIA agents to torture and interrogate Crescencio Galañena Hernández and Jesús Cejas Arias, both employees of the Cuban embassy in Argentina.[94]

Orletti's owner, local businessman Santiago Cortell, rented the property to the Argentine SIDE, whose officers maintained the facade of an auto mechanic shop, including the original sign reading "Cortell S.A." Located adjacent to a schoolyard, the sounds of school bells and children laughing were audible throughout the day. Orletti's operators used this point of reference when agreeing on the codename for the site's name, El Jardín (The Garden). However, detainees knew the site as "Orletti" after word spread among them that a fellow prisoner caught glimpse of the front sign from under the hood used to cover his face by the kidnappers. Struggling to gain awareness of his surroundings while being dragged from the van, he read "Orletti" out of the figures "Cortell S.A."

Guards, mostly members of the Triple A disguised as auto mechanics, rotated cars in and out of the front garage to give the appearance of an operating mechanic shop. The torturers lived in a lodging area upstairs alongside a collective holding room for detainees, keeping watch over prisoners through three small peepholes in the wall.[95] Stripping detainees naked, the torturers prohibited them from speaking to one another; if they heard any sounds of communication, they would arrive at the cell entrance and fire shotguns above the detainees' heads, hitting the wall to intimidate them. This dynamic was meant to create the ultimate form of alienation: together but divided. Survivors recall the sentiment of being trapped inside of themselves, alongside their comrades with whom they had previously worked with intimately, as one of the most distressing feelings. Alongside members of off-duty military in Task Force 18, Colonel Gavazzo interrogated and tortured prisoners in a small room adjacent to the guards' living quarters. Gavazzo spoke openly about his identity and sometimes allowed detainees to remove their blindfolds. Indeed, he acted with impunity because he and others had no intentions of releasing detainees alive. Instead, the SID brought PVP detainees to Orletti to extract information, specifically regarding the location of the ransom money, and to later murder them. In one case, a militant's father was detained and tortured in quest of information regarding his son, who remained adjacent in the holding cell throughout the torture session. The father, Enrique Rodríguez Larreta, recalls the experience:

> The next night was my turn to go to the top floor, where they interrogated me under torture, like all the other women and men who were there. They got me completely naked, and, placing my hands toward my back, they hung me by my wrists above the floor for about twenty minutes at thirty cm [centimeters]. At the same time they placed a sort of loincloth over me so that I received various electric shocks. When the electricity hits them, the victim receives an electric shock to multiple places at the same time. The apparatus that they called *la maquina* [machine] was connected while they asked questions and made insults and threats, carrying shocks to one's most sensitive parts. The floor under where they hung the detainees was wet and covered with glass the size of coarse salt for the purpose of adding to the torture if a person tried to support themselves by putting their feet on the floor. Various people that were with me got themselves out of the rig and kicked against the floor, which produced series injuries. I remember a special case of someone who I later realized was Edelweiss Zahn, who suffered deep wounds to her temples and ankles that later got infected.
>
> While they tortured me they asked me questions about the political activities of my son and about my participation in the People's Victory Party (PVP), to which they claimed

my son belonged. It was in this room where I could see, at one moment when the blindfold began to fall due to the intense perspiration, that on the wall there was a regular-sized portrait of Adolf Hitler.[96]

The Koch Amendment

Amid the wave of disappearances in Argentina and Uruguay, the US State Department's assistant secretary for inter-American affairs, Hewson A. Ryan, sent a letter to Representative Koch to deter him from pursuing the May 7 resolution that was still alive on the Senate floor and threatening to refuse Uruguay USAID funds for 1977. After denying the classification of the Uruguayan government as a military dictatorship, Ryan insisted that the human rights issues be taken on in private, claiming,

> We believe that our private diplomatic representations have had a positive effect in strengthening the Uruguayan Government's resolve to improve the human rights situation in that country . . . the Department does not believe that a legislated denial of assistance to Uruguay would serve the cause of human rights in that country or the interests of the United States in international affairs.

Throughout the letter, Ryan repeatedly emphasized that the human rights situation had improved greatly since the mass sweep of Tupamaros in mid-1972.[97] One day later, Ryan messaged Kissinger to assure him that the military's recent removal of President Juan Bordaberry would not affect US interests in Uruguay. He proclaimed, "The armed forces are moving quickly to restructure the government" and acknowledged that the Uruguayan military had hinted at remaining in power for at least a decade. He highlighted the military government's fragility due to frequent disagreements over political restructuring and emphasized that "friendly relations with Uruguay" could potentially become strained due to Koch's amendment because it would grant "military hardliners" an upper hand and "make it difficult for the moderate civilians and military leaders to improve Uruguay's human rights performance."[98]

Yet Representative Koch continued pursuing the goal of withdrawing USAID support and voicing concern for the lack of reporting on human rights violations. On July 19, Koch published an article in the *New York Times* claiming the US embassy "shuns the idea that there is a human rights problem in Uruguay." Ambassador Siracusa responded internally by declaring the claim to be "totally unwarranted, uninformed, and unfair." While the *Times* article triggered Siracusa's response, Secretary of State Kissinger also encouraged him to take a more active role refuting the narrative of US complicity.[99] Meanwhile, the US Bureau of Inter-American Affairs continued to intervene on the resolution and wrote Koch a letter calling his claims of US embassy complicity to be "completely unfounded."[100] On July 20, Ambassador Siracusa reiterated that Southern Cone military governments blamed an international Communist conspiracy for the rise in human rights campaigns and suggested that hostility and/or lack of sympathy from the US government would only further isolate its allies. He concluded:

> The US had long urged these countries to increase their cooperation for security. Now that they are doing so our reaction should not be one of opprobrium. We must condemn their abhorrent methods, but we cannot condemn their coordinated approach to common perceived threats, or we could well be effectively alienated from this part of the world. When Pinochet, Bordaberry, and Banzer spoke of their deep concern of new forms of intervention in their internal affairs and of the need for more effective hemispheric security, they were addressing these same problems— and talking to us.[101]

In response to the pressure induced by the Koch amendment, Uruguayan high government officials called for a handful of detainees to be relocated from Orletti back home to Uruguay.

On July 24, a flight left from Buenos Aires to Montevideo carrying twenty-six hooded and handcuffed PVP militants alongside dozens of boxes of household goods obtained by officials during the June raids. Ana Quadros recalls overhearing conversations about the decision to transport detainees:

> I heard things, including from the place where they held reunions between Argentine and Uruguayan servicemen, military, and paramilitary. That place was right next to where they held me. I heard all of their conversations. The Uruguayans wanted to bring us back to Uruguay, and I had no idea why, but they wanted to bring us. But the Argentines were firmly against it—they said that one day "this," "all of this," could be known. They debated until, clearly, the Uruguayan position won. And they decided to transport us back to Uruguay.[102]

A tour bus brought detainees to a home located at Rambla República de México 5515, in Barrio Punta Gorda. Authorities eventually relocated detainees to holding cells at the SID headquarters, where they met with José Nino Gavazzo to continue discussions about the ransom money and the location of the independence flag.[103]

Now the growing evidence of Uruguay's international collaboration and human rights violations could not be ignored. In a July 30 meeting between members of the CIA and US State Department, participants recognized that Plan Cóndor had developed beyond serving as a shared intelligence network and instead morphed into a "more activist role, including specifically that of identifying, locating, and 'hitting' guerrilla leaders."[104] Thus, members of the US State Department grew more aware of the atrocities taking place in the region and the potential for such a climate to force a change in the US's relationship with Southern Cone governments.

On August 3, head of the US Bureau of Inter-American Affairs Harry W. Shlaudeman warned of a "siege mentality shading into paranoia" that had swept over the region, including in

Chile, Uruguay, and Argentina, where "despite near decimation of the Marxist left" the governments insisted that "the war must go on." He continued by referencing Uruguayan foreign minister Blanco, declaring, "Some talk of the 'Third World War,' with the countries of the southern cone as "the last bastion of Christian civilization." For Shlaudeman, the Third World War discourse that had begun circulating within more radical circles of the military regimes demonstrated "bothersome parallels with National Socialism" and a growing antagonism with the United States as a failed ally in the struggle against Communism due to internal government infiltration, growing domestic instability around civil rights, and a failed military venture in Vietnam. While the region's looming threat of a right-wing bloc threatened its further isolation from the West, the United States would indeed benefit as "casual beneficiaries." But such benefits would not come without consequences, given the international perception that the United States was responsible for and closely aligned with the Chilean government of Pinochet. To keep the region within the US sphere of influence yet distant enough to avoid enmeshment, Shlaudeman suggested four policy recommendations: (1) emphasize the differences between the six countries, (2) depoliticize human rights, (3) oppose rhetorical exaggerations, and (4) use systemic exchanges to keep potential bloc members in the US cognitive universe.[105]

Shlaudeman's first recommendation proved key for understanding the importance of maintaining strategic ties with the government of Uruguay. While the Argentine and Chilean military governments continued to attract negative attention internationally, the Brazilian military government had remained stubbornly in power for over a decade and, although less prone to extremism due to its self-perceived role as a rising global power, continued "cooperating short of murder operations." Uruguay thus proved to be highly important to prevent formation of a bloc of the four largest economies in the region. While Shlaudeman suggested a policy that refrained from broad generalizations and instead favored highlighting "what the countries do not have in common rather than what they do," Koch's bill shed light on a human rights crisis in Uruguay that had gone under the radar for more than three years, during which both governments had enjoyed what Ambassador Siracusa repeatedly emphasized as friendly relations. Thus, the bill threatened those amicable relations by lumping together Uruguay with its far more belligerent neighbors, Argentina and Chile, and perhaps pushing them to join such a bloc. Although still a civil-military government with civilians "up front," Uruguayan foreign minister Blanco's coinage of the "Third World War" discourse demonstrated the government's growing eagerness to cooperate with its neighbors. The loss of Uruguay potentially left only Bolivia and Paraguay within the US's sphere of influence. Both majority nonwhite nations with highly underdeveloped economies, the former hovered on the verge of military intervention due to paranoia of a left uprising to avenge the country's role in Che Guevara's death, and the latter maintained a cryptic nineteenth-century-style dictatorship under the rule of Alfredo Stroessner.[106] Neither proved strategic for asserting a strong presence in the region or shifting foreign perceptions.

As news about the growing brutality of the Argentine dictatorship circulated globally alongside an Amnesty International report on human rights violations in Uruguay, Ambassador Siracusa confronted Uruguayan Army chief of staff Queirolo and Army commander in chief Vadora more directly. This time, Ambassador Siracusa clearly changed his tone regarding the reality of Plan Cóndor operations. Instead of trivializing the disappearances of roughly thirty Uruguayan exiles and their subsequent torture at the hands of a Uruguayan officer, Siracusa acknowledged that the Uruguayan government's public silence on the matter continued to raise suspicion. Yet he continued to paint a positive picture of human rights within Uruguay, specifically referencing the decreased number of political prisoners and state policy against the use of torture: he stubbornly debated that the official number of political prisoners sat at 2,017, as opposed to the 5,500 claimed in the Amnesty International report. Regarding torture, he denounced two reports of "psychological" torture by the hooding of prisoners but insisted that the cases did not reflect standard practice.[107]

By late August, the reports of human rights violations in the Southern Cone became so rampant that many US officials felt they had lost control. The US State Department warned embassies in Argentina, Uruguay, Chile, and Bolivia against sharing information about "individual subversives" while still encouraging information exchange about "general level" subversive activity. The telegram concluded, "It is essential that we in no way finger individuals who might be candidates for assassination attempts." More specific to Uruguay, the State Department suggested that Ambassador Siracusa begin communicating with General Vadora instead of Foreign Minister Juan Carlos Blanco, who it marked as an extremist after he became one of the region's main proponents of the Third World War thesis.[108] In mid-September Ambassador Siracusa met with both Foreign Minister Blanco and newly installed Uruguayan president Aparicio Méndez.[109] All parties agreed that recent approval of the Koch resolution, though detrimental to Uruguay's public image, was much preferred vis-à-vis executive implementation of the Harkin Amendment, which would block $85.4 million of Inter-American Development Bank loans while giving a clear impression of executive opposition rather than dissent by a congressional fringe. According to Foreign Minister Blanco, such a measure could spark a reaction that was "not only bitter and resentful, but highly nationalistic."[110] President Méndez confessed to the validity of various human rights violations reported in the Koch amendment but expressed confidence in the US government's commitment to maintaining a "friendly disposition toward Uruguay," one rooted in the "understanding and sympathy due to a friend." While President Méndez also admitted that transition to democracy in Uruguay depended greatly on the success of the Argentine and Brazilian governments' counterrevolutionary campaigns, all parties agreed on the importance of President Méndez's announcement to replace the Prompt Security Measures (MPS) with a new law on a "State of Danger" and right to due process.[111]

On September 16, the US Senate introduced a bill containing the Koch Amendment. After two weeks of debates in the House and Senate, Congress passed the Koch Amendment prohibiting USAID money, military training, and weapons sales to the Uruguayan government due to its human rights violations. President Méndez responded by publicly criticizing Uruguayan exile Wilson Ferreira Aldunate for being menaced by "foreign ideology." He also denounced Representative Koch for having ties with "international communism."[112]

However, the resolution's approval came too late to save the lives of roughly two dozen PVP militants, who were permanently disappeared during the final days of the congressional debates. The late-September offensive led to the recovery of $6 million of the ransom money after the capture of PVP militants Beatriz Castellonese and Elena Laguna. Two Joint Forces officers coerced the women and their children on a commercial flight to Montevideo, during which the officers posed as their husbands.[113] Three days after the congressional vote, the US Department of Defense shared an Intelligence Information Report from Buenos Aires announcing that, beginning September 24, the Argentine SIDE and Uruguayan SID had conducted a three-day joint operation to "eliminate" the entire infrastructure of the "OPR-33" in Argentina. While the report did not provide details regarding the fate of OPR-33 militants, it did acknowledge a "third and reportedly very secret phase" that included state collaboration with "special agents" to carry out assassinations of terrorists and "supporters of terrorist organizations," including the expansion of counterinsurgency networks to both France and Portugal. The report recognized that Plan Cóndor had become normalized throughout the region and that military officers had begun to speak openly about the project after previously keeping silent about the topic, stating, "A favorite remark is that, 'one of their colleagues is out of the country because he is flying like a condor.'"[114] The militants likely disappeared on an October 5 "second flight" from Buenos Aires to Montevideo, shortly after the recovery of the outstanding other $2 million.[115]

The Koch Amendment's congressional support prompted a meeting between high officials of the US State Department and Foreign Minister Blanco in Washington, DC. Regardless of the abundance of information regarding Uruguay's participation in transnational human rights violations, State Department officials maintained a sympathetic tone, choosing to focus instead primarily on domestic improvements in the treatment of political prisoners. US acting secretary of state Charles W. Washington declared:

> One of the basic problems Uruguay faces in the United States with regard to human rights is the absence of appreciation for the difficulties with which the country has had to cope. Human rights are relatively academic until a system has been established that permits individual freedoms. When subversive activities threaten the overthrow of a government, that government must take appropriate steps, and when it does so these steps are interpreted here as violations of human rights. This perspective is reflected in our Congress. The United States is a stable country and thus the people have very broad rights; consequently, U.S. citizens react when people abroad do not enjoy the same human rights. The U.S. believes in human rights but must see them in relation to the problems existing in any particular place.[116]

Foreign Minister Blanco seized the opportunity to situate Uruguay as victim by reiterating that charges of human rights violations had been trumped up and that the political violence in Uruguay was minimal compared to places like Lebanon and Cambodia. He celebrated the Uruguayan government's successful bid at countering armed left organizations with a death count on both sides totaling below two hundred people, and thus lamented the fact that Uruguay remained branded as a "chamber of torturers." He noted that the recent release of 1,800 political prisoners had cut the total number of jailed militants in half, and that the Amnesty International reports on human rights abuses would have never existed had the Uruguayan government "simply killed the terrorists and dumped them in the Río de la Plata" rather than holding them in jail "under better conditions than ordinary criminals." He assured State Department officials of the Uruguayan military's sensitivity toward human rights, proclaiming, "These are people who go to Church and take Holy Communion."[117]

After the Storm, the Spectacle: Military Simulacra and "Chalet Suzy"

While Uruguayan officials continued to play down the negative consequences of the Koch bill vis-à-vis the use of the Harkin Amendment, word of a July 1976 death threat against Representative Koch circulated in communications between the US Embassy in Uruguay and US State Department. On October 20, FBI agent Richard T. Taylor finally notified Koch of a July 23 comment made by Uruguayan Colonel José Fons, in which he declared, "Maybe Uruguay would have to send someone to the United States to get him."[118] After the recent car bomb assassination of ex–Chilean ambassador Orlando Letelier in Washington, DC, the CIA took what had previously been considered a drunken comment much more seriously and finally reported it to the FBI and State Department. While US officials previously understood that Cóndor-linked governments would not realize "operations" outside of the region, recent activities, including a Uruguayan and Argentine joint plot to "operate against" Hugo Cores in his Paris home, demonstrated that this was no longer the case.[119]

The comment raised even more questions due to the Uruguayan government's appointment of Fons as vice president of the Inter-American Defense Board and Gavazzo as defense attaché in the Uruguayan embassy, which would relocate both officers to DC. While the former was designated as a "plum to a Senior Colonel not likely to make General," Gavazzo received the appointment "to get him out of the day-to-day fight with terrorists because he had been burned and is known." The appointments also served as a reward for the men's service in recovering the PVP ransom funds. While Fons had previously informed Ambassador Siracusa that the Uruguayan government never seriously considered Cóndor operations within the United States due to the high risk and inevitable blowback, the officers' coincidental assignment stirred suspicion in DC, where officials sought to refuse them entry to the country. Ambassador Siracusa, who felt offended about being last to receive word of the assassination plot, reaffirmed that the probability of a Uruguayan attack on US soil remained slim and highlighted Fons's reputation as a "loose talker." He begrudg-ingly advised State Department officials to deny access to both Uruguayans due to the potential for political violence. Fons had already expressed fears of being subject to attack due to his partic-ipation in anti-terrorism campaigns. Thus, Siracusa suggested to play off those fears to avoid having to give further explanations.[120]

The Uruguayan government's anxiety about loss of US finan-cial support peaked on October 26, when officials staged a raid on a fake FAU-PVP safe house in the Montevideo suburb of Shangrila. Three days prior to the raid, Joint Forces officers had transported detainees Asilú Maceiro, Ana Quadros, Sara Méndez, Elba Rama, and Sergio López from the First Battalion deten-tion facility to a fictitious safe house named "Chalet Suzy." Upon arriving to the temporarily rented house, officers insisted that the militants eat well and groom themselves since they remained in poor physical health, having returned months prior on the first flight from Orletti. Officers curated the space with PVP propa-ganda and ViloX products. They stored guns and ammunition in the fireplace and built a small bunker below the living room to emulate a people's prison. Finally, they frequently shook furni-ture, banged walls, and yelled suspiciously to give neighbors the impression of something strange was occurring on their block. The militants witnessed the performance as they anticipated the government's next move.

On the morning of October 26, two female militants accom-panied their officer captors to the meat market and corner store. While sharing a meal that afternoon, the officers warned the detainees of the arranged military operation at 3 p.m. Upon finish-ing the meal, officers covered the detainees' faces with hoods and instructed them to wait in the living room. A team of television reporters set up their equipment in front of the house before the arrival of military units shortly after. True to schedule, a squadron of vehicles surrounded the house and General Ricardo Medina stepped forward with a megaphone, announcing, "Subversives, give up. Present yourselves!" Officers inside responded by shout-ing slogans, like "Hasta la victoria siempre." Detainees remained hooded inside the house as the officers made more suspicious sounds and shouted back to Medina. After the short verbal exchange, the forces outside staged a siege. They received the hooded militants and escorted them out of the house where they were de-hooded and instructed to present themselves before the squadron.[121] Upon leaving the house, the detainees were greeted by Uruguayan press, who took their photos and requested their names to publish in media outlets, which they readily supplied. The detainees then left the site in paddy wagons and headed toward a large field across from the Centennial Stadium. There, they met with other militants who had also been "recently captured" in what Joint Forces presented as a large, organized raid on various safe houses and hotels. The officers took advantage of the large crowd that had gathered at the stadium to witness a championship match between domestic football clubs Defensor and Peñarol. Hooded and shackled, militants were unloaded from the vehicles and lined up in the field, which resembled a temporary military camp. Police and military vehicles arrived one by one with sirens blaring to capture the spectators' attention. Once all detainees were present at the field, the Joint Forces loaded them back in the trucks and caravanned down Montevideo's main avenues with sirens blaring. The procession finally arrived at a press conference, where officers presented militant Ana Quadros as the face of the sixty-two guerrillas they claimed to have captured in the day's raids. The list of detainees included many militants who remained disappeared or secretly murdered in Buenos Aires, including Gerardo Gatti and other FAU-PVP militants "transferred" on the second flight.[122]

On October 30, 1976, the Italian National Associated Press Agency (ANSA) and US-based Associated Press published the story of the sixty-two captured PVP militants, basing the content on a press release from the Uruguayan Joint Forces. Argentina's *La Nación* printed the story in an article titled "The plans of the group recently destroyed in Uruguay," which claimed that the PVP had been plotting to assassinate at least eight government officials and businessmen both within Uruguay and the exterior, including Foreign Minister Juan Carlos Blanco, Ambassador to Brazil Carlos Manini Rios, and president of Club Atletico Peñarol Washington

Cataldi, among others. The report further claimed that the PVP planned to set up foreign bases of operation, specifically in Buenos Aires and Southern Brazil, to shelter other guerrillas upon returning from assassination operations within Uruguay. The text concluded with a declaration from General and Comander of the Fourth Division Gregorio Àlvarez:

> We are mending the gaping wounds in Uruguayan society. Subtly, thanks to our politicians, Marxism has infiltrated and seeped into Uruguayan society during the last thirty years, specifically among the most sensitive classes in a way that these wounds are going to take some time. At this time, Uruguay is gaining back consciousness that it should be the owner of its own destiny and that it shouldn't draw on foreign and alienating slogans nor ideas to move into the future.[123]

Realistically, PVP had no plans to assassinate any government officials aside from José Nino Gavazzo, who they passed up after trailing his whereabouts for nearly five weeks earlier that same year. While many PVP militants saw such an operation as an opportunity to seek personal vengeance, they remained committed to a strategy of mass movement building, even as their comrades faced violence at the hands of government officials.[124]

However, the theatrics took place too late to win over either US congressional opinion regarding USAID money or State Department officials' acceptance of the DC appointments. Assistant Secretary Shlaudeman still recognized that the appointment of Fons and Gavazzo would bring "unfavorable publicity damaging to relations between the two countries."[125] The situation spun even more out of control when two orphaned children mysteriously appeared in Valparaiso's Plaza O'Higgins on December 29. The siblings, Antatole Julien Grisona (four years old) and Victoria Julien Gisona (one year old), had been flown to Chile after being abducted from their parents, PVP militants Victoria Grisona and Roger Julien, who were permanently disappeared during the September 1976 offensive in Buenos Aires.[126] With the curtain swiftly raising on the Uruguayan government, the US State Department could not afford to risk the backlash of another potential attack on US soil by officers from a Cóndor-affiliated nation. On December 31, Shlaudeman finally informed the Uruguayan ambassador of the decision to deny visas to Fons and Gavazzo—a development that marked a clear turning point in US-Uruguayan relations.[127]

In January 1977, Jimmy Carter assumed the US presidency, launching a shift in relations with the Southern Cone due to his emphasis on human rights. While Southern Cone military governments became increasingly antagonistic to the United States for the duration of Carter's regime, the Chalet Suzy case shows that tensions had already begun during the government of his predecessor, Gerald Ford. When Lawrence Pezzullo took over duties as US ambassador to Uruguay, he recalled:

> It was really shocking. We had an embassy in Uruguay that was an apologist for the Uruguayan government. . . . They knew nothing. . . . You've got to sift out fact from fiction. An embassy can find things out if you want to. Once you find them out you can stand your ground. We had no factual evidence at the embassy. . . . How many in prison? In what conditions? Who does it? Who tortures? Where? Who gives instructions?[128]

While the Carter administration provided a shift in tone, the Uruguayan government continued smaller scale Plan Cóndor operations for the duration of his presidency without US backing. The disappearing of PVP militants would continue for the next two years, extending across borders into Paraguay and Brazil. In March 1977, Paraguayan authorities detained militants Gustavo Inzaurralde and Nelson Santana at the Argentine border. Both were permanently disappeared. In November 1978, militants Lilián Celiberti and Universindo Rodríguez were kidnapped in Porto Alegre, Brazil, as part of a campaign to locate Hugo Cores, who had been moving between France, Mexico, and Brazil in order to meet with exiles to devise an updated political strategy.

Brazilian military forces held the couple hostage in their Porto Alegre home for five days before extraditing them to Uruguay, where the government announced their imprisonment and detention upon encountering prohibited political material at the border. Brazilian journalist Luiz Cláudio Cunha challenged the government's narrative by testifying to having been held hostage upon visiting the couple's home while authorities occupied it. He utilized his platform in the magazine *Veja* to contest the government's fabrication. Given that the government of João Figueiredo had supposedly initiated a transition to democracy four years prior, Brazilian citizens felt shocked and deceived by the news.[129]

Plan Cóndor would not conclude until in the mid-eighties with the fall of the Argentine, Brazilian, and Uruguayan military governments. By then, Southern Cone dictatorships would combine to permanently disappear upward of thirty-five thousand people.

Conclusion

On December 10, 1976, Hugo Cores penned a letter while exiled in Paris in which the first use of the word "disappeared" surfaced in the public lexicon.[130] He used the word twice to describe his experience in detention, both times in quotation marks—an indication that the word had not yet been normalized, as it would be in the next few years. Cores declared:

> Just as it began happening in our country beginning three years ago, and as it happens in Argentina to hundreds of labor militants, students, and revolutionaries, I was tortured for eight days. During those long days for my family, I was "disappeared.". . . Dozens and dozens of declarations, proclamations, and telegrams demonstrated the broad concern around my case to the Argentine authorities. That is how we managed to break not only the fence of silence that existed about the situation of the "disappeared" in Argentina, but also what allowed for my freedom.[131]

Yet, internal communications between regional military officials and members of the US State Department began utilizing the term "disappeared" as early as August 1976.[132] The use of the term among state actors several months before its surfacing in public discourse demonstrates a degree of consensus around the tactic of disappearance.

Although the Uruguayan military government earned the infamous title of "Latin America's Torture Chamber" primarily due to its treatment of domestic political prisoners, an exploration of its anti-subversion policy abroad sheds new light on its logic of disappearance. From 1968 to 1978, the Uruguayan government detained upward of fifty-five thousand political prisoners for varying periods of time. Stunningly, one in thirty adult Uruguayans spent time in prison; 80 percent of those imprisoned experienced torture—that's one in sixty-two adult Uruguayans.[133] Throughout the Dirty War, 172 Uruguayans were permanently disappeared in eight different countries. Of the total number disappeared, 136 belonged to political organizations: the MLN-T (42), FAU-PVP (35), PCU (23), GAU (19), Revolutionary Communist Party (9), Montoneros (5), and three additional independent anarchists.[134] The vast majority, 138 Uruguayans, were disappeared from 1976 to 1978, of whom 119 were disappeared in Argentina.[135] Of the thirty-five disappeared FAU-PVP militants, thirty-four were disappeared in Argentina between April 1976 and April 1977. Notably, their cases provide the first examples of transnational cooperation to detain and disappear Uruguayan political militants during the Plan Cóndor era. While the GAU and MLN-T also suffered substantial losses in Argentina during this time (eighteen and twenty-five members respectively), state offensives against both organizations occurred well after those against the FAU-PVP.[136] Because the FAU-PVP suffered more disappearances than any other Uruguayan political organization while in exile, the cases of permanent disappearance of their militants provide key evidence for understanding Plan Cóndor's logic, infrastructure, and practical application.

While both academic and popular narratives about the global Cold War accurately recognize the centrality of the dualistic narrative of capitalism versus communism—most commonly represented by the struggle between the United States and Soviet Union for global geopolitical hegemony—such a narrative fails to capture the wide range of political ideologies and actors who were historical protagonists in this era. While the FAU-PVP remained peripheral to long-term US political interests and intervention in the region, the group became a central concern for early Cóndor-era US foreign policy. The FAU-PVP's transnational infrastructure, mass movement presence, and armed apparatus situated the small organization as among a powerful Southern Cone New Left—a movement of movements.

Conclusion

Un Pueblo Fuerte and All Power to the People

During an interview with Augusto Andrés, I asked him to look at my spreadsheet of labor conflicts and recall whether or not he remembered if they ended victoriously or not. In my effort to quantify workplace conflicts throughout the era, I hoped to encounter a pattern that proved direct action tactics were more apt for "winning" conflicts vis-à-vis negotiation. Upon receiving this question, Andrés responded, "What do mean you want to know if we won? You only win when you make the revolution." While the rarity of a Cold War–era armed anarchist organization stirred my initial interest in the project, I learned quickly from the militants themselves that the importance of the armed apparatus was secondary to everyday people's organizing in their workplaces. Yet, for the sake of an investigation, this stance proved the most difficult to narrate and analyze due to its diffused and under-documented nature. Most importantly, such a posture shifted the focus away from political organizations and toward everyday people as catalysts for social transformation. The FAU accompanied and encouraged everyday people who confronted their workplace conditions, as these experiences proved vital to understanding the logic of the market and state, and their place within such nexus of power. Indeed, it was through collective struggles that everyday people experienced subjective transformation more in line with the values and skills necessary for a revolutionary society. Ultimately, as Andrés's response to my question illustrated, the success or failure of a given workplace conflict proved trivial, as the underlying, irresolvable systemic contradictions would only produce more

conflicts in the immediate future. While "victories" were important for building working-class morale, the only true victory would
come when such battles would become unthinkable because the
contradictions that produce them would be obliterated.

Anarchism's unique influence in Cold War–era Uruguay can
only be explained by the FAU's willingness to transform the ideology into something relevant for the time. Those who envisioned
these changes did so with the intention of building popular power,
toward *un pueblo fuerte* (a strong people). These strong people
would produce and reproduce the utopian continent-wide anarchist federation of workers and consumers councils. They would
follow a pattern of transformation already in stride and alive in the
Cuban model. While the FAU remained critical of *foco*, they had to
recognize its relevance for encouraging everyday people take on a
role as historical protagonists. The heyday of anarcho-syndicalism
had ended, but a new mass politics was sweeping the continent,
and the FAU recognized its spirit to be shaped by libertarian ideals
of autonomy, emancipation, and self-determination.

However, the conditions in which the FAU organized were
unique to the massive shifts taking place in Uruguay's political
economy. Certainly, everyday people were influenced by the revolutionary fervor taking hold throughout the continent. But they
were also organically responding to a devolving material reality
that forewarned of the broader neoliberal crisis that would plague
Latin America for the latter quarter of the twentieth century.
While the FAU never overtook the Communist Party as majority representatives of the labor movement, Uruguayan workers
organically confronted their declining conditions with a rep-
ertoire of tactics advocated for by the FAU. At many work sites,
colleagues shared diverse, and often opposing, political views.
Certainly, very few people identified as anarchists. But ideology
showed its limitations when official channels proved insufficient
for resolving a crisis brought on by global historical forces, both
political and economic, that most everyday people couldn't care
less to understand. Meanwhile, they faced the realities of factory
closures, mass layoffs, wage theft, back pay, and anti-union policies, and they responded to them with a rage and dignity that

mirrored anarchist values of direct action and mutual aid. As such, the FAU did not concern themselves with growing membership or votes in support of the organization. Instead, militants aimed to free the social and political climate of its hegemonic influences, encouraging everyday people to react to their realities as they saw fit for themselves, on their own terms. Although everyday people were certainly not prepared to take up arms and face the military, their willingness to challenge oppressive conditions at their workplaces demonstrated a move toward dissident counter-hegemonic subjectivity that prefigured social relations in a revolutionary society. These "new men" would sustain collectivized production in the rear guard while the FAU's "little motor" confronted the state's armed forces. But things never got that far. Although the prospect of revolution remained far in the distance, even beyond the curve of the horizon, the FAU saw everyday people's accumulated experiences as integral to achieving any real alternative in the first place.

They certainly did enough to receive the full wrath of the market and state. Evidence of everyday people's outrage can be seen in the number of people who passed through the carceral system at the time. While we know very little about who these people were—in most cases we do not even know their names—the exceptionally high proportion of imprisonment (one in thirty adults) and torture (one in sixty-two adults) shows the degree to which the Uruguayan state saw a potential threat in the entirety of the population. Whereas the total number of PCU, MLN-T, and FAU militants likely totaled less than thirteen thousand, a total of fifty-five thousand people passed through Uruguay's prisons in the decade after 1968. With the onset of dictatorship on June 27, 1973, this process of building revolutionary popular power was brought to a halt by a violent civic-military government that permanently left in question the full potential of these everyday people.

Postscript

It was midday overlooking the Hamburg docks. Two men chatted over a beer. One was Phillip Agee, who was the CIA director in Uruguay. The other was me.

The sun does not appear much at these latitudes, but the table was soaked with light.

One beer after another, I asked about the fire. Some years prior, Época, the newsletter where I had worked, went up in flames. I wanted to know if the CIA had anything to do with it.

No, said Agee. The fire was a gift from God. He later said: "We received a lot of money to burn printing presses, but we couldn't use it."

The CIA could not get through to a single affiliate of our newsletter's workshop, nor could they recruit a single one of our graphic artists. The director of our workshop did not let a single one pass. He was a great goalkeeper, Agee recalled. Era un gran arquero.

Yes, he was. I said.

Gerardo Gatti, with such a gentle look on his face, was a great goalkeeper. He also knew how to play the attack. When we encountered one another in Hamburg, Agee had split with the CIA, a military government ruled over Uruguay, and Gerardo had been kidnapped, tortured, killed, and disappeared.

—EDUARDO GALEANO, *CERRADO POR FÚTBOL*

261

Some survivors of the mid-1976 offensive in Argentina fled to countries throughout Latin America and Europe. Other survivors were fortunate enough to fall prisoner in Uruguay prior to the coup and thus remained incarcerated throughout the massacre. While all imprisoned militants suffered torture, those arrested prior to the coup were released at the fall of the dictatorship in 1985. Exiles maintained written communication and sent care packages to captive comrades back home in Uruguay. Some even sent monthly economic contributions to prisoners' families to supplement the lack of income. Only Gilberto Coughlan and Elena Quinteros, both arrested during the dictatorship era, died while imprisoned in Uruguay.

Upon the fall of Uruguay's civic-military government in 1985, militants reconvened from all over the world and set out to rebuild the FAU. Some came from Bolivia, where they participated in the formation of a local cell of the Túpac Amaru Revolutionary Movement and organized miners alongside longtime anarchist ally Liber Forti. Some ventured from Costa Rica, later convening in Nicaragua, where they connected with the Sandinista National Liberation Front. Others arrived from Europe, where they had met up with Basque anarchist Lucio Urtubia to counterfeit $20 million worth of Citibank traveler's checks—money used to finance left struggles globally, including Italy's Red Brigades, Nicaragua's Sandinistas, Basque territory's ETA, and the ongoing human rights campaigns in Latin America. Numerous protagonists in this story continue doing political work as members of the FAU. Others saw their politics shift to more Marxist-Leninist tendencies and joined Hugo Cores in the PVP electoral party, which was a part of the Broad Front coalitional governments of José "Pepe" Mujica (2010–15) and Tabaré Vázquez (2005–10; 2015–20). The party formed in 1978 when Cores and other exiles in Europe abandoned the prospect of revolution and formalized a new political coalition around the fight to return to liberal democracy. Cores, who passed away in 2006, maintained that anarchists inevitably mature politically toward a vanguard party politics over time. Cores has been widely recognized as the brain behind the Marxist-anarchist synthesis of the late sixties.

When the topic of the split surfaced in conversations with interlocutors, I got the impression that they were exhausted talking about it. Conflicting narratives surface regarding the PVP's formation as a party. Those who currently belong to the PVP argue that exiled militants participating in the 1975 congress in Buenos Aires voted to transform into a vanguard party rather than maintain an anarchist politics. Current FAU members, in contrast, say that the decision was made after ROE absorbed militants from FER-FRT who formed a vanguardist politics through their experiences in MLN-T. Moreover, a handful of the FAU's old-guard militants were imprisoned in Uruguay at the time of this vote and could not participate in the congress. In discussing such sentiments with younger FAU militants and others in the region who have investigated the FAU's trajectory, I get the feeling that there remains a deep wound among those who experienced the split. My impression is that the wound is related less to political strategy and more to a sense of betrayal. The FAU was like a family. Its underground clandestine nature tended toward a structure of many cells made up of romantically involved couples and family members. Militants grew to know one another intimately, especially those who had belonged to the organization for nearly two decades by the time of the 1976 crackdown in Buenos Aires. Cores himself belonged to that generation of FAU militants, which made the split even more emotionally difficult and confusing to his comrades. In writing this book, I intentionally avoided extensive attention to the dynamics of the congress and the subsequent split because I do not find it relevant to understanding the FAU's prior decade of activity in an explosive labor movement—the core focus of this study.

Regardless of which side of the split they fell on, all survivors continued participating in the ongoing human rights campaign by offering court testimonies condemning Argentine and Uruguayan politicians and military officers. In 2010, a Uruguayan court sentenced both ex-president Juan María Bordaberry and ex-foreign minister Juan Carlos Blanco to twenty years in prison. While the former was convicted of treason against the Uruguayan constitution, the latter was sentenced specifically for his role in the disappearance of FAU militant Elena Quinteros. Bordaberry's incarceration marks only the second time in Latin American history that an ex-dictator was sentenced to prison by his own country's judicial system.

For over a decade, courts in Argentina, Uruguay, and Rome have pursued justice for the atrocities committed at Orletti and other clandestine detention, torture, and extermination sites in Argentina. In March 2011, Raúl Guglielminetti was sentenced to twenty years in Argentine prison for the kidnapping and torture of over twenty people.[1] Guglielminetti, an Argentine military officer and member of the Triple A taskforce operating Orletti, was involved in selling off property from the disappeared and managing a Miami-based money laundering operation that funneled tens of millions of dollars in Bolivian drug money to the Nicaraguan contras after the Cocaine Coup of 1980.[2] Dozens of FAU and PVP militants provided key testimonies in an Argentine trial to condemn the murderers and torturers who operated Automotres Orletti. On May 27, 2016, eighteen Argentine military officers received prison sentences of varying lengths for their ties to Plan Cóndor.[3] The most recent conviction concluded on September 11, 2017, when four Argentine ex–federal police were each sentenced to sixteen years in prison. One, Rolando Oscar Nerone, was extradited for trial from Brazil, where he was living a secret life in Rio de Janeiro's bohemian neighborhood of Santa Teresa. While there, he had informed neighbors that he was an exiled leftist militant who had escaped the Argentine military junta. The fortunate timing of my research has granted me the opportunity to accompany many interlocutors as they experienced the joy, relief, and satisfaction of the legal victory. Militants, many in their early seventies, still have chronic health issues from their experience with being tortured.

Yet many officers, high political authorities, and civilian accomplices from both countries have yet to be convicted. In the late eighties, Santiago Cortell, who owned the workshop in which Automotores Orletti was located, returned to inhabit the space with his family, using wallpaper and plaster to cover hundreds of bullet holes. In 2006, Argentina's government under President

Nestor Kirschner expropriated the building and converted it into one of various spaces for historical memory of the country's Dirty War. In a 2011 trial, Cortell denied having any knowledge of what had occurred at his property. He relocated to a new house only five blocks away, where he still lives today.[4]

Notes

Preface

1. Susana Draper and Verónica Gago, "Las Luchas como escuela," *Jacobin*, August 2, 2022, https://jacobinlat.com/2022/08/02/las -luchas-como-escuela.
2. "Platformism" is the name attributed to an approach to anarchist organization developed after the defeat of the working class during the Russian Revolution, and subsequent growth of Marxist-Leninism.
3. José Batlle y Ordóñez was in power from 1903 to 1907 and 1911 to 1915.
4. The Peronist era ran from 1946 to 1955. It saw General Juan Domingo Perón integrate organized labor into the state and make working-class culture, identity, and interests synonymous with that of the Argentine nation. The Peronist model drew input from unionized labor in state economic planning.

Introduction

1. David Harvey's *A Brief History of Neoliberalism* declares, "All forms of social solidarity were to be dissolved in favor of individualism, private property, personal responsibility, and family values." The emphasis on the hyper-individual is best captured in Francis Fukuyama's *The End of History and the Last Man*, which argues that the conclusion of the Cold War had broken humanity from the constraints of history, leaving individuals free to make their own futures by one's own merit. This new subject, an individual, is imagined as a rational actor who places economic motives at the forefront of decision making rather than any moral obligation to a particular ideology or responsibility to a collective or group. In the conclusion of *The Last Colonial Massacre: Latin America during the Cold War*, Greg Grandin recognizes how this process played out in Cold War Latin

America, declaring: "[The] divorce between self and solidarity—two qualities that are, after all, the defining essences of liberal democracy and socialism—was the fundamental requirement of Latin America's neoliberal regimes. Democracy is now by a shade of its former substance. This is Cold War terror's most important legacy." David Harvey, *A Brief History of Neoliberalism* (New York: Oxford University Press, 2009); Francis Fukuyama, *The End of History and the Last Man* (New York: Free Press, 1992); and Greg Grandin, *The Last Colonial Massacre: Latin America during the Cold War* (Chicago: University of Chicago Press, 2004), 198.

2.   The FAU departed from the reform-versus-revolution debate emblematized by the Moscow-inspired Uruguayan Communist Party (PCU)'s electoral strategy and the Cuba-inspired MLN-T's guerrilla strategy. Uruguayan historians Jaime Yaffe and Aldo Marchesi recognize how scholars reproduce this debate by speaking monolithically about the Uruguayan labor movement and by giving too much weight to the MLN-T. While both the PCU and MLN-T were indeed hegemonic, they saw strong competition from the FAU, who challenged the PCU's electoral strategy and the MLN-T's paramilitary strategy. As anarchists, the FAU saw an equivalent shortcoming among both political rivals due to their emphasis on taking over the state. The FAU were strong proponents of coalition building and collaboration with both the PCU and MLN-T, but they remained autonomous; they saw both rivals' strategies as inevitably leading to failure. While New Left organizations globally gained a reputation for refusal to dialogue and/or collaborate with political rivals, instead writing them off as reactionary or reformist, the FAU set out to debate the ideological foundations and subsequent strategies of each rival organization in the spaces where they were hegemonic and did so with a significant amount of success and popularity among working-class and student demographics. See Aldo Marchesi and Jaime Yaffe, "La violencia bajo la lupa: Una revisión de la literatura sobre violencia y política en los sesenta," *Revista Uruguaya de Ciencia Política*, vol. 19, no. 1 (2010): 95–118.

3.   Christian Ferrer, "Misterio y jerarquia: Sobre la inasimable del anarquismo," in *Cabezas de tormenta: Ensayos sobre el ingobernable* (Buenos Aires: Anarres, 2004), 66.

4.   Benedict Anderson, preface to Steven Hirsch and Lucien van der Walt, eds., *Anarchism and Syndicalism in the Colonial and Postcolonial World, 1870–1940* (New York: Brill, 2010).

5.   Ferrer, "Misterio y jerarquia," 71.

6.   Most research on mid- to late-twentieth-century anarchism has been conducted by nonacademics located within the movement. There are a few exceptions to this trend among scholars, such as

Andrew Cornell's *Unruly Equality: U.S. Anarchism in the Twentieth Century* (Oakland: University of California Press, 2016), which explores US anarchist militants' contributions to civil rights, anti-war, feminist, and environmental movements of the New Left.

7.   Among the existing historiography, most works that touch significantly on the FAU focus specifically on the organization, especially its internal politics. They are especially interested in (1) the organization's ideological contributions syncretizing anarchism with Third World Marxism and (2) their unique conceptualization of armed struggle. Texts include Rodrigo Vescovi, *Anarquismo y acción directa en Uruguay, 1968–1973* (Barcelona: Editorial Descontrol, 2015); and Daniel Agusto de Almeida Alves, "Arriba los que luchan! Sindicalismo revolucionario e luta armada. A trajectória da federaçao anarquista uruguaia: 1963–1973," unpublished PhD diss., Universidade Federal do Rio Grande do Sul, Porto Alegre, 2016. Rafael Viana da Silva's recent dissertation compares anarchist responses to Dirty War dictatorships in Argentina, Brazil, and Uruguay. While the study is unique in offering a comprehensive examination of regional anarchism in the Cold War era, it is still primarily concerned with internal debates and dynamics within the movement. Rafael Viana da Silva, "Um anarquismo latino-americano: Estudo comparativo e transnacional das experiencias na Argentina, Brasil, e Uruguai (1959–1985)," unpublished PhD diss., Universidade Federal Rural do Rio de Janeiro, 2018.

Many ex-militants of the FAU have contributed well-researched studies of the time period and organization. While they intersect archival research, interviews, and personal anecdote to provide rich narratives, they lack often lack analysis and thus may be better categorized as primary sources rather than historiographical contributions. See Raúl Olivera and Sara Méndez, *Hugo Cores: La memoria combatiente* (Montevideo: Editorial Trilce, 2007); Ivonne Trías, *Hugo Cores: Pasión y rebeldía en la izquierda uruguaya* (Montevideo: Editorial Trilce, 2008); Hugo Cores, *Memorias de la resistencia* (Montevideo: Ediciones Banda Oriental, 2002); Ivonne Trías, *Gerardo Gatti: Revolucionario* (Montevideo: Editorial Trilce, 2008); Augusto Andrés, *Estafar un banco—que placer! Y otras historias* (Montevideo: AlterEdiciones, 2009); Juan Carlos Mechoso, *Acción directa anarquista: Una historia de FAU*, vol. 4 (Montevideo: Ediciones Recortes, 2005).

8.   James Baer, *Anarchist Immigrants in Spain and Argentina* (Champagne: University of Illinois, 2015); José Moya, *Cousins and Strangers* (Berkeley: University of California, 1998); Osvaldo Bayer, "The Influence of Italian Immigration on the Argentine Anarchist Movement," Quilian Vos, trans., Libcom.org, https://libcom.org/library/influence-italian

-immigration-argentine-anarchist-movement-osvaldo-bayer, originally published in *Gli italioni fuori d'Italia*, Bruno Bezza, ed. (Milan:
Franco Angeli, 1983); Pascual Muñoz, *Antonio Loredo: Aletazos de Tormenta (El anarquismo revolucionario a comienzos del siglo XX)* (Montevideo: La Turba Ediciones, 2017).

9.   See Anton Rosenthal, "The Arrival of the Electric Streetcar and the
     Conflict over Progress in Early Twentieth Century Montevideo,"
     Journal of Latin American Studies, vol. 27, no. 2 (1995).

10. Carlos Rama and Ángel J. Cappelletti's *Anarquismo en America Latina*
     (1990) dedicates a chapter to the political ideology's development
     in Uruguay. The chapter recognizes the ideology's strong influence
     in literary circles, especially playwriters and poets, on both sides of
     the River Plate. Moreover, the authors paint a picture of frequent
     migration, communication, and exchange among anarchists in
     the River Plate beginning as far back as the ideology's arrival. See
     Ángel J. Cappelletti, *Anarchism in Latin America*, Gabriel Palmer-
     Fernández, trans. (Oakland: AK Press, 2018).

11. Geoffroy de LaForcade, "Federative Futures: Waterways, Resistance
     Societies, and the Subversion of Nationalism in the Early 20th-
     Century Anarchism of the Río de la Plata Region," *E.I.A.L.*, vol. 22,
     no. 2 (2011).

12. Gonzalo Zaragoza Ruvira, "Errico Malatesta y el anarquismo prole-
     tario," in *Historia y Bigliografia Americanistas*, vol. 16, no. 3 (1972).

13. de Laforcade, "Federative Futures," 73.

14. Ruth Thompson, "The Limitations of Ideology in the Early Argen-
     tine Labor Movement: Anarchism in Trade Unions, 1890–1920,"
     Journal of Latin American Studies, vol. 16, no. 1 (1984): 98.

15. Carlos M. Rama, "El movimiento obrero y social uruguayo y el Presi-
     dente Batlle," *Revista de Historia de América*, no. 46 (1958); Jorge Buscio
     and José Batlle y Ordoñez, *Uruguay a la vanguardia del mundo* (Mon-
     tevideo: Fin de Siglo, 2004); Ronaldo Munck, Ricardo Falcón, and
     Bernardo Galitelli, *From Anarchism to Peronism: Workers, Unions and
     Politics, 1855–1985* (London: Zed Books, 1987); Daniel James, *Resis-
     tance and Integration: Peronism and the Argentine Working Class, 1946–
     1976* (Cambridge, UK: Cambridge University Press, 1988).

16. For an in-depth exploration of anarchist historiography, see Peter
     Marshall, *Demanding the Impossible: A History of Anarchism* (London:
     Harper Perennial, 2008).

17. Arif Dirlik, *Anarchism in the Chinese Revolution* (Berkeley: University
     of California Press, 1993); Cornell, *Unruly Equality*.

18. Arif Dirlik recognizes that many of the arguments moved forth
     by postcolonial thinkers in the eighties had long existed in aca-
     demic and political circles. According to Dirlik, the term "postco-
     lonial" "mystifies both politically and methodologically a situation

that represents not the abolition but the reconfiguration of earlier forms of domination. "The complicity of postcolonial in hegemony lies in postcolonialism's diversion of attention from contemporary problems of social, political, and cultural domination, and in its obfuscation of its own relationship to what is but a condition of its emergence, that is, to a global capitalism that, however fragmented in appearance, serves as the structuring principle of global relations. . . . Now that postcoloniality has been released from the fixity of Third World location, the identity of the postcolonial is no longer structural but discursive." Whereas postcolonialism has arisen out of the postmodern condition of global production unity, specifically deterritorialization and the disappearance of a global center of capitalism, Third Worldism developed out of an attempt to link social movements throughout the Global South. Arif Dirlik, "The Postcolonial Aura: Third World Criticism in the Age of Global Capitalism," *Critical Inquiry*, vol. 20, no. 1 (1994).

19. Vijay Prashad, "The Third World Idea," *Nation*, May 17, 2007.

20. Rodolfo Porrini's "La historia de la clase obrera y los sindicatos en el siglo XX: Experiencias y aportes" provides a brief, yet informative, macro-level labor history of the twentieth century. The work, produced in collaboration with the PIT-CNT, focuses primarily on the various attempts to unify the labor movement under a single confederation. The work relies primarily on secondary literature for the first half century then turns to memoirs and auto-historiography for the Cold War era. While the work remains a helpful guide for understanding labor movement quantitative and qualitative turning points, it does not help us further understand everyday people's protagonism nor the *actual* functioning of state institutions. Similarly, Robert Jackson Alexander and Eldon M. Parker's *A History of Organized Labor in Uruguay and Paraguay* offers a wonderful chronology of the CNT's formation and identifies key tendencies and moments within it. Jackson Alexander, a foreign agent of the AFL-CIO's anti-communist Free Trade Union Committee, ventured to various Latin American countries to collect information on dissident communists within the labor movement. Both works have offered an important foundation for writing the work at hand.

Other scholars have offered enlivening works focused on the histories of specific unions. For instance, Susana Dominzain's edited volume *Así se forjó la historia: Acción sindical e identidad de los trabajadores metalurgicos en Uruguay* shares a detailed narrative of the development of Uruguay's metalworkers's union (UNTMRA). The union, a Communist Party stronghold, underwent a series of splits in some key industries, such as radio electricity, where workers broke away to form an independent union with a more combative spirit. The union also saw significant radicalization by the eve of the military takeover. Most of these works were produced by historical protagonists themselves. Yamandú González Sierra, an ex-FAU militant and historian, presents a detailed history of FUNSA in *Un sindicato con historia*. The book relies heavily on oral testimonies from both officers and rank and file to recount some of the union's key moments. Ivonne Trías, another ex-FAU militant, produced two biographies of FAU-affiliated unionists Gerardo Gatti, a graphic artist, and Hugo Cores, a bank employee. The works triangulate between personal experience, archival data, and oral testimonies. They have provided substantial detail regarding the relationship between the FAU and labor unions, especially those at small and medium-sized plants. Hugo Cores's unpublished *Sobre la tendencia combativa* (1983) offers a wonderful sketch of the dissident inter-local coalition, the Tendencia Combativa, but only presents brief description and profile of each union. Mario Tonarelli and Jorge Chagas's *El sindicalismo uruguayo bajo la dictadura, 1973-1984* details the June 1973 general strike and the next two years of union politics. Both union officers, they especially succeed at capturing the dialog between the state and the labor union movement in the months leading up to and after the military takeover.

See Rodolfo Porrini, "La historia de la clase obrera y los sindicatos en el siglo XX: Experiencias y aportes," in *Trabajo y utopía*, no. 22 (2002): 18; Robert Jackson Alexander and Eldon M. Parker, *A History of Organized Labor in Uruguay and Paraguay* (Westport, CT: Greenwood Publishers, 2005); Susana Dominzain, ed., *Así se forjó la historia: Acción sindical e identidad de los trabajadores metalurgicos en Uruguay* (Montevideo: Ediciones Primero de Mayo, 2016); Yamandú González Sierra, *Un sindicato con historia* (Montevideo: CIEDUR, 1991); Ivonne Trías, *Hugo Cores: Pasión y rebeldía en la izquierda uruguaya* (Montevideo: Ediciones Trilce, 2008); Hugo Cores, *Sobre la tendencia combativa* (unpublished, 1983), CEIU, Hugo Cores Archive; Jorge Chagas and Mario Tonarelli, *El sindicalismo uruguayo bajo la dictadura, 1973-84* (Montevideo: Ediciones del Nuevo Mundo, 1989).

21. Gilbert Joseph and Daniela Spencer's edited volume *In from the Cold* has encouraged historians to move away from assessing blame for the Cold War and instead toward examining how people fought at local levels, or "contact zones." Gilbert Joseph and Daniela Spencer, *In from the Cold: Latin America's New Encounters with the Cold War*, (Durham: Duke University Press, 2008). Hal Brands has identified the region's Cold War as a "multilayered conflict"—one that recognizes US hegemony in the Western Hemisphere but also emphasizes the role of Latin American actors throughout the epoch: Hal Brands,

Latin America's Cold War (Cambridge, MA: Harvard University Press, 2010). Jadwiga Pieper Mooney and Fabio Lanza insist we explore "street level" politics throughout the continent to add complexity to maneuvers of the "big players": Jadwiga Pieper Mooney and Fabio Lanza, *De-centering Cold War History: Local and Global Change* (New York: Routledge, 2013), 3. Tanya Harmer has called this approach the "Latin Americanization of the Cold War." Harmer also advocates for a global history of the Cold War, one that is interested in regional internal dynamics and how they played out beyond the continent and within it: Tanya Harmer, "The Cold War in Latin America," in *The Routledge Handbook of the Cold War*, Artemy M. Kalinovsky and Craig Daigle, eds. (New York: Routledge, 2014), 133–48.

22. de LaForcade, "Federative Futures," 73.
23. Autonomous Meatpackers Federation, Union Obrera Textil, BAO, GAS, FOEB, AEBU, ADEOM, SUAutomovil, FOMY, ADER (radioemisoras), UECU (cinematográficos), Vendedores de Diarios y Revistas, F. Ferroviaria, COAlpargatas, APPU, FUECI, Papeleros y Cartoneros, Aceiteras, Telecomunicaciones, Vidrio, General Electric, Bakers, CMNavales, etc.
24. Proportions taken from a personal data set compiled from archived editions of the Communist Party daily newspaper, *El Popular*. The data set consists of 550 recorded work actions between July 1969 and June 1973. While official numbers are indeed much higher due to press censorship, the PCU paper dedicated page 5 of each edition to reporting on labor conflicts.
25. Howard Handelman, "Labor-Industrial Conflict and the Collapse of Uruguayan Democracy," *Journal of Interamerican Studies and World Affairs*, vol. 23, no. 4 (1981).
26. US Ambassador to Uruguay Ernest Siracusa, Telegram 2164 from US Embassy in Uruguay to US Department of State, "Subj: Defense Minister's View on Current Situation," Montevideo, July 13, 1973, US Department of State Office of the Historian, https://history.state.gov/historicaldocuments/frus1969-76ve11p2/d337.
27. US Ambassador to Uruguay Ernest Siracusa, Telegram 2164.
28. See Van Gosse, "A Movement of Movements: The Definition and Periodization of the New Left," in *A Companion to Post-1945 America*, Jean Christopher Agnew and Roy Rosenzweig, eds. (London: Blackwell, 2002); Van Gosse, "Introduction: A Movement of Movements," in *The Movements of the New Left, 1960-1975: A Brief History with Documents* (Boston: Bedford, 2005).
29. George Katsiaficas, *The Imagination of the New Left: A Global Analysis of 1968* (Boston: South End Press, 1987), 18.
30. Jeremi Suri, *Power and Protest: Global Revolution and the Rise of Détente* (Cambridge, MA: Harvard University Press, 2003); Paul Berman, *A*

Tale of Two Utopias: The Political Journey of the Generation of 1968 (New York: W.W. Norton, 1996); Forrest D. Colburn, *The Vogue of Revolution in Poor Countries* (Princeton, NJ: Princeton University Press, 1994).

31. Grandin, *Last Colonial Massacre*, 15. Other scholars share a similar definition of the New Left, including Ricardo Melgar Bao, who defined the New Left as groups that "glorified violence … and distanced themselves from the political traditions of opposition movements that came before them, whether Marxist, reformist, or pacifist." Ricardo Melgar Bao, "La memoria sumergida: Martirologio y sacralización de la violencia en las guerrillas latinoamericanas," *Movimientos armadas en México, siglo xx*, vol. 1, Verónica Oikión Solano and Marta Eugenia García Ugarte, eds. (Zamora: El Colegio de Michoacan, 2006), 37.

32. Jonathan C. Brown, *Cuba's Revolutionary World* (Cambridge, MA: Harvard University Press, 2017).

33. Régis Debray, "Latin America: The Long March," *New Left Review*, no. 33 (1965).

34. Eric Zolov, "Expanding our Conceptual Horizons: The Shift from an Old to a New Left in Latin America," *Contracorriente*, vol. 5, no. 2 (2008): 51.

35. John Beverley, "Rethinking Armed Struggle in Latin America," *Boundary* 2, vol. 36, no. 1 (2009): 48-49. Christina Gerhart's recent book, *Screening the Red Army Faction: Historical and Cultural Memory (New York:* Bloomsbury Academic, 2018) also makes a point to write against mainstream media representations of Germany's Red Army Faction and other armed left organizations as driven by sex, drugs, and rock 'n' roll.

36. Zolov, "Expanding our Conceptual Horizons," 52.

37. Vania Markarian's *Uruguay, 1968: Student Activism from Global Counterculture to Molotov Cocktails* (Oakland: University of California Press, 2017), 152, explores the relationship between youth counterculture and the Uruguayan left.

38. Jeffrey J. Gould, "Solidarity under Siege: The Latin American Left, 1968," *American Historical Review*, vol. 114, no. 2 (2009).

39. Clara Aldrighi, *La izquierda armada: Ideología, ética e identidad en el MLN-Tupamaros* (Montevideo: Ediciones Trilce, 2001); Arturo Porzecanski, *Uruguay's Tupamaros: The Urban Guerrilla* (Westport: Praeger, 1974); Aldo Marchesi, *Latin America's Radical Left: Rebellion and Cold War in the Global Sixties* (New York: Cambridge University Press, 2018).

40. The broader critique of foco initially came from within the New Left itself. Samuel Farber, a Cuban anarchist exile and author of *The Politics of Che Guevara: Theory and Practice* (Chicago: Haymarket, 2016),

criticizes Che and foco strategy for never having been interested in growing a social revolution among the working class and instead holding a technocratic interpretation of communism. Trotskyists in the United States made an abundance of pronouncements regarding the MLN-T's strategy. Among them, Martin Glaberman critiqued Régis Debray for representing foco as a panacea and for neglecting to find a role for urban working classes in Latin America's capitol cities. Similarly, Frank Roberts claimed that a movement without deep roots in the working class, "roots which enable it to defend itself with the threat of massive strikes, can prove an easy prey to direct governmental violence." Martin Glaberman, "Régis Debray: Revolution without a Revolution," in *Speak Out*, April 1968; Frank Roberts, "The Tupamaros: Rise and Fall," in *Socialist International* (London: Socialist Review Publishing Co., 1974).

41. María José Moyana, *Argentina's Lost Patrol: Armed Struggle, 1969-1979* (New Haven: Yale University Press, 1995).

42. See Samuel Huntington, *Political Order in Changing Societies* (New Haven: Yale University Press, 1968); Ted Gurr, *Why Men Rebel* (Princeton: Princeton University Press, 1970).

43. Porzecanski, *Uruguay's Tupamaros*, 29.

44. Pablo Pozzi, *Por las sendas argentinas: El PRT-ERP; La guerrilla marxista* (Buenos Aires: Imago Mundi, 2009), 11.

45. Marchesi, *Latin America's Radical Left*, 15.

46. Anthony Arblaster writes: "There has been some kind of revival of anarchism. I put it as loosely at that, since while there has been a modest though appreciable revival of specifically anarchist groupings, what is of much greater importance has been the revived influence of anarchist thought and attitudes on the left generally, among many who neither call themselves anarchists nor would want to." Anthony Arblaster, "The Relevance of Anarchism," *Socialist Register*, vol. 8 (1971): 59.

47. Paul Goodman remarks: "The wave of student protest in the advanced countries overrides national boundaries, racial differences, the ideological distinctions of fascism, corporate liberalism and communism. Needless to say, officials of the capitalist countries say that the agitators are Communists, and Communists say they are bourgeois revisionists. In my opinion, there is a totally different political philosophy underlying—it is Anarchism." Paul Goodman, "The Black Flag of Anarchism," *New York Times Magazine*, July 14, 1968.

48. Felipe del Solar and Andrés Pérez, "El anarquismo en los orígenes del MIR y las Brigadas del Pueblo," in *Anarquistas: Presencia libertaria en Chile*, Felipe del Solar and Andrés Pérez, eds. (Santiago: RIL editores, 2008), available at https://cedema.org/digital_items/4753.

49. Gould, "Solidarity under Siege," 370.

50. Ana Rosa Amoros, interview with author, Montevideo, May 10, 2017.

51. Zelmar Dutura, "Prólogo: Contexto en que aparecen las CARTAS," in *Cartas de FAU*, vol. 1 (Montevideo: Ediciónes Recortes, 2016), 10.

52. I have benefited greatly from use of the Uruguayan Center for Inter-disciplinary Studies at the University of the Republic, where I have accessed archived documents and received mentorship from Profes-sor Aldo Marchesi. There, I found the personal archives of Hugo Cores (member of the FAU and general secretary of the bank teller's union) and Héctor Rodríguez (Communist Party dissident-defector and general secretary of the Textile Workers Congress). Both pro-vide important references to the Tendencia Combativa, specifically by identifying those unions who belonged to the coalition at a given historical moment. I also accessed folders with contents from FAU exiles in France, including propaganda documents smuggled from Buenos Aires to Montevideo when the organization relocated to Argentina in exile. The folders also consist of various human rights testimonies from members of the FAU who shared their stories with the Bertrand Russell Tribunal and Amnesty International.

53. The back page contained a small section called "This is the response," which consisted of short annotations of ongoing strug-gles compiled by Mauricio Gatti, who gathered reports from net-works among labor unions. Beyond debates and activities internal to the left, the documents contained blacklists of employers and reports about state-led repression, such as detentions and torture. Dutra, "Prólogo," 7–13.

54. Alessandro Portelli, "What Makes Oral History Different," in *Oral History Reader*, Robert Perks and Alistair Thompson, eds. (New York: Routledge, 2006), 68.

55. Howard Kimeldorf, "Bringing the Unions Back in (or Why We Need a New Old labor History)," *Labor History*, vol. 32 (1991): 96.

56. Kimeldorf, "Bringing the Unions Back in," 91–129.

57. FAU, "Pueblo fuerte: Poder popular desde el libertario" (Montevi-deo: Ediciones Recortes, 2017), 7.

58. See Edward Andrew, "Class in Itself and Class against Capital: Karl Marx and his Classifiers," *Canadian Journal of Political Science*, vol 16, no. 3 (1983).

59. E. P. Thompson, *The Making of the English Working Class* (New York: Vintage, 1966), 9.

60. Vladimir Lenin proposed a solution to these cycles of spontaneity in *What Is to Be Done?* (1902).

61. C. L. R. James and Grace Lee Boggs, *Facing Reality* (Detroit: Corre-spondence Press, 1958).

62. Martin Glaberman, *The Struggle against the No-Strike Pledge in the UAW during World War II* (Detroit: Bewick/ed, 1980).

63. James and Boggs, *Facing Reality*, 10.
64. Mario Tronti, "The Strategy of Refusal" (Thesis 12), in *Operai e Capitale* (Turin: Einaudi, 1966), 234–52.
65. Alain Touraine, "An Introduction to the Study of Social Movements," *Social Research*, vol. 52, no. 4 (1985): 775–76.
66. Mariarosa della Costa and Selma James, "The Power of Women and The Subversion of the Community," (n.p., 1972), available at https:// libcom.org/library/power-women-subversion-community-della -costa-selma-james.
67. Léon Rozitchner, "La izquierda sin sujeto," *La rosa blindada*, vol. 2, no. 9 (1966): 8.
68. Sandro Mezzadra and Verónica Gago, "In the Wake of the Plebeian Revolt: Social Movements, 'Progressive' Governments, and the Politics of Autonomy in Latin America," *Anthropological Theory*, vol. 17, no. 4 (2017): 482.

1.   Anarchy, *Patria, o Muerte*

1. Yamandú Gonzalez Sierra, *Un sindicato con historia*, vol. 2 (Montevideo: CIEDUR, 1991), 106.
2. Sierra, *Un sindicato*, 106.
3. Sierra, *Un sindicato*, 106.
4. Sierra, *Un sindicato*, 153.
5. While the UOESF endorsed a combative position shared by members within the FAU, León Duarte never shared his anarchist political orientation openly. Moreover, the seventeen delegates from the Lista 1 caucus represented a mixed bag of politics. Thus, UOESF's positions were the product of a growing militancy among workers within the plant as opposed to the product of one or two anarchists steering the direction of the union. Rodolfo Porrini and Mariela Salaberry, *León Duarte: Conversaciones con Alberto Márquez y Hortencia Pereira* (Montevideo: Editorial Compañero, 1993), 27.
6. Óscar Delgado, interview with author, Montevideo, December 20, 2017.
7. Megan Strom, "Transnational Youth: The Federation of Uruguayan University Students in the Early Cold War, 1941–1958," unpublished PhD diss., University of California, San Diego, 2015, 100.
8. Howard Handelman, "Labor-Industrial Conflict and the Collapse of Uruguayan Democracy," *Journal of Interamerican Studies and World Affairs*, vol. 23, no. 4 (1981): 375.
9. David R. Struthers, "The Batlle Era and Labor in Uruguay," MA thesis (Austin: University of Texas, 1990), 7.
10. Struthers, "The Batlle Era and Labor in Uruguay."

11. Rodolfo Porrini, "El sindicalismo uruguayo en el proceso histórico nacional (1870–2006)," in *Bicentenario Uruguay 1811–2011* (Montevideo: n.p., 2011).

12. Alexis Capobianco, "La concepción de Rodney Arismendi sobre las viás al socialismo," *Hemisferio Izquierdo*, November 21, 2017, https://www.hemisferioizquierdo.uy/single-post/2017/11/21/La-concepci%C3%B3n-de-Rodney-Arismendi-sobre-las-v%C3%ADas-al-socialismo.

13. Robert Jackson Alexander and Eldon M. Parker, *A History of Organized Labor in Uruguay and Paraguay* (Westport, CT: Greenwood Publishers, 2005), 44–46.

14. Handelman, "Labor-Industrial Conflict and the Collapse of Uruguayan Democracy," 375.

15. The El Cerro and La Teja neighborhoods became a hotbed for anarchism after the influx of southern and eastern European working-class migrants in the first half of the twentieth century. Inhabitants included famous militants Antonio Laredo and Pedro Boadas Rivas. Laredo, who founded the local Modern School after the ideas of Catalan anarchist Francisco Ferrer, was deported over ten different times from Argentina, Spain, and Uruguay. His photograph circulated to police departments throughout southern Europe and Latin America as part of an international database of anarchist militants started after the 1898 Rome Anti-Anarchist Conference and 1904 St. Petersburg Protocol. See Richard Bach Jansen, *Battle against Anarchist Terrorism: An International History, 1878–1934* (New York: Cambridge University Press, 2015).

El Cerro was later home to Boadas Rivas, a Catalan anarchist immigrant who arrived in Uruguay in 1926. Boadas Rivas was one of the famous anarchist expropriators—a member of the Durruti group within the Spanish National Confederation of Labor (CNT), which eventually laid the foundation for establishing the Iberian Anarchist Federation (FAI) in 1927. He participated in over one hundred bombings while in Spain, primarily noncompliant bosses during labor conflicts. Upon arriving to Uruguay with two other Catalan anarchists, Boadas Rivas linked up with anarchist expropriators in the Río de La Plata and began participating in bombing campaigns against various sites of United States presence in protest of the Sacco and Vanzetti trial. After a botched attempt to rob a *casa de cambio* (currency exchange) in the center of Montevideo left three killed and three seriously wounded, Boadas Rivas was captured alongside six other anarchist expropriators, who were sentenced to jail time in Punta Carretas. In March 1931, all six anarchists escaped from Punta Carretas by way of tunnel constructed by fellow anarchists from the outside, who had collectively purchased a home and coalyard across the street from the prison in August 1929, which was eventually used as the exit gate for the engineering feet. Boadas Rivas escaped to Buenos Aires but was soon extradited back to Uruguay, where he spent twenty years in prison. Upon release in 1952, he moved to El Cerro and worked there as a newspaper vendor.

16. *Tercerismo* responded to US intervention in Korea in the early 1950s, but it also rejected Moscow's role in the Korean War. While students outright denounced US imperialism in Korea, the broader public shied away from such militancy due to Uruguay's unique relationship with the US military as a supplier of wool for uniforms. The ideology eventually gained more popularity throughout the Cold War as a rejection of US and Soviet interests in the Americas. Strom, "Transnational Youth," 59.

17. For detailed narrative of the FAU's founding, see Eduardo Rey Tristán, *La izquierda revolucionaria uruguaya, 1955-1973* (Sevilla: Universidad de Sevilla, 2005), 195-205. The workers settled in El Cerro, and laborers of the neighborhood's six refrigeration plants, including the nationalized Frigorífico Nacional, joined them. The strike was declared in opposition to low wages and gross mismanagement in the private sector, where industrialists were eventually caught evading taxes by claiming only half their sales. The strike, coordinated across firms by the Autonomous Meat Federation (FAC), called for a unified labor central but this did not catch hold. Instead, the FAC showed its strength by coordinating nine industry-wide strikes involving the nation's most combative unions over the next two years. Porrini, "El sindicalismo uruguayo," 3.

18. Delegates included: Federación Libertaria de Argentina (2), Nossa Chaçara Sao Paulo (1), Agrupaçao Libertario Porto Alegre (1), Federación Anarquista Internacional de Chile (1), Asociasión Libertaria Cubana (2), Federación Anarquista Uruguaya (3). The conference also received declarations from anarchist organizations in Bolivia, Dominican Republic, Haiti, Mexico, Panama, Peru, and the United States. FAU, "Pimera conferencia anarquista Americana: Pronunciamientos, acuerdos, recomendaciones, declaraciones; April 1957" (Montevideo: Comunidad del Sur, June 1957).

19. FAU, "Pimera conferencia anarquista Americana," 13-15.

20. While Uruguayan scholar Aldo Marchesi recognizes that the Cuban Revolution marked an anti-imperialist turn that was not present in the calls for an *international* working-class fraternity among the early-twentieth-century left, the conference provides one small case of how anarchists embedded anti-imperialist struggle as part of a humanist internationalism. Aldo Marchesi, "Writing the Latin American Cold War: Between the 'Local' South and the 'Global' North," *Estudios Historicos*, vol. 30, no. 60 (2017). Opposition to

colonialism and imperialism was common in mid-nineteenth-century anarchist thought. Elise Reclus's *Nouvelle Geographie Universelle* (1876–94) provides one clear example of anti-colonial thinking in early anarchism. Federico Ferretti's recent examination of the text shows a distinction between his use of the words "colonization" and "conquest." For Reclus, the former represented the migration of European working classes to the Global South and the potential for a global fraternity in those new encounters; the latter represented the domination and subjugation of foreign peoples to a European ruling political class. Federico Ferretti, "'The Murderous Civilisation': Anarchist Geographies, Ethnography and Cultural Differences in the Works of Élie Reclus," *Cultural Geography*, vol. 24, no. 1 (2017).

21. Juan Carlos Mechoso, *Acción directa anarquista: Una historia de FAU*, vol. 3 (Montevideo: Editorial Recortes, 2006), 66.

22. Juan Carlos Mechoso, "Por qué apoyamos y de qué defendemos a la revolución cubana," in *Acción directa anarquista: Una historia de FAU*, vol. 4 (Montevideo: Ediciones Recortes, 2005), 130–31.

23. Mechoso, "Por qué apoyamos," 128.

24. Mechoso, "Por qué apoyamos," 128.

25. Some of the "traditionalist" groups' most well-known militants included Lucce Fabbri (Union Group), Jorge Errandonea (School of Fine Arts), Alfredo Errondanea (professor of sociology), and Ruben Prieto (founder of Comunidad del Sur); Those in the "New Left" camp included Gerardo Gatti (CNT delegate, SAG), León Duarte (general secretary, UOESF), Roberto Franano, Fernando O'Neill, Juan Carlos Mechoso, Alberto Mechoso, and Mauricio Gatti.

26. "Pleno FAU adoptó importantes acuerdos: Al replantearse R. Cubana," *Lucha Libertaria*, no. 206 (May 1962), quoted in Eduardo Rey Tristán, "La renovación del anarquismo en el Uruguay: La Federación Anarquista Uruguaya entre 1956 y 1967," *Estudos Ibero-Americanos*, vol. 30, no. 1 (2004): 174.

27. Tristan, "Pleno FAU adoptó importantes acuerdos," 175.

28. Juan Carlos Mechoso, "Continuidad histórica de una orientación revolucionaria" *Lucha Libertaria*, no. 206 (May 1962; José Jorge Martínez, "Trascedencia y superficialidad del año político 1962 *Lucha Libertaria*, no. 206 (May 1962; Gerardo Gatti, "La revolución y el burocratismo," *Lucha Libertaria*, no. 206 (May 1962), quoted in Tristán, "La renovación del anarquismo," 176.

29. A list of anarchist victims includes Augusto Sánchez (imprisoned and murdered), Rolando Tamargo (shot), Ventura Suárez (shot), Sebastián Aguilar Jr. (shot), Eusebio Otero (found dead in room), Raúl Negrín (burned alive), Francisco Aguirre (found dead in jail cell), Victoriano Hernández (blinded by prison torture,

eventually committed suicide). Those imprisoned included Casto Moscú, Modesto Piñeiro, Floreal Barrera, Suria Linsuaín, Manuel González, José Aceña, Isidro Moscú, Norberto Torres, Sicinio Torres, José Mandado Marcos, Plácido Méndez. and Luis Linsuaín. Rafael Uzcategui, "Authoritarian Chimeras: Cuba and the Gaona Manifesta," *Tierra y Libertad*, vol. 283 (2012).

30. For more on the treatment of anarchists during the years following the Cuban Revolution, see Sam Dolgoff, *The Cuban Revolution: A Critical Perspective* (Montreal: Black Rose, 1996); Frank Fernandez, *Cuban Anarchism: The History of a Movement* (Tucson: See Sharp Press, 2001).

31. A handful rejoined the organización after the polemic settled down, including Zelmar Sutra and Roger Julien (Fine Arts), Washington Peréz, Robert Larrasq, Ruben Prieto, and Víctor Gutiérrez (Comunidad del Sur). Guillermo Reigosa Pérez, "La Federación Anarquista Uruguaya," *Postaporteñ@*, November 16, 2010, 15; Zelmar Dutra, interview with author, Montevideo, June 13, 2017; Comando General del Ejercito, *Testimonio de una nación agredida* (Montevideo, 1978), 294.

32. Workers and students in the confederation sought to find common ground in the first two years of the FAU's existence. The intergenerational relationship flourished when anarchist students and workers acted as some of the main protagonists in the 1958 student and labor conflicts.

33. Traditionalists wanted to hold publicly accessible assemblies with decision-making power available to anyone present, whereas New Leftists advocated for a central organizing committee of veteran members.

34. In 1965, members of Communidad del Sur and the School of Fine Arts collaborated to publish a magazine, titled *Tarea*, which circulated four editions during that year. In a July 27, 1965, article titled "Las dos FEUU," the author cites a long history of social change brought about by student militants within the FEUU, specifically the end to mandatory military service and 1958 Organic University Law. The author argues that prior to the early sixties, the FEUU was its own political force, free of outside influence from parties and labor unions. The student government body was anarchic in the sense that students first and foremost represented themselves and debated among one another regarding how to enact political change and larger social transformation most effectively. The author critiques parties and labor unions for having created a culture of block voting within the student assemblies, which lead to a dogmatism and sectarianism rooted in outside influence rather than open debate amongst one another to provide student-specific answers to student-specific problems. The article does not mention the FAU by

name, but surely such former experiences influenced the piece. "Las dos FEUU," *Tarea*, vol. 1, no. 1 (1965): 16–19.

35. "Al diablo con la cultura: Bellas Artes en el Barrio Sur," *Tarea*, vol. 1, no. 4 (1965): 37–38. As director of fine arts, Jorge Errandonea organized students to replicate the project again in 1990. They chose the location of Montevideo's traditional Jewish neighborhood, Barrio Reus Norte. The street has since become one of Montevideo's landmarks.

36. The "Visible Sensibility" project was heavily critiqued among the left, including the FAU, who saw it as detached from the reality of growing forms of state repression. Augusto Andrés recalls a conversation with Marcelino Guerra, an Afro-Uruguayan involved with the School of Fine Arts, who highlighted that the work done in Palermo and Barrio Sur had reached more poor people of color in a few months than the Communist Party had in the entirety of the 1950s. Augusto Andrés, "Bellas Artes es hija de '58," email to author, June 21, 2018.

37. Gabriel Oyhantcabal Benelli and Matias Carambula, "Lucha por la tierra en el norte de Uruguay," in *Astrolabio: Nueva Época*, no. 7 (2011): 299.

38. Participants from the FAU included Juan Carlos Mechoso, León Duarte, Gerardo Gatti, and Mauricio Gatti.

39. Eleutorio Fernández Huidobro, *Historia de los Tupamaros*, vol. 1 (Montevideo: TAE Press, 1988), 132.

40. Huidobro, *Historia de los Tupamaros*, 62–64.

41. Huidobro, *Historia de los Tupamaros*, 106.

42. Huidobro, *Historia de los Tupamaros*, 83.

43. Marysa Gerassi, "Uruguay's Urban Guerrillas," in *New Left Review*, no. 62 (1970): 25.

44. Rolando Sasso, *Tupamaros, los comienzos* (Montevideo: Fin de Siglo, 2010), 230.

45. Carlos Quijano, "Contra cualquier malón," *Marcha* (Montevideo, ca. 1964), quoted in Huidobro, *Historia de los Tupamaros*, 117.

46. CIA Directorate of Intelligence, "Weekly Summary Special Report: The Uruguayan Government and the Left," Washington, DC, May 10, 1968, 3, available at https://www.cia.gov/library/readingroom/docs/CIA-RDP79-00927A006400060003-5.pdf.

47. Eleutorio Fernández Huidobro, *El tejedor: Héctor Rodríguez* (Montevideo: Editorial TAE, 1995), 240.

48. Comando General del Ejercito, *Testimonio*, 295.

49. Huidobro, *Historia de los Tupamaros*, 107.

50. Andres Cultelli, *La revolucion necessaria: Contribucion a la autocritica de los MLN-Tupamaros* (Buenos Aires: Colihue, 2006).

51. Tristán, *La izquierda revolucionaria uruguaya*, 114–16.

52. Hugo Cores, *Sobre la tendencia combativa* (unpublished, 1983), CEIU, Hugo Cores Archive, 4–5.

53. Alexander and Parker, *Organized Labor in Uruguay and Paraguay*, 61.

54. Huidobro, *El tejedor*, 243.

55. Delgado, interview with author.

56. Beginning 1961, the country's largest unions began coalescing around the PCU-specific CTU, but no more than 50 percent of organized labor remained affiliated with the confederation. Raúl Ivan Acuña, *¿A donde va el sindicalismo uruguayo?* (Montevideo: ARCA, 1967), 12.

57. Alexander and Parker, *Organized Labor in Uruguay and Paraguay*, 52–57.

58. Acuña, *¿A donde va el sindicalismo uruguayo?*, 12–16.

59. CIA Directorate of Intelligence, "Weekly Summary Special Report," 3.

60. The seven other officers included including José D'Elía (FUECI), Wladimir Turiansky (AUTE), Luis Nadales (FOL), Enrique Pastorino (CTU), Gerardo Cuesta (UNTMRA), Alberto Ramos Ferro (AEBU), and Juan Melgarejo (COFE).

61. Congreso del Pueblo–Mesa Organizadora, "Programa de soluciones a la crisis" (Montevideo), ca. August 1965, CEIU, Héctor Rodríguez Archive B1.

62. Joint Chiefs of Staff of the Uruguayan Armed Forces, *Subversion: Uruguayan Armed Forces Summary of Subversive Movement in Latin America*, Part I (Montevideo, August 23, 1977), 211; Handelman, "Labor-Industrial Conflict," 375.

63. Héctor Rodríguez, "Cronologia" (Montevideo, ca. 1965), CEIU, Héctor Rodríguez Archive B1.

64. Philip Agee, *Inside the Company: CIA Diary* (New York: Simon & Schuster, 1975).

65. Mesa Representativa del CNT, "Material preparatorio de la asamblea nacional de sindicatos" (Montevideo, December 3, 1965), 2.

66. Mesa Representativa del CNT, "Material preparatorio," 7.

67. "Hay una sola respuesta," in *Rojo y Negro (I)*, Gerardo Gatti, ed. (Montevideo, May 1968), FAU Library, 20.

68. The 1966 election would be the first to break from the National Council of Government. While the ballots offered options for filling the presidency and parliament, parties also scrambled to advance proposals for constitutional reform. With 75 percent of votes, the Blanco and Colorado "orange reform" initiative established a single-office presidency. The election also saw President Óscar Gestido (Colorado) asume office. Marcelo Sosa Gabito, "La (im)probable reforma constitucional en el escenario político uruguayo hacia 2019: Un análisis desde la trayectoria y la estabilidad

política," thesis (University of the Republic, Faculty of Social Sciences, Montevideo, 2017), 25-26.

69. Quoted in Cores, *Sobre la tendencia combativa*, 5.

70. Quoted in Cores, *Sobre la tendencia combativa*, 5-6.

71. Gerardo Gatti, "Electoralismo y parlamentarismo: Trabas para la izquierda" (Montevideo, October 28, 1966), available at http://www.cedema.org/ver.php?id=6470.

72. Gerardo Gatti, "Acción sindical y lucha armada," *Punta Final*, no. 96 (Santiago, January 20, 1970), available at http://www.cedema.org/ver.php?id=3177.

73. The FORA V faction would remain committed to the anarchist communist politics of the 1905 congress.

74. Quoted in Ivonne Trías and Universindo Rodríguez Díaz, *Gerardo Gatti: Revolucionario* (Montevideo: Trilce, 2012), 101.

75. CIA Directorate of Intelligence, "Weekly Summary Special Report," 5-7.

76. Quoted in Raúl Iván Acuña, *¿A donde va el sindicalismo uruguayo?* (Montevideo: ARCA, 1967), 61.

77. Hugo Cores, interviewed in Tristán, *La izquierda revolucionaria uruguaya*, 389.

78. Pascual Muñoz, "Antonio Laredo," book presentation, Montevideo, September 29, 2017.

79. "Importante documento del sindicato FUNSA sobre plan de lucha," in *La Historieta* (Montevideo, 1974), 35-42, Mechoso Family Archive.

80. Raúl Zibechi, *De multitud a clase: Formación y crisis de una comunidad obrera, Juan Lacaze (1905-2005)*, (Montevideo: Ediciones IDEAS, 2006); Leandro Kierszenbaum, "Estado peligroso y medidas prontos de seguridad: Violencia estatal bajo democracia, 1945-68," *Contemporánea*, vol. 3, no. 3 (2012): 107-10.

81. Detainees included Lilián Celiberti, Elena Quinteros, Yamandú González, and Gustavo Inzaurralde. Kierszenbaum, "Estado peligroso," 107-10.

82. Héctor Rodríguez, "Despues de las medidas de seguridad," in *La Historieta*, 11-14, Mechoso Family Archive.

83. "Acto FAU," *Marcha*, July 7, 1967.

84. Central Intelligence Agency, "Special Report: Cuban Subversion in Latin America," Office of Current Intelligence, Washington, DC, August 9, 1963, 5, available at https://www.cia.gov/library/reading room/docs/CIA-RDP79-00927A004100090003-7.pdf.

85. CIA Directorate of Intelligence, "Weekly Summary Special Report," 6.

86. Central Intelligence Agency-Intelligence Information Cable, "Plans of the Communist Party of Uruguay (PCU) to Attack United States

Property," Washington, DC, January 25, 1966, available at https://www.cia.gov/library/readingroom/docs/DOC_0000578597.pdf.

87. Other delegates included Edmundo Súa de Netto, Alberto Caymaris (MAPU), José Díaz Chávez (secretary general, Socialist Party), Adalberto González (MPJ); Carlos Domingo Elichirigoity (Avanzar), Juan A. Iglesias Villar, Elbio Baldovino, and José Jorge Martínez Fontana. Comando General del Ejército, *Testimonio*, 75.

88. Comando General del Ejército, *Testimonio*, 75.

89. "Acto FAU."

90. CIA Directorate of Intelligence, "Weekly Summary Special Report," 6.

91. Cores, *Sobre la tendencia combativa*, 13.

92. Comando General del Ejército, *Testimonio*, 78.

93. "Fidel Castro, OLAS, Publicación Especial de la FAU," (Montevideo, 1967); Juan Carlos Mechoso, interview with author, Montevideo, December 26, 2017.

94. Aldo Marchesi, "Political Violence and the Left in Latin America, 1967-1979," in *Oxford Encyclopedia of Latin American History* (New York: Oxford Press, 2016).

95. "Hay una sola respuesta," 35.

96. Gonzalo García, "Mijail Bakunin y Ernesto Guevara: En dos épocas una misma intransigencia revolucionaria," in *Rojo y Negro (II)*, Gerardo Gatti, ed. (December 1968), 107-39.

97. "Presencia del Che Guevara: Poema de Idea Vilariño y versos de Carlos Molina," in *Rojo y Negro (I)*, 35.

98. In fact, the PCB had not been in contact with Che since 1965 and did not even know of his presence in the country until December 1966. All PCB-affiliated participants in the guerrilla joined based on individual conviction. The party did declare solidarity with the campaign until March 30, 1967, when a group of less than a dozen members Communist Youth arrived. Mario Monje, "Mario Monje explica por qué su partido no apoyo al Che," in *Rojo y Negro (I)*, 125-44.

99. CIA Directorate of Intelligence, "Weekly Summary Special Report," 7.

100. "A un año se comprueba la justeza de la línea" (December 12, 1968), in *Cartas de FAU*, 122-23.

101. CIA Directorate of Intelligence, "New Deal in Uruguay?" Special Report-Weekly Review, Washington DC, December 1, 1967, available at https://www.cia.gov/library/readingroom/docs/DOC_0000578180.pdf.

102. "El acuerdo de *Época*," in *La Historieta*, 22-25, Mechoso Family Archive.

103. Augusto Andrés, interview with author, Montevideo, July 8, 2017.

104. Idea Vilariño met members of the FAU while attending talks and performances at the Ateneo del Cerro, where she became an anarchist sympathizer. She lived and wrote from the front room of the house and, for security purposes, did not know the details of who was meeting in the back room; she was merely aware that they were members of the FAU. Zelmar Dutra, "Prólogo: Contexto en que aparecen las CARTAS," in *Cartas de FAU*, 12.

105. Dutra, "Prólogo," 7.

106. "Eleven years of more or less public life. One year of more or less clandestine life. We have learned from the examples of Mikael Bakunin and Errico Malatesta, from the old anarchist workers, the martyrs of Chicago, from Sacco and Vanzetti, from Simon, from Durruti, from the comrades in the CNT and FAI, from the direct action groups, propagandists, and labor militants in the River Plate. This fight and its teaching are always present in our Organization." "Nutrirse para el combate aquí . . .," in *Cartas de FAU*, 126-27.

107. Dutra, "Prólogo," 7-9.

108. CIA Directorate of Intelligence, "Weekly Summary Special Report," 7.

109. "La lucha aclara las cosas" (August 12, 1968), in *Cartas de FAU*, 42.

110. Quoted in Trías and Rodríguez, *Gerardo Gatti*, 100.

111. Vania Markarian, *Uruguay, 1968: Student Activism from Global Counterculture to Molotov Cocktails* (Oakland: University of California Press, 2017), 161.

2. Dark Red, Light Black

1. See Aldo Marchesi, "The May '68 That Was Not May '68: Latin America in the Global Sixties," *Verso Blog*, May 24, 2018, https://www.versobooks.com/blogs/3846-the-may-68-that-was-not-may-68-latin-america-in-the-global-sixties.

2. For firsthand testimony of the expropriation, see Juan Carlos Mechoso, *Acción directa anarquista: Una historia de FAU*, vol. 4 (Montevideo: Ediciones Recortes, 2005), 245-53.

3. Mechoso, *Acción directa anarquista*, 239.

4. FAU's *especifismo* is often misunderstood and misrepresented, including among Uruguayan scholars. For example, when referring to FAU's experience in exile, historian Vania Markarian declares, "These former anarchists admitted that their previous disregard for mass politics and party organization had hampered the development of an effective popular mobilization against authoritarianism in Uruguay." Vania Markarian, *Left in Transformation: Uruguayan Exiles and the Latin American Human Rights Network, 1967-84* (London: Routledge, 2005), 72.

5. Robert Jackson Alexander and Eldon M. Parker, *A History of Organized Labor in Uruguay and Paraguay* (Westport, CT: Greenwood Publishers, 2005), 69. The IMF 1969 Annual Report blamed the price surge on "the steep rise in private sector wages during the period": International Monetary Fund, "Annual Report of the Executive Directors for the Fiscal Year Ended April 30, 1969" (Washington, DC, 1969), 117, available at https://www.imf.org/external/pubs/ft/ar/archive/pdf/ar1969.pdf.

6. Students at the Uruguayan University of Work (UTU) and Normal Institute (Teaching School) expressed grievances regarded over-enrollment and underfunding. For a thorough description of student grievances and Mayday actions, see Vania Markarian, *Uruguay, 1968: Student Activism from Global Counterculture to Molotov Cocktails* (Oakland: University of California Press, 2017), 29–34.

7. "Hay una sola respuesta," in *Rojo y Negro (I)*, Gerardo Gatti, ed. (Montevideo, May 1968), FAU Library, 32.

8. "Hay una sola respuesta," 4–5.

9. "Hay una sola respuesta," 25–26.

10. "Organización y método en el trabajo cotidiano (2)" (September 30, 1968), in *Cartas de FAU*, vol. 1 (Montevideo: Ediciónes Recortes, 2016), 72–73.

11. "Hay una sola respuesta," 32.

12. Peter Kropotkin, *Fugitive Writings*, George Woodcock, ed. (Montreal: Black Rose, 1993), 50.

13. For more on the FACA and Spartacus Workers Alliance, see Nicolás Iñigo Carrera, "Programa de investigación sobre el movimiento de la sociedad argentina: La alianza obrera Spartacus," Documento de Trabajo No. 26 (Buenos Aires: Pablo Editor, 1986), available at http://www.pimsa.secyt.gov.ar/publicaciones/DT26.pdf.

14. "Hay una sola respuesta," 29.

15. Mario Tronti, "Our *Operaismo*," *New Left Review*, no. 73 (2012), https://newleftreview.org/II/73/mario-tronti-our-operaismo.

16. "Rojo y Negro, dos colores que marcan un camino" (December 12, 1968), in *Cartas de FAU*, 127.

17. Felix de la Uz, "Algunos problemas acerca de la unidad de acción del movimiento revolucionario en America Latina" (May 1968), in *Rojo y Negro (I)*, 105, 115.

18. de la Uz, "Algunos problemas," 123.

19. Alexander and Parker, *Organized Labor in Uruguay and Paraguay*, 68.

20. Various well-known radical left militants belonged to the 1955 caucus, including Carlos Hébert Mejías Collazo and Kimal Amir (MLN-T), Hugo Cores (FAU), and Anibal Collazo, brother of MRO leader Ariel Collazo. Although the "1955" caucus and PCU-affiliated "Lista 3" caucus agreed on pushing for nationalization of the

banking sector, the former went further by advocating universal basic income to compensate for the half decade of sacrifices imposed upon the working classes to pay for the nation's economic crisis. Eduardo Rey Tristán, *La izquierda revolucionaria uruguaya, 1955-1973* (Sevilla: Universidad de Sevilla, 2005), 380-84, 391.

21. "Borradores de apuntes sobre el movimiento obrero del Uruguay, año 1968" (ca. 1974), in *La Historieta*, Mechoso Family Archive.

22. "El claro sentido de las medidas: Hechos y opiniones que lo evidencian" (June 20, 1968), in *Cartas de FAU*, 16.

23. Hugo Cores, *Sobre la tendencia combativa* (unpublished, 1983), CEIU, Hugo Cores Archive, 16.

24. Quoted in "El claro sentido," 15. Flores Mora left his position as minister of labor on June 1, 1968, but served in office throughout the May '68 mobilizations.

25. The next day, he threatened to fire all striking government employees. Quoted in "El claro sentido," 16.

26. According to Handelman, the MPS were a direct response to the prolongation of the bank workers' strike. Howard Handelman, "Labor-Industrial Conflict and the Collapse of Uruguayan Democracy," *Journal of Interamerican Studies and World Affairs*, vol. 23, no. 4 (1981): 381. Markarian, in *Uruguay, 1968*, also recognizes that the MPS were likely a response to various strikes already underway, especially those of civil servants and bank workers.

27. Quoted in "El claro sentido," 16.

28. The MPS were retracted between March and June 1969. Leandro Kierszenbaum, "Estado peligroso y medidas prontos de seguridad: Violencia estatal bajo democracia, 1945-68," *Contemporanea*, vol. 3, no. 3 (2012): 107-10.

29. On October 9, 1967, Gestido implemented MPS but canceled the decree two weeks later in the face of a CNT general strike. Alexander and Parker, *Organized Labor in Uruguay and Paraguay*, 68.

30. "Actuar ahora, único modo de frenar la represión" (June 26, 1968), in *Cartas de FAU*, 19. Uruguayan historian Álvaro Rico labels the June 13 decree as marking a shift to "conservative liberalism" and toward a long path to consolidating authority that eventually culminated in the 1973 coup. Álvaro Rico, *1968: El liberalismo conservador* (Montevideo: Banda Oriental, 1989).

31. Cores, *Sobre la tendencia combativa*, 17.

32. "Carta a la CNT," in *Rojo y Negro (II)*, Gerardo Gatti, ed. (December 1968), 177-90. Participating caucuses include Grupo AREA (Architecture), Grupo 58 (Medicine), Agrupación 26 (Humanities), Lista 11 (Engineering), Grupo AGU and Grupo Universitario de Izquierda (Natural Sciences), Economicas, Lista 68 (Law), and Grupo Militante (Chemistry).

33. Electrical workers in the UTE generator sector also used factory occupation as a tactic. "Así se está respondiendo" (June 20, 1968), in *Cartas de FAU*, 17.
34. Handelman, "Labor-Industrial Conflict," 381; Markarian, *Uruguay, 1968*, 35.
35. "Así se está respondiendo" (Montevideo), June 26, 1968, in *Cartas de FAU*, 20.
36. Image from *El Popular* (Montevideo), ca. 1968, Center of Photography.
37. "Así se está respondiendo," (Montevideo), July 5, 1968, in *Cartas de FAU*, 24.
38. "Confundir-disinformar, un medio más de 'hacer polítíca'" (July 11, 1968), in *Cartas de FAU*, 25.
39. "La represión continuá" (July 11, 1968), in *Cartas de FAU*, 27.
40. "El torno al oportunismo" (August 5, 1968), in *Cartas de FAU*, 38.
41. "Así se está respondiendo" (August 5, 1968), in *Cartas de FAU*, 40–41.
42. "Propusieron plan de lucha" (August 12, 1968), in *Cartas de FAU*, 46.
43. "Propusieron plan de lucha," 45–46.
44. "Así se está respondiendo" (August 12, 1968), in *Cartas de FAU*, 47.
45. Markarian, *Uruguay, 1968*, 37; While all five faculties became associated with the MLN-T, they also had sizeable groupings of militants belonging to the FAU and GAU. The School of Fine Arts remained affiliated with strands of anarchism.
46. "Hay ahora más dificultades para difundir esta carta" (August 12, 1968), in *Cartas de FAU*, 43.
47. "Así se está respondiendo" (August 19, 1968), in *Cartas de FAU*, 50.
48. "Así se está respondiendo" (September 2, 1968), in *Cartas de FAU*, 60.
49. "Así se está respondiendo" (September 2, 1968), 60.
50. "Así se retrocedió" (September 2, 1968), in *Cartas de FAU*, 5.
51. "Así se está respondiendo" (September 9, 1968), in *Cartas de FAU*, 65; Markarian, *Uruguay, 1968*, 5.
52. "Negociar sin lucha es traición" (September 9, 1968), in *Cartas de FAU*, 62–63.
53. "Negociar sin lucha es traición," 62–63.
54. Beyond street confrontation, authorities also detained and tortured militants and fellow travelers of organizations. In one case, ex-FAU member Leo Gerner was detained and tortured in efforts to retain information about the organization. Gerner, an employee of the Medical Union, ex-officer of the Nocturnal School Student Union, and member of the Uruguayan Health Federation (FUS), had quit the organization due to health issues over two years prior to his detention. "Los anarquistas no hablan" (October 28, 1968), in *Cartas de FAU*, 94.

55. The government never referenced the guerrilla organization MLN-T as reason behind the protests. Markarian, *Uruguay, 1968*, 39–40, 60; "El objetivo es desmoralizar al pueblo" (September 30, 1968), in *Cartas de FAU*, 76.

56. "El objetivo es desmoralizar al pueblo," 75–6.

57. Targets included the home of an executive cabinet member, the Chamber of Commerce, and the Banco Mercantil del Río de la Plata (Salto). "3 explosiones" (October 14, 1968), in *Cartas de FAU*, 90. CAP cells struck again in late January by burning four locals of the Colorado Party throughout Montevideo. They also exploded bombs at the Ministry of Finance, Ministry of Foreign Relations, and Metropolitan Guard Headquarters. The CAP left behind fliers claiming the attacks and declaring solidarity with the workers facing police repression at BAO and Bataioli, and workers facing unemployment at Frigorifico Nacional, Nervion, Vidplan, and various textile plants. The statement ended declaring, "We will do it like in 1952: we will put up a new 38th parallel." "Así se está respondiendo" (Febuary 3, 1969), in *Cartas de FAU*, 166; "Así se está respondiendo" (September 30, 1968), in *Cartas de FAU*, 76–77.

58. "Los coches pagaban peaje" (October 7, 1968), in *Cartas de FAU*, 82.

59. Markarian, *Uruguay, 1968*, 41–42.

60. USAID chief public safety advisor Charles C. Guzmán, "Police Riot Control Readiness—Uruguay," GEIPAR, September 19, 1972, available at http://www.geipar.udelar.edu.uy/index.php/2016/08/27/ips-14-1-riot-control-uruguay-1967-72.

61. "Asi se esta respondiendo" (November 18, 1968), in *Cartas de FAU*, 110.

62. Workers at Riplan (wool factory) and Ipusa (textile plant) occupied in protest of layoffs, radio workers (ADER) denounced the firing of various union officers, and metalworkers at the TEM factory implemented slowdown strikes to pressure a salary increase. "Así se está respondiendo" (December 16, 1968), in *Cartas de FAU*, 133–34.

63. Strikes were prohibited in "essential services." "COPRIN: Restricción al derecho de huelga," *El Popular* (Montevideo), June 24, 1970.

64. Alexander and Parker, *Organized Labor in Uruguay and Paraguay*, 69.

65. "Rausa no se presentó al Coprin," *El Popular* (Montevideo), June 14, 1970.

66. See Jorge Maureira Lagos, *Ideologia sindical cirstiana para America Latina* (Santiago: Editorial Juridica de Chile, 1968), 64–72.

67. Henceforth referred to as the Tendencia.

68. Cores, *Sobre la tendencia combativa*, 3–4.

69. Aside from Héctor Rodríguez, the GAU's most notable militants included Victor Bacchetta (SAG), Martin Ponce de León (AUTE), Carlos Fassano (AEBU), and Ricardo Vilaró (FUM).

70. Diego Castro, "Héctor Rodríguez, tejedor de un tradición negada," *Zur* (Montevideo), August 13, 2018.

71. María Julia Alcoba, interview with author, Montevideo, October 28, 2018. For more on women in the textile industry, see María Julia Alcoba, *Las mujeres ¿dónde estaban?* (Montevideo: Primero de Mayo, 2014).

72. "Plan de Lucha 1969," reprinted in Tristán, *La izquierda revolucionaria uruguaya*, 375.

73. Ivonne Trías and Universindo Rodríguez Díaz, *Gerardo Gatti: Revolucionario* (Montevideo: Trilce, 2012), 115.

74. The Tendencia had other strongholds in the interior aside from UTAA, such as the Plenario Intergremial in Mercedes, the Sindicato de Frutas y Verduras in Salto, and the AEBU Lista 1955 in Paysandu. Trías and Rodríguez, *Gerardo Gatti*, 112-14.

75. Trías and Rodríguez, *Gerardo Gatti*, 106.

76. Susana Dominzain, ed., *Así se forjó la historia: Acción sindical e identidad de los trabajadores metalurgicos en Uruguay* (Montevideo: Ediciones Primero de Mayo, 2016), 160-61.

77. Ghiringhelli, a tire factory under the elected leadership of Trotskyist militant Hugo Bianchi, maintained independence from the Radioelectricity Table but played a strong role in the Tendencia Combativa. Dominzain, *Así se forjó la historia*, 164-65.

78. Dominzain, *Así se forjó la historia*, 167-72.

79. Trías and Rodríguez, *Gerardo Gatti*, 112-14.

80. CIA Directorate of Intelligence, "Weekly Summary Special Report: The Uruguayan Government and the Left" (Washington, DC), May 10, 1968, 7.

81. "Sindicatos y tendencia" (April 27, 1970), in *Cartas de FAU*, April 27, 1970.

82. The best historical example of such practice can be found in turn-of-the-century Spain, where the anarcho-syndicalist CNT organized peasants of Aragon, factory workers in Catalonia, and street peddlers in Barcelona.

83. Trías and Rodríguez, *Gerardo Gatti*, 114.

84. "80 empresas claves controlan los yanquis en el Uruguay," *El Popular* (Montevideo), January 11, 1972; Alcoba, interview with author.

85. Regusci Voulminot was the largest private-owned floating dock in all Latin America.

86. Cores, *Sobre la tendencia combativa*, 47.

87. "¡A resistir! 6 sindicatos llaman a la lucha" (July 29, 1968), in *Cartas de FAU*, 33.

88. For example, a coalition of FAU and MLN-T bank workers linked up to launch bombing and petty vandalism campaigns directed toward scabs and management. Attacks were recorded at the Banco

de Londres, Banco 18, Banco Roxlo, the Stock Exchange, and television broadcasting station Channel 4. The small faction, called People's Self-Defense Commandos (CAP), carried out the actions independently and even against the will of most of the workers, who, regardless of demonstrating an intense labor militancy and willingness to struggle, sought to remain autonomous from political organizations, whether parties or clandestine armed groups. Tristán, *La izquierda revolucionaria uruguaya*, 391.

89. "Hay una sola respuesta," 22.

90. "Hay que optar: Acumular debilidad o fortalecerse luchando" (July 5, 1968), in *Cartas de FAU*, 26.

91. "Hay una sola respuesta," 20.

92. "Hay que optar," 25.

93. On November 14, the Frente Izquierda (FIdeL) transmitted a statement via PCU organ *El Popular* and other mainstream media sources, such as *El País, El Día, Acción, BP, Color*, and various radio news channels. The declaration declared: "They implement methods that were employed last century by anarchist groups. [These methods] are condemned ... erroneous, and totally intolerable for the development of the labor movement. . . . They lead to isolation and facilitate repression from the dominant. . . . They are doing them a favor." Untitled (November 18, 1968), in *Cartas de FAU*, 109.

94. "El torno al oportunismo," 39–40.

95. Comando General del Ejército, *Testimonio de una nación agredida* (Montevideo, 1978), 13.

3.   Alejandra and the Eagle

1. Augusto Andrés, "Recorder es volver a querer," presentation, Montevideo, 2014.

2. "Esplosión en refugio de Tupamaros: Cuatro heridos," *El Día* (Montevideo), April 27, 1969.

3. Whereas the MLN-T and Argentina's Montoneros were made up primarily of middle-class membership. See Daniel James, *Resistance and Integration* (Cambridge, UK: Cambridge University Press, 1993); Richard Gillespie, *Soldiers of Perón: Argentina's Montoneros* (New York: Oxford University Press, 1982); Lindsey Churchill, *Becoming Tupamaros: Solidarity and Transnational Revolutionaries in Uruguay and the United States* (Nashville: Vanderbilt University Press, 2014).

4. An MLN-T document recalled a case when PCU president Rodney Arismendi accused FAU militants León Duarte and Washington Pérez of treason and collaboration with management during an occupation of the FUNSA plant. The Supreme Court charged the union

with a financial penalty after ruling against their use of occupation to combat the police's attempt to evict. "Apuntes sobre la accion frente a las masas" (Documento 3, 1968), in *Movimiento de Liberación Nacional (Tupamaros): Documentación propia* (Caracas: Indal, 1972), 52.

5. "Se eligió la lucha," *Cartas de FAU*, June 16, 1969.

6. Lilián Celiberti, interview with author, Montevideo, July 5, 2017.

7. "Tarea que debe realizar cada militante, cada equipo, todos los días" (Montevideo, ca. 1970), Mechoso Family Archive.

8. Vania Markarian's *Uruguay, 1968: Student Activism from Global Counterculture to Molotov Cocktails* (Oakland: University of California Press, 2017) explores the relationship between youth counterculture and the Uruguayan left. The author argues that the PCU equally embraced counterculture in an effort to appeal to a growing middle-class base, specifically among students (see pages 146–47). The trend serves the author's broader argument, which claims that Uruguay's student movements maintained close relations with traditional left organizations. However, the work falls victim to using trends within the PCU and MLN-T to make broader claims about the left. While FAU militants recall debating among themselves regarding their tastes for music and art, the organization insisted that militants refrain from exhibiting such open markers of counterculture because of their estrangement from working-class culture and their potential to mark themselves as subversives.

9. Anonymous, interview with author, Montevideo, May 31, 2017. Such discipline was rather common among other revolutionary left organizations in the River Plate; see Vera Carovale, "Disciplinamiento interno: Moral y totalidad," in *Los combatientes: Historia del PRT-ERP* (Buenos Aires: Siglo Veintiuno, 2011).

10. Many First World anarchist groups of the sixties and seventies were much more influenced by anarcho-individualism and the Situationist International. Most groups were more oriented toward petty terrorism and/or a "politics of play" than toward a disciplined and organized collective movement. See, for instance, Provos (Amsterdam), Up Against the Wall Motherfucker (New York), the Diggers (San Francisco), and the Angry Brigade (United Kingdom).

11. The Normal School is a system of teacher training schools that prepares its students to work in marginalized public school systems. The model remains common throughout Latin America.

12. Celiberti, interview with author, July 5, 2017.

13. Beginning as early as 1958, a team of about two dozen FUNSA union leaders and rank and file workers took on the responsibilities of communicating between the combative labor unions and militant student organizations, laying the foundation for what would eventually become the ROE (the most notable of those involved

in networking include León Duarte, Miguel Gromaz, Jacinto Ferreira, Gerardo de Avila, Luis Romero, Riaño, Márquez, Bidigaray, Berrusi, and Washington Pérez. Many of them also belonged to the FAU. Hugo Cores, *Sobre la tendencia combativa* (unpublished, 1983), CEIU, Hugo Cores Archive, 45.

14. Twenty percent of Uruguayan university students participated in a political organization. Most channeled political energies into the FEUU, which was dominated by the PCU. CIA Directorate of Intelligence, "The Uruguayan Government and the Left," (Washington, DC, May 10, 1969), 3.

15. "Ficha ROE" (1972), Mechoso Family Archive. As compared to the UJC, Vania Markarian claims, "[m]ost members worked, but the prevalence of students among the more active militants suggests that the sectors that set the tone of the organization were not strictly working class but rather wage-earning middle-class youths." Markarian, *Uruguay, 1968*, 148.

16. The lack of direct reference can cause difficulty for investigation. Eduardo Rey Tristán also mentions such hang-ups when examining the student movement that he openly stated these limitations within his text, declaring: "Existing documentation about student groups is limited, mainly existing in fliers and handouts for quick printing by mimeograph, so it is only possible to partially compose the organizational panorama of these groups." He instead limits his inquiry to the groups' general tendencies and their relationships with revolutionary organizations. Eduardo Rey Tristán, *La izquierda revolutionaria uruguaya, 1955–1973* (Seville: Universidad de Seville, 2005), 398.

17. Untitled, (June 30, 1969), in *Cartas de FAU*, vol. 1 (Montevideo: Ediciónes Recortes, 2016), 250.

18. Marina Mechoso, interview with author, Montevideo, June 26, 2017.

19. "Actos relámpago: Definiciones y generalidades" (Montevideo, ca. 1972), Mechoso Family Archive.

20. "Limites de la zona" (Montevideo, ca. 1972), Mechoso Family Archive.

21. Note the term *ama de casa* (housewife) is particular to the time and should be more appropriately understood in today's lexicon as *domestic worker*. "Sindicatos y tendencia," *Cartas de FAU*, April 27, 1970.

22. Gerardo Leibner identifies a "masculinization" of the PCU, in which "the invisibility of women and their demands during the 1960s was due to a power-centred vision of revolution, reproducing a patriarchal division of roles inspired by the success of the Cuban Revolution." While the party saw an increase in women's participation in

its ranks throughout the 1960s, its growth as a mass party led to the lack of a women's-specific agenda attuned with a larger social reality in which working class families had yet to radically change the gendered division of domestic labor. He recognizes that challenging gender conceptions was among the first issues to be sacrificed in the left's transformation from small avant-garde into mass politics in the sixties. Gerardo Leibner, "Women in Uruguayan Communism: Contradictions and Ambiguities, 1920s–1960s," *Journal of Latin American Studies*, no. 50 (2017): 643–72.

23. "La Teja: Un barrio solidario," *Compañero* (Montevideo), May 28, 1971.
24. Lilián Celiberti, interview with author, Montevideo, October 16, 2018.
25. Ernesto Laclau, *On Populist Reason* (London and New York: Verso, 2005).
26. Clara Aldrighi, *Memorias de insurgencia: Historias de vida y militancia en el MLN-Tupamaros, 1965–1975* (Montevideo: Ediciones de la Banda Oriental, 2009), 252.
27. Augusto Andrés, "Un Testimonio de vida," presentation, Montevideo, May 2018.
28. Juan Gómez Casas, *Anarchist Organization: The History of the F.A.I.* (Montreal: Black Rose Books, 1986), 150.
29. By the beginning of the twentieth century, transatlantic state repression of organized anarchist movements led to the rise in popularity of anarcho-individualism and anti-organizationalist anarchism. This anarchist current saw working-class organizations as impotent and incapable of making revolution on their own, and thus envisioned small cells of anarchist affinity groups as harbingers of violence during moments of popular mobilizations. Tactics like bombings, vandalism, and assassinations earned anarchists a reputation as terrorists and provocateurs from outside of working-class organizations. Nevertheless, they maintained the position that the working class would be the primary protagonists in the revolution, but the anarchist militant's role was to escalate working-class mobilization toward revolutionary insurrection through use of propaganda by the deed. Such normalization of violence would serve as preparation for the revolutionary moment. Pascual Muñoz, *Antonio Laredo: Aletazos de tormentas* (Montevideo: La Turba Ediciones, 2017).
30. Internal documentation accounts for the existence of at least nine cells. "Lista de propuesta para integrar la dirección del sector" (Montevideo, ca. 1972), Mechoso Family Archive.
31. In one case, the directorate considered assassinating the police officer who shot FAU/ROE militant Heber Nieto in 1971, but they later called the action off after realizing it was driven too much by

ego. Juliana Martínez, interview with author, Montevideo, May 31, 2017.

32. Edelweiss Zahn, interview with author, Montevideo, June 11, 2017.

33. Augusto Andrés, interview with author, Montevideo, June 11, 2017.

34. CIA Office of National Estimates, "Varieties of Political Violence in Latin America: The Case of the Tupamaros in Uruguay" (Washington, DC), January 3, 1972.

35. Decolonial struggles throughout the Global South drew strong inspiration from Che Guevara and Frantz Fanon, both of whom conceived of a "new man" who could be liberated by violently confronting his oppressors.

36. Juan Carlos Mechoso, interview with author, Montevideo, June 28, 2017.

37. Celiberti, interview with author, July 5, 2017.

38. Juan Carlos Mechoso, *Accion directa anarquista* (Montevideo: Editorial Cortes, 2009), 189–90; Zelmar Dutra, interview with author, Montevideo, June 13, 2017.

39. "Lista de propuesta para integrar la dirección del sector" (Montevideo, ca. 1972), Mechoso Family Archive.

40. "Article 27: Inferior units will be subordinated to superior units. The directives from them [superiors] are obligatory for them [inferiors]. Failure to comply is a discipline violation. Similarly, the lower ranks within any organism should comply with any command from their superiors." "Reglamento" (ca. 1968), in *Movimiento de Liberación Nacional (Tupamaros)*, 69.

41. *Pozo* directly translates to "well."

42. Mechoso, interview with author; Dutra, interview with author; América García, interview with author, Montevideo, April 22, 2017.

43. Mechoso, interview with author.

44. Mechoso, interview with author.

45. "OPR: Información pasada por pastilla" (Montevideo, ca. 1972), Mechoso Family Archive.

46. "Algunos criterios para el trabajo al nivel de masas (1)" (May 19, 1969), in *Cartas de FAU*, 226–28.

47. FAU's insistence on recognizing the applicability and necessity of both tactics situates its position among a broader New Left debate around the use of violence and popular mobilization. See "Movimiento Nacional de Liberacion–Tupamaros," and "Partido o Foco, un falso dilema," in *Uruguay: La estrategia de los Tupamaros* (Buenos Aires: Los Libros, 1971).

48. Public opinion remained a longtime obsession of Uruguayan anarchists. In 1911, Montevideo's anarchist-led streetcar union initiated a conflict that morphed into the country's first general strike. The streetcar workers insisted that the city's electric trolleys were a

public good and invaluable "connector of public space." See Anton Rosenthal, "Spectacle, Fear, and Protest: A Guide to the History of Urban Public Space in Latin America," *Social Science History*, vol. 24, no. 1 (2000).

49. Contrarily, FAU condemned the PCU for exploiting any small gain for labor as a victory for the working class and for using their hegemony among the left to gather more party support via electoral votes. "Algunos criterios."

50. Abraham Guillén, *Estrategia de la guerrilla urbana* (Montevideo: Manuales del Pueblo, 1966).

51. For more on Guillén, see Donald Hodges's introduction to *Philosophy of the Urban Guerrilla: The Revolutionary Writings of Abraham Guillén* Donald C. Hodges, ed. and trans. (New York: William Morrow & Co., 1973); and Tommy Lawson, "Abraham Guillén: Between Bakunin and Marx; Anarchism, Socialism, and the Economics of Self-Management," Red and Black Notes, August 10, 2020, https://www.redblacknotes.com/2020/08/10/abraham-guillen-between-bakunin-and-marx-anarchism-socialism-and-the-economics-of-self-management.

52. Carlos Marighella, *Minimanual do Guerrilheiro Urbano* (Brazil: n.p., 1969).

53. "Apuntes sobre la accion frente a las masas" (Documento 3, 1968), in *Movimiento de Liberación Nacional (Tupamaros)*, 52.

54. MLN-T writings called for guerrilla leadership to be made up of militants with the highest levels of consciousness because they would be the ones to eventually take power and implement the revolutionary project. Unlike the FAU, the MLN-T did not have a political "party" under which to organize the masses. As a result, they joined the Broad Front for the 1971 election campaign, which brought about further contradictions between anti-legal armed struggle and legal institutional politics. "Foco o partido—falso dilema," in *Movimiento de Liberación Nacional (Tupamaros)*, 87–91.

55. "Arriba los que luchan" (June 30, 1969) in *Cartas de FAU*, 254; "Arriba los que luchan" (July 14, 1969) in *Cartas de FAU*, 263.

56. Doneschi Family, interview with author, Montevideo, October 17, 2018; Mechoso, interview with author.

57. "Ferroviarios amplian sus paros," *El Popular* (Montevideo), June 20, 1969.

58. "Son tiempos de pelea" (June 2, 1969), in *Cartas de FAU*, 237.

59. Augusto Chacho Andrés, *Estafar un banco—que placer!* (Montevideo: Alter Ediciones, 2009), 60.

60. "Son tiempos de pelea," 237.

61. Although the meat processing plant workers strike inspired solidarity actions across the nation, they were primarily directed towards

aiding the site-specific struggle in El Cerro rather than fighting for a universal program that captured the entirety of the labor movement. But this grievance remained unsettled and represented a major symbolic blow to the labor movement broadly.

62. "Mocion de la Tendencia al primer congreso de CNT" (May 1969), in *La Historieta* (Montevideo, ca. 1974), 12, Mechoso Family Archive.

63. Asociacion de Bancarios del Uruguay, "A los compañeros delegados del 1er congreso de la CNT" (Montevideo, May 1969), CEIU, Héctor Rodríguez Archive.

64. Howard Handelman, "Labor-Industrial Conflict and the Collapse of Uruguayan Democracy," *Journal of Interamerican Studies and World Affairs*, vol. 23, no. 4 (1981): 382; "Algunos criterios."

65. Workers selected List 1 with 52 percent of the total vote.

66. The rivalry also spawned two nonaligned lists, which won 7 percent and 25 percent of the vote respectively. "Se eligió la lucha" (June 16, 1969), in *Cartas de FAU*, 244.

67. Censorship did not remain unique to press organs, as distribution of fliers and pamphlets by everyday people was also prohibited.

68. Cores, *Sobre la tendencia combativa*, 34. The censorship continued until the end of the year, during which the newspaper primarily reported on legalized strike actions based on communiques from the Ministry of the Interior. For the second half of 1969, the newspaper reported only nineteen work conflicts nationwide. Of the nineteen reported actions, seven were less than half-day strikes by municipal workers (ADEOM) in the interior, and five were notifications of partial train services (AFE). The other seven work actions reported on were lockouts in Tendencia-affiliated industries, such as glassworks, meatpacking, and textiles. For example, textile workers at HISISA and HYTESA responded to layoffs by organizing forty-five- and eighty-day strikes respectively. Both maintained campaigns in face of a lockout.

69. "Se prohibe la difusión de noticias sobre determinados actos," *El Popular* (Montevideo), July 9, 1969.

70. "Arriba los que luchan" (June 30, 1969), 254.

71. "Arriba los que luchan," (July 14, 1969), 263.

72. "Unanime rechazo a misionero imperial," *El Popular* (Montevideo), July 9, 1969.

73. "Balance de nuestra lucha," *La Historieta* (Montevideo, ca. 1974), 15, Mechoso Family Archive.

74. "Lo que no cambia" (July 7, 1969), in *Cartas de FAU*, 256.

75. Hugo Cores, *Uruguay hacia la dictadura, 1968-1973: La ofensiva de la derecha, la resistencia popular y los errores de la izquierda* (Montevideo: Banda Oriental, 1999), 30.

76. Cores, *Sobre la tendencia combativa*, 32–33.

77. Walter Turiansky, "Continua la respuesta a Héctor Rodríguez: La huelga de UTE," in *Lucha y polémica sindical, 1968–1973*, vol. 2, Hector Rodríguez (Montevideo: Centro Uruguay Independiente, 1985), 56.

78. "Bastión de dignidad y coraje" (July 14, 1969), in *Cartas de FAU*, 264.

79. "Los que luchan" (July 28, 1969), in *Cartas de FAU*, 273.

80. "Desgravio a la bandera" (July 21, 1969), in *Cartas de FAU*, 269.

81. Mechoso, *Accion directa anarquista*, vol. 4 (Montevideo: Editorial Cortes, 2009), 207–8.

82. "Rige la militarización de los bancos," *El Popular* (Montevideo), July 28, 1969.

83. "Arriba," (August 4, 1969), in *Cartas de FAU*, 278.

84. "Arriba," 278.

85. "Arriba los que luchan" (August 11, 1969), in *Cartas de FAU*, 285; "Arriba los que luchan" (August 18, 1969), in *Cartas de FAU*, 289.

86. "Arriba los que luchan" (August 11, 1969).

87. Pellegrini Giampietro was released after seventy-three days in captivity. His friends paid U$15 million to a workers' hospital and primary school as ransom.

88. Eduardo Rey Tristán, *La izquierda revolucionaria uruguaya, 1955–1973* (Sevilla: Universidad de Sevilla, 2005), 387–88; Hugo Cores, *Memorias de la resistencia* (Montevideo: Ediciones Banda Oriental, 2002), 100.

89. Raúl Zibechi, "La dignidad en la acción colectiva: Centenario de Hectór Rodríguez," *Brecha* (Montevideo), August 10, 2018.

90. Like in June 1968, many striking workers were again drafted for the military. Handelman, "Labor-Industrial Conflict," 383.

91. Handelman, "Labor-Industrial Conflict," 383.

92. "Balance de nuestra lucha," *La Historieta* (Montevideo, ca. 1972), 15, Mechoso Family Archive.

93. "Bancarios: La lista No. 3 obtuvo mayoría de votos," *El Popular* (Montevideo), April 17, 1970.

94. Eleutorio Fernandez Huidobro, *El tejedor: Héctor Rodríguez* (Montevideo: Editorial TAE, 1995), 289.

95. Tristán, *La izquierda revolucionaria uruguaya*, 385.

96. Cores, *Memorias de la resistencia*, 100.

97. Cores, *Memorias de la resistencia*, 100.

98. Untitled (July 28, 1969), in *Cartas de FAU*, 273.

99. Hectór Rodríguez, "La táctica sindical en 1969," *Marcha* (Montevideo), February 6, 1970, reprinted in *Lucha y polémica sindical*.

100. Mario Acosta, "La verdadera faz de 1969 y la tactica C.N.T.," *El Popular* (Montevideo), January 23, 1970; Mario Acosta, "La definición política popular y la táctica de la C.N.T.," *El Popular* (Montevideo), February 20, 1970, reprinted in *Lucha y polémica sindical*.

101. "Lucha Popular" (Montevideo, March 9, 1970), quoted in Cores, *Sobre la tendencia combativa*, 15.

102. For more fulsome debate, see *Lucha y polémica sindical*.

103. Cores, *Memorias de la resistencia*, 99.

4. ¿Tiempo de Lucha? ¿Tiempo de Elecciones?

1. Comando General del Ejército, *Testimonio de una nacion agredida* (Montevideo: El Comando, 1978), 300.

2. Augusto Chacho Andrés, *Estafar un banco—que placer!* (Montevideo: Alter Ediciones, 2009), 63–65.

3. Augusto Andrés, "Flashes de otros tiempos," *Brecha* (Montevideo), August 12, 2016.

4. Howard Handelman, "Labor-Industrial Conflict and the Collapse of Uruguayan Democracy," *Journal of Interamerican Studies and World Affairs*, vol. 23, no. 4 (1981): 374.

5. "Asi entiende la 'estabilizacion' el gobierno," *El Popular* (Montevideo), June 16, 1970.

6. "Textiles: En 14 meses se redujo en 31% el valor real del salario," *El Popular* (Montevideo), April 21, 1970.

7. "Everfit: Todo el personal quedará desocupado," *El Popular* (Montevideo), May 20, 1970.

8. "La desocupacion invade los barrios del Cerro y La Teja," *Compañero* (Montevideo), April 29, 1971.

9. Law 13.730, "Cercenan derecho de huelga," *El Popular* (Montevideo), June 25, 1970.

10. Juan Carlos Mechoso, *Acción directa anarquista: Una historia de FAU*, vol. 4 (Montevideo: Ediciones Recortes, 2009), 166.

11. "La gente no está quieta," *Cartas de FAU*, March 2, 1970, Mechoso Family Archive.

12. "Expresión de militante solidaridad," *El Popular* (Montevideo), June 16, 1970; "Obreros de Erosa enfrentan el hombre en sus hogares," *El Popular* (Montevideo), January 30, 1970.

13. "Atma: Hay firmeza y mucha solidaridad," *El Popular* (Montevideo), December 12, 1970.

14. Hugo Cores, *Uruguay hacia la dictadura, 1968–1973: La ofensiva de la derecha, la resistencia popular y los errores de la izquierda* (Montevideo: Banda Oriental, 1999), 51.

15. "En Divino: Todos o ninguno," *Compañero* (Montevideo), October 20, 1971.

16. "La lucha decidio: La patronal fue derrotada," *Compañero* (Montevideo), October 30, 1971.

17. TEM was owned by foreign enterprises Castleton and Hoover.

18. *Cartas de FAU*, July 27, 1970, Mechoso Family Archive.

19. Hugo Cores, *Sobre la tendencia combativa* (unpublished, 1983), 42–46, CEIU, Hugo Cores Archive.

20. During the first days of the strikes, police forces launched stones at buses from inside the TEM factory due to the CUTCSA union's strong showings of solidarity, including horn honking and banner waving upon passing by. "Omnibus: No se detienen en TEM," *El Popular* (Montevideo), June 7, 1970.

21. One OPR-33 militant recently encountered an exposé on the Viet Cong, in which the author included a recipe for a Molotov cocktail used by guerrilla fighters. The recipe required gasoline and coconut oil, which was supplemented with coconut soap instead, creating quite the spectacle as firefighters took two hours to put out the flames. Andrés, *Estafar un banco*, 97; *Cartas de FAU*, July 27, 1970.

22. María Esther Gilio, "TEM: Union en la lucha," *Marcha* (Montevideo), July 1970, 15.

23. *Cartas de FAU*, July 27, 1970.

24. Workers poked fun at the June 1969 COPRIN ruling as providing them the means to buy two bus tickets and a box of matches. Regardless, management remained incompliant with the ruling until after the 1970 conflict. "Citaran a la patronal de TEM," *El Popular* (Montevideo), May 6, 1970; Cores, *Sobre la tendencia combativa*, 46.

25. *Cartas de FAU*, July 27, 1970.

26. "TEM: Una recia moral de victoria," *El Oriental* (Montevideo), August 7, 1970, quoted in Susana Dominzain, *Así se forjó la historia: Acción sindical e identidad de los trabajadores metalurgicos en Uruguay* (Montevideo: Ediciones Primero de Mayo, 2016), 170.

27. "TEM: Una recia moral de victoria."

28. María Esther Gilio, "TEM: Union en la lucha," *Marcha* (Montevideo), July 1970, 15.

29. "Desde un principio dimos la solidaridad a los obreros de TEM," *El Popular* (Montevideo), August 18, 1970.

30. Dominzain, *Así se forjó la historia*, 167.

31. Rodney Arismendi, *Lenin, la revolución, y América Latina* (Montevideo: Ediciones Pueblos Unidos, 1970).

32. Rodney Arismendi, "Ahora, mas que nunca, unidad para asegurar y ganar la elección," *El Popular* (Montevideo), July 9, 1971.

33. Speech transcript, "Seregni: No nos dejaremos trampear nuestro destino," *El Popular* (Montevideo), March 27, 1971.

34. "Llamado desde las fabricas," *Marcha* (Montevideo), December 24, 1970.

35. "Adquiere renovada viegencia la declaración del M.L.N. de adhesión al Frente Amplio" (December 1970), in *Movimiento de Liberación*

Nacional (Tupamaros): Documentación propia, 2nd ed. (Caracas: Indal, 1972), 184–85.

36. Movimiento Nacional de Liberacion-Tupamaros, "Partido o Foco, un falso dilema," in *Uruguay: La estrategia de los Tupamaros* (Buenos Aires: Los Libros, November 1971).

37. "El acto mas grande de la historia del país," *El Popular* (Montevideo), March 27, 1971.

38. "Gallup: Medio millon de votos para la unidad popular," *El Popular* (Montevideo), November 30, 1970.

39. Lilián Celiberti, interview with author, Montevideo, July 5, 2017.

40. Robert Jackson Alexander and Eldon M. Parker, *A History of Organized Labor in Uruguay and Paraguay* (Westport, CT: Greenwood Publishers, 2005), 61.

41. In a gesture of good faith leading up to the election, President Pacheco Areco legalized the FAU along with the five other revolutionary left organizations banned in 1967. This allowed the organization to print and circulate material freely. After the closure of *Época*, the organization circulated the *Cartas de FAU* via underground networks to over five thousand recipients. On April 29, 1971, the FAU began circulating a biweekly newspaper called *Compañero*. Under the editorial lead of León Duarte, the publication documented and analyzed the ROE-Tendencia Combativa's campaigns.

42. Augusto Andrés, "En 1971 aparece el FA," email correspondance with author, August 14, 2017.

43. "Cuidado con los desvios, lo central es la lucha" (June 2, 1969), in *Cartas de FAU*, vol. I (Montevideo: Ediciónes Recortes, 2016), 234.

44. Andrés, email correspondence.

45. "El F.A. pasó en Montevideo del 17,10 al 30.89%," *El Popular* (Montevideo), November 29, 1971.

46. *Tiempo de elecciones? Tiempo de lucha?* (Montevideo, May 1971), Mechoso Family Archive, 18.

47. *Tiempo de elecciones? Tiempo de lucha?*, 19–21.

48. "Unirse en la lucha—no dividirse en el voto," in *Cartas de FAU*, November 9, 1970, Mechoso Family Archive.

49. Juan Pilo, interview with author, Montevideo, June 22, 2017.

50. Eduardo Rey Tristán, *La izquierda revolucionaria uruguaya, 1955–1973* (Sevilla: Universidad de Sevilla, 2005), 352; "Emulando a Hitler," *El Popular* (Montevideo), ca. May 1971.

51. "Indignación en Colón ante la agresión de ayer," *El Popular* (Montevideo), June 1, 1971.

52. "En un establecimiento donde se esgrimen armas de fuego los profesores niegan a dar clases," *Marcha* (Montevideo), October 4, 1971.

53. Raúl Olivera, interview with author, Montevideo, July 25, 2017.

54. Rodney Arismendi, "Del P. Comunista a la C.N.T.," *El Popular* (Montevideo), June 24, 1971.
55. "Congreso de la CNT," *Compañero* (Montevideo), July 22, 1971.
56. "Congreso de la CNT."
57. Although the cells collected no more than four arms from each site, the operations were the first public acts signed off on by OPR-33. Mechoso, *Acción directa anarquista*, 293.
58. "Sobre el uso de un local sindical," *Compañero* (Montevideo), April 29, 1971.
59. Rodolfo Porrini and Mariela Salaberry, *León Duarte: Conversaciones con Alberto Márquez y Hortencia Pereira* (Montevideo: Editorial Compañero, 1993), 105.
60. "Resistencia obrera en FUNSA," *Sol* (Montevideo), ca. October 1971.
61. Juan Carlos Mechoso, *Acción directa anarquista: Una historia de FAU*, vol. 4 (Montevideo: Ediciones Recortes, 2005), 323–25.
62. "Refutan a patronal yanqui de Pepsi," *El Popular* (Montevideo), September 3, 1970.
63. "Nueva negativa de Pepsi-Cola," *El Popular* (Montevideo), September 4, 1970.
64. "Pepsi: Rechazan plan represivo de la patronal," *El Popular* (Montevideo), September 16, 1970.
65. "Pepsi: Formula inaceptable," *El Popular* (Montevideo), September 22, 1970.
66. "Hirieron de bala a obrero de Pepsi Cola," *El Popular* (Montevideo), September 26, 1970.
67. A women's committee from Barrio Peñarol donated U$2,000 worth of foodstuffs.
68. "Jornada solidaria con trabajadores de Pepsi el jueves en Zona Norte," *El Popular* (Montevideo), September 15, 1970.
69. The rally hosted speeches from representatives of FUNSA, TEM, and FOEB; "Pepsi: Rechazan plan represivo."
70. "Pepsi-Cola intenta romper sindicato," *El Popular* (Montevideo), September 5, 1970.
71. "Triumfaron obreros de Pepsi: Se firmó anoche la solución," *El Popular* (Montevideo), October 16, 1970.
72. Including the British hospital, American hospital, Italian hospital, Spanish hospital, IMPASA, Larghero, Evangélico, Fraternidad, and CASMU.
73. Cores, *Sobre la tendencia combativa*, 47–48; "Conflicto en las mutualistas replantea crisis asistencial," *Sur* (Montevideo), October 26, 1971.
74. "Hospital de clinicas: Situacion angustiosa," *El Popular* (Montevideo), October 28, 1970.

75. The Uruguayan Federation of Public Health Administrators and Staff (FUFEMM), a subsidiary of ADEOM, was responsible for services at all government supported clinics, including those at the university.

76. "Salud: Sigue conflictos por salarios," *El Popular* (Montevideo), November 15, 1970.

77. In the early 1960s, the Ciclo Básico program of the Faculty of Medicine began sending students to poor communities to offer health services free of charge as part of the curriculum. Students, who primarily came from the Catholic school system and drew influence from liberation theology, developed relationships with Montevideo's impoverished communities and fostered a more holistic analysis of the place of health services in a market economy. Augusto Andrés, interview with author, Montevideo, July 8, 2017.

78. In November 1970, Gramon, Bayer, Bio, and Atenas pharmaceutical laboratories fell under worker control after management failed to fulfill COPRIN's ruling for an U$8,000 monthly wage increase. The ruling affected some three thousand workers in the country's thirty-nine pharmaceutical laboratories. Management at twenty-four plants responded to the ruling by declaring a lockout. Workers further decried the industry's growing foreignization; within two years, foreign ownership of medical laboratories had increased from 48 to 63 percent. "Medicamento: Levantan el lock-out," *El Popular* (Montevideo), December 16, 1970; Cores, *Sobre la tendencia combativa*, 49.

79. "El conflict en Warner podria involucrar a todo el medicamento," *Sur* (Montevideo), ca. November 1971.

80. "Solucion en el sanitorio Español ayer," *El Popular* (Montevideo), November 13, 1971.

81. "La salud y su contexto," *Marcha* (Montevideo), September 22, 1972.

82. "Cicssa: Triunfo de la linea combative," *Compañero* (Montevideo), August 7, 1971.

83. "Secuestran a conocido abogado," *El Día* (Montevideo), June 24, 1971.

84. Mechoso, *Acción directa* anarquista, vol. 4 (Montevideo: Ediciones Recortes, 2005), 317–19.

85. "Ahora, mas que nunca, toda la solidaridad," *Compañero* (Montevideo), July 22, 1971.

86. "CICSSA: Triunfo de la línea combativa," *Compañero* (Montevideo), August 7, 1971.

87. Roger Rodríguez, "Heber Nieto fue asesinado con un rifle que Dan Mitrione le encargó a la DNII," *La red 21* (Montevideo), March 12, 2009.

88. CICSSA, FEUU, UOESF, SIMA, COT, TEM, FUS, Seral, ATMA,

UTAA, Ghiringhelli, Frigorífico Nacional, Administrative Federation of Textile Industry, List 1955 AEBU, Assoc. Funcionarios de Subsistencias, URDE (Union de Destajistas del Espinillar), Union Ferroviaria, General Electric, List 9 of Hospital Clinics. "16 sindicatos impulsan lucha," *Compañero* (Montevideo), July 26, 1971.

89. "Lo que piensa un obrera," *Compañero* (Montevideo), August 18, 1971.

90. "Cuando un periodista libre se convierte en usurpador de las libertades," *Flecha* (Montevideo), September 10, 1971.

91. "Detenidos en Playa Ramirez por platar bandera de Otorgues," *El Popular* (Montevideo), October 30, 1971.

92. O. A., "El prosteletismo, la legislación, y la propaganda," *Flecha* (Montevideo), September 10, 1971.

93. Alongside Cores, four other AEBU militants remained in detention. All were members of the 1955 List. "Libertad para Cores y todos los presos," *Compañero* (Montevideo), November 16, 1971.

94. Judges even made this clear to prisoners after serving their sentences, informing them that they would likely be detained again in the future for "security purposes." Augusto Andrés recalls having been detained in September 1972 by Captain Manuel Cordero, who sought to extract more information about those who participated in failed "Operation Apretesis" one year prior. Upon arriving to the Fifth Artillery, Captain Cordero personally carried out waterboarding and other methods of torture. Andrés, *Estafar un banco*, 74-75.

95. On November 19, GAU published a statement condemning the arbitrary detentions. Although the two organizations took different positions on the elections after working closely together for nearly a decade, GAU remained in solidarity with FAU. "Libertad para los presos politicos," *Marcha* (Montevideo), November 19, 1971.

96. "Huelga de hambre en cuarteles: Los secuestados por el gobierno no podrán votar hoy," *Ahora* (Montevideo), November 28, 1971.

97. "Está detenido en el CGIOR dirigente de FUNSA," *El Popular* (Montevideo), January 7, 1971; SAG general secretary Gerardo Gatti was also detained arbitrarily for two weeks in mid-March. "Confinan a Gerardo Gatti," *El Popular* (Montevideo), ca. March 1971.

98. Associated Press, "Michele Ray Kidnapped from Uruguay Home," *New York Times*, December 1, 1971, available at https://www.nytimes.com/1971/12/01/archives/michele-ray-kidnapped-from-uruguay-home.html.

99. Gerardo Gatti, "El llamamiento de enero! A pelear juntos compañero!," *Compañero* (Montevideo), January 12, 1972.

100. Martin Weinstein, "Uruguay: Military Rule and Economic Failure," in *Politics, Policies, and Economic Development in Latin America*, Robert Wesson, ed. (Stanford, CA: Hoover Press, 1984), 42.

101. "La alimentacion ancarecio el 50.3% en 1971," *El Popular* (Montevideo), January 31, 1972.

102. "Cientos de empresas reclaman aumentos de precios para sus productos ante la COPRIN," *El Popular* (Montevideo), October 16, 1971.

103. The wool industry downsized from four thousand to eight hundred employees by 1971, "El contraband de lana acrece desocupación," *El Popular* (Montevideo), February 12, 1972.

5.   To Know Half a Person

1.   Comando General del Ejército, *Testimonio de una nacion agredida* (Montevideo: El Comando, 1978), 475.

2.   Robert Jackson Alexander and Eldon M. Parker, *A History of Organized Labor in Uruguay and Paraguay* (Westport, CT: Greenwood Publishers, 2005), 63–64.

3.   Delegates behind the proposal included: FUNSA, BAO, COT, UTAA, Palacio de la Luz (UTE), Ghiringhelli, Serratosa, Coca-Cola (FOEB), Plenario Juan Lacaze, Plenario Mercedes (ADEOM), Anda, Español (FUS), Casmu (FUS), Tem, Seral, Atma, Alpargatas, SIMA, Aceiteros, Tanners Union (UOC), Ubur (AEBU), OMTUTU (UTU), and Professors Liceo No. 13, among others. Juan Carlos Mechoso, *Accion directa anarquista*, vol. 6 (Montevideo: Editorial Cortes, 2009), 355.

4.   Interview with Raúl Sendic, "Los Tupamaros hacia una alternativa de poder," *Punta Final*, no. 157 (1972): 4.

5.   President Areco formed OCOA on September 9, 1971, at which time he called upon the military to take over matters of subversion. While police and military began collaborating against left opposition in 1969, less than 20 percent of military resources and personnel went toward anti-subversion efforts. Prior to the formation of OCOA, Armed Forces involvement primarily included the organizing and sharing of US intelligence documents to form profiles of Uruguayan political activists who traveled to socialist countries, such as Cuba. The United States also helped by training servicemen. Between 1950 and 1979, nearly three thousand Uruguayan military men trained at the US Army School of the Americas (SoA). Between 1970 and 1975, roughly 310 trained at the SoA, with nearly half dedicated to "Internal Security Operations." The Uruguayan military recruited primarily from poor rural regions that had not been exposed to the left ideologies and struggles centered in Montevideo. Wolfgang S. Heinz and Hugo Fruhling, *Determinants of Gross Human Rights Violation by State and State-Sponsored Actors in Brazil,*

Uruguay, Chile, and Argentina, 1960–1990 (Cambridge, MA: Martinus Nijhoff Publishers, 1999), 354–57.

6. While authorities largely turned a blind eye to the PCU's hidden stockpile of six hundred AR-15 rifles, they hoped to provoke the party to pick up arms to justify its illegalization and subsequent violence against it. Sergio Israel, *La enigma Tribal: Una investigación periodística sobre el coronel Ramon Trabal; su persona, su actividad militar política, y su nunca aclarado asesinato en Paris* (Montevideo: Ediciones Trilce, 2002), 75.

7. Aldo Marchesi, "Political Violence and the Left in Latin America, 1967–1979," *Oxford Research Encyclopedia of Latin American History*, William Beezley, ed. (New York: Oxford Press, 2015).

8. Comisión de Constitución, Códigos, Legislación General y Administración, *Familiares de víctimas de los enfrentamientos armados ocurridos entre los años 1962 y 1976*, President Tabaré Vázquez et al., folder no. 1628, March 2007, https://legislativo.parlamento.gub.uy/temporales/D2007030926-004897406.pdf.

9. Over the next few years, the MLN-T's organizational framework was shattered not only due to state repression, but also due to a lack of strategical coherence among members; militants continued many of the debates regarding class struggle, syndicalism, and mass mobilization that caused friction within El Coordinador in 1964. The weakened organization and disparate communication between militants led to an effort to reform the organization under a more centralized structure, pro-Moscow disposition, and Marxist-Leninist vanguard strategy. Eleutorio Fernández Huidobro, *Historia de los Tupamaros*, vol. 1 (Montevideo: TAE Press, 1988), 112.

10. Abraham Guillén, the MLN-T's main intellectual and strategic point of reference, echoed the FAU's critique in his impactful *Strategy of the Urban Guerrilla*, originally published as *Estrategia de la guerrilla urbana* (Montevideo: Ediciones Liberación, 1969). Guillén recognized the FAU's tactical support for workplace conflicts as more accurately reflecting the ideas moved forth in his text. He drew parallels between their approach to armed action and that of the Iberian Anarchist Federation (FAI) in the years prior to the Spanish Civil War. Abraham Guillén, *Philosophy of the Urban Guerrilla: The Revolutionary Writings of Abraham Guillén*, Donald C. Hodges, ed. and trans. (New York: William Morrow, 1973), 273.

11. From internal strategy document, *COPEI* (Montevideo, 1972), 4.

12. *COPEI*, 4.

13. *COPEI*, 5, 7.

14. *COPEI*, 5, 9.

15. Guillén, *Philosophy of the Urban Guerrilla*, 269.

16. *COPEI*, 15.

17. *COPEI*, 3.

18. *COPEI*, vol. 2 (Montevideo, 1972), 14–15.

19. Vania Markarian, *Uruguay, 1968: Student Activism from Global Counterculture to Molotov Cocktails* (Oakland: University of California Press, 2017), 141.

20. Women members of the FAU/OPR-33 rarely participated directly in armed direct action tactics, such as kidnappings and robberies. They sometimes served as lookouts, but they primarily acted in the rear guard by information gathering.

21. This sentiment can be traced to early-twentieth-century anarchist-feminist perspectives on the domestic sphere. In the case of Spanish women anarchists in Andalucia, they resisted accumulation into the labor force and fought to maintain their home life, albeit in a socially emancipated way. In other words, they resisted subsuming their labor under capital. See Martha Ackelsberg, *Free Women of Spain: Anarchism and the Struggle for the Emancipation of Women* (Oakland: AK Press, 2004).

22. In twenty-six interviews with ex-members of OPR-33, only one recognized a practice of gendered division of labor within the organization. All others insisted that the organization never intentionally divided tasks by gender. Various works on the MLN-T have encountered a similar negation of such practice. Yet members of OPR-33 unanimously agreed that women were not present in the armed direct actions for safety purposes—something they insisted had more to do with questions of seniority, experience, and the small number of armed militants, or, more broadly, the organization's primary focus on building popular power. The MLN-T, which saw armed struggle as the revolutionary vanguard, emphasized an equal role for women in armed direct actions. They even wrote about this in a November 1971 text with a section dedicated to "revolutionary women." The text declared: "It is essential for the militant woman to find in her own revolutionary comrades the just understanding of her limitations, in order that her revolutionary role be efficacious and in order that the work of the group overcome prejudices so that there will no longer exist 'male' jobs and 'female' jobs, but rather the necessary complementarity which the revolutionary task as a whole requires." Both organizations insisted that carrying arms leveled the gender hierarchy between men and women militants. Jane Jaquette, "Women in Revolutionary Movements in Latin America," *Journal of Marriage and Family*, vol. 35, no. 2 (1973), 351; Lindsay Churchill, *Becoming the Tupamaros: Solidarity and Transnational Revolution in Uruguay and the United States* (Nashville: Vanderbilt University Press, 2014); Edelweiss Zahn, interview with author, Montevideo, June 11, 2017; "Lista de propuesta para

integrar la dirección del sector," OPR-33 folder, Mechoso Family Archive.

23. Edelweis Zahn, interview with author; Juliana Martínez, interview with author, Montevideo, May 31, 2017; Ana Rosa Amoros, interview with author, Montevideo, May 10, 2017; América López, interview with author, Montevideo, April 22, 2017.

24. Amy R. Baehr, "Liberal Feminism," *Stanford Encyclopedia of Philosophy*, Edward N. Zalta, ed. (Palo Alto: Stanford University Press, 2018).

25. Linda Reif's telling work on women guerrillas throughout the continent identifies two key barriers to women's participation in armed organizations: (1) structural disenfranchisement via resource maldistribution along gendered lines and (2) organizational attitudes regarding women, including lack of attention to women's issues and patriarchal internal dynamics among guerrillas themselves. She recognizes that Latin American men deferred to and recognized women as experts of the home. Such attitudes, combined with their ability to raise less suspicion than men, situated them in what the author calls "supportive roles." Linda Reif, "Women in Latin American Guerrilla Movements: A Comparative Perspective," *Comparative Politics*, vol. 18, no. 2 (1986).

26. Ana Laura de Giorgi, "La otra nueva ola: Jóvenes mujeres comunistas en el Uruguay de los 60," *Revista Izquierdas*, no. 22 (2015): 222.

27. Each cell had one *encargado* who was responsible for keeping contact with the Fomento (directorate) by way of an intermediary and for organizing information within the group. "Lista de propuesta para integrar la dirección del sector" (Montevideo, ca. 1972), Mechoso Family Archive.

28. Amoros, interview with author.

29. Daniel Guérin, *L'anarchisme: De la doctrine à l'action* (Paris: Gallimard, 1965). It is unclear what edition Juliana would have read at the time.

30. The FAU broke from orthodox anarchism after declaring support for the Cuban Revolution in 1962. They operated with a central committee rather than general assembly.

31. Martínez, interview with author.

32. Amoros, interview with author. After a raid of a FAU/OPR-33 safehouse in El Cerro, neighbors remembered the home's occupants as three youths who "lived a normal life, planting vegetables and raising chickens in a small, improvised coop of bricks and blocks." "Descubrieron un cubrir donde estuvo Molaguero," *El País* (Montevideo), August 7, 1972.

33. Amoros, interview with author.

34. Martínez, interview with author.

35. Some visitors were high-profile clandestine militants and had to participate in meetings behind a ski mask.

36. Like the MLN-T, the FAU/OPR-33 saw both maternity and romantic relationships as burdensome and distracting.

37. Martínez, interview with author.

38. Lilián Celiberti, interview with author, Montevideo, July 5, 2017.

39. Martínez, interview with author.

40. This story incorporates an intricate look at the Seral shoe factory conflict by request of the protagonists themselves, who continue to see their activity as embedded in popular social conflict. They insisted that their protagonism be situated as part of a broader narrative of the conflict to avoid misrepresentations of heroism and adventurism. The workforce included ninety women and eighty-three minors.

41. "Seral: Mas de 300 despidos," *Compañero* (Montevideo), September 10, 1971.

42. Sergio Molaguero, *Conocer la verdad: La historia de mi secuestro* (Montevideo: Artemisa Editores, 2008), 60; "El 'benefactor' Molaguero pierde una batalla," *Compañero* (Montevideo), April 29, 1971.

43. The ROE affiliates included José Estevez, Rogelio Álavarez, Omar Fernández, Rodolfo Páez, and Joaquín Texeira. Juan Carlos Mechoso, correspondence with author, September 11, 2018.

44. Juan Carlos Mechoso, "Seral" (Montevideo, n.d.), Mechoso Family Archive.

45. "Obreros de Seral ¡Firmes en la pelea!" *Compañero* (Montevideo), January 12, 1972.

46. "Seral: Mas de 300 despidos."

47. "La leccion de FUNSA ocupada," *Marcha* (Montevideo), July 7, 1972.

48. "Desde Santa Lucia llega la marcha de la dignidad," *Compañero* (Montevideo), November 23, 1971.

49. "Santa Lucia: Los tiempos cambian," *Compañero* (Montevideo), October 20, 1971.

50. "Casa Sanz: Los incendiarios eran empleados de Seral," *Acción* (Montevideo), December 24, 1971.

51. "The FAU Version of Story of the Seral Dispute and Molaguero Kidnapping (as published in *Lucha Libertaria*)," in *The Federación Anarquista Uruguaya (FAU): Crisis, Armed Struggle, and Dictatorship, 1967-1985* (London: Kate Sharpley Library, 2009), 41.

52. "Reglamento" (ca. 1968), in *Movimiento de Liberación Nacional ('Tupamaros'): Documentación propia*, 2nd ed. (Caracas: Indal, 1972), 69.

53. Juliana Martínez, interview with author, Montevideo, October 11, 2017.

54. The task required that Juliana draw upon her subjugated knowledge to avoid drawing unwarranted attention. She remembers

paying close detail to her clothing style to avoid resembling an urban dweller. She drew reference from her upbringing in Chuy to recall the social codes specific to a small town, such as the infrequent use of makeup purses by women inhabitants. She feared running into friends or family members during the outing; such encounters would require an explanation for why she had ventured so far from the capitol alongside a male companion.

55. Passing information required precision and vigilance. In a prior exchange with the same intermediary, the military police arrived and stopped Juliana's car prior to passing the information. The authorities searched the car, to no avail, and the intermediary left the scene. The militants knew to return the next day at the same time for what was called the *automatico*, a normalized practice to assure the exchange in the case of a botched prior attempt. Martínez, interview with author, May 31, 2017.

56. On the first attempt (May 6), Molaguero elected a different route. On May 8, the teams failed to communicate Molaguero's departure due to the receiving team forgetting to turn on their walkie-talkie. On May 9, the walkie-talkie was interfered with by crossing radio signals. On May 10, the intercepting team mistakenly stopped the car of Deputy Bari González. Molaguero, *Conocer la verdad*, 40.

57. "Descubrieron un cubrir donde estuvo Molaguero," *El País* (Montevideo), August 7, 1972.

58. "Dr. . . . El dia 11 del corriente" (Montevideo, May 12, 1972), Mechoso Family Archive.

59. "FUNSA ocupada," *El Popular* (Montevideo), June 23, 1972.

60. "Molaguero: Estuve un mes encadenado y hambriento; en deplorable estado, ayer habló para los periodistas," *El País* (Montevideo), July 21, 1972. A member of the FAU/OPR-33 later shared that the food ration was comparable to that of working poor folks of the time.

61. The women knew to glance at the bathroom window to check for the bottle's presence before entering. Its absence signified that the house was unsecure and surveilled. Amoros, interview with author.

62. Juliana Martínez, interview with author, Montevideo, June 13, 2017; Amoros, interview with author, May 10, 2017.

63. Amoros, interview with author.

64. "La situación en FUNSA," *Marcha* (Montevideo), June 30, 1972.

65. Although they participated in the same cell, authorities could not draw the connection; while authorities first detained Andrés for his role in Operation Apretesis, Trías escaped after serving as lookout on the street, rather than entering the building. Andrés, *Estafar un banco—que placer!* (Montevideo: Alter Ediciones, 2009), 74-75.

66. Secretaría de Derechos Humanos para el Pasado Reciente (ex-Secretaría de Seguimiento de la Comisión para la Paz), Legajo LDD 111.

67. "CNT Denuncia Acción Provocadora de la ROE," *El Popular* (Montevideo), August 9, 1972.

68. Hugo Cores, "Después de cuatro meses de barbarie, somos capaces de reencontrarnos," in *Luchar Ahora*, Comité Obrero Sacco y Vanzetti, ed. (Montevideo, August–September 1972), Mechoso Family Archive.

69. The Argentine visitor greeted the crowd with words of solidarity from Raimundo Ongaro, CGT-A general secretary and secretary of the Buenos Aires Graphic Artists Federation (FGB), and Augustín Tosco, Luz y Fuerza secretary and leader of the Cordobazo. The CGT-A formed a militant sector of Peronism that sought to resignify the ideology around an anticapitalist, anti-imperialist, and anti-bureaucratic practice. The CGT-A shared many similarities with the Tendencia, especially its use of direct action tactics, including armed intervention in labor conflicts by the People's Revolutionary Army (ERP). The CGT-A also reflected a synthesis of left ideas around "unity in action." The FGB was originally founded by anarchists in 1857. Like in Uruguay, anarchist influence in graphic arts unions remained steady. In the late sixties and early seventies, an unnamed tendency with strong influences from the ROE formed within the union. Two of its members, Hugo Quijano and Raúl Olivera, were Uruguayan anarchists who grew up participating in the student movement with close ties to the FAU/ROE. Rafael Viana da Silva, "Um Anarquismo Latino-Americano: Estudo comparativo e transnacional das experiências na Argentina, Brasil e Uruguai, 1959–1985," PhD diss. (Universidade Federal Rural do Rio de Janeiro, 2017), 140.

70. Quoted in Hugo Cores, *Sobre la tendencia combativa* (unpublished, 1983), xvii, CEIU, Hugo Cores Archive.

71. Zelmar Michellini, "Les duele que no todos sean mansos," in *Luchar Ahora*.

72. Gerardo Gatti, "Convocamos a todos a pelear unidos," in *Luchar Ahora*.

73. Cores, "Después de cuatro meses de barbarie."

74. Hugo Cores, *Memorias de la resistencia* (Montevideo: Ediciones Banda Oriental, 2002), 126.

75. Daniel Augusto de Almeida Alves, "Arriba los que luchan! Sindicaismo revolucionário e luta armada a trajetória da Federaçao Anarquista Uruguaia: 1963–73," PhD diss. (Porto Alegre: Universidade Federal Rio Grande do Sul, 2016).

76. María Eugenia Jung and Universindo Rodríguez, *Juan Carlos Mechoso: Anarquista* (Montevideo: Ediciones Trilce, 2006), 80–86.

77. Eduardo Galeano, interview with Alberto Mechoso, "Desde el fondo del abismo," in Juan Carlos Mechoso, *Acción directa anarquista:*

Una historia de la Federación Anarquista Uruguaya, vol. 4 (Montevideo: Ediciones Recortes, 2005), 387–92.

78. Jung and Rodríguez, *Juan Carlos Mechoso*, 86–88.

79. For full transcription of both texts, see "Los comunicados 4 y 7 presente," *El Muerto* (Montevideo), February 11, 2011, available at http://elmuertoquehabla.blogspot.com/2011/02/los-comunicados -4-7-1973-presente.html.

80. The meetings consisted of General Gregorio Álvarez, Coronel Ramón Trabal, General Hugo Chiappe Posse, Brigadier Pérez Caldaz, Vice Admiral Olazábal, Gerardo Cuesta (PCU), Wladimir Turiansky (PCU), and José D'Elía. Jorge Chagas and Mario Tonarelli, *El sindicalismo uruguayo bajo la dictadura, 1973–84* (Montevideo: Ediciones del Nuevo Mundo, 1989), 31; US Ambassador to Uruguay Ernest Siracusa, Telegram 436 from US Embassy in Uruguay to US Department of State, "Preliminary Analysis of Possible External Orientation of Uruguayan Military," February 11, 1973, US Department of State Office of the Historian, https://history.state .gov/historicaldocuments/frus1969-76ve11p2/d330.

81. Cores, *Memorias de la resistencia*, 127.

82. Cores, *Memorias de la resistencia*, 128.

83. Ernest Siracusa, Telegram 453 from US Embassy in Uruguay to US Department of State, "Preliminary Recommendations Re U.S. Posture in New Uruguayan Situation," February 13, 1973, US Department of State Office of the Historian, available at https://history .state.gov/historicaldocuments/frus1969-76ve11p2/d331.

84. CIA memorandum, "The Future Role of the Military in Uruguay," April 10, 1973, Washington, DC, available at https://history.state .gov/historicaldocuments/frus1969-76ve11p2/d333.

85. Chagas and Tonarelli, *El sindicalismo uruguayo*, 32.

86. Ernest Siracusa, Telegram 1176 from the US Embassy in Uruguay to the US Department of State, "Uruguay Two Months After the Crisis," April 18, 1973, US Department of State Office of the Historian, https://history.state.gov/historicaldocuments/frus1969-76ve11p2/ d334.

87. "Ferrocarril: Dos meses de directorio militar," *Compañero* (Montevideo), June 13, 1973.

88. "Nuestra opinión sindical," *Compañero* (Montevideo), May 22, 1973.

89. "Mas sindicalistas de la Tendencia detenidos," *Compañero* (Montevideo), May 22, 1973.

90. "El sindicato de FUNSA responde al comando general del ejercito," *Compañero* (Montevideo), June 5, 1973.

91. "Nuestra opinión sindical: El plan aprobado por el secretario de la CNT dispersa las movilizaciones y debilita el peso de la clase obrera en la situación political," *Compañero* (Montevideo), June 5, 1973.

92. Aurelio González, *Una historia en imagenes, 1957–1973* (Montevideo: Alter Ediciones, 2012), 260.

93. "Resolution 1.102/973 of 30 June 1973," Robert K. Goldman, Joaquin Martínez Bjorkman, and Jean-Louis Weill, "Memorandum from Mission of Inquiry to URUGUAY from December 12–18, 1977," folder 24, CEIU, Waksman.

94. "Decree 466/973 of 27 June 1973," Robert K. Goldman, Joaquin Martínez Bjorkman, and Jean-Louis Weill, "Memorandum from Mission of Inquiry to URUGUAY from December 12–18, 1977," folder 24, CEIU, Waksman.

95. Francois Graña, *Los Padres de Mariana: María Emilia Islas y Jorge Zaffaroni* (Montevideo: Editorial Trilce, 2011), 130.

96. Chagas and Tonarelli, *El sindicalismo uruguayo*, 50.

97. Chagas and Tonarelli, *El sindicalismo uruguayo*, 63–65.

98. Chagas and Tonarelli, *El sindicalismo uruguayo*, 63–65; Chagas and Tonarelli are careful to distinguish the Tendencia's July 1973 negotiations from those between the CNT majority and Coronel Bolentini beginning in February 1973. The PCU had long sought to identify military sectors that would side with the people in the event of a civil war. This strategy was best reflected in the party's support for General Seregni as Broad Front presidential candidate in 1971 elections.

99. "El documento de los tres 'F': FUS, FOEB, FUNSA" (Montevideo), August 1973, Mechoso Family Archive.

100. "El documento de los tres 'F.'"

101. "Clausuras," *Marcha* (Montevideo), June 27, 1973.

102. Susana Dominzain, *Así se forjó la historia: Acción sindical e identidad de los trabajadores metalurgicos en Uruguay* (Montevideo: Ediciones Primero de Mayo, 2016), 332–33.

103. "Mientras se comercializan lana sucia hay 2,500 trabajadores textiles desocupados" *Compañero* (Montevideo), September 25, 1973; "Una olla sindical no es solo para comer sino para continuar la lucha," *Compañero* (Montevideo), September 25, 1973; "Movilización Ascendente en torno a los despedidos" *Compañero* (Montevideo), September 18, 1973.

104. "Festival de la solidaridad en el sindicato de FUNSA," *Compañero* (Montevideo), October 2, 1973; "Los Viernes haga llegar su solidaridad," *Compañero* (Montevideo), September 18, 1973.

105. Cores, *Memorias de la Resistencia*, 133.

106. "Prohiba la union de los sindicatos," *Compañero* (Montevideo), August 28, 1973.

107. Ricardo Vilaró, *Uruguay y sus sindicatos* (Holland, March 1979), 56, CEIU, Ricardo Vilaró Archive.

108. Ivonne Trías, *Hugo Cores: Pasión y rebeldía en la izquierda uruguaya* (Montevideo: Editorial Trilce, 2008), 141.

109. Andrés, *Estafar un banco*, 80.
110. "Decree 1.026/973 of 28 November 1973," Robert K. Goldman, Joaquin Martínez Bjorkman, and Jean-Louis Weill, "Memorandum from Mission of Inquiry to URUGUAY from December 12–18, 1977," folder 24, CEIU, Waksman.
111. Chagas and Tonarelli, *El sindicalismo uruguayo*, 123–24.
112. Although my sample of 343 total work actions represents only a fraction of those recorded in official data, the set, taken from *El Popular*, offers a rather accurate look at an increasing militancy among CNT majority-affiliated unions.
113. Ernest Siracusa, Telegram 3712 from US Embassy in Uruguay to US Department of State, "Subj: Conversation with President Bordaberry," December 26, 1973, US Department of State Office of the Historian, https://history.state.gov/historicaldocuments/frus1969-76ve11p2/d339.
114. Ernest Siracusa, Telegram 2164 from US Embassy in Uruguay to US Department of State, "Subj: Defense Minister's View on Current Situation" (Montevideo), July 13, 1973, US Department of State Office of the Historian, https://history.state.gov/historicaldocuments/frus1969-76ve11p2/d337.
115. Howard Handelman, "Labor-Industrial Conflict and the Collapse of Uruguayan Democracy," *Journal of Interamerican Studies and World Affairs*, vol. 23, no. 4 (1981): 378.
116. José Nun, "The Middle Class Military Coup," in *The Politics of Conformity in Latin America*, C. Veliz, ed. (New York: Oxford University Press, 1967), 66–118.
117. Comité de Solidaridad–Casa del Pueblo Uruguayo, "Noticias Noticias Noticias Noticias Noticias Noticias … Cono Sur—1976: Resumen servicio especial" (Montreal, ca. 1976), folder 26, CEIU, Waksman; Martin Weinstein, "Uruguay: Military Rule and Economic Failure," *Politics, Policies, and Economic Development in Latin America*, Robert Wesson, ed. (Stanford, CA: Hoover Press, 1984), 43.
118. Vilaro, *Uruguay y sus sindicatos*.

6. The Garage Was Not a Garden

1. Tournier would later become Uruguay's most famous animated film director.
2. Daniel Agusto de Almeida Alves, "Arriba los que luchan! Sindicalismo revolucionario e luta armada. A trajectória da federaçao anarquista uruguaia: 1963-1973," unpublished PhD diss., Universidade Federal do Rio Grande do Sul, Porto Alegre, 2016; Ivonne

Trías, *Hugo Cores: Pasión y rebeldía en la izquierda uruguaya* (Montevideo: Editorial Trilce, 2008), 95.

3. Other members of the OPR-33, such as Juan Carlos Mechoso, Alfredo Pareja, and Raúl Cariboni, were imprisoned in March 1973.

4. After leaving the MLN-T to participate in the formation of the OPR-33, Hébert Mejías Collazo shared his knowledge of how to counterfeit paper documents. Members of the FAU with training in graphic arts replicated these methods to produce a variety of fake state-issued documents. Augusto Andrés interview with author, Montevideo, December 27, 2017.

5. Much has been written about the role of exiled anarchists residing in the Río de La Plata region, specifically the development of transnational networks to both support resistance in the homeland and to build and influence the development of revolutionary left movements in their countries of residence, whether Argentina or Uruguay. The historiography focuses primarily on Italian and Spanish exiles who arrived in the region and played key roles in both native and host countries. Once arriving in the Río de La Plata, anarchists often found themselves moving back and forth between Argentina and Uruguay to escape right-wing dictatorships that seized power during different historical moments in both countries. For example, during the Mussolini era, Italian anarchists fled to the Río de La Plata to sustain the movement and launch resistance from abroad, in an effort that María Migueláñez Martínez has labeled as "exile as a political strategy against fascism." María Migueláñez Martínez, "Atlantic Circulation of Italian Anarchist Exiles: Militants and Propaganda between Europe and Río de La Plata (1922–1939)," *Zapruder World*, vol. 1 (2014). One Argentine scholar argues that the FAU-PVP's activity abroad resignified "exile" to mean more than merely "retreat": Fabiola Labrolla, "El exilio combatiente: La fundación del Partido de la Victoria del Pueblo del Uruguay en la Argentina," conference paper, *Jornadas XIV* (Montevideo: University of the Republic, 2013), 12.

6. See John Dinges, *The Condor Years: How Pinochet brought Terrorism to Three Continents* (New York: New Press, 2005); Fernando López, *The Feathers of the Condor: Transnational State Terrorism, Exiles, and Civilian Anticommunism in South America* (New York: Cambridge University Press, 2016); Patrice McSherry, *Predatory States: Operation Condor and Covert War in Latin America* (Lanham, MD: Rowman & Littlefield Publishers, 2005).

7. Aldo Marchesi's *Latin America's Radical Left: Rebellion and Cold War in the Global Sixties* (New York: Cambridge University Press, 2018) acknowledges four important sites for the development of the Southern Cone left: Montevideo (mid-1960s), Havana (1967), Santiago

(1970-73), and Buenos Aires (1973-76). The latter is the focus of this chapter due to its importance as a refuge for exiles. Although Allende's Chile offered refuge to militants in the three years prior, Argentina's unique condition as the last country to fall under dictatorship enabled militants to find shelter there after having exhausted the potential of armed struggle in their home countries.

8. Vania Markarian, *Left in Transformation: Uruguayan Exiles and the Latin American Human Rights Network, 1967-1984* (London: Routledge, 2005).

9. Álvaro Rico, *Investigación histórica sobre la dictadura y el terrorismo de estado en el Uruguay (1973-1985)*, vol. 1 (Montevideo: UDELAR, 2008), 769-83.

10. Dinges, *Condor Years*, 210.

11. Scholars tend to downplay the impact of the Uruguayan dictatorship because of its relative low numbers of permanent disappearances compared to other Plan Cóndor governments. For example, political scientist Paul Sondrol (1992) challenged Alfred Stephen and Martin Weinstein for having classified the dictatorship as "totalitarian." He distinguishes between totalitarian and authoritarian patterns of repression, claiming that the former seeks to eliminate entire categories of people viewed as threats to the national project for their mere existence, whereas the latter targets individuals due to their political activity (196). Yet, combined with previous offensives against the Comunidad del Sur and the closure of the School of Fine Arts, the mid-1976 offensive against the FAU had successfully eliminated nearly all anarchists from Uruguay. Paul C. Sondrol, "1984 Revisited? A Re-Examination of Uruguay's Military Dictatorship," *Bulletin of Latin American Research*, vol. 11, no. 2 (1992): 187-203.

12. Sikkink argues that human rights activists disillusioned by the failure in Vietnam and inspired by the success of civil rights activism pressured the US government to take up human rights policy globally beginning in 1973. The "global human rights idea" was an outward extension of rights allotted to US citizens based on the country's founding documents. However, the United States struggled to balance its staunch anti-communism while simultaneously attempting to support human rights abroad. The author continues, "There was no one US policy, no single vision of who or what the United States was and what it stood for. . . . Since the 1950s, intense anticommunism had informed all aspects of US policy in the region. This anticommunism was often justified by referring to abysmal human rights practices of communist regimes. But by the 1970s, anticommunism led the United States to support, arm, and train authoritarian regimes that carried out massive human rights abuses against their citizens. In principle, anticommunism could

be made compatible with a commitment to human rights, but US policy makers in Latin America had come to accept as an article of faith that anticommunism required strong support for authoritarian military regimes." Kathryn Sikkink, *Mixed Signals: U.S. Human Rights Policy in Latin America* (Ithaca: Cornell University Press, 2007), xviii; 5–7, 18.

13. Interview with Hugo Cores from Trías, *Hugo Cores*, 139.

14. "A los comptriotas [*sic*], a los amigos del pueblo uruguayo" (Paris, May 1975), CEIU, French Exile Organizations Politique, folder 12.

15. They drew comparisons between the Italian, Spanish, German, Polish, and Jewish anarchists who founded the first workers' organizations in the Río de la Plata with Che Guevara's transnational organizing efforts in Cuba, Bolivia, Guatemala, and Africa. "En exilio hay mucho por hacer," *Boletín de la Resistencia*, no. 23 (Buenos Aires), August 20, 1975, CEIU, Hugo Cores Archive.

16. "A los comptriotas."

17. "A los comptriotas."

18. "A los comptriotas."

19. The paper served as one of various internal media organs within the military and was edited by Luis Michelini, a PCU fellow traveler. The primary-source compilation of Uruguayan police and military files *Testimonio de una nacion agredida* (Montevideo: El Comando, 1978), 110, claims the paper was clandestinely funded by the PCU but that Michelini also served as a double agent for the CIA. Perhaps the best indication of the PCU's financial backing can be found in a statement in the October 19, 1973, edition, which declared, "The weekly paper 9 *de Febrero* does not correspond to any military orientation, nor is it sponsored by the Armed Forces. We have taken up this task with an enormous amoung of sacrifice to support the national cause. Surely, the pueblo Oriental will judge our work. But with independence and clean consciousness we take on this responsibility during this difficult time." FAU militant Juan Carlos Mechoso recalls a conversation with a party leader and labor union official in prison, who showed him a copy of the newspaper and declared, "Look what my organization is doing!" Conversations about the meaning of "Communiques 4 and 7" continued into 1976, when the ROE held debate in Paris regarding the two cryptic messages to commemorate three years passing. "3 años de los comunicados 4 y 7" (Montevideo, March 1976), CEIU, French Exile Organizations Politique, folder 12.

20. US ambassador to Uruguay Ernest Siracusa declared, "With the armed forces having recently moved formally into the economic decision-making process through the economic and social council and having placed a number of military officers in important

government posts, it would seem that the military is the driving force in the nation's efforts towards economic and political change. However, a better description of the present state of affairs is that the military presence is the spur prodding such efforts but no one hand is on the reins." Ernest Siracusa, "Telegram 2224 from the Embassy in Uruguay to the Department of State, Subj: The Uruguayan Military: A Lack of Cohesion," August 8, 1974, US Department of State Office of the Historian, https://history.state.gov/historicaldocuments/-frus1969-76ve11p2/d340.

21. While exiled in Chile in 1973, MLN-T leadership recognized the organization's shortcomings, specifically their inability to build around a mass movement strategy. Andrés Cultelli's self-critique declares: "In the end, the mass political wing March 26 could do very little once it was decided that everything would revolve around a military strategy. . . . The question of unions . . . was left to the Communist Party. The question of the role of masses as a necessary condition for revolution never entered the consciousness of the MLN-T leadership nor its members, who were all fascinated by the armed apparatus and its 'indestructability.'" Andrés Cultelli, *La revolución necesaria, contribución a la autocrítica del MLN-Tupamaros* (Montevideo: Colihue, 2006), 51.

22. See Aldo Marchesi, *Latin America's Radical Left: Rebellion and Cold War in the Global Sixties* (New York: Cambridge University Press, 2018).

23. Throughout the late sixties, the FER student organization served informally as a front for the MLN-T. In 1970, the FER divided over questions of strategy, autonomy, and their affiliation with the Tupamaros. This "microschism" formed the FER68, which eventually morphed into the MLN-T popular organization 26 de Marzo. The members of the FER who maintained the organization's name linked with the newly formed FRT social movement. Both of the latter eventually merged with the ROE. Eduardo Rey Tristán, *La izquierda revolucionaria uruguaya, 1955-1973* (Sevilla: Universidad de Sevilla, 2005), 403.

24. Markarian, *Left in Transformation*, 74.

25. According to Argentine scholar Fabiola Labrolla, the FAU grew away from the FNR/UAL after successfully obtaining a $10 million kidnap ransom in August 1974. The organization subsequently built an independent exile infrastructure utilizing their own resources. Labrolla, "El exilio combatiente," 12.

26. While the Federacion Libertaria Argentina remained hegemonic in Argentine anarchist political circles, their position on Perón, specifically their collaboration with various right-wing factions to support the ouster of Perón in 1955, spawned a rift within the anarchist

movement. Anarchist veterans, including famous turn-of-the-century expropriator Emilio Uriondo, formed a small circle under the name La Protesta, which they borrowed from the FORA's newspaper, *La Protesta Humana*. Moreover, some members of the Fuerzas Armadas Peronistas, such as Alva Castillo, were born of anarchist parents and remained anarchist sympathizers. Castillo frequently visited imprisoned members of the FAU in Buenos Aires jails and offered her home as refuge when members of the FAU-PVP became targets of a state offensive in 1976. Juan Carlos Mechoso, interview with author, Montevideo, December 26, 2017.

27. Hugo Cores, interview, in Markarian, *Left in Transformation*, 71.

28. Augusto Andrés, interview with author, Montevideo, June 11, 2017.

29. Sara Méndez, interview with author, Montevideo, July 13, 2017.

30. CIA Intelligence Memorandum, "Subj: The Roots of Violence: The Urban Guerrilla in Argentina," June 9, 1975, Washington, DC, available at https://www.cia.gov/library/readingroom/docs/CIA-RDP85 T00353R000100180001-6.pdf.

31. The mythical JCR-1 was a replica version of the Swedish-made Carl Gustav M-45. The 1975 JCR "Plan 500" set out to build five hundred submachine gun models, a small arms factory, two fully equipped gun stores with indoor shooting ranges, and one tech laboratory to fabricate police interceptors. Marchesi, *Latin America's Radical Left*, 162.

32. Many ERP operations were extremely ambitious and high risk, including a 1974 siege on the Azul C-10 Armed Calvalry Regiment only three months after Perón's return to presidency and a 1975 guerrilla offensive in rural Tucuman, in which militants sought to liberate 310 kilometers of space, including some parts of southern Bolivia. Robert L. Sheina, *Latin America's Wars: The Age of the Professional Soldier, 1900–2001*, vol. 2 (Washington, DC: Potomac Books, 2003), 102–103.

33. Mechoso, interview with author.

34. The Laurino kidnapping resulted in the arrest of OPR-33 militants Pablo León and Anibal Griot. Another failed kidnapping attempt shortly after resulted in the arrest of Omar Zina. All three had the luck of passing as ordinary criminals without affiliations with a political organization. Ruben "Pepe" Prieto, interview in *The Federación Anarquista Uruguaya (FAU): Crisis, Dictatorship, and Armed Struggle, 1967–1985* (London: Kate Sharkey Library, 2009).

35. Property in the center costed as little as $30,000, and homes in peripheral neighborhoods sold for as little as $8,000. François Graña, *Los padres de Mariana: María Emilia Islas y Jorge Zaffaroni; la pasión militante* (Montevideo: Ediciones Trilce, 2011), 169–70.

36. Erro was likely referring to the efforts of the FAU-ROE and GAU

militants to maintain a communication structure during the 1973 general strike while PCU delegates remained committed to reaching an agreement with the Armed Forces.

37. "Carta presumiblemente redactada por un informante de la policía sobre las actividades de políticos uruguayos en Argentina y sobre el acto organizado por la ROE y realizado en la Federación de Box el 19 de abril de 1974," May 6, 1974, Archive of the Uruguayan National Directorate of Information and Intelligence (DNII), folder 7065, available at https://medios.presidencia.gub.uy/jm_portal/ 2011/noticias/NO_B889/tomo1/2-sec2-cronologia-documental -anexos/2_partido_victoria_pueblo/PVP_crono_larga.pdf.

38. Seven of the arestees had outstanding arrest warrants, and twenty-six had criminal records in Uruguay. Cores, interview in Triás, *Hugo Cores*, 143.

39. "Realización de un acto público en Buenos Aires. Documentos que informan sobre el 'Operativo Gris' de la Policía Federal Argentina, vinculado a la detención de 101 uruguayos participantes de una reunión realizada en calle México No. 2936," June 2, 1974, Archive of the Uruguayan National Directorate of Information and Intelligence (DNII), box 60, available at https://medios .presidencia.gub.uy/jm_portal/2011/noticias/NO_B889/tomo1/ 2-sec2-cronologia-documental-anexos/2_partido_victoria_pueblo/ PVP_crono_larga.pdf.

40. US ambassador Hill and José López Rega held a televised press conference regarding US funding for the drug-related policing in Argentina, during which the minister of social welfare declared, "The anti-drug campaign will automatically be an anti-guerrilla campaign as well," McSherry, *Predatory States*, 74, 78.

41. Most houses were purchased in Buenos Aires suburbs for as little as $6,000. Juan Carlos Mechoso, interview, "Anarchists Had More of a Stomach to Fight," In *The Federacion Anarquista Uruguaya (FAU): Crisis, Armed Struggle and Dictatorship, 1967–1985*, Kate Sharpley Library, 2001.

42. All militants received a one-month stiped to spend on pension lodging while searching for more permanent residence. Some continued to receive stipends after facing difficulties encountering work due to the need to maintain a low profile. The first wave of exiles produced a late 1972 report acknowledging the difficulty of balancing wage labor with political militancy. The odd jobs that many encountered, such as ice cream vending in the street, required shift availability for up to twelve hours a day. Those who continued receiving monthly stipends were required to live in homes with kitchen equipment available to keep cost of living down. Stipends enabled up to six bus rides, two coffees, one packet of cigarettes,

and one newspaper daily. Militants also received monthly money for hygiene products and one trip to the movie theater. Finally, militants received an annual stipend for one pair of pants, two shirts, one sweater, and two pairs of underwear. "Contestación de la nota recibida el 9/10/72" (Montevideo, ca. December 1972) Mechoso Family Archive; "Criterios Generales" (Montevideo, ca. March 1974), Mechoso Family Archive.

43. Augusto Andrés, "Aquella Locura," *Brecha* (Montevideo), May 20, 2016. In a private conversation on December 28, 2017, Andrés also shared information about how and where the FAU-ROE printed material while abroad.

44. Graña, *Los Padres de Mariana*, 132.

45. Andrés, interview with author; Robert K. Goldman, Joaquin Martínez Bjorkman, and Jean-Louis Weill, "Memorandum from Mission of Inquiry to URUGUAY from December 12-18, 1977," folder 24, CEIU, Waksman.

46. Graña, *Los Padres de Mariana*, 131; "En exilio hay mucho por hacer," in *Boletín de la Resistencia* (Buenos Aires), August 20, 1975, CEIU, Hugo Cores Archive; "Como dice ésta carta: Con ingenio y cuidado difundir la inform no. 23 ación popular," in *Boletín de la Resistencia*, no. 29, March 1976, CEIU, Hugo Cores Archive.

47. Participants in the congress concealed their faces with hoods to avoid leaking any of the identities of their comrades. The sudden numerical growth of the organization after the merger with the FER-FRT and heightened risk of arrest and torture, especially within Uruguay, necessitated an increased vigilance around security. Militants coalesced around subgroups of twelve to fifteen. Drivers used the organization's vehicles to pick up militants from arranged locations, where they were immediately covered by a hood and driven to the meeting space. There, they deliberated around various topics and eventually came to conclusions by vote. Notetakers compiled documentation of the discussions and decisions, and sent the information along to the Buenos Aires-located Fomento. All documentation from the congress was burned upon completing the final deliberation in June 1975. Anonymous, interview with author, Montevideo, May 15, 2017.

48. Director of SID General Amauri E. Prantl (OCOA Military Division I), "Análisis sobre el Partido por la Victoria del Pueblo," from *Investigación histórica sobre la dictadura y el terrorismo de estado en el Uruguay (1973-1985)*, vol. 3, 75-83.

49. Yvonne Trías and Universindo Rodríguez, *Gerardo Gatti: Revolucionario* (Montevideo: Trilce, 2012), 261-63.

50. Augusto Andrés, interview, in Trías and Rodríguez, *Gerardo Gatti*, 237.

51. "Prontuario Policial N. 252, 27-v-75," in Trías, *Hugo Cores*, 151.

52. The April-to-May sweep also captured the Etchinique brothers (MLN-T) and Enrique Erro (UP). During this same period, authorities at the Ezeiza airport prevented Zelmar Michelini from traveling to the United States and detained his passport on site. "Un dirigente acusa," in *Tribunal Russell: La dictadura civico-militar uruguaya en el blanquillo de los acusados*, Hugo Cores (Paris, February 1976).

53. "Demandamos a las autoridades argentinas el resguardo de su vida y su libertad, hoy en serio peligro," in *Ultima Hora* (Buenos Aires), vol. 1, no. 67 (1975), CEIU, Movimiento Laboral (Héctor Rodríguez).

54. "Solo la protesta y el repudio internacional a los crímenes de la dictadura Uruguaya, pueden salvar la vida y la libertad de Carlos Coitiño," May 6, 1975, CEIU, French Exile Organizations Politique, folder 12.

55. Memorandum of Conversation, "Subject: Uruguayan Foreign Minister's Bilateral Meeting with the Secretary," May 10, 1975, US Department of State Office of the Historian, https://history.state. gov/historicaldocuments/-frus1969-76ve11p2/d341.

56. Memorandum of Conversation, "Uruguayan Foreign Minister's Bilateral Meeting with the Secretary."

57. In the first months of 1976, Kissinger and the US State Department moved away from their previous "New Dialogue" strategy, which recognized Latin America as a monolithic bloc, and turned instead toward bilateral foreign relations that dealt with each country separately.

58. Russell E. Olson, "Letter to Aurelia A. Brazeal" (Montevideo), August 8, 1975, US Department of State Office of the Historian, https://history.state.gov/historicaldocuments/frus1969-76ve11p2/ d342.

59. News of Coghlan's death and others imprisonment gained publicity throughout Europe via the ROE network established abroad by Presno and Cores. Images of Coghlan's face lined Parisian streets, and news of the five detainees surfaced in the Swedish press. "Campaña por la libertad de los compañeros ferroviarios presos," *Boletín de la Resistencia* (Buenos Aires), April 4, 1975, CEIU, French Exile Organizations Politique, folder 12.

60. All attendees reaffirmed commitment to cooperating between countries to fight continental subversion. Argentine representative Jorge Rafael Videla declared, "To be precise, as many people [as] necessary will die in Argentina to ensure the security of our country." Although many PCU leaders went into exile after the party was illegalized in November 1973, roughly forty organizers remained in Uruguay, and meetings continued with the active involvement of a couple hundred members. The party operated in the first years of

324NOTES TO PAGES 229–231

the dictatorship with a de jure prohibited status but did not suffer severe repression until Operation Morgan.

61. "Contra el enemigo vale todo," *Boletín de la Resistencia* (Buenos Aires), no. 28 (February 1976), CEIU, Hugo Cores Archive.

62. "Tribunal Russell: La dictadura cívico-militar uruguaya en el blanquillo de los acusados" (Paris, February 1976), CEIU, Hugo Cores Archive, 11–12.

63. Resolution 1.804/973 of October 15, 1973, Robert K. Goldman, Joaquin Martínez Bjorkman, and Jean-Louis Weill, "Memorandum from Mission of Inquiry to URUGUAY from December 12–18, 1977," folder 24, CEIU, Waksman.

64. Markarian, *Left in Transformation*, 92.

65. Memorandum of Conversation, Ambassador Siracusa and Foreign Minister Juan Carlos Blanco, "Subj: Ambassador Siracusa speaks to Juan Carlos Blanco about Human Rights concerns in US" (Montevideo), January 27, 1976, US Department of State Office of the Historian, https://history.state.gov/historicaldocuments/frus1969-76ve 11p2/d347.

66. This sentiment extended to all but one other worker in the US Embassy in Uruguay. Katherine Sikkink recalls, "I was curious about what people in the embassy in Uruguay were saying about human rights. Only one of the embassy staff people I interviewed admitted that they thought the Amnesty International report was accurate. The others told me that their boss, Ambassador Ernest Sircausa, assured them that the report was highly misleading. Sikkink, *Mixed Signals*, xvi.

67. Secretary of State Henry Kissinger, "Memorandum of Conversation," March 26, 1976, National Security Archives, 20, 23. Similar to Kissinger, US ambassador to Argentina Robert Hill viewed the junta's economic program as "encouragingly pragmatic" and assured, "The US government should not become overly identified with the junta, but so long as the new government can hew to a moderate line the US government should encourage it by examining sympathetically any requests for assistance." He saw promise in Videla's quick attention to opening the country to foreign investment and resolving "various investment problems," such as Exxon, Chase Manhattan, and Standard Electric. "Telegram 2061 From US Embassy in Argentina to US Department of State, Subj: Videla's Moderate Line Prevails," National Security Archives, March 29, 1976, US Department of State Office of the Historian.

68. Luis Gutiérrez, "Primera Reunion de Trababajo de Inteligencia Nacional" (Santiago), October 29, 1975, 1, National Security Archives.

69. Gutiérrez, "Primera Reunion."

70. McSherry, *Predatory States*, 9.

71. USAID workers began expressing concern about losing congressional support for continuing the flow of Public Safety Program funds to Uruguay as early as July 1973. Reports about torture in the interior province of Paysandu caused a USAID representative to write to US deputy chief of mission in Uruguay Frank Ortiz regarding a foreseeable difficulty in continuing the program. The memo acknowledged the growing difficulty of maintaining a US presence in the country after the negative publicity brought on by the Council of Churches' "investigation" (scare quotes in original) and Costas Gavras's film *State of Siege*. Copy of Memo, Rhoads to Ortiz, "Possible Efects of Uruguayan Torture Charges on the AID Public Safety Program, and Other U.S. Relationships with the GOU," July 1, 1973, National Security Archives, available at https://nsarchive2.gwu.edu//NSAEBB/NSAEBB309/-index.htm. Moreover, ex–CIA officer Philp Agee's book *Inside the Company: CIA Diary* (New York: Simon & Schuster, 1975) confessed to personally sharing names and information of Uruguayan leftists with local police officers. He vividly details hearing screams from an adjoining room while waiting in a Montevideo police station in 1965.

72. "Telegram 1610 From the Embassy in Uruguay to the Department of State, Subj: Amendment Against Military Assistance to Uruguay," May 7, 1976, US Department of State Office of the Historian https://history.state.gov/-historicaldocuments/frus1969-76ve11p2/d348.

73. Markarian, *Left in Transformation*, 97–98.

74. "Uruguay: Muertos pasados por agua," *Cambi6* (Buenos Aires), May 31, 1976.

75. On March 28, four days after the military coup in Argentina, FAU-PVP militants Ricardo Gil (twenty-eight, an economics professor working with the UN in Buenos Aires), Elida Alvarez (twenty-eight, a law student who fled to Argentina after detention and torture alongside her still-imprisoned husband in Uruguay), and Eduardo Ferreira (twenty-seven, a factory worker and union organizer) were detained in the port of Colonia transporting propaganda into Uruguay. On April 3, Ary Cabrera (twenty-one, AEBU) was detained in her Buenos Aires home. On April 16, Telba Juárez (twenty-nine, a teacher) and Eduardo Chisella (twenty-five, also a teacher) were detained in Barracas (Buenos Aires). Amnesty London, "Urgent Message to AIUSA: ATTN Bill Whipfler," May 6, 1976, CEIU, French Exile Organizations Politique, folder 12.

76. Héctor Romero (UOESF, twenty-eight) had been detained since 1970, while the other three men entered prison in 1973. Mechoso, Romero, and Pareja suffered intensive torture in 1975, leaving the

latter with a heightened level of asthma and difficulty walking. Amnesty London, "Urgent Message to AIUSA."

77. Amnesty London, "Urgent Message to AIUSA."

78. Amnesty London, "Urgent Message to AIUSA."

79. "Sediciosos 'asesinados' con la prensa: Un desmentido rotundo a falaz acusación," *El País*, May 23, 1976, CEIU, Ponce de León Vilaro, folder 19.

80. "Memorandum of Conversation (Santiago Chile)," June 6, 1976 (Secretary's Suite, 8:10am–9:15am), Participants: US Secretary Henry Kissinger, US Under Secretary Waters, US Under Secretary Maw, Argentine Foreign Minister Guzzetti, Argentine Ambassador Carasales, Argentine Ambassador Pereyra, and "Mr. Estrada," transcribed by Luigi R. Einaudi.

81. Harold M. Saunders, "Department of State Briefing Memorandum: Secretary of State Harry Kissinger" (Buenos Aires), June 4, 1976, National Security Archives, https://nsarchive2.gwu.edu/NSAEBB/ NSAEBB73/760604.pdf.

82. Ernest Siracusa, "Telegram 2046 From the US Embassy in Uruguay to the Department of State, Subj: Possible International Implications of Violent Deaths of Political Figures Abroad," June 7, 1976, US Department of State Office of the Historian, https://history .state.gov/historicaldocuments/frus1969-76ve11p2/d349.

83. "Transcripción literal de las declaraciones de Wáshington Pérez en ALVESTA, Suecia," recorded September 1, 1976, and transcribed on September 4 in London, 10, CEIU, French Exile Organizations Politique, folder 12.

84. Gordon initially approached Carlos Gromaz, a FAU militant who took on negotiations to free union officers from detention in Uruguay during the pre-coup years, to represent the FAU-PVP in the negotiations. However, recognizing the extent to which the Argentine authorities had discovered the organization's networks, he refused to take on the role. Instead, he made use of Amnesty International networks to go into exile in Europe. Trías and Rodríguez, *Gerardo Gatti*, 275.

85. "Transcripción literal de las declaraciones de Wáshington Pérez."

86. Trías and Rodríguez, *Gerardo Gatti*, 274.

87. Augusto Andrés, "Aquella Locura," *Brecha* (Montevideo), May 20, 2016.

88. "Transcripción literal de las declaraciones de Wáshington Pérez. On August 12, 1976, Pérez and his family arrived in Sweden as refugees with support from the UN High Commission of Human Rights, 26.

89. "On 30th Anniversary of Argentina Coup: New Declassified Details on Repression and US Support for Military Dictatorship," John Dinges, ed., March 23, 2006, National Security

Archive, Washington, DC, https://nsarchive2.gwu.edu/NSAEBB/ NSAEBB185/index.htm.

90. Andrés, "Aquella Locura."

91. The crossover between the Argentine military and paramilitary organizations is perhaps most visible in the SIDE's "Operaciones Tacticas 18" (Task Force 18), also known as "Gordon's Men," which consisted of both members of the military intelligence service and civilian members of the Triple A's Grupo de Tareas.

92. McSherry, *Predatory States*, 75–77.

93. Angelo Angelopoulos, the Greek national and owner of Comargen, hired Gavazzo after striking a deal with him while in exile in 1975. In 1973, the Uruguayan government placed Comargen under administrative intervention after detecting widespread fraud and tax evasion. Angelopoulos avoided trial by fleeing to Buenos Aires, where he linked with Triple A leader Aníbal Gordon. Shortly after, Gordon introduced him to Gavazzo, who advocated for his return within the Uruguayan military government. In 1975, Angelopoulos returned to oversee his factory in Uruguay, placing Gavazzo at the floor's helm. Gavazzo fired and imprisoned the union's most dedicated militants. Comargen workers protested layoffs with a six-month-long encampment and hunger strike in 1969. The factory eventually closed in the late 1980s, leaving hundreds of workers unemployed. "Gavazzo, Arab, y Aníbal Gordon," *LaRed21* (Montevideo), July 15, 2007.

94. The CIA and Latin American authorities were especially interested in extracting information about the JCR. In late August 1976, the CIA Buenos Aires office learned of the detentions of the two Cubans alongside two members of the Chilean MIR, Patricio Biedma and "Mauro." Eager to extract information about potential Cuban funding for the JCR, Michael Townley, a CIA agent working in Chile as part of Pinochet's secret police force (DINA), and Guillermo Novo, a Cuban American exile living in Miami, flew to Buenos Aires to interrogate the Cubans. The duo participated in the Coordination of United Revolutionary Organizations, a CIA-sponsored paramilitary organization of anti-Castro Cuban exiles. In a 2001 case opened by Argentine judge María Servini de Cubría, ex-director of the DINA Juan Manuel Contreras Sepúlveda testified that both men utilized torture techniques to extract information from the Cuban embassy workers. Under the orders of Augusto Pinochet less than one month later, Townley and Contreras Sepúlveda orchestrated the assassination of ex–Chilean ambassador to the United States and leading Pinochet opponent Orlando Letelier. The Cubans' remains were found thirty-six years later, hidden in cement barrels that washed ashore in the northern Buenos Aires

suburb of Virreyes. Cecilia Devana, "En el marco del Plan Cóndor: La CIA torturaba cubanos en Argentina," *Infojus Noticias* (Buenos Aires), July 29, 2013.

95. The collective holding cell at Orletti diverged dramatically from other holding methods at Argentina's larger clandestine detention centers like ESMA and "La Perla," where prisoners were isolated in casket-sized boxes and only released to eat. There were no clear feeding schedules nor forced labor like at other detention sites of the epoch.

96. Torture sessions lasted between thirty minutes and three hours. One of the few survivors of the center, Edelweiss Zahn, remains completely deaf in one ear due to the torture she endured while in detention. "Informe Enrique Rodríguez Larreta Piera," Equipo de trabajo Sitio de memoria Ex CCD y Automotores Orletti.

97. Robert W. Zimmermann, Director of the Office of East Coast Affairs, ARA/ECA, and the Deputy Assistant Secretary of State for Inter-American Affairs (Ryan) to the Assistant Secretary of State for Inter-American Affairs (Shlaudeman), "Briefing Memorandum. Subj: Congressman Koch—Bureau Contacts," June 22, 1976, US Department of State Office of the Historian, https://history.state.gov/historicaldocuments/frus1969-76ve11p2/d354.

98. Hewson A. Ryan, "Briefing Memorandum, Subject: Uruguay—Current Political Situation," June 18, 1976, US Department of State Office of the Historian, https://history.state.gov/historical documents/frus1969-76ve11p2/d352.

99. Ernest Siracusa, "Telegram 2722 from US Embassy in Uruguay to US Department of State, Subj: Congressman Koch's Charges," July 21, 1976, US Department of State Office of the Historian https:// history.state.gov/-historicaldocuments/frus1969-76ve11p2/d355.

100. In a July 14, 1976, letter from Senior Deputy Assistant Secretary of Inter-American Affairs Hewson Ryan to Representative Koch, the former accusses the latter of being uninformed of embassy reports and/or chosing to ignore them in favor of the Wilson Ferreira and Amnesty International narratives. Ambassador Ernest Siracusa, Telegram 2722 From US Embassy in Uruguay to the Department of State, "Subj: Congressman Koch's Charges," July 21, 1976, US Department of State Office of the Historian, https://history.state.gov/historicaldocuments/frus1969-76ve11p2/d355.

101. Ernest V. Siracusa, Telegram 2702 from US Embassy in Uruguay to US Embassy in Brazil, US Embassy in Argentina, US Embassy in Paraguay, US Embassy in Bolivia, US Embassy in Chile, "Subj: Trends in the Southern Cone," July 20, 1976, US Department of State Office of the Historian, https://nsarchive2.gwu.edu/NSAEBB /-NSAEBB125/condor03.pdf.

442724347

329

102. Ana Quadros, interview with Bianca Ramírez Rivera, in "En ese lugar que era tan frío: Sobre la (im)posibilidad de comprender la experiencia de Ana Inés Quadros, ex detenida del centro clandestino de detención Automotores Orletti," *Testimonios*, vol. 7, no. 7 (2018): 132-33.

103. Sergio López, Testimony in *La Gran Farsa*, dir. Alejandro Figueroa, available on YouTube, 45:00-50:00, https://www.youtube.com/watch?v=TtceMAHEzfU.

104. US Department of State Memorandum for the Record, "Subject: ARA-CIA Weekly Meeting, 30 July 1976," August 3, 1976, US Department of State Office of the Historian.

105. ARA Harry H. Shlaudeman, "Monthly Report (July): The 'Third World War' in South America," August 3, 1976, US Department of State Office of the Historian, https://nsarchive2.gwu.edu//NSAEBB/NSAEBB309/-19760803.pdf.

106. Shlaudeman, "Monthly Report (July)."

107. Ernest V. Siracusa, Telegram 2941 From the Embassy in Uruguay to the Department of State, "Subj: Human Rights Discussion with Lt. Gen. Vadora and Gen. Queirolo," August 7, 1976, US Department of State Office of the Historian, https://history.state.gov/historicaldocuments/frus1969-76ve11p2/d357.

108. US Department of State, Telegram 209192 From the Department of State to the Embassies in Argentina, Uruguay, Chile, and Bolivia, "Subj: Operation Condor," August 23, 1976, US Department of State Office of the Historian, https://history.state.gov/historicaldocuments/frus1969-76ve11p2/d241.

109. Ernest Siracusa, Telegram 3123 From the Embassy in Uruguay to the Department of State, "Subj: Operation Condor. Ref: State 209192," August 24, 1976, US Department of State Office of the Historian, https://history.state.gov/historicaldocuments/frus1969-76ve11p2/d358.

110. Ernest V. Siracusa, Telegram 3388 From the Embassy in Uruguay to the Department of State, "Subj: Meeting with Foreign Minister," September 11, 1976, US Department of State Office of the Historian, https://history.state.gov/historicaldocuments/frus1969-76ve11p2/d360.

111. Ernest V. Siracusa, Telegram 3451 From the Embassy in Uruguay to the Department of State, "Subj.: Meeting with President Aparicio Mendez. Ref.: Montevideo 3388," September 15, 1976, US Department of State Office of the Historian, https://history.state.gov/historicaldocuments/frus1969-76ve11p2/d361.

112. Support for the bill totaled 216-155 in the House and 56-24 in the Senate. Markarian, *Left in Transformation*, 97-98.

113. Rico, *Investigación histórica sobre la dictadura*, 36.

114. Department of Defense Intelligence Information Report Number 6 804 0334 76, "Subject: (U) Special Operations Forces (U)," October 1, 1976.

115. Rico, *Investigación histórica sobre la dictadura*, 36.

116. Memorandum of Conversation, "Subj: US-Uruguay Relations" (Washington, DC), October 8, 1976, US Department of State Office of the Historian, https://history.state.gov/historicaldocuments/frus1969-76ve11p2/d363.

117. Memorandum of Conversation, "Subj: US-Uruguay Relations" (Washington, DC), October 8, 1976, US Department of State Office of the Historian, https://history.state.gov/historicaldocuments/frus1969-76ve11p2/d363.

118. Ernest Siracusa, Telegram 4652 From the Embassy in Uruguay to the Department of State, "Subj: Threat Against Congressman Koch. Ref: State 292202," December 2, 1976, US Department of State Office of the Historian, https://history.state.gov/historical-documents/frus1969-76ve11p2/d365; Edward Koch, "Letter to US Attorney General," October 19, 1976, National Security Archives, https://nsarchive2.gwu.edu/NSAEBB/-NSAEBB112/koch01.pdf.

119. Ernest Siracusa, Telegram 4755 From the Embassy in Uruguay to the Department of State," December 10, 1976, US Department of State Office of the Historian, https://history.state.gov/historical documents/frus1969-76ve11p2/d367; A US Department of State top-secret document from July 22, 1976, discussed an early July plan to "liquidate" Latin American exiles living in France. The author proclaimed, "Condor operations in France would simply be an extensive of the recently intensified cooperation among Southern Cone governments to eradicate terrorism," US Department of State, "INR Afternoon Summary," July 22, 1976, National Security Archives, https://nsarchive2.gwu.edu//dc.html?doc=3238657-1-Department-of-State-INR-AFTERNOON-SUMMARY-Top.

120. Ernest Siracusa, Telegram 4652 From the Embassy in Uruguay to the Department of State, "Subj: Threat Against Congressman Koch. Ref: State 292202," December 2, 1976, US Department of State Office of the Historian, https://history.state.gov/historical documents/frus1969-76ve11p2/d365.

121. Although late October marks a transition to late spring in Uruguay, the militants presented themselves dressed in winter clothing that they had gathered from other prisoners along the journey. All FAU-PVP members were detained in the thick of Buenos Aires winter. Alicia Cadenas, interviewed in *La Gran Farsa*.

122. Juan Ferreira, son of Wilson Ferreira Aldunate, notified the US State Department of the Chalet Suzy episode and proclaimed that the event was meant to embarrass the US government. He

acknowledged that all those detained in the simulacra belonged to the list of thirty Uruguayans recently disappeared in Buenos Aires. Henry Kissinger, Telegram to US Embassies in Argentina and Uruguay, "Subject: Arrested Uruguayans," October 29, 1976, available at https://wikileaks.org/plusd/cables/1976STATE267364_b.html.

123. "Los planes del grupo desbaratado en Uruguay," *La Nación* (Buenos Aires), October 31, 1976.

124. Juan Carlos and Mariana Mechoso, conversation with author (unrecorded), Montevideo, December 12, 2017.

125. Henry Kissinger, Telegram 306332, US Department of State to the Embassy in Uruguay, "Subj: Condor," December 18, 1976, US Department of State Office of the Historian, https://history.state.gov/historical-documents/frus1969-76ve11p2/d368.

126. Without knowledge of their backstory, an image of the orphaned children "with strange accents" appeared in Santiago's *El Mercurio* newspaper. A middle-class Chilean family adopted the children within a few days of their appearance, but the eerie occurrence led to more questions than answers. Without knowledge of her grandchildren's appearance in Chile, Angelica Grisona spent two years appealing to Argentine military courts and even obtained various meetings with President Jorge Rafael Videla, who declared, "Don't look anymore. We do not do those sorts of things. In the end, if there was a confrontation and your son was involved, who knows, but we do not have anything to do with those things. In July 1979, Clamor, a Sao Paulo-based human rights organization headed by Archbishop Paulo Evaristo Arns, discovered the children and contacted their grandmother, who traveled to Valparaíso to claim them. Eduardo Gentil, "Children of Couple Kidnapped in Argentina in 1976 Found in Chile," *Latin America Daily Post* (São Paulo), August 1, 1979, CEIU, French Exile Organizations Politique, folder 12.

127. Harry W. Shlaudeman, Action Memorandum to the Undersecretary of State for Political Affairs, "Subj: Uruguayan Intelligence Personnel to the US," December 31, 1976, US Department of State Office of the Historian, https://history.state.gov/historicaldocuments/frus1969-76ve11p2/d369.

128. Quoted in Sikkink, *Mixed Signals*, xvi. Kissinger remained supportive of the region's anti-subversion efforts. His position eventually conflicted with President Jimmy Carter's *discursive* emphasis on Human Rights. During Kissinger's visit to Argentina to view the 1978 World Cup, he applauded the government for their efforts against subversion during a private conversation with President Videla. The comments raised concern among US representatives in the Organization of American States, who reported that Kissinger's repeated praise surely went to official's heads and undermined

President Carter's human rights agenda. However, the Carter administration recognized Videla as a "moderate" option and began privately supporting his government as early as September 1977. Robert Pastor, National Security Council Memorandum, "Subj.: Kissinger on Human Rights in Argentina and Latin America," July 11, 1978, National Security Archives, https://nsarchive2.gwu.edu//dc.html?doc=3010641-Document-04-National-Security-Council-Kissinger.

129. Washington Office on Latin America, "Brazil and Uruguay: Repressive Illegal Cooperation," November 29, 1978, Washington, DC, CEIU, Collection Waksman, folder 26.

130. Sandra Pintos Llovet, "Trayectorias de las investigaciones antropológica forenses sobre detenidos desaparecidos en Uruguay y Argentina," MA thesis (University of the Republic [Uruguay], Latin American Studies, 2018).

131. Letter from Hugo Cores, December 10, 1976, Paris, CEIU, Hugo Cores Archive, box 4.

132. Ernest Siracusa, Telegram 2941 From the Embassy in Uruguay to the Department of State, "Subj: Human Rights Discussion with Lt. Gen. Vadora and Gen. Queirolo," August 7, 1976, US Department of State Office of the Historian, https://history.state.gov/historical documents/frus1969-76ve11p2/d357.

133. Ricardo Vilaró, *Uruguay y sus sindicatos* (Holland, March 1979), 56, CEIU, Ricardo Vilaró Archive; Howard Handelman, "Labor-Industrial Conflict and the Collapse of Uruguayan Democracy," *Journal of Interamerican Studies and World Affairs*, vol. 23, no. 4 (1981): 373.

134. The rest were common citizens, members of the FEUU, or independent union militants. Three children were also disappeared.

135. Rico, *Investigación histórica sobre la dictadura*, 769–83.

136. Offensives in Argentina disappeared seventeen GAU militants in 1977. Of the twenty-five members of the MLN-T disappeared in Argentina, eleven disappeared in 1977 and ten disappeared in 1978. Only ten members of the PCU disappeared during these years—four in Argentina. Rico, *Investigación histórica sobre la dictadura*, 769–83.

Postscript

1. "Juicio a Los Represores de Automotores Orletti: Gulielminetti fue condenado a 20 años de prisión, Rufo y Martínez Ruiz a 25 y Cabanillas a perpetua," *Pagina 12*, March 31, 2011, https://www.pagina12.com.ar/diario/ultimas/20-165283-2011-03-31.html.

2. Peter Dale Scott and Jonathan Marshall, *Cocaine Politics: Drugs,*

Armies, and the CIA in Central America (Berkeley: University of California Press, 1998), 50.

3. Carlos Osorio and Peter Kornbluh, "Operation Condor Verdict: GUILTY!," National Security Archive, May 27, 2016, https://nsarchive.gwu.edu/briefing-book/southern-cone/2016-05-27/operation-condor-verdict-guilty.

4. Natalia Biazzini, "Inspección ocular al centro clandestino: Una visita a Orletti, la sede del Plan Cóndor en la Argentina," Archivo InfoJus Noticias, June 22, 2013, http://www.archivoinfojus.gob.ar/nacionales/una-visita-a-orletti-la-sede-del-plan-condor-en-la-argentina-607.html.

Index

AK PRESS is small, in terms of staff and resources, but we also manage to be one of the world's most productive anarchist publishing houses. We publish close to twenty books every year, and distribute thousands of other titles published by like-minded independent presses and projects from around the globe. We're entirely worker run and democratically managed. We operate without a corporate structure—no boss, no managers, no bullshit.

The **FRIENDS OF AK PRESS** program is a way you can directly contribute to the continued existence of AK Press, and ensure that we're able to keep publishing books like this one! Friends pay $25 a month directly into our publishing account ($30 for Canada, $35 for international), and receive a copy of every book AK Press publishes for the duration of their membership! Friends also receive a discount on anything they order from our website or buy at a table: 50% on AK titles, and 30% on everything else. We have a Friends of AK ebook program as well: $15 a month gets you an electronic copy of every book we publish for the duration of your membership. *You can even sponsor a very discounted membership for someone in prison.*

Email **friendsofak@akpress.org** for more info, or visit the website: **https://www.akpress.org/friends.html**.

There are always great book projects in the works—so sign up now to become a Friend of AK Press, and let the presses roll!